The Center Must Not Hold

The Center Must Not Hold

White Women Philosophers on the Whiteness of Philosophy

George Yancy

LEXINGTON BOOKS
A division of
ROWMAN & LITTLEFIELD PUBLISHERS, INC.
Lanham • Boulder • New York • Toronto • Plymouth, UK

Published by Lexington Books
A division of Rowman & Littlefield Publishers, Inc.
A wholly owned subsidiary of The Rowman & Littlefield Publishing Group, Inc.
4501 Forbes Boulevard, Suite 200, Lanham, Maryland 20706
http://www.lexingtonbooks.com

Estover Road, Plymouth PL6 7PY, United Kingdom

Copyright © 2010 by Lexington Books

All rights reserved. No part of this book may be reproduced in any form or by any electronic or mechanical means, including information storage and retrieval systems, without written permission from the publisher, except by a reviewer who may quote passages in a review.

British Library Cataloguing in Publication Information Available

Library of Congress Cataloging-in-Publication Data
The center must not hold : White women philosophers on the Whiteness of philosophy / [edited by] George Yancy.
   p. cm.
  Includes bibliographical references and index.
  ISBN 978-0-7391-3881-6 (cloth : alk. paper) — ISBN 978-0-7391-3883-0 (electronic)
 1. Race—Philosophy. 2. Race relations—Philosophy. 3. Racism. 4. Women philosophers. I. Yancy, George.
  HT1523.C46 2010
  108.9'09—dc22   2009054092

∞™ The paper used in this publication meets the minimum requirements of American National Standard for Information Sciences—Permanence of Paper for Printed Library Materials, ANSI/NISO Z39.48-1992.

Printed in the United States of America

This book is dedicated to Samuel Alexander Yancy
—an absolute sap for affection

Contents

Foreword	Sandra Harding	ix
Acknowledgments		xiii
Introduction	Troublemaking Allies *George Yancy*	xv
Chapter 1	White Ignorance and the Denials of Complicity: On the Possibility of Doing Philosophy in Good Faith *Barbara Applebaum*	1
Chapter 2	Reading Black Philosophers in Chronological Order *Audrey Thompson*	27
Chapter 3	On Intersectionality and the Whiteness of Feminist Philosophy *Alison Bailey*	51
Chapter 4	The Man of Culture: The Civilized and the Barbarian in Western Philosophy *Lisa Heldke*	77
Chapter 5	Whiteness and Rationality: Feminist Dialogue on Race in Academic Institutional Spaces *Crista Lebens*	99
Chapter 6	Appropriate Subjects: Whiteness and the Discipline of Philosophy *Alexis Shotwell*	117

Chapter 7	Color in the Theory of Colors? Or: Are Philosophers' Colors All White? *Berit Brogaard*	131
Chapter 8	The Secularity of Philosophy: Race, Religion, and the Silence of Exclusion *Shannon Sullivan*	153
Chapter 9	Philosophy's Whiteness and the Loss of Wisdom *Susan E. Babbitt*	167
Chapter 10	Against the Whiteness of Ethics: Dilemmatizing as a Critical Approach *Lisa Tessman*	193
Chapter 11	The Whiteness of Anti-Racist White Philosophical Address *Cris Mayo*	211
Chapter 12	Colonial Practices/Colonial Identities: All the Women are Still White *Sarah Lucia Hoagland*	227
Chapter 13	Is Philosophy Anything if it Isn't White? *Cynthia Kaufman*	245
Index		265
About the Contributors		273

Foreword

"Virtually no one intends to be racist," points out one contributor to *The Center Must Not Hold*, writing about philosophers in general. Indeed, perhaps the most difficult thing for white philosophers to recognize is that being smart and well-intentioned isn't enough to make our work innocent of racist assumptions or claims. We can still be "part of the problem" for people of color, in spite of our smarts and our good intentions. This challenge is especially difficult to countenance for philosophers with social justice commitments, such as feminists. It is a bitter pill to have to learn to swallow. What are we to do if being smart and having good intentions doesn't enable us to avoid producing philosophical writing that is complicit with white supremacy?

Our situation today reminds me of the anger and frustration articulated by many of our colleagues on the left when we (mostly white) women philosophers pointed out several decades ago their persistent male-supremacist attitudes and assumptions. It also reminds me that many of them learned how to contribute philosophic work that we female feminists could honestly value. Moreover, many young men in subsequent generations cut their philosophic teeth in feminist philosophy classes (among others), found that an exciting experience, and emerged as professional philosophers with far less expectation of male-supremacist entitlement than was exhibited by most colleagues in our own generation. Today I always find such young men in my feminist philosophy classes. These days I think we are somewhere in the middle of this kind of process as whites begin to learn how to engage seriously with philosophical assumptions, concerns, methods, and styles grounded in the experiences of African Americans and other peoples of color.

These illuminating and courageous essays contribute to a long history of white women's writings against racism—in the U.S., in South Africa and the rest of the settler colonies of the former British empire, and elsewhere around the globe. Drawing on the anti-racist work of women and men of color in the U.S. and elsewhere, as well as of white women and men, these writings make important interventions into what is regarded as the appropriate priorities, conceptual assumptions, and methods of Anglo American philosophy. These authors build on the work of pioneering white women philosophers such as Marilyn Frye, Vicky Spellman and Carole Pateman, as well as of women of color philosophers such as Gloria Anzaldua, Katie G. Cannon, Angela Davis, bell hooks, Maria Lugones, Sylvia Marcos, Chandra Talpade Mohanty, Uma Narayan, Nikiru Nzegwu, Oyeronke Oyewumi, Meyda Yegenoglu and Naomi Zack, and the anti-racist work of men such as David Goldberg, Walter Mignolo, Charles Mills, and Cornel West.

What I found especially exciting about so much of this work is its focus on two kinds of sources of resistance to anti-racist philosophy. One kind is the structural, material conditions of everyday life that generate priorities, standards, and social practices of philosophy departments and institutions such as philosophy conferences. These conditions ensure that white philosophers and their white audiences will find perfectly reasonable the racist assumptions, practices, and claims that ground mainstream Anglo-American (and other Western) philosophies. That is, the interests of these authors is not so much in racist individuals or particular racist claims in philosophic writing, though we learn a lot about these. Nor is their interest in "studying the Other," though we also learn a great deal about the experiences and thought of philosophers of color. Rather, their concerns are with the material conditions and structural arrangements that enable smart and well-intentioned white philosophers and their similar white students, colleagues, readers and audiences to find perfectly acceptable the persistent silencing and disvaluing of any human experiences but their own, and then to claim universality for their own claims that are grounded in only their own white experiences in a white-supremacist society. These essays identify the material and institutional aspects of "life in philosophy" that insure complicity with existing institutional, societal, and civilisational forms of racism. We must change the social worlds in which we live as philosophers so that they discourage whites' perception that our experiences in white-supremacist social relations provide the desirable route to discovering philosophic truths and universally valuable wisdom.

Another focus that I found illuminating in many of these essays is on the sources of resistance to anti-racist work to be found in our distinctively white subjectivities—especially in the senses of self for philosophers committed to advancing social justice, such as feminists. How are we created as subjects of philosophy—as the speakers of radically new kinds of philosophic truths and wisdom—who nevertheless do not usually notice that the truths and wisdom we come upon will be grounded only in our own white experiences in a white-supremacist society—experiences uninformed by critical race theories? What would philosophy look like if—regardless of the race of the author—it started off from the experiences of people of color in a white-supremacist society—and of people of any and every color who lived in a society that was not white-supremacist? What would such feminist philosophies look like?

These authors critically engage with assumptions and practices of Anglo-American philosophy, Rawls and Habermas, logic, the Enlightenment and

Western rationality, Liberal and left conceptions of democracy, equality, freedom, justice, autonomy and the individual, rights discourses and the ethical life, secularism, the philosophy of religion, and philosophers' and psychologists' theories of color. They critically examine philosophers' fear of pluralism, the prioritization of epistemology over morals and politics, the silence in philosophy about Black experiences and the experiences of other peoples of color, Western exceptionalism and triumphalism, the division of interests between philosophy and anthropology, and philosophic ideals of speaking with certainty and authority. In short, these essays delineate how the epistemological, ethical, and political crisis of the modern West that has been so widely recognized outside philosophy has not yet been fully recognized within the discipline.

These essays do not present a coherent collective argument—thank goodness! There are fascinating tensions and conflicts within and between these writings as their authors push against the conventional boundaries of "proper philosophy" to struggle with some of the most difficult and important questions about U.S. and global social relations today as these appear in philosophic work. Is Anglo-American philosophy capable of producing wisdom, as it claims to do? Or is it only capable of producing white-supremacist correctness, as one white graduate student is quoted as claiming? What are the limitations for anti-racist goals of purely intellectual arguments? What is the importance of personal experiences and of living in different ways to the production of anti-racist philosophy? Should epistemological issues be prioritized over ethical and political ones? How are philosophy's typical forms of addressing readers complicitious with racist assumptions? Approaching such questions from various kinds of anti-racist philosophic and social concerns, these essays generate provocative questions that can stimulate further research and classroom discussions.

I found these essays deeply moving, intellectually illuminating, and strategically challenging. I am looking forward to teaching them in my own feminist philosophy course. Along with the powerful philosophic work already done by women and men of color and by some white men, these essays point to directions the discipline of philosophy must take if our field is to combat its current condition as "part of the problem" for peoples of color in the U.S. and around the globe. This is an especially propitious moment for the discipline to move forward in such projects. Across the world oppressed peoples are gazing with mixtures of hope and often puzzlement at recent shifts in our federal personnel and policies and at the U.S.'s newly emerging vision of itself and its place in global social relations. Can the field of philosophy share such a vision of itself and its place in global thinking? *The Center Must Not Hold* can help us and our students imagine and produce philosophies that move us toward anti-racist worlds.

Sandra Harding
Los Angeles, California
June, 2009

Acknowledgments

I would like to thank the women of this text for contributions that are philosophically bold and insightful. Each contributor is cognizant of the complexity of what it means to be an *ally* and how such a relationship is mediated by conflicting interests, philosophical differences, normative assumptions, and political outlooks. Yet, each contributor shares the collective vision regarding the importance of de-centering the whiteness of philosophy. That the center *must* not hold bespeaks the necessity and imperativeness of action; it says that we *can't* go on re-inscribing the raced (white) center of philosophy through the maintenance of hegemonic repetitive white epistemic and axiological orders. As such, I would like to thank the contributors to this text for their ethical diligence and profound care for issues of justice.

I would like to thank Dr. Matthew R. Adam, former Philosophy Acquisitions Editor, for his dedication to this project. Thanks to Rebecca McCary, Editorial Assistant, for her energy and professionalism. Thanks to Jana M. Wilson, Assistant Acquisitions Editor, for her efforts and enthusiasm. Sandra Harding's willingness to write the Foreword to the text was icing on the cake for me. I respect the rigor of her philosophical work and its profound ethical and political import. I would like to thank Fred Evans and Jim Swindal for their continued support of my work. A special thanks for support and friendship to four extraordinary human beings: Eleanore and John Holveck, Wilhelm S. Wurzer, and to Acting Dean and internationally recognized John Milton scholar Albert Labriola. Each will be sadly missed. I would like to thank my students (graduate and undergraduate) for their mutual show of enthusiasm and passion for learning. A special thanks is given to Taine Duncan for her assistance with the index. Taine is a burgeoning philosopher who will no doubt make important philosophical contributions to both feminism and critical theory. Thanks to my mother, Artrice, and Carson, who are dearly loved. James G. Spady is thanked for his creative leadership. And John McClendon is thanked for his co-struggle in our effort to strengthen the American Philosophical Association *Newsletter on Philosophy and the Black Experience* as we continue to publish significant work in the area of African American philosophy and philosophy of the Black experience.

Charles Berlin is thanked for giving me a safe space for self-discovery and through whom I've learned the cognitive importance of metaphor. I thank the Yancy boys who are loved fiercely. And my wife, Susan, is much appreciated and loved for her labor on this book, particularly in terms of the sheer mechanics of putting the text together. I thank you to the Nth Degree! And then some.

Introduction: Troublemaking Allies

George Yancy, Duquesne University

> Challenging white supremacy in philosophy is a struggle that nonwhite philosophers should not have to take on by themselves. White philosophers should choose to be "bad" philosophers, too. White philosophers should put pressure on other philosophers, as many "bad" nonwhite philosophers have already done, to end white supremacy in philosophy.
> —Anna Stubblefield

> Individually and collectively philosophers must take responsibility for what is taught, who does the teaching, and who is taught. The whiteness of philosophy must be addressed with the same energy as the maleness of philosophy is beginning to be.
> —Robert Bernasconi

I think that I will begin with me—a *Black male*. The self that "I am," which is always already in the subjunctive mode, is not trapped or securely situated within a solipsistic bubble and does not function as an Archimedean point of absolute certainty. The self that I am is historically situated, contingent, vulnerable, relational, raced, *embodied*, and constituted through various processes of interpellation,[1] which is Louis Althusser's term that denotes processes of being hailed whereby one is constituted by pre-given norms and institutional forces. So, even as I speak from a raced and gendered *here*, I recognize my identity as part of a long, complex, and confluent prior discursive history in the making. I am also a transversal self, a self grounded within the sphere of sociality. The space of sociality always already presupposes the existence of others. While the self needs moments of privacy and moments to be alone, the process of withdrawal presupposes the anterior reality of others. The process of distancing oneself from others in the form of withdrawal into spaces of relative solitude presupposes a self-other dialectic. In short, even private spaces are pre-marked by the social; they carry the trace of the public. Deploying the self as a point of critical embarkation need not take the form of escapism or narcissism; indeed, it can function as an invitation—a call. Within the context of this introduction, I think of this strategy as an act of *trust*. Indeed, as I hope to show in the following introductory reflections, marked by a brief excursus, *The Center Must Not Hold: White Women Philosophers on the Whiteness of Philosophy* is fundamentally predicated upon trust.

The phenomenon of trust involves levels of openness, honesty, transparency, self-disclosure, and risk. Within the context of my pedagogical efforts, I always try to create a critical space within which there is trust. The demands that I place upon my students, I place upon myself. Part of this pedagogy is designed to complicate the illusion that teachers/professors transcend the fray of everyday life. There is the recognition that all of us are incomplete, complicated, and complex. It says: *I am all too human*.

To engage in educational practices that are liberating, trust is indispensable. My pedagogy emphasizes the important point that an engaged form of *collective elenchus* or cross examination has the potential for creating conditions that help to make us into better human beings, not simply better scholars or intellectuals. Because I teach at a university where the majority of students are white,[2] and because I teach undergraduate and graduate philosophy courses that deal with issues of race and embodiment, I encourage them to think about the various ways in which they have undergone processes of white racialized interpellation. And even as most of them resist this way of re-conceptualizing/re-positioning the self, there is often some movement. After all, as white, they have come to see themselves as simply persons, autonomous and self-made. In fact, for many whites, there is no need or no interest in critically engaging the ways in which they have *become* the *white* selves that they are. Getting my students to see the epistemological and ethical orders of whiteness—to grasp whiteness as the transcendental norm—is fraught with so many difficulties, especially as whiteness is constituted through processes of repetition and normalization that actually militate against seeing the white self as needing disruption or critical analysis. Whiteness, as a site of power, obfuscates self-scrutiny. By the time most white students take my courses, they have come to see their identities as the result of individual effort, an act of "auto-genesis." I encourage them to see their whiteness as a site of regulation, a form of hailing that initiates them into the selves that they have become. We discuss how "*hailing* is an act of forming the subject to comply with and obey the laws of its discursive or social domain."[3] This, of course, is threatening. They are forced to rethink much of their history, both personal and collective. There is often a feeling of vertigo and uncertainty. There is also the task of admitting to the reality of a white self that has been complicit in being bequeathed unearned power and privilege. It is at this point that I trouble my own identity; I become a troublemaker. In doing so, trust emerges as a bridge, as a stimulus to disclosure on their part. Within the context of my classroom, being a troublemaker functions as a prelude to forming alliances.

Introduction: Troublemaking Allies xvii

It is not unusual for me to ask my students the question: "Are there any white students in here who see themselves as white racists?" All hands remain at their sides or on their desks. There have been a few times, and very few, when a white student will raise his/her hand. This single act often creates an opening for fruitful discussion. I will then pose the question: "Are there any males in here who see themselves as sexists?" There are usually one or two hands that go up. Typically, my hand is the only one. Part of the objective is to expose another axis of hegemony or dominance. By raising my hand, my effort is to communicate to my students that I am not afraid to discuss the ways in which I am positioned by sexist norms that confer patriarchal power. My students are often surprised by my candor and yet profoundly appreciative. Of course, there is always risk. I discuss with them how my own male identity is constantly under the process of interpellation, how I am positioned by sexist epistemological orders. We discuss how men come to fragment the bodies of women into bits of flesh. I share with them how it is difficult to go into most bookstores or approach most newsstands and not have one's identity positioned as the subject of a pornographic narrative. After all, the pornographic material is displayed for our visual consumption, though the cover shots are slightly concealed. The suggestiveness of the poses of the women on the cover places the male in the position of gazer, in the position of sexual aggressor-subject—the "fuckor." The exposed woman on the cover is positioned as the gazed upon, the passive-object—the "fuckee."[4] This leads to fascinating and productive discussions about how women in the class feel about having their bodies objectified, made into sexual playthings. They begin to identify male hegemony as constituting an entire visual culture, one in which they are typically *the looked at*. In fact, many of them begin to recall moments of having their bodies distorted while walking down the street. While I stress that I am an anti-sexist, I critically and openly talk about the ways in which all men are still complicit within a set of practices that hail women as sexual objects and how being hailed as a sexual object is inflected relative to race and class. I point out to the class that the best that men can achieve is the status of anti-sexist sexists. It is at this point that many students begin to see parallels, though without flattening the two "isms," between male anti-sexist sexism and white anti-racist racism. I also discuss with them how it is that white myths have positioned me as the super-sex addict, noting the intersections between racism and sexism. Even as I contest the ways in which women are objectified in our society, through the lens of white racism my body is stereotyped as the frightening Black penis. I am re-presented as the essence of bestiality and hyper-sexuality by many of the same women for whom I have taken up the fight against their objectification and my participation in it. Before the end of class, many of my white students raise their hands when it comes to self-identification as racist and sexist—some, of course, raise their hand twice.

Movement has taken place. A certain level of trust has occurred. Throughout the semester, I begin to see students engage in troublemaking. They actively engage in interrogating sites of white privilege, questioning what they previously thought to be a priori true about themselves and others. They refuse to accept problematic aspects of the status quo, especially around race, and reach beyond their narrow views of themselves and try, as best as possible, to imagine themselves and the world differently. Demonstrating to my students that I can engage in public self-critique, revealing aspects of myself that are incomplete, they get to see levels of honesty that are discouraged in academia. After all, especially as a philosopher, I am taught to remain dispassionate and distant, while the ugliness of life should always take the form of hypothetical thought experiments. Within this chimerical or fanciful space where "free-floating" minds allegedly meet, embodiment is believed to be an encumbrance. To understand the effects of sexism and racism, however, presupposes the reality of one's embodiment and the embodiment of others. It is as embodied that one suffers the injurious evils of sexism and racism. My students learn the importance of bringing their entire complex selves to class—selves that often falter, get ambushed,[5] say the wrong things, and become passionate and emotional. My own display of pedagogical passion is *not* about ego-aggrandizement or indicative of processes of self-mortification—what has been called the self-flagellator.[6] My pedagogical interventions into sexism are not a manifestation of a theatrics of repressed male guilt. I would like to think that what I am doing is acting in good faith by exemplifying critical practices that might fuel their own efforts at refusing to approach the multitudinous problems of our social existence with a passive attitude. My aim is to encourage them to respond to the *call*, the invitation to trouble their lives and not settle for mediocrity. For the most part, I believe that I have had some success. And while I emphasize the significance of remaining resolute and vigilant, etymologically, "to keep watch," the struggle continues, new misunderstandings arise, and the operations of sexist and racist power endure.

To begin the introduction of this text through an act of self-identification as a Black male is a relational act. It involves an act of conscious self-positioning vis-à-vis the aims of the text as a whole—it says that I am existentially and politically invested. It is also relational in that there is a specifically strained history between white women and Black men. In this way, I am also relationally positioned by,[7] located within, a historical narrative that is anterior to my existence. From the support and complicity of white women in the enslavement of Black bodies, the anger and racist discourse against granting the vote to Black men in 1870,[8] participation and perpetuation of the myth of the Black male rapist, to the show of trepidation that we, as Black males, get as we encounter white women on the street, in banks, on elevators, and perhaps even at American Philosophical Association conferences, there is tension. Some may argue that this is old rhetoric, old news. Yet, this history continues to mediate our transactions. Knowing this strained history full-well, *The Center Must Not Hold: White Women Philosophers on the Whiteness of Philosophy* is an invitation, a call by a Black male philosopher, to white women to take seriously the various ways in which whiteness gets perpetuated through the activity of philosophizing by whites. "For decades," according to Angela Davis, "white women activists have repeated the complaint that women of color frequently fail to respond to their appeals."[9] Such appeals had to be rejected, because the center of whiteness continued to hold. Such appeals entailed the erasure of Black women and the dismissal of their unique forms of marginalization and oppression. The appeal that I make within this text is fueled by my own efforts at not only challenging the whiteness of philosophy, but also its male hegemony. Both must be critiqued lest white women's philosophizing continues to replicate white hegemony and thereby explicitly or implicitly marginalize philosophers of color, their philosophical sensibilities, conceptual problematics, epistemic standpoints, and worldviews.

Sandra Harding asks, "What are we to do if being smart and having good intentions doesn't enable us to avoid producing philosophical writing that is complicit with white supremacy?"[10] This text explores and critiques the *whiteness* of philosophical knowledge-production. Charles Mills, addressing why it is that Black people find philosophy so alienating, argues that it has to do with "the self-sustaining dynamic of the 'whiteness' of philosophy, not the uncontroversial whiteness of skin of most of its practitioners but what could be called, more contestably, the *conceptual* or *theoretical* whiteness of the discipline."[11]

As I began to think about the ways in which white women philosophers have boldly and importantly challenged the *center* of white male philosophy, I noticed that the critique was primarily directed at the *maleness* of philosophy, leaving the whiteness of philosophy unquestioned and elided. In such areas as epistemology, ethics, philosophy of mind, social and political philosophy, philosophy of science, aesthetics, philosophy of religion, philosophical conceptualizations of the person, and so on, the critique has been directed at the various ways in which patriarchal norms have shaped these areas and how they have been and are predicated upon androcentric perspectives on the world. Such critiques have been powerful and indispensable in terms of demonstrating how philosophy, that presumed "pure" and a-historical domain of inquiry, is defined by and invested in male axiological frames of reference. Such critiques have also opened up new spaces for doing philosophy in different voices, voices that are often deemed ersatz and concerned with particularity only. The efforts of white women philosophers[12] (self-ascribed as feminist or not) have provided ways of rethinking the canon, rethinking identity and power, rethinking issues of embodiment vis-à-vis philosophical cognition, and rethinking the very nature of what constitutes a philosophical problem. These efforts have led to the disruption of various epistemic orders that have proven detrimental to such dynamic processes as women's self-understanding and self-imagining. Yet, the conceptual whiteness of philosophy remains. While its maleness has been and continues to be identified and critiqued, whiteness continues to get performed through various modes of philosophical engagement, value-laden assumptions, and epistemological orders. Hence, in critiquing one site of power—maleness—many white women philosophers are complicitous with whiteness, marking the former as the latter remains unmarked and invisible. While white women have engaged in important acts of philosophical self-authorization that challenge sites of male philosophical discourse, the center of whiteness continues to hold as white women re-inscribe a form of hegemonic sameness. Sarah Hoagland asks white feminists, "What if we ceased animating colonial practices and identities? Would the center, our racialized gender center, still hold?"[13] Hoagland's question is an urgent one. Given the complex ways in which whiteness conceals its tracks, and given the insidiousness of its trappings and unexpected re-animation, I think that the question that Hoagland leaves us with is a challenge. She recognizes the fragility of the answer, but affirms the strength of the call to action embedded within an interrogative form of address.

I see this call to action as a space for a critical alliance between white women philosophers and philosophers of color. In the end, both groups are victims of white hegemony, though philosophers of color have experienced white imposed trauma differently. This distinction is important to acknowledge for fear that we flatten our histories and homogenize our differences. Embracing the importance of unshared locationalities of pain and suffering militates against meta-narrative supremacy, a meta-narrative that ostracizes and silences. The white women philosophers within this text are troublemaking allies. Each bears witness to the complexity of whiteness within the domain of philosophy. This act of bearing witness, though, eschews déjà vu white arrogance in the form of feigned white exceptionality and white self-congratulatory posturing.[14] As white allies (*alligare*, "to bind to"), there is a binding to the efforts of philosophers of color to expose the whiteness of philosophy, even as this whiteness confers privilege and power upon them. Yet, they bear witness; they provide critical evidence for the problematic existence of philosophy's conceptual whiteness—a false universal indeed. As *white* philosophers, they are cognizant of the traps and snares of the re-inscription of whiteness as the center. The concept of alliance, "to bind to," is complicated by the seduction of whiteness and its own insidious call to bad faith. Troublemaking is a continuous effort, though not Sisyphean. "To bind to" in a collective effort to nominate whiteness requires mutual trust/faith. Reflective of the dynamic of religious faith (*religare*, "to tie fast"), we proceed together and leap forward even as there is no guarantee. With Hoagland, however, the strength of the call is still there. The other side of her interrogative is the realization of a future where whiteness is no longer a continuously animated center and where whiteness as a form of repetition loses its rhythm—permanently.

Notes

1. See Louis Althusser's "Ideology and Ideological State Apparatuses" in *Lenin and Philosophy and Other Essays* (New York: Monthly Review Press, 2001).
2. Indeed, though not lately, many of my classes have been *all* white.
3. Alecia Youngblood Jackson, "Performativity Identified," *Qualitative Inquiry* 10, no. 5 (2004): 673–690, quotation on 677.
4. For an analysis of these two terms ("fuckor" and "fuckee") and how they speak to Catharine MacKinnon's view that woman don't seem to be able to escape the totality of male violence, see Drucilla Cornell's *Transformations: Recollective Imagination and Sexual Difference* (New York: Routledge, 1993), specifically chapter 5.
5. For more on the conceptualization of ambush within the context of white anti-racist efforts, See George Yancy's *Black Bodies, White Gazes, The Continuing Significance of Race* (Lanham, MD: Rowman & Littlefield, 2008), especially chapter 7.
6. More on this concept in relationship to male feminists, see David J. Kahane's "Male Feminism as Oxymoron," in *Men Doing Feminism*, ed. Tom Digby (New York: Routledge, 1998), especially 227.
7. See Stuart Hall, "Cultural Identity and Cinematic Representation," *Framework* 36 (1989): 68–81.
8. This right was challenged over and over again by racist whites in the form of forcing Blacks to take literacy tests, pay poll taxes, and through acts of intimidation and actual beatings. This is why the Voting Rights Act of 1965, almost one-hundred years later, was so incredibly important.
9. Angela Y. Davis, *Women, Culture, & Politics* (New York: Random House, 1984/1989), 7–8.
10. See Harding's Preface within this volume.
11. Charles W. Mills, *Blackness Visible: Essays on Philosophy and Race* (Ithaca, NY: Cornell University Press, 1989), 2.
12. This is not to imply that philosophers who are women of color have not critically engaged the *patriarchal* assumptions of western philosophy. My point is that white women philosophers must not simply critique sites of patriarchy while leaving uncritiqued and unchallenged sites of whiteness, which are sites of power that are conferred upon both white women and white men even if they are inflected differently based upon gender.
13. See Hoagland's chapter within this volume.
14. I would like to thank Sarah Hoagland for an important observation regarding the structure of the book, particularly in terms of her advice regarding the avoidance of the pretense of white anti-racist self-glorification.

1

White Ignorance and Denials of Complicity: On the Possibility of Doing Philosophy in Good Faith

Barbara Applebaum, Syracuse University

> I wish to examine what does (or does not) go on in the minds of "nice" white people which allows them to ignore the terrible effects of racism, and, to the extent that these effects are recognized at all, to deny that they bear any responsibility for their perpetuation.
> —Sandra Lee Bartky [1]

> How were people able to consistently do the wrong thing while thinking that they are doing the right thing?
> —Charles W. Mills [2]

Introduction

A number of philosophers of late have provocatively suggested that doing what is considered "good" philosophy can have pernicious effects. Charles Mills[3] contends that ideal theory, the traditional method of moral theory, is ideology that benefits the privileged and he maintains that white ignorance is an inherent feature of the mainstream philosophical discipline.[4] Building on the work of Lewis Gordon, Robert E. Birt[5] examines the "bad faith of whiteness" as it is manifested in philosophy and Clevis Headley[6] speaks about strategies of denial in philosophy that function "to distort objective features of the social world in order to make the social world more psychologically comforting."[7] Although she does not target the discipline of philosophy specifically, Sandra Bartky[8] discusses what she refers to as a white culpable ignorance or more specifically, a *white refusal to know what one ought to know because to know would implicate one in the perpetuation of systemic injustice.* It is such a *systemically supported reluctance to know what one does not know (a relentless readiness to ignore consideration of one's ignorance)* that is the focus of this chapter.

Study of such resistance is not new. White feminist philosophers have been extremely diligent about exposing the androcentrism of philosophical theories. Yet, we/they had to be pressed by women of color to examine our/their own presumed white innocence. In their discussion of white feminists, although not specifically white feminist philosophers, Mary Louise Fellows and Sherene Razack[9] note the "consistent surprise" and resistance to consider one's complicity when women of color view them as agents of oppression. Perhaps the most extensive examination of such white resistance can be found in the scholarship around social justice pedagogy, particularly as manifested in teacher education. What can these two areas of study contribute to the understanding of how the whiteness of philosophy can "insulate itself against refutation"[10] and how such whiteness can be more effectively challenged?

This chapter takes up a type of reaction to the theories of philosophers of race that may not be exceedingly prevalent within published scholarship but will not be uncommon in discussions within and among philosophers themselves. The following case is a hypothetical one but I believe it will resonate with many who have become embroiled in discussions with some white philosophers who, for example, *disagree* that their whiteness affects their epistemology or that their social location plays a crucial role in their continued ignorance about the meaning and reality of systemic oppression and privilege. The hypothetical case involves a philosopher of education who tried to introduce his colleagues to the work of Charles Mills in which Mills attempts to expose and challenge the whiteness of philosophy. The response was both incredulity and dismissal. "The *whiteness* of philosophy?" a hypothetical white philosopher rhetorically replies. "This is just a generalization that is an excuse for not being able to get one's hands dirty in details." In response to Mills' provocative observation that Rawls does not address racial injustice in his celebrated opus, *A Theory of Justice*,[11] another white philosopher protests, "That's because Rawls is focused on ideal theory." In utter disbelief, the white philosopher charges, "What? Is Mills implying that Rawls is complicit in systemic injustice?" When the philosopher who introduced Mills work to his colleagues counters that yes, this is what Mills contends and he adds that Mills also argues that ideal theory, so prevalent in moral theory, perpetuates the whiteness of philosophy, the response he receives from his colleagues is to argue so extensively about how Mills caricatures Rawls that the critique of moral theory as grounded in ideology becomes peripheral, almost dismissed without serious discussion. (Which is particularly regrettable since Mills unabashedly admits to defending a liberal framework.[12])

Were these white philosophers just doing what "good philosophers" do—providing warrant for their disagreement with some of the arguments that Mills makes? Are these philosophers just disagreeing or does their disagreement function as defensiveness and dismissiveness? Was this merely an uncharitable reading of Mills' work by a few individual philosophers? And/or are these instances of *patterns of discursive moves* connected to the race of these philosophers that derail the discussion and protect them from having to consider their complicity in systemic racism? Of course it is important to get Rawls right, but by focusing predominantly on whether or not Mills understands Rawls were these white philosophers able to ignore and ultimately dismiss without discussion arguments that might compel them to consider their complicity in racism, especially since these white philosophers did not express a similar urgency about getting Mills right? What underlies the expressed *incredulity* about the possibility that Rawls (or themselves) could be complicit in the perpetuation of systemic oppression and privilege? Sandra Bartky maintains that part of the problem of *"the shameful livery of white incomprehension"*[13] is that white people think that they already have knowledge of the Other and that what they know absolves them of any complicity with racism. Yet what they know is not only incomplete and selective but also frequently false and ideological because such knowledge functions to protect privilege. Are white philosophers immune to such criticism?

In the first two sections of this chapter the notion of white ignorance and its connection to denials of complicity will be explored. The third part will raise and consider some important questions with epistemological implications that notions such as white ignorance invite. Are arguments that support the prevalence of white ignorance question-begging? How can those who argue for the existence of white ignorance avoid the "everything is resistance problem"? To address these questions the meaning and possibility of engaged disagreement will be discussed. More specifically, what distinguishes "disagreement as resistance" from "engaged disagreement"? Finally, it will be argued that the type of engagement necessary for white individuals to consider their complicity in systemic racism requires a shift in one's conception of moral responsibility. With the help of Iris Marion Young's Social Connection Model of Responsibility,[14] I argue that the contours of such a shift can be elucidated.

I acknowledge how provocative and challenging these questions seem. A well-intentioned philosopher might even argue that these are questions of interest to psychologists but not something of *philosophical* interest. It is important to highlight that to evade the questions posed in this chapter by reassigning them to the realm of psychology and as outside of philosophical concern is exactly the danger that this chapter is trying to underscore. Such strictly erected boundaries around the philosophical realm might in some instances be justified but in others can function to support and sustain the type of disengagement that validates denials of complicity. These are questions, therefore, that white philosophers cannot avoid seriously engaging.

White Ignorance

What is this white ignorance that Mills and others are referring to and how does such ignorance contribute to denials of complicity? We can elucidate white ignorance by contrasting two incidences:

Story #1: I am a white person. On vacation, I decided not to check my email. You know, if you check, you feel obligated to respond—I preferred to remain ignorant.

Story #2: In his "Fragments of a Social Ontology of Whiteness,"[15] George Yancy describes how a white philosopher whom he deeply respected cautioned Yancy with deep concern and out of good intentions not to get pegged as someone who pursues issues in African-American philosophy. Yancy immediately thinks:

> "Pegged! I'm doing philosophy!" It immediately occurred to me that the introductory course in philosophy that I had taken with him some years back did not include a single person of color. Yet, *he did not see* his own philosophical performances—engagements with European and Anglo-American philosophy as "pegged"; he simply taught philosophy qua philosophy. Such a philosophy only masquerades as universal.[16]

Race is not a factor in all types of ignorance. As Mills explains it, "At all times . . . there will be many facts about the natural and social worlds on which people, including white people, have no opinion, or a mistaken opinion, *but race is not directly or indirectly responsible*."[17] Race, for instance, does not play a role in my decision to ignore email. Yet race is a factor in the type of ignore-ance exhibited by the white philosopher in Yancy's narrative. Moreover, white ignorance does not refer exclusively to the type of ignorance prevalent in overtly racist white individuals but additionally covers the type of "not knowing" existing in even those who are well-intended and "educated" which "after the transition from de jure to de facto white supremacy, it is precisely this kind of white ignorance that is most important."[18] In order to understand how race was relevant, a number of characteristics of such ignorance must be emphasized.

In the second story, the exhibited ignorance is not merely a lack of knowledge resulting from a cognitive flaw of a particular individual. Such ignorance is not merely an individual's bad epistemic practice but, as Linda Alcoff explains, is "a substantive epistemic practice itself."[19] In other words, white ignorance is a product of an *epistemology* of ignorance, a systemically supported, socially induced pattern of (mis)understanding the world that is connected to and works to sustain systemic oppression and privilege. Most important, such ignorance functions to mystify the consequences of such unjust systems so that those who benefit from the system do not have to consider their complicity in perpetuating it. There are benefits for the dominant social group of such ignorance. In her analysis of willful ignorance in literary characters, Vivian May writes, "there are many things those in dominant groups are taught *not* to know, encouraged *not* to see, *and the privileged are rewarded for this state of not-knowing*."[20] Quoting from Peggy McIntosh, May explicates that willful ignorance involves *a pattern of assumptions* that privileges the dominant group and gives license to members of those groups "to be ignorant, oblivious, arrogant, and destructive"[21] all the while thinking themselves "as good."

Well-intentioned white people are often surprised when they encounter experiences that compel them to consider what they do not know about systemic racism. Willful ignorance, May continues, "is . . . a carefully constructed, narrow vision of reality that *denies its narrowness*"[22] and involves socially authorized "inscribed habits of (in)attention."[23] In a distressing illustration of such habits of selective attention outside the realm of philosophy, Tyron Foreman and Amanda Lewis[24] underscore the intense surprise that many white Americans expressed after Hurricane Katrina about the social reality of racial inequality in New Orleans. Foreman and Lewis attribute this astonishment to a racial apathy that is a consequence of the white ignorance manifested in the ideology of color ignore-ance.

Mills contends that one's social positionality will influence what questions one believes are important to ask and the problems one believes are valuable to pursue. White ignorance involves not asking or not having to ask (i.e., having the privilege not to need to ask) certain questions. In his 1997 book, *The Racial Contract,* Mills argues that a Racial Contract underwrites the modern Social Contract. The Racial Contract is a covert agreement to misinterpret the world and white people are both the signatories and benefactors of the contract. The Racial Contract, according to Mills, involves:

> . . . simply a failure to ask certain questions, taking for granted as a status quo and baseline the existing color-coded configurations of wealth, poverty, property, and opportunities, the pretence that formal, juridical equality is sufficient to remedy inequities created on a foundation of several hundred years of racial privilege, and that challenging that foundation is a transgression of the terms of the social contract.[25]

White ignorance, therefore, generates specific types of delusions—wrong ways of perceiving the world that are socially validated by the dominant norms.

Such delusions, or an "inverted epistemology" as Mills terms it, are an "officially sanctioned reality"[26] that is a divergence from actual reality. According to Mills, the racial contract is an agreement to:

> . . . *mis*interpret the world. One has to learn to see the world wrongly, but with the assurance that this set of mistaken perceptions will be validated by white epistemic authority . . . . Thus, in effect, on matters related to race, *the*

> Racial Contract prescribes for its signatories an inverted epistemology, an epistemology of ignorance, a particular pattern of localized and global cognitive dysfunctions (which are psychologically and socially functional), producing the ironic outcome that whites will in general be unable to understand the world they themselves have made.[27]

One of the significant features of white ignorance is that it involves not just *not knowing* but *not knowing what one does not know and believing that one knows*. Thus, following Eve Sedgwick,[28] systemic ignorance is not passive but is an activity. Extending Sedgwick's insights to the discourse of color ignorance, Cris Mayo contends that such ignoring is not a "lack of knowledge" but "a particular kind of knowledge."[29] It is this latter phenomenon, fueled by a refusal to consider that one might be morally complicit, that promotes a resistance to knowing.

Echoing insights from Standpoint Theory, Mills explicates the process by which this occurs. Dominant concepts that constitute one's framework of meaning can obscure certain realities, "blocking them from sight, or naturalizing them." Concepts "necessary for accurately mapping these realities," however, "will be absent."[30] In a provocative but evidently correct observation, Mills notes, "the crucial conceptual innovation necessary to map nonideal realities has *not* come from the dominant group."[31] While it is important to emphasize that it is not only white people who are susceptible to white ignorance, white people are particularly susceptible because they are the one's who have the most to gain from remaining ignorant. As Sandra Harding argues, it is members of oppressed groups, those who have direct experience with oppression, who "have fewer interests in ignorance about the social order and fewer reasons to invest in maintaining or justifying the status quo than do dominant groups."[32]

This is not to imply that all members of oppressed groups automatically have such knowledge. Alcoff explains:

> ... identity does not determine one's interpretation of the facts, nor does it constitute fully formed perspectives, but rather, to use the hermeneutic terminology once again, identities operate as horizons from which certain aspects or layers of reality can be made visible. In stratified societies, differently identified individuals do not always have the same access to points of view or perceptual planes of observation. Two individuals may participate in the same event, but have perceptual access to different aspects of that event. Social identity is relevant to epistemic judgment, then, not because identity determines judgment but because identity can in some instances yield access to perceptual facts that themselves may be relevant to the formulation of various knowledge claims or theoretical analyses.[33]

In other words, there is a greater tendency for those who experience racial exclusions than those who are privileged by such exclusions to be more troubled by the universalization of white space and to be more affected by white norms that are mystified as universal but are not.

If the systemically privileged have the privilege to ignore systemic inequalities and if privilege itself is sustained by such ignore-ance, how would this affect knowledge production in the discipline of philosophy? Focusing specifically on moral theorizing, for example, Mills argues:

> Such communities will not usually experience these injustices directly; they will have a vested interest in the system's perpetuation and thus be prone to evasions, bad faith, and self-deception about its true character. They will be more receptive to dominant social ideologies whose conceptual structure ignores, blurs over, or justifies the plight of the subordinated.[34]

An insidious consequence, as Mills points out, is that there may be serious recognition difficulties in spotting racial problems that are philosophically relevant.

As an illustration of such recognition problems, again outside of philosophy, recall the uproar in the media when in the early part of 2007 Joseph Biden, a white Senator, publicly described fellow Democratic presidential contender Senator Barack Obama as "the first mainstream African-American who is articulate and bright and clean and a nice-looking guy."[35] Biden insisted that he meant it as an innocent compliment. Indeed, white people, drawing on their own experience, do not normally object when they are described as "articulate" and "clean" and the adjectives are most often intended as a form of praise. Yet some African-Americans were outraged and offended that someone could think that the former president of the *Harvard Law Review* should be complimented by being described as "articulate." As a subtle form of insidious racism, the descriptor has the subtext of amazement (even bewilderment) that implied this person is articulate "for a Black person." Mills, focusing on philosophy, argues that when moral theory is based on examples or paradigms of examples drawn from white experience then there arises:

> ... recognition problems in identifying certain racial practices as violations of those same principles or as instantiations of prohibited behaviors. Hence the familiar dispute, marked by mutual frustration and anger toward the other, in which whites and blacks disagree on how X should be categorized.[36]

White ignorance contributes to such recognition problems and has to be acknowledged and countered. As Mills counsels:

> Tracking these failures and transforming one's practice so as to avoid them in the future will then be facilitated if one understands their systemic architecture, knows in advance the cognitive and affective grooves within which

one's mind is likely to run. It becomes easier to do the right thing if one knows the wrong things that, to one's group, will typically *seem* like the right thing.[37]

Yet this is not always easy as denials of complicity work to sustain white ignorance. What are denials of complicity and how are they related to moral ignorance?

Before moving on to argue for the connection between white ignorance and denials of complicity, I want to pause briefly to remark on a tendency to assimilate white ignorance with willful ignorance. In their discussion of epistemologies of ignorance, both Alcoff and May often refer to white ignorance as willful ignorance. What is willful ignorance and how is it connected to white ignorance? My email decision previously mentioned appears to be an example of willful ignorance because I preferred, desired or wanted to remain ignorant of something. But in common parlance willful ignorance is more insidious. Willful ignorance often refers to a blatant avoidance or disregard of facts or well-founded arguments because they oppose one's personal beliefs, values or worldviews. Willful ignorance has also been used to refer to a laziness or a fear to examine critically one's personal point of view. In other words, it is to remain intentionally ignorant of something that one *should* know but one does not want to know. Willful seems to imply a level of knowing, i.e., that one wants to ignore knowing and is aware of what one is doing. Thomas Green defines willful ignorance as:

> ... that condition that I note from time to time in those who (1) are ignorant on some matter important to their lives, (2) *are aware of their ignorance*, but even more than that, are (3) resolved to remain in their ignorance, (4) not the least because it is such a source of enjoyment and pleasure to them. I suppose that each of us can recall someone who fits this description. It is a bit more difficult to admit what is probably no less true, that there are traces of this sort of thing in ourselves.[38]

White ignorance may be but is not always the result of a deliberate and conscious decision. Often such ignorance does not seem willful at all but rather the product of a socially induced tendency to ignore that involves being unaware that one does not know. Why categorize white ignorance as willful?

Another characteristic of willful ignorance that might better capture why white ignorance might be understood to be a form of willful ignorance is that willful ignorance is *culpable* ignorance. Interesting and complex questions about culpable ignorance can be found in the ethical debates around moral responsibility but will not be addressed here.[39] By and large, involuntary ignorance is often thought to excuse one from moral culpability unless one knowingly contrives one's own ignorance, then one is culpable even if one is ignorant. White ignorance may be a type of willful ignorance because there is a sense in which white people deliberately contrive their own ignorance. But white ignorance might also be willful not necessarily because the ignorance is consciously or deliberately manufactured but instead willful because such ignorance benefits the person or the social group the person is a member of. Members of the dominant group, for instance, have *a vested interest* in not knowing. Linda Alcoff[40] emphasizes that white people not only have less interest in understanding their complicity in social injustice than those who are victimized by such systems but also that white people have a *positive interest* in remaining ignorant. The point is that even if one does not deliberately manufacture such ignorance, white ignorance does not release one from moral responsibility and might be in that sense something willful in the sense that it is something that someone *would* want.

One of the types of vested interests that such ignorance serves is the sustaining of one's moral self-image. The type of white ignorance that is the focus of this chapter, therefore, involves not only "not knowing what one does not know and thinking that one does know" that is socially sponsored. In addition, such ignorance benefits members of the dominant group and protects their moral sense of self. Both these features of white ignorance promote denials of complicity.

White Ignorance and Denials of Complicity

> . . . most white people in this country are complicit in an unjust system of race relations that bestows unearned advantages on them while denying these advantages to racial Others. Complicity in this system is neither chosen nor, typically, is it acknowledged, because there are both powerful ideological systems in place that serve to reassure whites that the suffering of darker-skinned Others is not of their doing and because the capacity of whites to live in denial of responsibility is very highly developed.[41]

As the recognition in academic circles grows that, even after the civil rights movement and the end of de jure segregation, racism is systemically endemic, many disciplines have shifted their focus from an exclusive concern with the victims of systemic injustice to acknowledging the need to turn the investigative gaze inward on all those who perpetuate and sustain such systems. The significance of the term "white supremacy," for example, is extolled by Mills because it focuses on "systematicity" of racism. White supremacy shifts the focus:

> . . . from the individual and attitudinal (the discourse of "racism") to the realm of structures and power, it facilitates the highlighting of the most important thing from the perspective of justice, which is how the white population benefits illicitly from their social location . . . .[42]

From the perspective of racism as prejudice, if one does not have any illicit attitudes against people of color, one can perceive oneself to be morally innocent. From the perspective of racism as a system of privilege, if one benefits from privilege, one's complicity is much more difficult to deny.

Questions of the complicity on the part of well-intentioned white people only arise when racism is understood macroscopically.[43] As Mills explains:

> ... with the decline in overt racism in the white population, the real issue for a long time has not been individual racism but, far more importantly, the reproduction of white advantage and black disadvantage through the workings of racialized social structures. The idea of white supremacy is intended, in part, to capture the crucial reality that the *normal* workings of the social system continue to disadvantage blacks in large measure *independently* of racist feeling.[44]

Along with the recognition in academic scholarship of racism as systemic, however, a burgeoning body of research has developed around white denials of complicity. Such denials involve discursive ways in which white people deny they have any role to play in systemic racism and in which white people proclaim their white innocence. Sandra Bartky[45] delineates a typology of such denials in which is included the culpably ignorant or those who fail to know what they ought to know because such knowledge would morally implicate them. Since people generally want to see themselves as morally good, any intimation that one plays a role in perpetuating unjust systems of oppression and privilege will likely be denied. Two ways, for example, that white people protect their moral sense of self is to maintain ideologies of color ignore-ance and meritocracy that in effect deny and dismiss how racism exists in the lives of the marginalized. Only those who do not experience racism can profess its non-existence or diminish its effects, consequently also relieving themselves of having to consider how they might be complicit in perpetuating a system that to them does not exist.

Educational researchers, especially researchers who study how white students engage in social justice education, have given serious attention to such denials. Many educational scholars[46] have explored how white students use discursive maneuvers to resist knowledge of their complicity. Such resistance is expressed in multifarious ways from emotional oppositional outbursts in class to passivity and silence. Kim Case and Annette Hemmings[47] observe that white women preservice teachers often use what they refer to as "distancing strategies" in order to avoid being positioned as racist or implicated in systemic oppression. They use these strategies to avoid acknowledging responsibility. Similarly, Elizabeth Higgenbothan[48] notes how it is not enough to explain different definitions of racism or to teach about the meaning of oppression. White students often resist this knowledge because the message they hear is "you are to blame."

Kathy Hytten and John Warren's[49] excellent ethnography of the rhetorical strategies their students performed in courses that attempt to teach about systemic oppression and privilege offers many examples of such tactics. Among the types of discursive strategies that Hytten and Warren discuss are: remaining silent, evading questions, resorting to the rhetoric of ignoring color, focusing on progress, victim blaming and focusing on culture rather than race. Hytten and Warren emphasize that these discursive moves are culturally sanctioned discourses of evasion that "were not original—that is, they are already available, already common forms of asserting dominance."[50] These rhetorical strategies work to obstruct engagement so that deliberations about one's complicity in systemic oppression are avoided.

Alice McIntyre[51] coined the phrase "white talk" to name discourse that functions to "insulate White people from examining their/our individual and collective role(s) in the perpetuation of racism."[52] In the same vein, Sandra Bartky explains the unwillingness to acknowledge complicity in racism is more than just a personal lethargy or a private failure but rather a culturally sanctioned discourse of evasion that protects the interests of the privileged and their moral composure. White ignorance, therefore, is sustained by denials of complicity but white ignorance also authorizes such denials. In effect, "resisters" believe they are just disagreeing with the material but their disagreement also functions as a refusal to engage.

While one can disagree and remain engaged in the material, for example, asking questions, searching for clarification and understanding, denials function as a way to distance oneself and dismiss without engagement. Hytten and Warren emphasize that such strategic denials are not only already available in the sense that they are socially authorized but also that they serve to protect the center, the location of privilege. Such discursive strategies of denial are an "implicit way of resisting critical engagements with whiteness."[53] When white students, for instance, refuse to acknowledge the depth of their privilege, their privilege is reflected in the very questioning of the social facts that are at odds with their experience. They have what Peggy McIntosh refers to as permission to escape[54] and what Alice McIntyre calls "privileged choice,"[55] i.e., the mere fact that they can question the existence of systemic oppression is a function of their privilege to choose to ignore discussions of systemic oppression or not.

Color ignore-ance is a widespread position of moral belief but is also a strategy of denial.[56] White students often refuse to "see" color as a way in which to establish their moral, non-racist credentials. Moreover, they become defensive when such beliefs are challenged because to challenge such beliefs would entail challenging their moral innocence.[57] The students believe they are just expressing their belief but that belief also functions as a way of "blaming the victim" and, thus, avoiding any consideration of their complicity. Woody Doane explains:

> "Color-blind" ideology plays an important role in the maintenance of white hegemony.... Because whites tend not to see themselves in racial terms and not to recognize the existence of the advantages that whites enjoy in American society, this promotes a worldview that emphasizes *individualistic* explanations, for social and economic achievement, as if the individualism of white privilege was a universal attribute. Whites also exhibit a general inability to perceive the persistence of discrimination and the effects of more subtle forms of institutional discrimination. In the context of color-blind racial ideology, whites are more likely to see the opportunity structure as open and institutions as impartial or objective in their functioning ... this combination supports an interpretive framework in which whites' explanations for inequality focus upon the cultural characteristics (e.g., motivation, values) of subordinate groups.... Politically, this blaming of subordinate groups for their lower economic position serves to neutralize demands for antidiscrimination initiatives or for a redistribution of resources.[58]

If white students believe that it is morally justified to refuse to consider race, they not only are authorized to ignore racial patterns of social injustice, they will also feel warranted in refusing to use racial labels to describe themselves. As a result, the unearned privilege that they are afforded because of their racial positionality can be disregarded or dismissed. Moreover, when they are confronted with marginalized voices recounting oppressive experience, they can easily interpret such narratives as "complaints" and dismiss them with the claim that this is an example of "being overly sensitive" or "playing the race card."[59]

Denials of complicity are not restricted to the classroom. While much has been written about the reactions of white feminists to the charge of racism from feminists of color, Sarita Srivastava[60] highlights how white feminists, who see themselves as committed to egalitarian principles *as feminists*, find it incomprehensible that they, who are themselves so "progressive," can be accused of racism. White feminists understand themselves as challenging systemic oppression not contributing to it. Srivastava quotes from Ruth Frankenberg's classic study, *White Women, Race Matters: The Social Construction of Whiteness*, "Because we were basically well-meaning individuals, the idea of being part of the problem of racism was genuinely shocking to us."[61] Yet even in social movements that are organized around social justice, difference can be sacrificed in the name of unity and thus relations of power and inequity among women can be overlooked. It is this deep investment in their own moral innocence that often makes it difficult for white feminists to engage with the inequalities that occur within their own movements. Sherryl Kleinman[62] contends that "we become so invested in our beliefs as radicals or 'good people' that we cannot see the reactionary or hurtful consequences of our behaviors."[63] And Srivastava cautions, "an alternative moral identity can both foster and impede social change."[64]

A need for moral innocence can encourage a profound resistance to knowing that entrenches ignorance further. There is a *passion for ignorance*, as Deborah Britzman[65] puts this, when it comes to learning "difficult knowledge" that challenges one's moral identity and compels one to consider one's complicity in systemic injustice. She maintains that such knowledge cannot be learned without emotional trauma. It seems that white ignorance and denials of complicity mutually reinforce each other and support a refusal to engage in learning. How can philosophy be informed by this scholarship and what can this scholarship help us to understand about the whiteness of philosophy?

Philosophy, White Ignorance and Denials of Complicity: Epistemological Concerns

"Reading *Drylongso, White Over Black, I Know Why the Caged Bird Sings, They Called Them Greasers, The Woman Warrior, Invisible Man,* etc., is not helpful in exploring racism and ethnocentrism *unless* these works are read from (*a racially) engaged position"* such that whites address our complicity *in racism* and seek to unravel "the connections between racism, ethnocentrism, white/Anglo self-esteem, (and) polite arrogance."[66]

Modern philosophy, largely through the influence of Descartes, has been predicated on the assumption that knowledge is exclusively a function of the mind and the discipline prides itself on a disembodied epistemology that abstracts away from the experiences of everyday life. Anna Stubblefield[67] notes the defense from some philosophers against the charge of the theoretical whiteness of philosophy: ". . . European philosophy is the study of the most general and universalizable questions—the nature of reality, of truth, of justice—that concerns all people."[68] Moreover, classically trained philosophers are taught to separate the personal from the scholarly. The impersonal style, as Annette Baier remarks, "has become nearly a sacred tradition in moral philosophy."[69] Epistemic warrant, not personal opinion, are the components of philosophical argumentation. Because the personal is understood as an area that does not require justification or defense—it remains outside of rational deliberation—it lacks any epistemic warrant and should not be a factor in philosophical reasoning.

Yet both feminists and critical race scholars warn that such abstraction and claims of objectivity are not what they seem to be. What is considered essentially and universally human is a mystified version of what is masculine, white, able-bodied, heterosexual and Western. The possibility of discursive patterns that conceal structures of oppression and privilege operative in philosophical argumentation is a most incendiary charge. Intimations of ideology and delusion that are assumed by notions of white ignorance raise a plethora of difficult questions. Is disagreement always resistance? Wouldn't such a charge of resistance undermine the possibility of criticism and legitimation altogether? If the claim is that philosophy insulates itself from the "complicity critique" is there not a danger that all disagreement will be labeled resistance and, thus, dismissed leaving the position of those who maintain the whiteness of philosophy beyond challenge? Does the argument about white ignorance and the whiteness of philosophy function itself as a way to refuse to engage with its critics and thus, insulates itself against challenge?

To expose the whiteness of philosophy, however, is not to reject the possibility of engaged disagreement. It does, however, call for a very special type of engagement. Putting one's own beliefs on hold, putting oneself in another's shoes, rational deliberation, reflection and consideration of all viewpoints are among the suggestions articulated by those who advocate for dialogue across difference. Some feminist scholars have problematized the liberal focus on dialogue across difference[70] while others point to the limitations of dialogue but do not necessarily call for its wholesale rejection.[71] Nonetheless, within this debate about dialogue and its limitations there are insightful analyses of components of communicative virtues that can help to flesh out the type of engagement I believe must precede any possibility of disagreement. I will focus on two features of engagement (clearly there may be more): listening and vulnerability.

Listening

Listening has not often been the focus of attention in academic scholarship. More often the act of speaking is central. Yet there is no mutual dialogue when those with power have the privilege to not actively listen well and especially when they have the privilege to doubt rather than believe.[72] Lisa Delpit opens her oft quoted essay, "The Silenced Dialogue: Power and Pedagogy in Educating Other People's Children,"[73] with a litany of complaints that teachers of color have about white teachers.

> "I'm tired of arguing with those White people, because they won't listen. Well, I don't know if they really don't listen or if they just don't believe you."

> "It's really hard. They just don't listen well. No, they listen, but they don't hear—you know how your mama used to say you listen to the radio, but you hear your mother? Well they don't hear me."[74]

What does it mean to actively listen well in the context of asymmetric positions of power?

Listening that is engaged involves learning not only about the other but also about oneself and being willing to be changed by what one hears. Since privilege involves the possibility of not having to engage, the systemically privileged must have an interest in working to understand what the marginalized can offer. As Maria Lugones and Elizabeth Spelman contend, ". . . there is nothing that necessitates that you understand our world: understand, that is, not as an observer understands things, but as a participant, as someone who has a stake in them understands them."[75] Similarly, Audrey Thompson insists that white people have to listen *desperately*, to listen, that is, with "faith and commitment."[76] This means it is not enough to tolerate benignly work that challenges whiteness or to add such work to the curriculum in a marginal way. Instead the work of scholars of color must be *seriously studied*, "tak(ing) it to heart, reading and attending to what we read in new ways."[77] This is not an issue of merely suspending judgment that would pose the danger of relativistic toleration, as Thompson underscores. Exercising any judgment of work that radically challenges one's own world requires first that one "knows how to listen, how to read different scholars."[78]

Engaged listening, however, requires a very special type of openness. In her critique of the politics of recognition that she claims perpetuates rather than challenges systemic oppression, Kelly Oliver[79] suggests the metaphor of witnessing, and more specifically "bearing witness" as a more constructive way of understanding the type of engagement in social relations that multiculturalism requires. Witnessing is understood as more than just a matter of eye-witness reporting. It also has an almost religious connotation of bearing witness to that which cannot be seen, to that which is "beyond recognition." Such engagement with the other involves a type of listening that can hear what is beyond one's recognition. Oliver distinguishes between eye-witnessing and bearing witness to what cannot be seen and illustrates this distinction using the work of Dori Laub, a psychoanalyst who does research on Holocaust survivors.

Laub notes a debate between historians and psychoanalysts after both had heard testimony from a woman who claims to have been an eyewitness to the Auschwitz uprising and who had described the four chimneys that were destroyed when Jewish prisoners set fire to the camp. The historians dismissed and discredited the woman's testimony because, as Laub explains, historical evidence points to only one chimney being destroyed at the time. The psychoanalysts, on the other hand, understood that the woman was not reporting historical facts but rather was describing the uprising at Auschwitz as something so radical and unimaginable, something beyond recognition. It is a mistake to think that such experiences can be captured by facts and figures. Oliver explains quoting Laub that "what the historians could not hear, listening for empirical facts, was the 'very secret of survival and of resistance to extermination.'"[80] While the historians were listening for confirmation of something that they already knew, the psychoanalysts were listening "to hear something new, something yet beyond comprehension."[81] An important facet of engaged listening is to be open to hear something new, beyond one's recognition. Genuine listening involves being open to hear something new, beyond recognition, but this also calls for a special type of vulnerability.

Vulnerability

Being willing to be vulnerable has affinities with what Emily Robertson, borrowing from Andrew Olenquist, refers to as being open to the possibility that one might be "obligated to lose."[82] In this sense, one is willing to be open to the possibility that one might be shown to be wrong and that someone else's reasons might be better than one's own. There is, however, another possibly related type of vulnerability that is acknowledged by Lugones and Spelman that involves a willingness to risk alienation and self-disruption. In order for white women to understand what women of color are trying to tell them, Lugones and Spelman argue, they:

> ... need to learn to become unintrusive, unimportant, patient to the point of tears, while at the same time open to learning any possible lessons. You will also need to come to terms with the sense of alienation, of not belonging, of having your world thoroughly disrupted, having it criticized and scrutinized from the point of view of those who have been harmed by it, having important concepts central to it dismissed, being viewed with mistrust, being seen as of no consequence except as an object of mistrust.[83]

Such openness requires being willing to be vulnerable to severe criticism and radical self-questioning without which white people will not be able to understand what voices of color are saying. As Thompson explains, the call to listen is "a radical call. It is a demand not just to register or include the voices of women of color but to change how we as white women act and think. It is a call to rethink our theories."[84]

Ann Diller,[85] in her 1998 Presidential Address to the Philosophy of Education Society, articulates a similar understanding of "being open." She maintains that a philosopher of one's own education must be willing to be torpified. The capacity to be torpified involves an:

> ... ability to be awed, to be surprised, to be astonished, to be moved in a deeply moral or ethical, or aesthetical, or epistemological or ontological way. It takes considerable courage, self-knowledge, a brave heart, and honest openness to face one's own ignorance and to stay present in the concomitant experience of discomfort.[86]

Delpit, as well, concludes her essay with a powerful call for white people to listen and to be vulnerable. Although:

> ... (b)oth sides do need to be able to listen, ... I contend that it is those with the most power, those in the majority, who must take the greater responsibil-

ity for initiating the process. To do so takes a very special kind of listening, listening that requires not only open eyes and ears, but open hearts and minds. We do not really see through our eyes or hear through our ears, but through our beliefs. To put our beliefs on hold is to cease to exist as ourselves for a moment—and that is not easy. It is painful as well, because it means turning yourself inside out, giving up on your own sense of who you are, and being willing to see yourself in the unflattering light of another's angry gaze . . . . We must learn to be vulnerable enough to allow our world to turn upside down in order to allow the realities of others to edge themselves into our consciousness.[87]

Calls for engagement require genuine listening and a willingness to be torpified but do not necessarily focus on agreement.

An interesting example of engaged disagreement, I maintain, can be found in the debate between Seyla Benhabib and Judith Butler in *Feminist Contentions*.[88] Initially focused on the tensions between postmodernism and feminism, the discussion quickly shifted to their opposing positions in regard to the subject, agency and autonomy. While they take opposing issues on many important issues, their exchange worked not only to clarify each other's positions but also to lay bare the advantages and disadvantages of both. From the exchange, it appears that they did not set out to dismiss each other's position—they did not just "come to say no"[89] but rather to engaged in thoughtful and theoretical work.[90]

Naomi Scheman provides some insight into the type of openness that encourages engagement. She cautions:

. . . Not to leave ourselves open and vulnerable to alternative understandings when our own come in part from locations of discursive privilege is to close ourselves to the possibility of learning from others whose social locations on the borders of intelligibility equip them precisely for dismantling the structures we may deplore but cannot ourselves see beyond—since they are, for those of us who are intelligible in their terms, the "limits of our language."[91]

If some retort, "but how can one be open to everything and everybody?" Scheman astutely responds that how we ought to chose what we give attention to is exactly the issue. She does not advocate "epistemic promiscuity" or being open to every passing argument but rather emphasizes that we must examine how we chose which arguments that challenge our beliefs we will seriously engage with, whose critique we try hard to understand, whom we read and where we might look for ways that "might shake us up."

Finally, a cue to what may help or obstruct the development of such engagement is to be found in the *incredulity* expressed in the rhetorical question, "Are you implying that Rawls is complicit in racism?" Such incredulity is a moral incredulity—"Are you implying that Rawls is a bad or immoral person?" Traditional conceptions of moral responsibility promote a defensiveness that may block off engagement. Engagement on the part of dominant group members, therefore, requires that they first make a shift in their conception of moral responsibility.

Rearticulating Moral Responsibility

In her 2002 PES Presidential Address,[92] Barbara Houston indicts the traditional conception of moral responsibility for encouraging the "moral lethargy of decent people" because it is too centered on individual intentions, backward-looking and essentially concerned with attributions of moral accountability. Other feminist philosophers have called for the rearticulation of moral responsibility in ways that can acknowledge white complicity. Lisa Heldke[93] distinguishes between being responsible to (marginalized people) and responsibility for (one's own social location), the latter relating to the type of white moral responsibility I am attempting to articulate. Although I do not pretend to offer a complete and wholly satisfying elucidation of how white moral responsibility can be delineated, I find Iris Marion Young's work on the Social Connection Model of Responsibility[94] helps to move this task forward.

Let me note that this is not a call for rearticulating white moral responsibility so that white people can feel comfortable. Instead the point is that traditional conceptions of agency and responsibility function to obscure rather than expose white complicity.

In order to articulate a model of responsibility that can accommodate the responsibility one bears under conditions of systemic injustice, Young distinguishes the social connection model from what she refers to as the liability model, which aligns with the more traditional version of responsibility. The liability model has three characteristic features. First and foremost, its objective is to isolate who is at fault and to assign blame. A person, under this model, is responsible to the degree that there is an action that connects the individual to the harm. The action must be voluntary and the agent must not be excusably ignorant. (Of course, this is an overly simplified account of an extremely complex debate in ethics but serves the purpose well enough to make the contrast between the two models clear.) Second, for an act to count as wrong, it must deviate from some acceptable norms, institutional practices and/or background conditions that constitute what is morally acceptable. The emphasis is on the deviation rather than on a critical examination of the norms themselves. Finally, since the concern is with assigning blame and fault, this model requires some action or event that can be isolated and has reached a terminus, something that can clearly be pointed to as what one is being held accountable for. The emphasis is more on isolated actions or events rather than structural or systemic patterns.

Young argues that the liability model is grounded in a notion of personhood that assumes we are atomistic individuals that have the capacity to strive for transcendence through rational autonomy. Such autonomy assumes that one can overcome external constraints and that one can stand outside of existing contingencies. The liability model of responsibility, Young contends, cannot capture the type of responsibility for harms that result from the convergence of actions of many individuals acting within generally accepted institutional rules and norms, as is the case with the harms of systemic social injustice. Young explains being complicit in systemic social injustice as the product of "proxy agency" and the system is sustained as the "collective results that no one intends, results that may even be counter to the best intentions of the actor."[95] Unlike a business partnership that one can dissolve at will, Young insists that no one can stand outside of existing contingencies. If moral responsibility is tied to individual intention and a transcendence of contingencies, the responsibility for the complicity or proxy agency in the perpetuation of systemic injustice will be concealed.

In contrast to the liability model, the social connection model of responsibility highlights how individuals *bear responsibility*[96] when they contribute in some way to the processes that produce and sustain systemic injustice. Unlike the liability model, it does not seek to isolate those responsible *in order to* distinguish them from those not responsible or from those less responsible. Even when individual agents can be found who are directly accountable for structural injustice (for example, blatant racists), this does not absolve others who *indirectly* contribute to structural injustice from bearing responsibility. The social connection model is not focused on how perpetrators' actions deviate from acceptable norms but rather "brings into question precisely the background conditions that ascription of blame or fault assume as normal."[97]

When we judge that structural injustice exists, we are saying precisely that at least some of the normal and accepted background conditions of action are not morally acceptable. Most of us contribute to a greater or lesser degree to the production and reproduction of structural injustice precisely because we follow the accepted and expected rules and conventions of the communities and institutions in which we act. Usually we enact these conventions and practices in a habitual way, without explicit reflection and deliberation on what we are doing . . . .[98]

Finally, the social connection model is more forward looking than backward looking. It does not require an isolated action or event that has reached a terminus. Such a model targets those processes that are likely to continue producing harms unless they are thwarted. Systemic injustice involves processes that produce ongoing harms that are often difficult to mark and isolate for blame. The social connection model uniquely draws our attention to the need to motivate those who participate in these processes to join to change the system collectively. Only by joining with others in collective action can one discharge one's responsibility for complicity. As Young stresses, "No one of us can do this on our own."[99]

Young's social connection model of responsibility helps us to understand how dominant group members are responsible for the maintenance of systemic social injustice and what types of actions are needed for social change. To use this model of responsibility as a lens can potentially diminish denials of white complicity, improve listening on the part of white people and, thus, enhance cross-racial dialogue. In addition, the possibility for the development of alliance identities might be increased.

In his *Bad Faith and Antiblack Racism*, Lewis Gordon[100] defines bad faith as a kind of self-deception and he notes how bad faith is a flight from responsibility. As an existential phenomenologist, Gordon problematically assumes that racism can be overcome by heroic individualism and destruction of racial identity. I have argued doing philosophy "in good faith" requires that those who benefit from white supremacy must seriously engage with philosophies of color that aim to destabilize philosophy's white center. I have also argued that such engagement will require a shift in the conceptions of moral responsibility that dominant group members rely upon. "The alternative to bad faith," as Linda Alcoff writes, is ". . . the enactment of an identity based on responsible, reflective choice within the context of a historical agenda larger than any individual life's project."[101] As I have argued in this chapter, this means that doing philosophy in good faith would require taking the whiteness of philosophy very seriously.

Notes

1. Sandra Lee Bartky, "Race, Complicity, and Culpable Ignorance," in *"Sympathy and Solidarity" and Other Essays* (Lanham, MD: Rowman & Littlefield, 2002), 151.
2. Charles W. Mills, *The Racial Contract* (Ithaca, New York: Cornell University Press, 1997), 94.
3. Charles W. Mills, "Ideal Theory as Ideology," *Hypatia: A Journal of Feminist Philosophy* 20, no. 3 (2005): 164–184.
4. Charles W. Mills, "White Ignorance," in *Race and Epistemologies of Ignorance*, ed. Shannon Sullivan and Nancy Tuana (Albany, New York: State University of New York Press, 2007), 13–38.
5. Robert E. Birt, "The Bad Faith of Whiteness," in *What White Looks Like: African-American Philosophers on the Whiteness Question*, ed. George Yancy (New York: Routledge, 2004), 55–64.
6. Clevis Headley, "Deligitimizing the Normativity of 'Whiteness': A Critical Africana Philosophical Study of the Metaphoricity of 'Whiteness'," in *What White Looks Like: African-American Philosophers on the Whiteness Question*, ed. George Yancy (New York: Routledge, 2004), 87–106.
7. Headley, "Deligitimizing the Normativity of 'Whiteness,'" 99.
8. Bartky, "Race, Complicity, and Culpable Ignorance."
9. Mary Louise Fellows and Sherene Razack, "Seeking Relations: Law and Feminism Roundtables," *Signs: Journal of Women in Culture and Society* 19, no. 4 (1994): 1048–83.
10. Mills, "White Ignorance," 19.
11. John Rawls, *A Theory of Justice* (Cambridge, MA: Harvard University Press, 1971).
12. Mills, "White Ignorance," 15; also see "Reply to Critics," *Small Axe: A Journal of Criticism* 2, no. 2 (1998): 191–201.
13. Bartky, "Race, Complicity, and Culpable Ignorance," 152.
14. Iris Marion Young, "Responsibility and Structural Injustice," http://socpol.anu.edu.au/YoungRespStrInj6.05.doc (accessed January 28, 2009). Also see "Responsibility and Global Justice: A Social Connection Model," *Social Philosophy and Policy* 23, no. 1 (2006): 102–130.
15. George Yancy, "Fragments of a Social Ontology of Whiteness," Introduction to *What White Looks Like: African-American Philosophers on the Whiteness Question*, ed. George Yancy (New York: Routledge, 2004), 1–24.
16. Yancy, "Fragments of a Social Ontology of Whiteness," 1, emphasis mine.
17. Mills, "White Ignorance," 20, emphasis mine.
18. Mills, "White Ignorance," 21.
19. Linda Martín Alcoff, "Epistemologies of Ignorance: Three Types," in *Race and Epistemologies of Ignorance*, ed. Shannon Sullivan and Nancy Tuana (Albany, New York: State University of New York Press, 2007), 39.
20. Vivian M. May, "Trauma in Paradise: Willful and Strategic Ignorance in *Cereus Blooms at Night*," *Hypatia* 21, no. 3 (2006): 113, emphasis mine.
21. Peggy McIntosh, "White Privilege and Male Privilege: A Personal Account of Coming to See Correspondences through Work in Women's Studies," in *Critical White Studies: Looking Behind the Mirror*, ed. R. Delgado and J. Stefancic (Philadelphia: Temple University Press, 1997), 292–299.
22. May, "Trauma in Paradise," 114, emphasis mine.

23. May, "Trauma in Paradise," 114.
24. Tyrone Foreman and Amanda Lewis, "Racial Apathy and Hurricane Katrina: The Social Anatomy of Prejudice in the Post-Civil Rights Era," *DuBois Review* 3, no. 1 (2006): 175–202.
25. Mills, *The Racial Contract*, 73.
26. Mills, *The Racial Contract*, 18.
27. Mills, *The Racial Contract*, 18, emphasis in the original.
28. Eve Kosofsky Sedgwick, *Epistemology of the Closet* (New York: Oxford University Press, 1980), 225.
29. Cris Mayo, "Civility and Its Discontents: Sexuality, Race, and the Lure of Beautiful Manners," in *Philosophy of Education 2001*, ed. Suzanne Rice (Urbana, Ill.: Philosophy of Education Society, 2002), 78–87, quotation on 85.
30. Mills, "Ideal Theory," 175.
31. Mills, "Ideal Theory," 175.
32. Sandra Harding, *Whose Science? Whose Knowledge? Thinking From Women's Lives* (Ithaca, New York: Cornell University Press, 1991), 126.
33. Linda Martin Alcoff, *Visible Identities: Race, Gender, and the Self* (Oxford: Oxford University Press, 2006), 43.
34. Charles W. Mills, "White Right: The Idea of a *Herrenvolk* Ethics," in his *Blackness Visible: Essays on Philosophy and Race* (Ithaca, New York: Cornell University Press, 1998), 142.
35. http://edition.cnn.com/2007/POLITICS/01/31/biden.obama/ (accessed January 28, 2009).
36. Mills, "Ideal Theory as Ideology," 150.
37. Mills, "Ideal Theory as Ideology," 149.
38. Thomas Green, "On the Illusion that We Can Choose to Believe," in *Philosophy of Education Society 1994*, ed. Michael Katz (Urbana, IL: Philosophy of Education Society, 1995), 70, emphasis mine.
39. Michael J. Zimmerman, "Moral Responsibility and Ignorance," *Ethics* 107 (1997): 410–426; Holly Smith, "Culpable Ignorance," *Philosophical Review* 83 (1992): 543–572.
40. Alcoff, "Epistemologies of Ignorance," 47.
41. Bartky, "Race, Complicity, and Culpable Ignorance," 154.
42. Charles W. Mills, "Racial Exploitation and the Wages of Whiteness," in *What White Looks Like: African-American Philosophers on the Whiteness Question*, ed. George Yancy (New York: Routledge, 2004), 31.
43. Marylyn Frye, "Oppression," in her *The Politics of Reality: Essays in Feminist Theory* (Trumansburg, New York: Crossing Press, 1983), 1–16.
44. Mills, "Racial Exploitation," 31.
45. Bartky, "Race, Complicity and Culpable Ignorance."
46. Estella Williams Chizhik and Alexander Williams Chizhik, "Are you Privileged or Oppressed? Students' Conceptions of Themselves and Others", *Urban Education* 40, no. 2 (2005): 116–143; Rudolfo Chavez Chavez and James O'Donnell, *Speaking the Unpleasant: The Politics of (non)Engagement in the Multicultural Education Terrain* (Albany: State University Press, 1998); Ann Berlak, "Teaching and Testimony: Witnessing and Bearing Witness to Racisms in Culturally Diverse Classrooms," *Curriculum Inquiry* 29, no. 1 (1999): 99–127; Audrey Thompson, "Entertaining Doubts: Enjoyment and Ambiguity in White, Antiracist Classrooms," in *Passion and Pedagogy: Relation, Creation, and Transformation in Teaching*, ed. Elijah Mirochick and Debora C. Sherman (New York: Peter Lang, 2002), 431–452; Kevin Kumashiro, "Teaching and Learning through

Desire, Crisis, and Difference: Perverted Reflections on Anti-Oppressive Education," *Radical Teacher* 58 (2000): 6–11; Kathy Hytten and Amee Adkins, "Thinking Through a Pedagogy of Whiteness," *Educational Theory* 51, no. 4 (2001): 433–450; Leslie G. Roman, "White is a Color! White Defensiveness, Postmodernism and Anti-racist Pedagogy" in *Race, Identity and Representation in Education*, ed. Cameron McCarthy and Warren Crinchlow (New York: Routledge, 1993), 71–88; Bonnie TuSmith, "Out on a Limb: Race and the Evaluation of Frontline Teaching," in *Race in the College Classroom*, ed. Bonnie TuSmith and Maureen T. Reddy (New Brunswick, New Jersey: Rutgers University Press, 2002), 112–125.

47. Kim Case and Annette Hemmings, "Distancing: White Women Preservice Teachers and Antiracist Curriculum," *Urban Education* 40, no. 6 (November 2005): 606–626.

48. Elizabeth Higginbotham, "Getting All Students to Listen," *American Behavioral Scientist* 40, no. 2 (November/December 1996): 203–211.

49. Kathy Hytten and John Warren, "Engaging Whiteness: How Racial Power Gets Reified in Education." *Qualitative Studies in Education* 16, no. 1 (2003): 65–89.

50. Hytten and Warren, "Engaging Whiteness," 66.

51. Alice McIntyre, *Making Meaning of Whiteness: Exploring Racial Identity with White Teachers* (Albany, New York: State University of New York Press, 1997).

52. McIntyre, *Making Meaning of Whiteness*, 45.

53. Hytten and Warren, "Engaging Whiteness," 65.

54. McIntosh, "White Privilege and Male Privilege," 295–6.

55. Alice McIntyre, "White Talk," in *Making Meaning of Whiteness: Exploring Racial Identity with White Teachers* (Albany, New York: State University of New York Press, 1997), 55.

56. Eduardo Bonilla-Silva, *Racism without Racist: Color-Blind Racism and the Persistence of Racial Inequality in the United States* (Lanham, MD: Rowman & Littlefield, 2003).

57. Nado Aveling, "Student Teachers' Resistance to Exploring Racism: Reflections on 'Doing' Border Pedagogy," *Asia-Pacific Journal of Teacher Education* 30, no. 2 (2002): 119–130.

58. Woody Doane, "Rethinking Whiteness Studies," in *White Out: The Continuing Significance of Racism*, ed. Ashley W. Doane and Eduardo Bonilla-Silva (New York: Routledge, 2003), 3–21, quotation on 13–14.

59. Amanda Lewis, "There is No Race in the School Yard: Color-Blind Ideology in an (Almost) All-White School," *American Educational Research Journal* 38, no. 4 (2001): 781–811; Tim Wise, "What Kind of Card is Race? The Absurdity (and Consistency) of White Denial." http://www.lipmagazine.org/~timwise/whatcard.html (accessed January 28, 2009).

60. Sarita Srivastava, "'You're Calling Me a Racist?' The Moral and Emotional Regulation of Antiracism and Feminism," *Signs* 31, no. 1 (2005): 29–62.

61. Ruth Frankenberg, *White Women, Race Matters: The Social Construction of Whiteness,* (Minneapolis: University of Minnesota Press, 1993), 3.

62. Sherryl Kleinman, *Opposing Ambitions: Gender and Identity in an Alternative Organization* (Chicago: University of Chicago Press, 1996).

63. Kleinman, *Opposing Ambitions*, 11.

64. Srivastava, "'You're Calling Me a Racist?,'" 41.

65. Deborah Britzman, *Lost Subjects, Contested Objects: Toward a Psychoanalytic Inquiry of Learning* (Albany: State University of New York Press, 1998).

66. Audrey Thompson, "Listening and Its Asymmetries," *Curriculum Inquiry* 33, no. 1 (2003): 79–100, quotation on 82 (Thompson is citing Maria Lugones, "Hablando Cara a Cara/Speaking Face to Face: An Exploration of Ethnocentric Racism," in *Making Face, Making Soul/Haciendo Caras: Creative and Critical Perspectives by Women of Color,* ed. Gloria Anzaldua [San Francisco, CA: Aunt Lute Foundation Books, 1990], 51) emphasis mine.
67. Anna Stubblefield, "Meditations on Postsupremacist Philosophy," in *White on White/Black on Black,* ed. George Yancy (Lanham, MD: Rowman & Littlefield, 2005), 71–82.
68. Stubblefield, "Meditations on Postsupremacist Philosophy," 76.
69. Annette Baier, *Moral Prejudices: Essays on Ethics* (Cambridge MA: Harvard University Press, 1994) 194.
70. Elizabeth Ellsworth, "Why Doesn't this Feel Empowering? Working Through the Repressive Myths of Critical Pedagogy," *Harvard Educational Review* 59, no. 3 (1989): 297–324.
71. Nicholas C. Burbules and Suzanne Rice, "Dialogue Across Differences: Continuing the Conversation," *Harvard Educational Review* 61, no. 4 (1991): 393–416; Alison Jones, "The Limits of Cross-Cultural Dialogue: Pedagogy, Desire, and Absolution in the Classroom," *Educational Theory* 49, no. 3 (1999): 299–316; Barbara Houston, "Democratic Dialogue: Who Takes Responsibility?" in *Democratic Dialogue in Education: Troubling Speech, Disturbing Speech,* ed. Megan Boler (New York: Peter Lang, 2004), 105–122.
72. Burbules and Rice, "Dialogue Across Differences."
73. Lisa Delpit, "The Silenced Dialogue: Power and Pedagogy in Educating Other People's Children." *Harvard Educational Review* 58, no. 3 (1988): 280–298.
74. Delpit, "The Silenced Dialogue," 280.
75. María C. Lugones and Elizabeth V. Spelman, "'Have We Got a Theory for You!' Feminist Theory, Cultural Imperialism, and the Demand for 'The Woman's Voice,'" in *Hypatia Reborn: Essays in Feminist Philosophy,* ed. Azizah Y. al-Hibri and Margaret A. Simons (Bloomington and Indianapolis: Indiana University Press, 1990), 18–33, quotation on 23.
76. Thompson, "Listening and Its Asymmetries," 91.
77. Thompson, "Listening and Its Asymmetries," 90.
78. Thompson, "Listening and Its Asymmetries," 91.
79. Kelly Oliver, *Witnessing: Beyond Recognition* (Minneapolis: University of Minnesota Press, 2001).
80. Shoshana Felman and Dori Laub, *Testimony: Crisis of Witnessing in Literature, Psychoanalysis, and History* (New York: Routledge, 1992), 62 (also see Oliver's "Witnessing and Testimony," *Parallax* 10, no. 1 (2004): 79–88, quotation on 83).
81. Kelly, *Witnessing,* 42.
82. Emily Robertson, "The Value of Reason: Why Not a Sardine Can Opener?" in *Philosophy of Education 1999,* ed. Randall Curren (Urbana, IL: Philosophy of Education Society, 2000), 1–14.
83. Lugones and Spelman, "'Have We Got a Theory for You!,'" 31.
84. Thompson, "Listening and Its Asymmetries," 89.
85. Ann Diller, "Facing the Torpedo Fish: Becoming a Philosopher of One's Own Education," in *Philosophy of Education 1998,* ed. Steven Tozer (Urbana, IL: Philosophy of Education Society, 1999), 1–9.
86. Diller, "Facing the Torpedo Fish," 8.

87. Delpit, "The Silenced Dialogue," 297.
88. Judith Butler, "Contingent Foundations," and "For a Careful Reading" in *Feminist Contentions: A Philosophical Exchange*, ed. Seyla Benhabib, Judith Butler, Drucilla Cornell and Nancy Fraser (New York: Routledge, 1995), 35–58 and 127–144, respectively; Seyla Benhabib, "Feminism and Postmodernism," and "Subjectivity, Historiography and Politics," in *Feminist Contentions*, 17–34 and 107–126, respectively.
89. Thompson, "Listening and Its Asymmetries," 92.
90. Amanda Anderson sees the debate differently as an "agonizing failed speech situation. Any reader of the text cannot fail to register, in particular, Butler's emphatic attempts to distance herself from the whole project" (1). "Butler at once fames and dismisses Benhabib, and in a sense refuses to debate her" (2). While related to the topic at hand, a more careful analysis of Anderson's specific claims is beyond the scope of this chapter. It must be noted, however, that although Anderson attempts to vindicate Benhabib's position, she becomes keenly aware of its limitation through her engagement with Butler's arguments.
91. Naomi Scheman, "Openness, Vulnerability, and Feminist Engagement," *American Philosophical Association Newsletter on Feminism and Philosophy* 00, no. 2 (2001): 92–96.
92. Barbara Houston, "Taking Responsibility," in *Philosophy of Education 2002*, ed. Scott Fletcher (Urbana, IL: Philosophy of Education Society, 2003), 1–13.
93. Lisa Heldke, "On Being a Responsible Traitor: A Primer," in *Daring to be Good: Essays in Feminist Ethico-Politics*, ed. Bat-Ami Bar On and Ann Ferguson (New York: Routledge, 1998), 87–99.
94. Iris Marion Young, "Responsibility and Global Justice: A Social Connection Model," *Social Philosophy and Policy* 23, no. 1 (2006): 102–130.
95. Young, "Responsibility and Global Justice," 114.
96. Young, "Responsibility and Global Justice," 115.
97. Young, "Responsibility and Global Justice," 120.
98. Young, "Responsibility and Global Justice," 120.
99. Young, "Responsibility and Global Justice," 123.
100. Lewis Gordon, *Bad Faith and Antiblack Racism* (Atlantic Highlands, New Jersey: Humanities Press, 1995).
101. Linda Martin Alcoff, Review of Lewis Gordon's *Bad Faith and Antiblack Racism*, *Philosophy in Review* 17, no. 2 (1997): 99.

2

Reading Black Philosophers in Chronological Order

Audrey Thompson, University of Utah

When her African American colleagues declared Catherine Clinton "an 'Honorary Octoroon,'" the white historian was delighted.[1] Although she treats the anecdote as an amusing aside, the imprimatur from black colleagues underscores her credentials as a white person who "gets it." Implicitly, it offers a rebuke to black students who claim that a white woman should not teach black history. To such students, the Honorary Octoroon label says, "You don't understand. She's one of us. She looks white, but she's really black." Much as Clinton values the playful compliment, though, she is troubled by the suggestion that a partial black heritage might explain or shore up her qualifications as a race scholar. A person's race, she believes, has no bearing on her ability to conduct research into African American experiences. Those who question Clinton's right to teach black history usually have decided what she can teach and write about based on her skin color, without knowing anything about her as a scholar or a person. Responding to an imaginary question as to who she thinks she is to do work in black history, Clinton says, "I am my own person."[2] The colorblind answer refuses the racial knowingness assumed by the question.

Asking whether a white professor can teach African American topics frames the issue in either/or terms. Although no one suggests that a white teacher ought to *omit* black topics from a course—that a white teacher of American literature, for example, ought to cover nothing but white-authored literature—it is often argued that whites should not teach courses devoted to black topics, in part because whites cannot understand the issues in the ways that African Americans would.[3] Like Clinton, Christie Farnham argues against this view. The teacher's "pigmentation," she says, is irrelevant; what matters is her scholarly expertise.[4] Frustrated at being challenged as scholars and teachers of black history because they are not black, Farnham, Clinton, and Jacqueline Jones all underscore their disciplinary credentials. What distinguishes competent historians, says Jones, are their "research and analytical skills," along with "the passion they bring to their work." "Psychic powers"—apparently referring to powers that would allow historians to intuit what African Americans might have felt and thought in particular circumstances—are not a professional consideration.[5]

Except insofar as black students bring inappropriate expectations to the encounter, whiteness has nothing to do with either research or teaching, Jones, Farnham, and Clinton argue. Although their analyses are in many ways specific to history as a discipline, their claims and assumptions are relevant to philosophy. A historian studies the evidence found in primary documents and other materials to understand particular patterns of events. Whereas Jones and Farnham characterize such study as a search for "truth," Nathan Huggins points out that "the historian chooses his subject, asks what he considers the most crucial and necessary questions, selects his data, and constructs his argument and narrative with an eye toward discriminating that which he finds compelling and essential and that which appears incidental and of no consequence."[6] Thus, the "truth" to be discovered is relative to what the researcher considers interesting questions and relevant data. The inquiry process frames not only what is known but how it is known.

In philosophy, what counts as a significant question depends in part on whether one takes racial diversity or sexual identity to be a special "problem" (for democracy, for example), or instead starts from race and sexuality as organizing frameworks. In mainstream ethics, "integrity" is regarded as a universal value. It is a touchstone for understanding human freedom: one of the measures of oppression is whether a person *can* act with integrity and survive. Yet because such an ideal assumes the perspectives of those in positions of power and privilege, it almost inevitably leads to understanding the oppressed as falling short of the ideal (albeit for reasons beyond individuals' control). "Black people live with severely limited ethical choices," Katie Cannon acknowledges, but this does not mean that their moral actions are to be understood merely as "defensive reactions to the oppressive circumstances" of white supremacy.[7] On the contrary, values and virtues grounded in black experience and culture "assert a human validity that is not derived from the white-male-norm."[8] Integrity is understood differently if moral agency is not keyed to a position of veiled dominance.

In philosophy, as in history, it is possible for researchers to learn to decenter dominant perspectives. But it is far easier to decenter the assumption that only white philosophy is worth studying than to interrogate the whiteness of disciplinary standards regarding what it means to define, inquire into, or analyze a topic. It may be more difficult still to recognize the whiteness of discipline-based values regarding what it means to listen, argue, tell a story, or teach.

Trusting White Teachers

When asked about her credentials for writing black history, Jones tells people, "'Let's begin the discussion with my footnotes, and go on from there.'"[9] The thoroughness of her research, she believes, attests to her ability to speak authoritatively about black history. Yet Jones's mastery of the subject does not always give black students sufficient reason to trust her voice. She tells us of two undergraduates who asked how she came to write *Labor of Love, Labor of Sorrow*. Disappointed to discover that the author is not black, the students sought some recognizable personal reason for a white woman's interest in black history. Either failing to recognize what the black students wanted to know or resisting their underlying question, Jones tells us that she "launched into an autobiographical tale that began with my childhood" and culminated in her undergraduate and graduate schooling. Becoming "increasingly impatient" with this narrative, the students eventually interrupted her to ask, "'Are you married to a black man?'"[10]

For Jones, the students' desire "for some personal—even intimate—connection between me and the story I told in the book" is anti-intellectual.[11] After all, her colleague who lectures about "nineteenth-century financial institutions" is not "asked, 'Are you married to a banker?'"[12] Being black, however, is not like being a banker. In dismissing the black students' longing to find some personal reason to trust her, Jones overlooks a crucial point: the students are not discounting her knowledge. They *want* some reason to trust her. They are looking for something to assure them that she is not just any white woman. Instead, she tells them a "long-winded" story that ignores their real question.[13] While it is understandable that Jones should resist giving the students pre-packaged indications of her trustworthiness, it is troubling that she refuses to take seriously their wanting to know about her personal investment in the issues she studies. When the students prompt her for the narrative that they are most prepared to recognize, she is irritated rather than interested.

It is not uncommon for students of color to want to know a teacher's stand on questions of race, sexuality, and gender. Without some specific knowledge of the teacher's investments in equity, students may wonder what degree of reliance they can place on her research or what risks they can afford to take in her classroom. A professed neutrality has not stood in the way of white teachers bonding with and protecting white students. Even an explicit affirmation of support for black and brown struggles does not indicate how someone in power will act to preserve or challenge the status quo. The passion to which Jones refers is a more reliable guide—although not if it is strictly intellectual. Knowing that a teacher is black or brown or is married to a person of color suggests a personal investment in race questions. Such knowledge is a problematic shortcut, to be sure; intimacy with minoritized racial experience hardly guarantees that a scholar knows the relevant research, is supportive of students of color, or knows how to teach.[14] Nevertheless, embodied racial commitments are easier to trust than intellectual enthusiasm.

Although whites tend to expect to be trusted, we also know that in cross-race relations we might not be. It is tempting, therefore, to resort to niceness to finesse any awkwardness. Not only does being nice offer to smooth the way, but it makes us feel good about ourselves. To the extent that niceness suggests an evasion of necessary struggle, however, it may signal untrustworthiness. From the perspective of cross-race relations, a nice person may be someone more interested in being liked (or seen as not racist) than in facing the challenges of racism. By contrast, personal interest and supportiveness represent ongoing involvement—but even these may be regarded with suspicion. Given whites' history of being interested in people of color for the wrong reasons, students of color may wonder whether a white teacher's supportiveness stems from genuine caring or from guilt, pity, rescue/hero fantasies, or a desire for affirmation as a good white person.[15]

In some cases, of course, a white teacher's support for a student of color is accepted as an expression of genuine interest and connection. Such success stories can lull us into believing that race is not an issue in working relationships. Especially when there is good rapport between a student and teacher (or between colleagues or friends), it is tempting for whites to think of the relationship as somehow beyond race. Personalities obviously make a difference, but personal harmony cannot guarantee that the relationship will not falter along lines of culture and power. What seems natural and comfortable to people in positions of dominance reflects our expectations of what is due us. As soon as individuals in a cross-race relation shift from their accustomed racial positions, any seemingly easy fit between personalities is likely to get messy. Deliberately working against the grain of white entitlement, for example, can make it difficult to find cross-race relational rhythms that feel spontaneous. Expectations of student–teacher trust drawn from universalistic assumptions about mentoring, caring, or dialogue often reinforce white entitlement, leading whites to become impatient with the messiness of cross-race hopes and doubts.[16] "It's too much to have to think about," we say. "There's nothing I can do about any of that." "Even if I tried to address all that, I would probably get it wrong."

This chapter explores the messiness of cross-race classroom relations when hopes are high. Specifically, it looks at cross-race relations and whiteness in an African American philosophy of education course I taught several years ago. The black students entered the class with high hopes. Whatever their private doubts, there was no initial indication that they mistrusted my ability to teach African American issues. At first, there was almost euphoria amongst the black students: never before had so many black graduate students enrolled in one of our department's courses. The black students felt empowered. By the middle of the semester, however, they grew frustrated with the whiteness of the course. The issue was not so much that the professor was white and that half the students were white (although both circumstances were problematic), but that my pedagogy failed to decenter the white students. As an African American student told me, "We thought it would be a space for *us*."

In what follows, I discuss whiteness theory as a framework for analysis before setting forth my understanding of the whiteness of my pedagogy. I took notes during or after most of my conversations with the students, but because the notes were for my own understanding, they should not be read as data. They reflect what I heard, and are not meant to represent what the students "really" thought. Quite possibly the students would characterize the class differently. Not all of the black students talked with me about their frustrations during the semester that the course was offered, and some may have changed their minds about particular issues over the years. There were twenty-five people in the class (including me), and there must be at least fifty versions of what happened. This is one version.

Whiteness Theory and Trust

Liberal views of race tend to equate whiteness either with skin color (an incidental property) or European heritage (a cultural value). By contrast, leftist approaches see whiteness primarily as a structural position—specifically, a position of dominance and privilege.[17] What looks normal, safe, innocent, friendly, logical, or fair to whites is likely to be articulated to our racial entitlement. Thus, "in white supremacist society, white people can 'safely' imagine" that they are not judged by black people, since their power accords whites "the right to control the black gaze."[18] Like maleness and heterosexuality in mainstream U.S. society, whiteness is powerful in part because it is equated with the "normal" human condition. At the same time, it represents a preferred status. In contrast with other groups, whites are likely to be credited with being objective, fair-minded, and hardworking. Although a white person may choose to renounce her racial power and privilege, and may work against the social systems that hold them in place, her very capacity to exercise anti-racist agency is organized by the system of white supremacy.[19]

Rather than conceiving of whiteness as a noun or adjective, as if it had a fixed quality, we are better off understanding it as a verb. The normalizing of whiteness is achieved by repeated actions that establish and reestablish whiteness as a taken-for-granted frame of reference. In material terms, this means that whites control access to social goods so that they have a greater share of whatever is considered universally desirable. Being white increases one's expectations of having access to higher education, for example, or an environmentally safe neighborhood. Whiteness also involves controlling symbolic forms of dominance and privilege, so that whites set the standards for beauty, intelligence, and morality. By exercising claims to centrality, authority, innocence, and trustworthiness, whites continually (re)position ourselves and other whites as more deserving than members of other racial groups.[20]

The belief that U.S. society is a democracy and a meritocracy offers hope to some, justification to others. Because seemingly fair and disinterested societal patterns of reward pay disproportionate dividends to whites, whites have an investment in rendering white privilege and dominance invisible.[21] In a democracy, the benefits reaped by whites must be explained and justified, and this is difficult to do if no person of color ever reaps similar rewards. The system works *for* whites, but it is vital that it appear open to all. The presence of occasional people of color in structural locations ordinarily reserved for whites helps provide society with an alibi. Although people of color as a group remain oppressed, the fact that the benefits of whiteness are extended to a few, "deserving" people of color allows the system of white dominance to remain invisible. Non-whites who benefit from white-privileging mechanisms are more or less on probation, however. One can lose one's status as an honorary white by challenging the racial status quo, for example, or by acting "too black."

Paradoxically, for Jones, Clinton, and Farnham, it is their probationary status as honorary *blacks* that is at issue. To achieve acceptance as "Honorary Octoroons"—as exceptions to the rule of white ignorance—the authors feel that they are asked to satisfy arbitrary, even racist expectations. For many whites, the idea that they would be distrusted "just because I happen to be white" is a violation of a deeply held expectation that they should be judged as individuals. Expecting to be judged on their merits as accomplished teachers and scholarly authorities, the historians fail to see that the privilege of being judged as an individual is contingent on being able to claim a status unmarked by race (i.e., white). Those accustomed to being judged on merit also may fail to see the degree to which white (as well as male, heterosexual, and middle-class) agency is bolstered by social and institutional supports that disproportionately serve dominant groups—what María Lugones calls the "back up" behind seemingly individual achievements.[22] It is because we benefit from being white that we are not judged merely as individuals.[23] Contrary to what Farnham assumes, black and brown distrust of whites is based not on skin color but on white dominance and privilege.[24] This is not to say that trust never develops in a cross-race relationship. Particular kinds of trust develop in a variety of situations, perhaps due to workplace proximity, personal friendship, or shared political work. Nevertheless, there are structural reasons for people of color to distrust whites' ability to decenter white entitlement from their sense of what is kind, logical, fair, appropriate, and intellectually stimulating.[25]

White scholars who are good teachers and who take race questions seriously may be successful in cross-race classrooms and assume, accordingly, that race is not an issue. But success can be misleading. Describing a course in which she introduced eighteen college freshmen (three of whom were African American) to the history of black and white race relations in the United States, Jones writes that she "faced a number of pedagogical challenges . . . , but my inadequacy as a white person teaching African American history was not high on my list."[26] Her description of her teaching suggests the richness of the intellectual and political work that her students learned to do. Yet I wonder if the seeming irrelevance of race for her pedagogy might be attributable in part to her having taught a class in which white expectations, entitlements, and concerns appeared normal because most of the students were white. In what follows, I focus not on whether white teachers can teach African American subjects but on what it means to teach as if students' whiteness did not matter.

African American Epistemologies and Pedagogies

The first time I taught the African American Epistemologies and Pedagogies class, LaShonda was the only African American in the class.[27] I was teaching it not because I was any sort of expert but because LaShonda needed a graduate student community in which she would not always be the only one to bring up black issues and the only one who knew anything about black students. I hoped that a course devoted to black education might provide the beginnings of such a community of inquiry.[28]

When I began working with LaShonda, my acquaintance with African American philosophy, sociology, and history of education was fragmentary. Over the following years, I began to immerse myself in the research, but by the first time that I taught the course, three years later, I still did not have much sense of African American philosophy as a field.[29] Four years after that, when I taught the course a second time, I was in a stronger position to offer an overview of black philosophies of education. Unfortunately, I was by now less aware of how problematic my understanding of the issues was. To avoid having a white-referenced approach to black education frame the terms of discussion, I had decided against including accommodationists such as Booker T. Washington in the syllabus. I am embarrassed to confess that I informed the class that the syllabus would reflect only authentically black positions—that I had chosen to omit philosophies rationalizing white supremacy. There were two black students in the class. Bernard, who was conservative, was outraged. "I like Booker T. Washington's position," he said. "My whole family likes his position. Are you telling me that you, a white woman, are going to decide for me and my family what is authentically black?" He was right, of course. In foregrounding the liberal and radical positions that I myself most admired, I had suppressed the diversity of black thought. Although the authors on the syllabus were not ventriloquizing my positions, they had to pass muster with me before I counted them as authentically black. In effect, I was treating my progressive politics as if they provided me with credentials as an "Honorary Octoroon" authorized to evaluate black authenticity.

The third time I offered the course, I made my whiteness an explicit consideration of my pedagogy. Framing my role as that of learner rather than expert, I told the students about some of my intellectual, political, and cultural challenges as a white teacher of a course on black thought. I called attention to my whiteness as a teacher. Yet I failed to consider the whiteness of a pedagogy that did not place the needs of black students at the center. Certainly I believed that I was meeting the needs of black students, but I assumed that those needs were primarily a matter of their being able to study black philosophies of education in a context in which white philosophies were not the point of departure. Six years later, people continue to talk about the course—not because it was a disaster (I have had some of those, but this wasn't one), but because so many hopes coalesced around it and then disintegrated. A few things worked well, but what stood out for many black students was what did not happen.

A Critical Mass of Black Students

On predominantly white campuses, students of color are "always . . . at the race-ready."[30] Because whiteness (in the guise of racelessness) organizes much of academic inquiry, students of color often "attempt to engage White students in discussions of race-related topics," but, by and large, white students "withdraw from such discussions."[31] An Asian American undergraduate in Ana Martínez Alemán's study reports that she would look around her classroom when a racially offensive statement was made and realize, "I'm the only person of color in the class and I'm, like, 'Oh, I guess I have to start representing people of color.'"[32] To avoid this kind of isolation, Geneva Gay advises students of color to "enroll in classes together as much as possible."[33] She points out that "courses that deal specifically with ethnic diversity," especially, may "provide cultural validation and renewal" and "places of refuge."[34]

It was at the first meeting of the African American epistemologies class that I learned that black students from across three departments had organized to take the class together. Half the students in the class were people of color; of these, most were black.[35] Some courses in my department have had a critical mass of students of color, but never before had there been a critical mass of black students. They told the class that they saw it as an opportunity to focus on black educational concerns with black students at the center, yet neither they nor I thought to confer about their expectations or how to meet their goals. Later, they told me that they had expected the class to be a refuge from the white-centeredness of the university. I am not sure whether they simply assumed that the course would be a place for them to thrive or whether they knew that it might not be, but thought the risk worth taking. They may have assumed that a core of black students could of itself create a black-centered space. Perhaps some students hoped that I would serve primarily as discussion facilitator and would avoid any authoritative role, allowing the black students to define the terms for the class in a way that a black professor might not.

It is not clear why the students chose this particular course as a refuge, other than that it happened to be offered at a time when there were enough black graduate students with related interests to form a critical mass. It was not that no other race-based courses were offered. The majority of the faculty in my department are scholars of color and we offer many courses on race, including several taught by black professors. In most of our classes, race and culture (and to a lesser extent class, gender, and sexuality) are key organizing topics. Our collective emphasis on race does not mean, however, that whiteness is automatically decentered. Our home disciplines (anthropology, sociology, history, philosophy, and social psychology) tend to normalize whiteness, and most of the faculty, as graduate students, experienced mainstream pedagogies. Insofar as we share dominant academic values concerning scholarly evidence and argumentation, and subscribe to individualistic beliefs about authentic learning, we risk normalizing white-referenced approaches to education. Even when we specifically seek to challenge white supremacy, it is all too easy, as my colleague Dolores Delgado Bernal has pointed out, for professors of any race to direct their attention to anxious or entitled white students or to pitch explanations to students with little experience in thinking about racial issues.

A Black-Centered Intellectual Space

My intent was for the class to center black experiences, black politics, black culture, and black thought. Like the black students, I wanted the class to be a "black space," but—despite believing that classroom dynamics are pivotal to how social justice courses interrogate race—I mostly approached the class as if black-centeredness had already been secured by the syllabus.[36] Setting forth requirements intended to address the multiple dimensions of African American experience, the syllabus explained that "a working assumption of the course is that knowledge is embodied, relational, contextual, *and* structural, political, and abstract." Among the requirements was a cultural project intended to take up embodied and artistic forms of black knowledge.[37] Apart from the students' projects, however, the class paid little explicit attention to classroom embodiments of racial culture and politics.

I had assumed, and some of the black students may have assumed, that reading great black writers would naturally be affirming for black graduate students. It was not. Over the course of the semester, most of the African American students in the class came to talk to me individually. Charles, who was particularly unhappy with the course, told me in some frustration, "This class isn't getting at our issues. The readings don't speak to my life. They're all written by dead people." I viewed his dissatisfaction in a similar way that Farnham, Jones, and Clinton view black students' demand for relevance: as a failure to grasp the nature of the discipline. Farnham writes that "Many African American students view black studies courses as 'theirs.' Thus, they feel that these courses should serve their perceived needs for self-validation." Yet while "self-esteem may well result from the study of the African American past," Farnham argues, "the discipline of history is not designed to serve this end."[38] Although I did not reduce Charles's desire for relevance to a quest for self-esteem, I shared Farnham's sense that the standards of the discipline transcend any student's personal expectations. It seemed to me anti-intellectual for Charles to claim that non-contemporary readings could not speak to his issues. The syllabus was philosophical, but also specifically cultural and political. As an African American intellectual, Charles surely had something to learn from Frederick Douglass, Carter

G. Woodson, Malcolm X, and W. E. B. Du Bois—not to mention Angela Davis, Cornel West, bell hooks, and Patricia Hill Collins. Reluctantly, Charles agreed with me. But he still maintained that the course was not speaking to his concerns.

At the time, it seemed to me that if Charles was not interested in the classics of black philosophy of education, then the problem was that he had chosen the wrong course. When I initially offered the course, I believed that what would make it powerful for students while legitimating it in the eyes of the academy would be for students to engage with the greats of African American education. Rather than approach black authors as occasional "raced" voices in a predominantly white conversation, I wanted to develop a course that would highlight black theorists in conversation with each other. The class would be similar in structure to a course on American pragmatism, demonstrating how particular intellectual and political conversations developed over time. I saw the readings as demanding, sophisticated, and complex pieces of writing best framed in a black cultural context.

Viewed from a perspective that values black philosophy but does not decenter whiteness, the symmetry in the argument works beautifully: if there are courses on white classics, there should be courses on black classics. But the argument turns upon a false parallelism. Black classics cannot be approached as if they were white classics, only black. Mainstream philosophy classics courses typically frame concepts and values in universal terms, but it is impossible to understand black-centered conceptions of authenticity, freedom, or alienation without starting from the specificity of black history, black experiences, and black politics. Their very status as *black* classics signals their refusal of universalism. Not infrequently, black texts claim to speak a universal black truth, but their refusal of colorblind universalism should remind us that any universal claim threatens to suppress a disturbing diversity. The texts in my class presumably did not speak to Charles in part because they did not reflect a blackness he could recognize. I still wonder to what extent Charles was being anti-intellectual, but it is an unanswerable question. The class was not working for him, intellectually or otherwise, and I should have thought more carefully about his longing for readings that would speak to his experience and his struggles.

Taking a chronological approach to black philosophy of education turned out not to work very well for any of the African American students. Only much later did I understand that the texts were not intrinsically interesting to most of the black students (few of whom would have called themselves philosophers). It therefore made little sense that I was presenting classic black ideas, arguments, and analyses in more or less chronological order, rather than organizing them in terms of the issues at stake. Moreover, if the readings were to be presented in chronological order, they needed to be framed in terms of the social and historical context to which they spoke. Only two students (one black, one white) had much knowledge of African American history. In a context in which historical knowledge could not be assumed and was not taught, reading black philosophers in chronological order invited abstraction from the messy, lived politics of race. In the absence of a rich and nuanced historical understanding of the issues, not only white students and the white teacher but black and brown students could invest historical race-based arguments with their own cultural and political assumptions and values.

Teaching black philosophers in chronological order also raises the question of where the chronology starts. In constructing my syllabus, I automatically started with slavery. Later, my colleague William Smith asked me about that decision. Why had I not started with the knowledge and wisdom that enslaved black people brought to the United States from Africa? Why had I started with slavery and the New World, as if that were the beginning of the black intellectual journey to human freedom and flourishing? Despite wanting the class to be immersed in black philosophy, I had assumed a white framework. As Michael Hanchard points out, "there has been a popular and academic tendency to diminish, deny, or neglect the impact that African peoples, practices, and civilizations have had on the West's development, as well as to forget the extent to which these populations have sought paths that have veered away from Western modernities even while being interlocked with them."[39] Although the roughly chronological approach to the syllabus was not intended to intimate a trajectory of racial "progress," almost inevitably the lack of historical complexity meant that earlier black thought was framed as a precursor to later, more recognizably "modern" thought. In addition, the unexamined white/black binary that organized that framework effectively suppressed consideration of black multiplicity—as well as cross-race relations between African Americans and other minoritized groups.

A Disembodied Pedagogy

In "The Silenced Dialogue: Power and Pedagogy in Educating Other People's Children," Lisa Delpit tells of a black man who, frustrated with his graduate courses, says, "It seems like if you can't quote Vygotsky or something, then you don't have any validity to speak about your *own* kids."[40] A black woman teacher concurs: "When you're talking to White people they still want it to be their way. ... [T]hey think they know what's best for *everybody*, for *everybody's* children. They won't listen."[41] Most of the white students in the African American epistemologies class understood this pattern and were on guard against it. Yet the pattern still emerged, because students of different backgrounds did not have comparable investments in the course.[42] This is not to say that the white students (and, in a different way, the brown students) did not have serious moral and political investments in liberatory approaches to black philosophy and pedagogy; for the most part, I think they did. But for many of the white students, the course readings were a chance to learn "about" African Americans at a distance. For the brown students, there was a certain amount of overlap between the readings and their various situations and histories, but there was also significant distance.[43] For the black students, the readings had burning personal and group implications. They had strong feelings about whom to read, how to read them, and with whom one could safely talk with about the readings.

Like Jones's class, mine took a discipline-based approach that managed to sidestep many of the complexities of racial classroom dynamics as long as only one or two black students were in the class. What had seemed to work in the past, however, no longer worked once there was a core group of black students. Their yearning to theorize from their own positionality now became a live expectation, but an expectation without back up. It lacked institutional and pedagogical support. I now realize that when a white student in the African American epistemologies class challenged Cornel West or bell hooks by invoking Derrida or Bakhtin, the effect was different than it would have been in another course. In a pragmatism course, it might be quite appropriate to invoke Paulo Freire to challenge John Dewey or Lisa Delpit to challenge Louise Rosenblatt, but in this course the importation of outside (white) theorists served to deflect the group's attention from the specific historical and political struggles of *these* theorists. The African American students did not object to these moves—they had read the same theorists themselves—but I think that the white (and sometimes brown) students' comfort in moving to white theorists to grapple with black theorists served to decenter black theorizing.[44] The student overtures clearly were intended to offer serious intellectual engagement with the readings, but the effect of these highly abstract exchanges was to move away from blackness as the ground of meaning-making, towards universal claims.

Stuart Hall has pointed out that "the theoretical encounter between black cultural politics and the discourses of a Eurocentric, largely white, critical cultural theory . . . is always an extremely difficult, if not dangerous, encounter. (I think particularly of black people encountering the discourses of poststructuralism, postmodernism, psychoanalysis and feminism.)."[45] What may seem to a white teacher and white students to be a shared intellectual struggle to master difficult and demanding materials may feel to black students like their peers' refusal to listen or an attempt to reclaim the center of inquiry. Black, brown, and white students who have struggled with pragmatism, poststructuralism, and critical pedagogy in other courses may find that, when what is at stake is the educational future of black children, the assumption that we can all figure this out together by working through it with our shared intellectual tools is just wrong: certain forms of thinking-through will seem like a hostile use of rationality and a privileging of universalism over the immutable fact that, for some of us, "these are our children."[46]

The Crisis

The tensions between black and white students came to a head halfway through the course, when we were discussing arguments for separate black schools. In 1935, W. E. B. Du Bois asked, "Does the Negro need separate schools?" In part, his answer was that:

> They are needed just so far as they are necessary for the proper education of the Negro race. The proper education of any people includes sympathetic touch between teacher and pupil; knowledge on the part of the teacher, not simply of the individual taught, but of his surroundings and background, and the history of his class and group; [and] such contact between pupils, and between teacher and pupil, on the basis of perfect social equality, as will increase this sympathy and knowledge.[47]

Like Carter G. Woodson in his 1933 *Mis-Education of the Negro*, Du Bois in 1935 viewed white education as largely hostile to the cause of black freedom.[48] Black children could not flourish in white schools where they were mocked, "despised and resented," "neglected or bullied," said Du Bois.[49] Although he acknowledged that the principles of equal educational access and cross-group democratic communication might be jeopardized by any educational concession to white supremacy, he saw black children as too vulnerable to be burdened with racist teachers in the name of equality. "For the kind of battle thus indicated, most children are under no circumstances suited. It is the refinement of cruelty to require it of them."[50]

My class read Du Bois's essay alongside contemporary articles making the case that white teachers commonly fail to meet the needs of black children.[51] A lively discussion ensued as to whether black children today need separate schools. Susan was one of the few whites in the class who had not previously studied whiteness theory or critical race theory. When several African American students spoke out in favor of voluntary all-black schools, Susan was visibly upset. From her perspective, segregation meant the failure of anti-racism. In an effort to clarify what she felt was at stake—namely, progress towards positive race relations—she argued that giving up on integrated schools meant giving up on racial change. If black students did not attend racially mixed schools, she said, white teachers such as herself would never unlearn their fear of blacks. The African American students were outraged. One student explained that she did not want her children in schools where white teachers had to unlearn their fear of blacks; she wanted them in schools where they did not have to face hostile white teachers. Other African American students pointed out that they were not concerned with the needs of white teachers; they wanted to get black *children* in schools where *their* needs would be met. When Tracie told Susan, "I understand your concern, and, believe me, it's not that I discount it. But I have to put our children first," Susan was appalled. "If you don't have to listen to my needs," she said, "why should I listen to yours?"

The following week's class meeting began with a guest lecture on Afrocentricity by an African American professor, then broke into three sub-groups for most of the second half of the class. The black students stayed in the main classroom with the black professor, who had volunteered to join them; the brown students went into an adjacent room by themselves; and the white students went with me into yet another classroom. For about an hour, we all met separately before returning to the large group. Although the black students were glad to have had an acknowledged space to themselves, their discussion was not as productive as they had hoped it would be. The brown students were happy; they had had a good conversation. The white students were distressed.

In our separate room, I asked the white students about their palpable unhappiness. A little self-consciously, they said that they felt excluded and inadequate; they knew that the black and brown students were relieved to have a space apart from them. Most of the white students understood why I had separated the groups. Far from contesting the decision, they supported it. Intellectually and politically, they understood what was at stake. Emotionally, it was wrenching.

In this all-white setting, Susan revisited her earlier position that her own needs ought to weigh equally with those of black students. As she had listened to the black and brown students in the class, she told us, and as she continued to read about African American students' experiences in integrated school settings, she changed her mind. "All I could see at first," she told us, "was what *I* needed and wanted. I really wasn't seeing what the black students were going through or that their children's need was greater than mine." Despite her initial defensiveness and lack of awareness, she did not retreat into wounded silence, nursing her objections privately, but continued to engage in the conversation. She was quieter than she had been, but it was an attentive, listening form of quiet, rather than a refusal to engage.

The experience of separation had a significant impact on most of the students. Yet because we did not weave the resulting knowledge, doubts, and anxieties into the course as a topic of inquiry, we lost much of its educational potential. It took courage for the black students to keep returning to a class in which their hopes of claiming a black-centered education were being undermined. It took courage for Susan to revisit her volatile exchange with the black students. Unfortunately, she did so only in the all-white space. Had I been more attentive to her relationship with the black students—and to their relationships with all the white students—I would have created a space for us to talk about these exchanges. At the time, it did not occur to me to try to discover what forms the classroom relationships might take if they were not merely contained but rearticulated. I did not see myself as an advocate and experimentalist, engaged in learning with the students how to listen across race; my role, as I saw it, was to serve as intellectual guide and discussion facilitator. Now I wonder why I assumed that facilitating cross-race conversations would not require calling into question our standing assumptions about listening, evaluating arguments, and claiming authority.

Conversations in a Crowd

There was an additional problem with the situation in which the crisis occurred. The class was large, and the question of voluntary self-segregation stirred up such intense debate that students had to wait in line to make their points. As students raised their hands, I would write down their names and then call on them in the order that they had signaled their desire to say something. I was thrilled with the discussion, as was a black colleague who was present that day. I assumed that the students also found the discussion politically and intellectually stimulating. Afterwards, however, some of the African American students told me that they had felt alienated by the turn-taking format. One student asked me why, in a class devoted to issues that vitally concerned African American students, they had to wait for five or ten minutes to have their say, only to have the urgency of their concerns dissipate while other students redirected the conversation.

In large classes, it can be difficult to achieve the distinctive type of intimacy that allows for productive race talk. Stanley Gaines describes teaching a course on interethnic relations in which he had almost thirty students. "The course . . . had grown so large that at times I felt almost like a traffic cop, striving to ensure that all students respected the interpersonal rules of the road (e.g., refraining from interrupting, mocking, or attempting to intimidate each other)."[52] Insofar as students "view each other as nothing more than nameless faces, as representatives of various racial groups rather than as unique persons," large classes may lend themselves to a kind of anonymity.[53] It is not surprising that students of color often experience large multicultural education classes as violent. In our class, however, the interactions for the most part were courteous and interested. Most students knew several other students; a number were friends. Some of the students may have assumed, as I did, that friendly cross-race relations outside of class would underwrite trust within the class. But the class provoked anxieties and expectations that we never explicitly faced together. One white woman who had been best friends with a black woman in the class for decades told me during break one day, "You're ruining our friendship." Although their friendship recovered, the class brought them and perhaps other students to a crisis point without acknowledging that studying black philosophies of education have lived consequences for both intra- and cross-race student relationships.

On the face of it, my decision to call on students in the order in which they raised their hands was fair. There was no question of privileging students I knew well or students who were simply louder than other people. But my belief that the process was fair was caught up, without my realizing it, with colorblindness. Fairness typically is interpreted as focused on process and indifferent to particularity. In some cases, first-come-first-served is a perfectly appropriate guideline.

In this case, however, it led me to overlook the legitimate claims of particularity. In an emergency room, it makes sense to take the most endangered patients first, regardless of the order in which they arrived. Our discussion about separate schools was not a matter of life and death, but it was an important conversation in which students' investments were strikingly different. The class was not organized to support recognition of those different investments.

Whiteness and the Black Curriculum

Not wanting the African American epistemologies class to function as a followup to the whiteness theory class I had taught the previous semester, I deliberately did not take up whiteness in the class. Tracie and Reed, African American students who had been in both classes, were disappointed that the African American epistemologies course did not explicitly address whiteness. Later, Reed told me that he thought I should have grounded the class in an understanding of white supremacy. When I explained that I had wanted to keep the focus on blackness rather than framing blackness in relation to whiteness, he pointed out that *not* talking about whiteness meant that I had let white students "off the hook." In the whiteness class, he said, there was never any question about white students hiding in or behind their whiteness. "They knew they were going to get called on it." In the African American philosophy of education class, white students were able to talk about black philosophy without addressing their own investments in whiteness.

Many commentators have written about situations in which white students were resistant or hostile to analyses of race and racism, but that was not the situation in our class. Most of the white students were neither unaware of white privilege nor, by standard measures, racially or culturally insensitive. Most were thoughtful, careful people who engaged respectfully with other students; many had taken whiteness theory or critical race theory classes, or both. Few were outwardly defensive. Yet this did not mean that white students were prepared to be partners in inquiry with the black students in the class. Not fully realizing what was at stake for the black (or brown) students, white students who contributed to the large group discussions usually jumped in as more or less equal partners in the search for "truth." Unlike the students of color, white students were able to treat the questions *as if* they were abstract. Like them, I had racial investments in the arguments and analyses being discussed, but we did not examine our investments in white privilege and dominance. Later, speaking of the white students, one of the African American students said, "They read but they didn't hear, if it challenged them as a white person. They didn't minimize it, but they sterilized it." That dynamic was supported by my framing the class as a black classics course. The effect was to "shellac" the texts, as Toni Morrison says, "immobilizing their complexities and power."[54]

For the most part, individual student performances of white privilege were not what stood out for the African American students. One black student said later that he did not even really remember most of the white students. Some of the white students spoke little or not at all, except in the small groups that focused on their projects. What was at issue for most of the black students was the larger racial group dynamic. As one black student put it, "White students needed to be in the background." At least one white student agreed. James told the class, "I think those of us who are white just have to accept that we will never understand these issues the way that people of color do. We should back off and shut up." Although this position appeared to show respect and deference towards people of color, it also rationalized a form of disengagement, providing James with an alibi for not studying outside his comfort zone.

My impression is that the black students did not want the white students either to disengage or to absent themselves. Before class every week, the black students met to discuss the readings among themselves; they already had a separate space. What they wanted was a shared classroom space in which they would be recognized as the primary stakeholders. They wanted to have *this* class oriented to their needs in the way that other classes were routinely oriented to white students' needs for growth and racial enlightenment. Dispassionate theoretical discussions displaced them from the center—but so did disengagement on the part of white students. Some of the African American students wondered, later, what would have happened if white students *had* been asked to take a back seat—if they would have engaged in new ways or if they would have bowed out of risky engagement and simply become spectators of the intense and sometimes painful debates among the black students.

The presence of white students as spectators exacerbated black students' anxieties about black-on-black conflicts. Presumably, however, whiteness would have organized black student relations to some extent even had whites not been present. Intraracial black and brown tensions are often explained in terms of "internalized racism," but as bell hooks points out, "'white supremacy' is a much more useful term for understanding the complicity of people of color in upholding and maintaining racial hierarchies."[55] Whereas "internalized racism" attributes skin color politics, for example, to mis-socialization, the term white supremacy recognizes black investments in how one works (or could work) the system. Although the language of black authenticity appears directly opposed to complicity with white supremacy, it is linked to an implied authority to represent black people as a unified group—and to declare those who do not fit the description not genuinely black. It authorizes the same surveillance of blackness that white supremacy does and does a different but devastating kind of damage.

In class and outside of class, there were painful, only partially suppressed conflicts regarding who could speak authentically about black experience. George Napper notes that black authenticity is commonly identified with the "street," on the assumption that those least successful in navigating the system are also those who have least assimilated to white culture.[56] Black college students, realizing that they enjoy "privileges and liberties that are not forthcoming to their brothers [and sisters] in the streets and ghettos," experience "conflict, contradiction, and guilt" about their blackness, Napper suggests.[57] I can speak only as an outsider to these feelings, but as an insider to the ways in which higher education helps to structure intraracial tensions. My reading of the black-on-black dynamics in the African American epistemologies class was that black students' status as a visible minority on a predominantly white campus had misprepared them for classroom discussions that explored a range of black philosophical positions.

This was the first time that the students were not in the position of being either the only or one of two black "representatives" in a class. Almost invariably, black students preface classroom statements about race with the disclaimer, "I can't speak for all African Americans"; nevertheless, they are often placed in the position of doing so by their white audiences. In time, black students may come to assume the implied but denied position of black spokesperson, for it is a way to claim authority in a context where little authority is likely to be granted. Finding themselves in the luxurious position of being part of a significant number of black students in a class on black philosophy, the African American students at first felt exhilaration, support, and solidarity. The feeling of solidarity diminished, though, as they began to experience the violence of mutual surveillance regarding what counted as an authentically black position. A black student who called for integrated schools risked being called a sell-out. A gay student or older woman or light-skinned African American or a black student with a "white" religion might be dismissed as "not getting it."

Ana Martínez Alemán points out that, for students of color on predominantly white campuses, friendships with others of the same race and/or ethnicity offer "a respite" and "refuge" from the white-centered institution. In principle, these relationships provide a "racial and/or ethnic safe haven."[58] But the intimacy fostered by the space of refuge can obscure the fact that the students may not have much in common. Speaking of women undergraduates at a Midwestern college, she says, "The scarcity of women of color on this campus may restrict to a degree the relationship to race and/or ethnic authentication and validation. Many women commented that the absence of a critical mass of women of color means that their female friendships are very often a consequence of their racial and/or ethnic similarity and not personality."[59] On predominantly white campuses, the kind of refuge available to students of color is not necessarily that of deep personal trust based on multifaceted relationships. It may be only "a form of developmental triage" that "stops the bleeding only long enough to send friends back into battle."[60]

Edén Torres makes a similar point about the Latinas in the partially segregated space of the experimental Chicana/Latina course.

> Happy to be with so many women of color, and confident that we had achieved a kind of cohesion rarely experienced in the academy, we settled smugly into a

period of infatuation with our exclusivity. What we had failed to consider was how deeply we might be affected by our class, racial, religious, sexual orientation, regional, skin color, and age differences, among other things.[61]

"The romance of solidarity" affords a honeymoon period in which students of color feel at one with each other.[62] As differences in personal assumptions, values, and investments emerge, however, the romance begins to fade. It can be difficult to sustain deep trust, because the trust was fostered by the shared experience of being embattled by white dominance and privilege. The small number of students of color on campuses like mine makes it difficult for students of color to experience blackness and brownness as not threatened but enriched by multiple, complex definitions and analyses.

Conclusion

Absurd though it would have been to have arranged the course readings in alphabetical order, doing so would have been less misleading than arranging them chronologically. Alphabetical arrangements are at least obviously arbitrary. As we gave no nuanced attention to the historical contexts in which the different positions emerged, the chronological approach had no point other than to suggest change through time—implicitly, "progress." The chronological structure of the epistemologies and pedagogies class helped suppress the multiplicity of black thought by not framing different positions as potentially coexisting.

I wonder now if it would have been possible to arrange the syllabus in a relational order: an order that might have allowed us to bring the arguments and analyses to bear on our classroom dynamics. How might the readings have helped us to trouble white entitlement and white centrality in academic settings more generally? The "classics" format encouraged us to frame our discussions around important social issues, but these were matters that whites often felt comfortable treating in the abstract. Insufficiently prepared to discuss race issues with black and brown students without reclaiming the center, white students learned "about" blackness but not about their relations to and implications in blackness. Black and brown students, too, read about blackness without necessarily troubling their own relations to blackness. By confining our discussion of the readings to their application to the world "out there," white, brown, and black alike, we missed the chance to think more carefully about our *ways* of thinking about the issues—and how those were caught up in often painful relations, including the relationships we were most sure were solid.[63]

Notes

1. Catherine Clinton, "Contents under Pressure: White Woman/Black History," in *Skin Deep: Black Women and White Women Write about Race*, ed. Marita Golden and Susan Richards Shreve (New York: Doubleday), 255.
2. Clinton, "Contents under Pressure," 238, 239.
3. This chapter focuses on what it means pedagogically and intellectually for whites to teach courses devoted to black topics, but there are also important political and institutional issues at stake. The pattern of whites teaching black and brown subjects can be seen as a form of colonization whereby whites reap the benefits of black and brown labor. Given that college courses on black literature and black history, for example, might never have existed were it not for the organized demands of black students and the pioneering intellectual work of black scholars, we need to ask, "What does it mean to hire white scholars to teach these courses after the battles for inclusion have been fought by others?" Although some white scholars also made important contributions to the development of black studies, the emergence of black studies is largely a black story.
4. Christie Farnham, "The Discipline of History and the Demands of Identity Politics," in *Teaching What You're Not: Identity Politics in Higher Education*, ed. Katherine J. Mayberry (New York: New York University Press, 1996), 108.
5. Jacqueline Jones, "Teaching What the Truth Compels You to Teach: A Historian's View," in *Teaching What You're Not: Identity Politics in Higher Education*, ed. Katherine J. Mayberry (New York: New York University Press, 1996), 181. The book to which the students refer is Jacqueline Jones, *Labor of Love, Labor of Sorrow: Black Women, Work, and the Family, from Slavery to the Present* (New York: Vintage, 1985).
6. Nathan Irvin Huggins, *Revelations: American History, American Myths*, ed. Brenda Smith Huggins (New York: Oxford University Press, 1995), 166.
7. Katie G. Cannon, *Black Womanist Ethics* (Atlanta: Scholar's Press, 1988), 145 and 11.
8. Cannon, *Black Womanist Ethics*, 145.
9. Jones, "Teaching What the Truth," 181.
10. Jones, "Teaching What the Truth," 177. Italics removed.
11. Jones, "Teaching What the Truth," 178.
12. Jones, "Teaching What the Truth," 178. Italics removed.
13. Jones, "Teaching What the Truth," 178.
14. Teacher education classes all too often proceed on the tacit assumption that color is an automatic passport to multicultural knowledge and culturally relevant pedagogy. Insofar as such classes teach multicultural education at all, they concentrate on teaching white prospective teachers to meet the needs of students of color. As Carmen Montecinos points out, though, there is no reason to assume that a student of color knows the history of her racial or ethnic group (let alone that of other groups), or comes equipped with pedagogical skills that will serve students of color. See "Multicultural Teacher Education for a Culturally Diverse Teaching Force," in *Practicing What We Teach: Confronting Diversity in Teacher Education*, ed. Renée J. Martin (Albany: State University of New York Press, 1995), 97–116. Also see Rosa Hernández Sheets and Laureen Chew, "Absent from the Research, Present in Our Classrooms: Preparing Culturally Responsive Chinese American Teachers," *Journal of Teacher Education* 53, no. 2 (March/April 2002): 127–41.
15. In her important work on entitlement among white students, Alison Jones identifies white students' needs for access to and absolution from students of color as a drain on the

time and energy of students of color. Alison Jones, "The Limits of Cross-Cultural Dialogue: Pedagogy, Desire, and Absolution in the Classroom," *Educational Theory* 49, no. 3 (Summer 1999): 299–316. However, she does not mention that white faculty also may seek affirmation, validation, and a multicultural experience from students of color. For a powerful discussion of how white faculty may position faculty of color as validating their claims to anti-racism, see Jeanne Perreault, "White Feminist Guilt, Abject Scripts, and (Other) Transformative Necessities," *West Coast Line* 28, no. 13/14 (Spring/Fall 1994): 226–38.

16. Black and brown faculty, too, may express frustration at black-on-black, brown-on-brown, black-on-brown, and brown-on-black student expectations, hopes, and disappointments; I believe these dynamics are also organized to some extent by whiteness. My focus in this chapter, however, is primarily on white professors.

17. Seeking to differentiate the performative from the structural aspect of whiteness, Marilyn Frye coined the term "whiteliness" to refer to cultural performances of whiteness. Just as "masculinity" is performed (as opposed to maleness), and can be interrupted and rescripted, whiteliness can be interrogated and reworked. See Marilyn Frye, "White Woman Feminist," in *Willful Virgin: Essays in Feminism, 1976–1992* (Freedom, CA: Crossing Press, 1992), 147–69.

18. bell hooks, "Representations of Whiteness," in *Black Looks: Race and Representation* (Boston: South End Press, 1992), 168.

19. See Cris Mayo, "Certain Privilege: Rethinking White Agency," in *Philosophy of Education 2004*, ed. Chris Higgins (Urbana, Ill.: Philosophy of Education Society, 2005), 308–16.

20. Although whites are not positioned similarly with regard to class, sexuality, gender, age, ability, or other dimensions of power and privilege, being white usually is a significant benefit. Even white criminals are likely to receive more lenient sentences than their black and brown counterparts. This is not to say that the benefits of whiteness are added onto other benefits; the kinds of power and privilege available to whites vary widely, depending on intersectionalities with class, gender, sexuality, ability, age, religion, and other positionalities.

21. On white investments in whiteness, see W. E. B. Du Bois, "The Souls of White Folk," in *W. E. B. Du Bois: A Reader*, ed. David Levering Lewis (New York: Henry Holt & Co., 1995), 453–65 [orig. 1920]; James Baldwin, *The Price of the Ticket: Collected Nonfiction 1948–1985* (New York: St. Martin's Press, 1985); and George Lipsitz, *The Possessive Investment in Whiteness: How White People Profit from Identity Politics* (Philadelphia: Temple University Press, 1998).

22. María Lugones, *Pilgrimages/Peregrinajes: Theorizing Coalition against Multiple Oppressions* (Lanham, MD: Rowman & Littlefield, 2003), 211.

23. For a discussion of these issues in the context of cross-race friendship, see Retha Powers, "Overhand and Underhand," in *Skin Deep: Black Women and White Women Write about Race*, ed. Marita Golden and Susan Richards Shreve (New York: Doubleday/Nan A. Talese, 1995), 47–59.

24. Conversations with Kathy Spencer Christy regarding black students' (dis)trust of white teachers and with Greg Bourassa concerning the structural dimensions of black–white trust have richly informed my thinking about cross-race trust.

25. An excellent example of the racial tensions in a committed educational partnership can be found in Jennifer E. Obidah and Karen Manheim Teel, *Because of the Kids: Facing Racial and Cultural Differences in Schools* (New York: Teachers College Press, 2001).

26. Jones, "Teaching What the Truth," 192–93.
27. The initial name for the course was "African-American Epistemology and Pedagogy," later changed to "African American Epistemologies and Pedagogies." I will often refer to an abbreviated version of the title or to synonyms like "African American philosophy of education." All names of students used in the text are pseudonyms.
28. For parallel reasons, I later developed a queer theory course.
29. The first two times that I taught the course, I was in a department that largely suppressed race as a topic for course work. Apart from a required undergraduate multicultural education course and its graduate counterpart, the department offered few courses explicitly devoted to race or culture, although several faculty addressed race and culture under generic-sounding course titles. By the last time I offered the course, the original department had been divided up. My current department focuses on social justice in education, and many of our courses center race, with several emphasizing African American issues.
30. Ana M. Martínez Alemán, "Race Talks: Undergraduate Women of Color and Female Friendships," *The Review of Higher Education* 23, no. 2 (Winter 2000): 141.
31. Stanley O. Gaines, Jr., "Color-Line as Fault-Line: Teaching Interethnic Relations in California in the 21st Century," *Journal of Social Issues* 60, no. 1 (March 2004): 182.
32. Martínez Alemán, "Race Talks," 143.
33. Geneva Gay, "Navigating Marginality en Route to the Professoriate: Graduate Students of Color Learning and Living in Academia," *International Journal of Qualitative Studies in Education* 17, no. 2 (March–April 2004): 277.
34. Gay, "Navigating Marginality," 277.
35. Although "black" as used in this chapter often overlaps with "African American," I do not use the terms synonymously, as one of the black students in the class was not African American. My primary focus in this chapter is on how my pedagogy conflicted with the hopes and expectations of the African American students.
36. The electronic syllabus for the class can be found at http://www.pauahtun.org/6623-Spring.2002.html
37. The syllabus asked students to immerse themselves in some aspect of African American culture with which they were relatively unfamiliar, such as black poetry, popular magazines, children's fiction, photography, sculpture, paintings, dance, historically black religions, or television. As much as possible, students were asked to immerse themselves in black versions of that medium "to the exclusion of other (especially mainstream) versions of the cultural or art form. For example, if you are concentrating on African-American movies, you should try to avoid other kinds of movies for the time being. My purpose in asking for this exclusivity is to promote the kind of fluency that comes with immersion rather than sampling, comparison, or 'translation' approaches." Students were asked to write about their responses to this material and class time was set aside for students to gather in small groups to talk about the projects. For some students (of different races), immersing themselves in the project and talking about it with their peers was the most significant dimension of the course, because it most effectively centered blackness.
38. Farnham, "Discipline of History," 114.
39. Michael Hanchard, "Afro-Modernity: Temporality, Politics, and the African Diaspora," *Public Culture* 11, no. 1 (1999): 246. Also see John K. Thornton, *Africa and Africans in the Making of the Atlantic World, 1400–1800* (Cambridge: Cambridge University Press, 1994); Basil Davidson, *The Black Man's Burden: Africa and the Curse of the Nation-State* (New York: Times Books, 1992); Paul Gilroy, *"There Ain't No Black in the Union Jack": The Cultural Politics of Race and Nation* (1987, reprint; Chicago: Univer-

sity of Chicago Press, 1991); and Paul Gilroy, *The Black Atlantic: Modernity and Double Consciousness* (Cambridge: Harvard University Press, 1993).
40. Lisa D. Delpit, "The Silenced Dialogue: Power and Pedagogy in Educating Other People's Children," *Harvard Educational Review* 58, no. 3 (August 1988): 280.
41. Delpit, "Silenced Dialogue," 280.
42. Students' investments in the course differed in a variety of ways. Age, religion, gender, sexuality, class, nationality, nationality, and regionality as well as academic background, all mattered. Although I focus primarily on the black/white divide, students' investments were multiple and complex.
43. I use the term "brown" in this context with misgivings, for these students did not share an identity. They came from very different cultural and religious backgrounds. Nevertheless, they shared a positionality, for they were conscious of being neither black nor white and of having no comfortable way into the classroom discourse.
44. It is possible, of course, for black students to make the same move, but in this class none of the black students did.
45. Stuart Hall, "New Ethnicities," in *Stuart Hall: Critical Dialogues in Cultural Studies*, ed. David Morley and Kuan-Hsing Chen (London: Routledge, 1996), 443.
46. White students also may be parents of black or mixed-race children, although in this class that happened not to be the case. The degree to which white parents of black, brown, or mixed-race children problematize their own whiteness varies considerably. See, for example, Ruth Frankenberg, *White Women, Race Matters: The Social Construction of Whiteness* (Minneapolis: University of Minnesota Press, 1993); and France Winddance Twine, "Transracial Mothering and Antiracism: The Case of White Birth Mothers of 'Black' Children in Britain," *Feminist Studies* 25, no. 3 (Fall 1999): 729–46.
47. W. E. Burghardt Du Bois, "Does the Negro Need Separate Schools?" *Journal of Negro Education* 4, no. 3 (July 1935): 328.
48. Carter Godwin Woodson, *The Mis-Education of the Negro* (1933; reprint, Washington, D.C.: Associated Publishers, 1972). Over the years, Du Bois took a range of positions on education for African Americans, but this particular article has several resonances with Woodson's book. Whereas Woodson's book focused on adults, Du Bois's article focused primarily on children.
49. Du Bois, "Does the Negro Need Separate Schools?" 330.
50. Du Bois, "Does the Negro Need Separate Schools?" 331.
51. The other two readings assigned were Joan Davis Ratteray, "The Search for Access and Content in the Education of African-Americans," in *Too Much Schooling, Too Little Education: A Paradox of Black Life in White Societies*, ed. Mwalimu J. Shujaa (Trenton, N.J.: Africa World Press, 1994), 123–41; and Michele Foster, "Educating for Competence in Community and Culture: Exploring the Views of Exemplary African-American Teachers," in *Too Much Schooling*, 221–44.
52. Gaines, "Color-Line as Fault-Line," 180.
53. Gaines, "Color-Line as Fault-Line," 181.
54. Toni Morrison, *Playing in the Dark: Whiteness and the Literary Imagination* (New York: Vintage, 1992), 91. Although Morrison is referring to white-authored texts, her imagery also suggests the ways in which black-authored texts may be positioned as powerful but inert. For example, as a brown student pointed out, our class's discussion of Malcolm X's writing honored his politics but seemed to erase his Muslim faith.
55. bell hooks, "Overcoming White Supremacy: A Comment," in *Talking Back: Thinking Feminist, Thinking Black* (Boston: South End Press, 1989), 113.
56. George Napper, *Blacker than Thou: The Struggle for Campus Unity* (Grand Rapids,

MI: William B. Eerdmans Publishing Company, 1973), 21.
57. Napper, *Blacker than Thou*, 29. Also see 21. Although Napper's account dates from the early seventies, it still has value for contemporary analyses.
58. Martínez Alemán, "Race Talks," 144.
59. Martínez Alemán, "Race Talks," 148.
60. Martínez Alemán, "Race Talks," 147.
61. Edén E. Torres, "The Virtues of Conflict: Challenging Dominant Culture and White Feminist Theory," in *Chicana without Apology/Chicana sin vergüenza: The New Chicana Cultural Studies* (New York: Routledge, 2003), 139.
62. Torres, "Virtues of Conflict," 139.
63. I owe a large debt to Deanna Blackwell and Ellen Correa, with whom I have had countless rich conversations about whiteness and pedagogy. We also have collaborated on papers that discuss several of the issues discussed here. In 2003, Deanna and I co-wrote "Quality Time with White Folks: Cross-Race Relationships in the Classroom," which was presented at the semi-annual spring meeting of the *Midwest Society for Women in Philosophy* in East Lansing, Michigan. In 2005, Ellen and I presented "The Whiteness at the Heart of Progressive Pedagogy: Costs for Students and Teachers of Color" at the annual meeting of the *American Educational Research Association* in Montréal. I also have had many wonderful conversations with Gregory Bourassa, Kathleen Spencer Christy, Thomasania Leydsman, Darron Smith, and Eugene Tachinni that have importantly informed this chapter. I thank all of them, as well as the students in the three African American Epistemologies and Pedagogies classes who taught me so much. Finally, I thank my colleagues, who constantly educate me.

3

On Intersectionality and the Whiteness of Feminist Philosophy[1]

Alison Bailey, Illinois State University

> Because white eyes do not want to know us, they do not bother to learn our language, which reflects us, our culture, our spirit.
> —Gloria Anzaldúa[2]

> When I do not see plurality stressed in the very structure of a theory, I know that I will have to do lots of acrobatics—like a contortionist or tightrope walker—to have this theory speak to me without allowing the theory to distort me in my complexity.
> —María Lugones[3]

Feminism and academic philosophy have had lots to say to one another. Yet part of what marks feminist philosophy as *philosophy* is our engagement with the intellectual traditions of the white forefathers.[4] As Naomi Zack observes "so much feminist theory rests on the ideas of the patriarchs."[5] For some, the authors we read, the ideas we engage, and the texts we cite determine whether feminist work really counts as philosophy. It makes sense—given our training—that feminist philosophers would draw first from our disciplinary legacy to understand our experiences. In the space of less than two generations we have generated a delightfully unruly corpus of work and ushered in a new generation of students eager to read, embellish and critique this flourishing canon. We have carved out new areas of inquiry in politics, epistemology and philosophy of science, ethics, and more recently in metaphysics. I'm not uncomfortable with these projects: Aristotle, Foucault, Sartre, Wittgenstein, Quine, Austin, and countless others have provided us with some very powerful conceptual tools for advancing our projects. The history of philosophy is rich and diverse. Overall it has served feminist philosophy well. However, as Sandra Harding observes, conventional standards for what counts as "good science" (or in this case "good philosophy") always bear the imprint of their creators.[6] If Anglo-European cultural frameworks and methodologies have crafted philosophical "best practices," and if feminist philosophers understand these as doing philosophy pure and simple, then we have (albeit critically) inherited our forefather's toolbox. The categories and concepts we borrow and adapt reflect prevailing political and social arrangements—including patriarchy, ableism, white supremacy and colonialism. When white feminists modify these tools to fit our projects we are certain to leave the fingerprints of domination on the conversations we begin. We may have de-centered the maleness of philosophy, but not its whiteness, not its colonial legacy—even in feminist contexts! More than a few scholars have commented on this phenomenon.[7] Charles Mills makes a strong case for philosophy's "theoretical whiteness" when he observes that our questions are composed, framed and answered in ways that completely ignore the position of women and men of color within white supremacist regimes. Bell hooks calls attention to the alliances between white women academics and their male peers, and asks why they continually turn toward the critical theory by white men while failing to engage the critical insights of black women and women of color. Uma Narayan offers strong evidence for academic feminism's tendency to aspire to Western epistemic and political standards. María Lugones patiently challenges politically-minded white feminists and progressive male scholars of all races on their indifference to women of color's struggles and the reluctance to embrace the alternative conceptual frameworks arising from those struggles.[8] So why is it that white feminists philosophers continue to reach almost exclusively into the forefather's toolbox? Why do we do this even when scholarship by Arab, Native, African-American, Asian, Latino/a, and African women speaks directly to our projects? Why do we turn to Aristotle instead of Anzaldúa?

Admittedly, there are some times when women and men of color's scholarship will not answer the questions feminist philosopher's pose. At other times we may be ignorant of the potential contributions scholars or communities of color can make to our projects. As a white philosopher I worry about the ways white ignorance continues to preserve our disciplinary boundaries. As a white feminist I'm concerned with what Marianna Ortega identifies as white feminists "loving, knowing ignorance" of women of color. In other words, there is the tendency for some white feminists who are involved in the production of knowledge about women of color—whether by citing their work, reading and writing about them, or classifying them—to use women of color's work to further their own desires and ends. Here white women, as perceivers, invent an account of women of color's realities that accords more with our desires [and conceptual frameworks] than with women of color's actual lived experiences.[9] So, I think about whether the tools my discipline hands me, combined with my well-meaning white feminist engagement with women of color, ever serve as strategies for exclusion.[10] This leads me to ask: Why haven't most white feminist philosophers engaged the conceptual frameworks from people of color's intellectual traditions and Anglo-European philosophy with equal vigor? Why is it that we always bring traditional disciplinary epistemological, metaphysical and normative values *to* the study of racism or colonialism, but almost never use the tools of diversity and pluralism to challenge the very racial or colonial structures of metaphysics, epistemology and ethics?[11]

In this chapter I want to explore some possible reasons why white feminists philosophers have failed to engage deeply the radical work being done by non-Western women, U.S. women of color and scholars of color outside of the discipline. My conversation begins with intersectionality, which, for feminists working outside of philosophy, is a predictable point of departure; but as a white feminist philosopher I have specific reasons for starting here. The fact that intersectionality is, at once, such a widely recognized strategy for making visible women of color's issues and concerns in academic and policy discussions, and so neglected by philosophers is telling.[12] I want to invite philosophers to think more seriously about intersectionality and other pluralist approaches as strategies for calling attention to whiteness of philosophy in general and feminist philosophy in particular. I want us to consider what feminist philosophy would be like if women of color's writing, experiences, and communities drove philosophical inquiry. Since most philosophers are unfamiliar with intersectional methodologies, I begin with a basic explanation of the foundational claims of this approach. Next, I explore some reasons why white feminists working in philosophy may be resistant to this method. I identify both disciplinary and personal reasons for this hesitancy and argue that intersectionality serves as a useful strategic tool for examining white authority in the emergent feminist canon. Finally, I explore the role intersectional thinking might play in creating a feminist critical race philosophy by outlining four projects that I think will challenge and enrich feminist work in the discipline.

A Primer on Intersectionality for Philosophers

Intersectionality has become as popular as it is problematic. Despite the fact that it is often treated as a methodological panacea, intersectionality is really a strategy for making plurality visible in academic conversations and policy discussions. In this sense it works more like a tool (e.g. a spell check program) for making inquirers mindful of complexity, than like a fully-developed methodology (e.g. socialist feminism, psychoanalytic feminism). Since philosophers are less familiar with intersectionality than, say, social scientists, I begin with a basic account of this influential method.

Contemporary feminist uses of intersectionality became popular in the early 1980s when U.S. academic feminism underwent a dramatic paradigm shift. At the time ground-breaking books such as Angela Davis's *Women, Race and Class* (1981), Gloria Anzaldúa and Cherríe Moraga's *The Bridge Called My Back: Radical Writings by Women of Color* (1983) and Gloria Hull, Patricia Scott and Barbara Smith's *But Some of Us are Brave* (1983), and Audre Lorde's *Sister Outsider* (1984) challenged the essentialist underpinnings of white academic feminism and its accompanying account of gender. U.S. women of color's writing demonstrated how white feminist's theoretically blending of white supremacist concepts of gender (all the women are white), with patriarchal concepts to race (all the men are dark) damaged women of color by either distorting their experiences with discrimination or allowing them to fall through the cracks. Using this basic insight, feminist critical race theorists, coined the term "intersectionality" to name approaches to discrimination that treated oppressions as multiplicative rather than additive. Kimberlé Crenshaw's crossroads metaphor grounds most popular discussions.

> Intersectionality is what occurs when a woman from a minority group tries to navigate the main crossing in the city.... The main highway is "racism road." One cross street can be Colonialism, the [other] Patriarchy Street.... She has to deal not only with one form of oppression, but with all forms, those names as road signs, which link together to make a double, a triple, multiple, a many layered blanket of oppression.[13]

Thinking intersectionally has the advantage of rendering homogenous categories and subjects politically suspect by situating individuals within networks of relations that complicate their social locations. It offers powerful, often historically based accounts, of the ways race, class, gender, sexuality and many other categories come into existence in and through their relationships to one another in contradictory and complicated ways. Intersectionality clears space for marginalized groups to articulate new realities from complex locations that reflect more accurately women's diverse social experiences. The approach has the additional virtue of demonstrating how privilege traverses and mitigates some individual's experiences with oppression—white privilege attenuates gender subordination; and, class privilege may take the edge off race oppression.

Intersectionality has both a methodological and a normative dimension. Ange-Marie Hancock observes that the term "refers to both a normative theoretical argument and an approach to conducting empirical research that emphasizes the interaction of categories of difference (including but not limited to race, gender, class and sexual orientation)."[14] Scholars working primarily in the social sciences, feminist theory, critical legal studies, and international human rights and public policy have used intersectionality to emphasize the interactions between categories of difference and complex systems of domination. The Working Group on Human Rights of the Center for Women's Global Leadership, for example, uses intersectional methodology as a strategy for mainstreaming gender into human rights policy discussion, considering the full diversity of women's lived experiences, and enhancing women's empowerment. Charlotte Bunch explains the value of this approach for human rights policy:

> The methodology of intersectionality—of looking at how different aspects of our identities such as race and gender affect each other—also helps to further work toward another basic human rights concept: indivisibility. The human rights system is based on the idea that human rights are indivisible and interre-

lated. But the treaties and mechanisms set up to defend and promote human rights tend to be linear—that is they tend to treat different aspects of abuse and discrimination (race, sex, age, migrant status, etc.) separately . . . . This work on methodology and guidelines for how to relate gender to issues such as torture, war crimes, freedom of expression, arbitrary execution, etc. can be useful to thinking about an intersectional approach that looks at how race and gender, as well as, other factors affect each other.[15]

Brunch's remarks point to an incongruity between human rights as ideally "indivisible and interrelated" and the practice of enforcing human rights through policies that understand rights additively. The unapologetically normative dimension of feminist theory is implicit in Brunch's remarks. If additive approaches distort, silence and exclude marginalized people's experiences, and if intersectional approaches include them, then the latter are better because they are fundamentally more democratic. If the underlying goal of feminism is to eliminate injustices, and if additive approaches fail to make visible the unique ways gendered racisms discriminate, then feminists *ought* to adopt intersectional or other pluralist methods.

A foundational account of intersectionality originates in Kimberlé Crenshaw's now-famous "Mapping the Margins" essay where she identifies three intersectional frameworks: structural intersectionality, political intersectionality, and an examination of intersectionality in the context of identity politics.[16] The structural approach is by far the most common. It focuses on the intersections among macro-level socio-political structures (e.g. white supremacy, patriarchy, ableism, hetero/sexism, colonialism, or capitalism) in an attempt to tease out how these *structures*—rather than *identities*—traverse one another to create new locations of interaction.[17] Structural intersectionality does not foreground all systems of oppression at once. The usual approaches highlight one feature (e.g. gender) and demonstrates how racism, classism, or colonialism run through it. Patricia Hill Collins's work in *Black Feminist Thought* (1990), for example, employs structural intersectionality as a strategy for making describing Black women's unique experiences with oppression visible. As Collins argues:

> Black feminist thought fosters a fundamental paradigmatic shift that rejects additive approaches to oppression . . . [and] sees these distinctive systems of oppression as being part of one overarching structure of domination . . . . Viewing relations of domination for Black women for any given sociohistorical context as being structured via a system of interlocking race, class, and gender oppression expands the focus of analysis from merely describing the similarities and differences distinguishing these systems of oppression and focuses greater attention on how they interconnect. Assuming that each system needs the others in order to function creates a distinct theoretical stance that stimulates the rethinking of basic social science concepts.[18]

If structural intersectionality offers a fuller understanding of the relationships among what Collins calls "matrices of domination," then it also makes sense to consider the relationships among the movements of resistance they foster.

Intersectionality's *political* approach "describe[s] the location of women of color both within overlapping systems of subordination and at the margins of feminism and antiracism."[19] It offers a helpful strategy for bringing out the tensions and connections between feminism, anti-racism, anti-colonialism and other resistance movements. According to Crenshaw, women of color frequently find themselves situated within at least two subordinated groups pursuing conflicting political agendas. And, "[t]he need to split [their] political energies between two sometimes-opposing groups is a dimension of intersectional disempowerment which men of color and white women seldom confront."[20] For example, during the 1970s Native women in the American Indian Movement (AIM) were torn between backing tribal politics, which were largely unconcerned with women's rights, and white feminist political projects that were unconcerned with colonialism. As Devon Abbott Mihesuah explains, Native women had "much to lose by publicly discussing the dysfunctional gender roles with their tribes during the 1970s and today. Native women could not whole-heartedly embrace the women's movement of the day because 'women's lib was a white, middle-class thing, and at this critical stage they had other priorities.' Despite sexism that pervades their societies, American Indigenous women . . . keep their secrets close and often fight for group rights more aggressively than the fight for gender rights."[21] In response to this double-exclusion some Native women formed Women of All Red Nations (WARN) to address social issues such as education, health care, and forced sterilization from a perspective that neither tribal leaders nor white feminists addressed.

Crenshaw hints at a third approach when she explains "intersectionality might be more broadly useful as a way of mediating the tension between assertions of multiple identity and the ongoing necessity of group politics."[22] What might be called *identity politics* intersectionality emphasizes how particular subjects and groups are constructed or construct themselves in response to structural barriers. This focus uses personal narratives and histories to explore the impact of structural inequalities on particular groups or individuals from a micro-level or material perspective. It incorporates an awareness of how racism, colonialism, or hetero/sexism shape how subjects answer the question "Who am I?" and how groups reply to the question "Who are we?" Philosophers might characterize this version as something close to an existential phenomenological approach that highlights human life from the inside, as lived experience, rather than pretending to understand it from an outside macroscopic point of view. *This Bridge Called My Back* (1983) popularized this approach by revolutionizing how U.S. women of color explored their identities in the wake of second wave feminism. *Bridge* authors clearly name the multiple displacements women of color experience by doing what Cherríe Moraga calls a "theory in the flesh."[23] Gloria Anzaldúa's account of her lived experiences in the borderlands illustrates this nicely: "Alienated from her mother culture, 'alien' in the dominant culture, the woman of color does not feel safe within the inner life of her Self. Petrified, she can't respond, her face caught between *los intersticios*, the spaces between different worlds she inhabits."[24] Evelyn Alsultany's echoes Anzaldúa's fragmented experience as she describes how her life as a Cuban Iraqi American is constantly reinvented by the context in which those who try to make sense of her are placed.

> My body becomes marked with meaning as I enter public space. My identity fractures as I experience differing dislocations in multiple contexts. Sometimes people otherize me, sometimes they identify with me. Both situations are equally problematic. Those who otherize me fail to see my humanity and those who identify with me fail to see difference; my Arab or Muslim identity negates my Cuban heritage. . . . Ethnicity needs to be recast so that our moving selves can be acknowledged.[25]

It's really quite difficult to distinguish between these three characterizations. All have served feminist projects well: They have awakened white feminists from our essentialist slumbers, generated almost three decades of academic scholarship by feminists of color, and reframed the ways most of us think about political issues.

Intersectionality and White Academic Analytic Feminist Philosophy

When it comes to addressing the ways racism and colonialism shape our intellectual traditions and practices, Western academic analytic philosophy remains decades behind other disciplines in the humanities and social sciences. Despite feminist philosophy's growing popularity, most white women are still lax about beginning our inquiry in plurality. Why does this continue to be the case? Naomi Zack offers one possible explanation. "Intersectionality," she says, "requires a redirection of philosophy, in method as well as subject matter," and not all philosophers—even feminist philosophers!—are comfortable with this shift.[26] Feminists interested in working toward what Anna Stubblefield calls a "post-supremacist philosophy" should examine the possible reasons for this hesitancy.[27] Do intersectional approaches compromise the "purity" of Anglo-European philosophy? Will a newfound pluralist voice reflect our nature and spirit in ways that make us feel uncomfortable? Do U.S. women of color and Third World women's challenges just complicate (mess up?) all we've thought about since the 1980s?

I think there are some clear disciplinary obstacles to using intersectional approaches. Philosophy's reputation for clear and well-orchestrated argumentation sometimes functions as a cover for our conceptual biases. Normally our persistent attention to soundness and validity are offered as evidence of impartiality and fairness, but they may also be read as strategies for preserving theoretical purity and erasing difference. Too often the traditional Western philosophical gaze is driven by arrogant perception, where arrogant eyes skillfully organize the world and its contents with reference to the desires and interests of the perceiver.[28] Philosophers are theory huggers: we are usually more comfortable talking about ideas than we are about people. As María Lugones observes, "white women theorists seem to have worried more passionately about the harm the claim [about women's differences] does to theorizing than about the harm the theorizing did to women of color."[29] Sometimes we hold concepts so tightly that our love for them replaces our love for one another. We care more for the coherence of our arguments than for the coherence of our relationships. Our desire to defend what we've worked so hard to gain sometimes eclipses our desire to listen. So, intersectional approaches can place feminist philosophers in a disciplinary double bind. If we theorize gender or race too abstractly we lose sight of the diverse material conditions of women's lives, and if we begin arguments in specific locations with women of color, then some will say that we are no longer doing philosophy. In the face of this bind (compounded by the pressures of finding a job, getting tenure, and publishing) many of us are compelled to take the philosophically safe route: we develop our ideas as they relate to the canon rather than our relations with one another.

White feminist philosophers would do well to examine the concepts we cling to and to think about why we value them. There is no question that many of us are more comfortable in our disciplinary comfort zones than we are engaging non-Western or non-white traditions of making meaning. Tight arguments and conceptual clarity are difficult to pull from unfamiliar spaces. White feminist philosophers must learn to be conceptually at home in worlds that challenge us. Starting inquiry in plurality demands a level of comfort and skill with ambiguity—the idea that identities are never fixed and that their meaning must be constantly negotiated. And so, we must name and explore how our "best practices" confine us to Western or white realities, logics and epistemologies. I'm slowly becoming aware of how my own whitely philosophical habits and choices maintain disciplinary boundaries. My analytic training moves me to value some authors, subjects, styles of writing, thinking, and knowing over others. I'm more comfortable with certainty than ambiguity. I'm drawn to writing that is analytically rigorous over memoir, poetry, prose or narrative. I'm suspicious of spiritual practices as sources of knowledge. I rely exclusively on visual metaphors for explaining difficult concepts. When I speak I often hear the voices of the forefathers echo in my words, and I wonder what other voices they may have drowned out. I'm curious about what it would be like for me to "[t]hrow away abstraction and the academic learning, the rules, the map and compass. Feel [my] way without blinders. To touch more people, the personal realities and the social must be evoked—not through rhetoric but through blood, pus, and sweat."[30] Would I still be doing philosophy if I did this? Does it matter?

Our reluctance to employ pluralist methodologies is also the product of the spaces most of us inhabit. When white feminists philosophers do pay attention to racism, colonialism, or white supremacy it is usually (but not always) in safe theoretical spaces where whiteness is centered: classrooms, conferences, workshops, and roundtables.[31] These conversations are very different when they happen on public transportation, in soup kitchens, refugee camps, prisons, on the third shift at the factory, or at tribal colleges. Almost all of our conversations take place in spaces that fail to challenge directly the irreconcilable material differences between women of color's lives and our own. I remember coming face to face with this realization on a trip I took with the Rio Bocay Project to transport medicine and school supplies to the Sumo and Miskito peoples of Nicaragua in the early 1990s. I was a graduate student at the time and my head was filled with theoretical questions about the social construction of gender and what at the time was called "the difference problem" in feminism. I remember talking with a Sumo woman about what she thought counted as women's issues in her village. She paused and replied that food and medicine were her most pressing concerns. At first I thought that perhaps she did not understand me, or that my Spanish was unclear, so I asked her again about what *women's* issues were most pressing in her village. Again she paused and plainly stated: "*We need food and medicine, these are the most important things for us.*" Why was it so difficult for me to hear her the first time? Simple. I couldn't see that her poverty and immediate needs were the products of a colonial history. I was more interested in theorizing her responses in a way that fit with a Western "First World" theoretical framework that directed my attention to patriarchal oppression before the effects of colonialism or U.S. imperialism. It was more convenient for me to fit her concerns into my theoretical framework than it was to admit that a strictly patriarchal reading was useless in this context.

White women must become better listeners. We cannot recognize our interdependency with women of color in any genuine way if we confine ourselves, our conversations and our writing exclusively to academic spaces where we feel reassured. For white feminist philosophers to make valuable contributions to a post-supremacist philosophy more of us must leave the comfort and safety of familiar spaces and texts and relocate ourselves outside of the academic, disciplinary, literary, political, and other environments that encourage the white solipsism of living [and doing philosophy] as if only white people, our worlds and our problems mattered.[32] We have to ask some difficult questions about how the topics, writing styles, and methods we choose mirror our affluence. Are we inspired exclusively by academic texts and conference presentations? How often are women of color part of our real or imagined audiences when we think, write and speak? Does our knowledge about women of color's lives come exclusively through books, articles, and documentaries? If so, what does this say about our relationships with the women of color in the communities where we live and work? Answering these questions requires the courage to seek new communities and theoretical tools. It means ignoring the voices in our heads that tell us we are "not doing philosophy."

Now, I don't want to lay the blame for white ignorance squarely at the foot of philosophy as a discipline. Building multiplicity into the heart of philosophical inquiry is challenging to white feminists for another reason: it prompts us to acknowledge our own plurality and the whiteness of feminist philosophy. María Lugones's observations are once again very helpful here. In her essay "On the Logic of Pluralist Feminism" she identifies a number of tricks that racism plays on white women, including our tendency to block identification with unflattering pictures of our white selves that compete with the accepted association of whiteness with being good, well-meaning, decent, and sensitive. This is only one account of whiteness. Many people of color often experience white folks as insensitive, self-centered, or greedy, untrustworthy. This facet of whiteness is only accessible though interactions with people of color. As Lugones puts it: "It is not that [people of color] are the only faithful mirrors, but I think we *are* faithful mirrors. Not that we show you as you *really* are. What we reveal to you is that you are many—something that may in itself be frightening to you .... You block identification with that self because you are afraid of plurality: Plurality speaks to you of a world whose logic is unknown to you and that you inhabit unwillingly."[33] When white women block identification with ourselves as plural, we block identification with women of color; and when we block our identification with women of color we shut out the part of ourselves that we don't want to see. It is uncomfortable and painful for white folks to recognize our plurality. It forces us to consider how our selves, the world, and how we come to know it, might be more varied and context dependent than we thought originally. Intersectionality obliges us to acknowledge our plurality, and once we do philosophical inquiry can no longer be just about us and the issues we find interesting. It's no wonder that dominant groups theorize from the comfort of our own histories, conceptual frameworks and worlds of meaning—speaking from this location keeps our identities whole, stable and in control.

Intersectionality also requires us to confront some very real fears about our authority and the fragility of the feminist canon we've struggled to create. I like the way Mariana Ortega makes this point.

> White feminists stand as the guardians of the doors of feminism, while women of color are those who remain homeless in this feminism, the ones who don't quite belong in this homeland .... It is easy to see that white feminists stand to lose if they give up being the guardians of the door; their very being would be at stake .... the inclusion of women of color who bring to light their difference is not welcomed precisely because the plurality that these women of color bring to light threatens the safety of white feminists' home.[34]

Our fear may be historically grounded. For over thirty years feminist philosophers have struggled to introduce issues of gender and sexuality into the discipline and our efforts have not always been met warmly. For instance, in the 1970s neo-Marxists and other progressive male scholars routinely responded to claims about women's oppression by arguing that gender oppression was nothing special (since everyone is oppressed in some way), or that all oppressions could be reduced to class oppression. So there was a time when "everyone is oppressed in different ways" responses to feminism were hostile.[35] There may be a lingering fear, for some of us, that we can't embrace plurality without loosing our feminist edge. This fear runs deeper when we realize that white feminists have yet to name the unseen ways whiteness functions to structure and maintain control over the conversations we've begun. When white feminist philosophers think about race some of us forget both our own multiplicity and our complex relationships with women of color. We turn inward to examine *ourselves*: we unpack the invisibility of privilege, interrogate white guilt and shame, articulate the social construction of whiteness, address the harms and habits of whiteness, or theorize ways to be traitorous.[36] What scholars of color have taught us about whiteness is acknowledged in these discussions, but people of color themselves are often present only as dim reflections.

What Should White Feminist Philosophers Do? Notes Toward a Critical Race Feminist Philosophy

If Anglo-European philosophical traditions disproportionately drive the agenda in feminist philosophy, then we must think carefully about whether our topical and theoretical choices produce and preserve whiteness. This requires that we hold tightly to the hope that philosophy can serve the ends of liberation rather than domination. If some (but certainly not all) Western conceptual frameworks risks discursive colonization of people of color's lives, then we must be mindful of this possibility. At the same time we must also remember that many scholars of color have put the forefather's tools to good library uses. One way to make room for these considerations is to develop critical race feminism in philosophy along the lines of critical race feminism in legal studies. It might be objected that critical race feminism would never have arisen had it not been for the significant increase of women of color entering the legal academy at the end of the last century, and that philosophy has not had parallel influx. Philosophy's largely white demographic should not prevent us from building interdisciplinary feminist coalitions.[37] Contemporary analytic philosophy and law are close cousins. We have similar complaints about exclusive categories, clear taxonomies, transcendent and ahistorical truths, abstract homogenous subjectivities, and pure methods and procedures that are standard in each of our disciplines.[38] A critical race feminist philosophy must have plurality stressed in its very structure. Intersectionality is one way of initially making plurality visible. Intersectional approaches allow us to understand how white solipsism shapes inquiry—thus decentering whiteness—by prompting us to engage questions of discrimination, domestic violence, or reproductive health services from the standpoint of many women's lives. Once the plurality of women's experiences becomes visible, new lines of inquiry will emerge. However, I don't think the foundational accounts of intersectionality I've outlined are by themselves robust enough to offer the full-fledged pluralist methodology a critical race feminist philosophy requires. Setting aside, for the moment, the question of what a complete pluralist methodology might look like, I'd like to begin sketching some of the basic issues I believe a critical race feminist philosophy might begin to address. In other words, what sorts of questions should feminist coalitions be considering if the white center of feminist philosophy is not to hold?

Naming The Ways Whiteness Shapes Feminist Philosophy

However we decide to address the whiteness of most feminist philosophy we must work coalitionally. Feminist interdisciplinary coalitions might begin by naming the Westerness or the whiteness of the philosophical sub-disciplines we've created. Two decades ago feminist philosophers took it upon themselves to explain why basic taken-for-granted-as-unproblematic concepts such as autonomy, persons, citizenship, rationality, and objectivity distorted and erased women's moral, political, and epistemic experiences; but, [white] gender and not plurality was at the heart of these projects. We can now think about whether the concepts feminist philosophers have amended and re-tooled have been imagined in ways that preserve whiteness and colonial relations.[39] This means thinking honestly about the ways white feminists may have framed philosophical problems in ways that marginalize women of color's voices and concerns.

Feminist work in reproductive bioethics illustrates my concern nicely. It's no accident that, from the 1980s on, feminist reproductive bioethics shifted its focus from abortion and contraception to high-tech solutions to infertility such as surrogacy, sex selection, In Vitro Fertilization (IVF), egg donation and other artificial reproductive technologies (ARTs). They draw moral attention to issues generated by technologically advanced medical fertility procedures that are accessible primarily to white affluent women in the West. For communities of color the moral issues raised by ARTs pale in comparison to the injustices suffered by their grandmothers, mothers, daughters and sisters who historically have been denied the right to become mothers on their own terms. Native women, Black women and Latinas have been sterilized against their will. Oral contraception was tested on Puerto Rican women before it was made available to all women on the U.S. mainland. Norplant was tested on poor women in India and Brazil. And, more recently, quinacrine has been used to sterilize women in developing countries.[40] Throughout the 20th century women of color have had their children taken from their families and placed into foster care or government-run boarding schools. When ARTs and surrogacy are the primary focus of feminist reproductive bioethics our moral attention is diverted away from the low-tech reproductive abuses that women of color continue to endure. The heavy ART focus of feminist reproductive bioethics reflects the fact that feminists do not have plurality at the heart of their inquiry: we have been thinking about reproduction along one axis—[white] gender—and have failed to address the racial and colonial dimensions of our projects.

Thinking intersectionally about ARTs and surrogacy does not mean extending our existing analyses to women of color's reproductive experiences. In many cases we must begin inquiry anew. For example, feminists have been writing about commercial surrogacy for over 20 years. Those in favor of the practice argue that surrogacy gives women (and gay men) additional reproductive options, and that surrogates should be free to choose this practice as a way of earning money. Opponents argue that gestational labor is morally different from other work practices and that surrogacy raises important questions about the commodification and exploitation of women's reproductive bodies. The questions become more complex when we think about surrogacy in a global context. Within the past five years commercial surrogacy services have been outsourced to clinics in India and Eastern Europe that charge $6000 rather than $60,000 for their services. Thinking intersectionally about surrogacy in a global context gets us to ask a different set of questions about the complex relationships between colonialism, capitalism, caste, and race that are not addressed by the earlier literature on white American women's experiences as surrogates. What's going on when American, Canadian and European women use Indian women's bodies to gestate their [white] children? How do lower-middle income Indian women negotiate the complex terrain that requires them to remain anonymous during the surrogacy process, so that they can make more money in nine months than they would in three years? What would our discussion look like if we began in the lives of Indian women who see this emerging market as both an opportunity to help others and to improve their lives?[41]

We also need to consider the language we use when we frame discussions of reproductive bioethics. Women of color have been active in the reproductive rights movement from the start; yet white women's choice of theoretical language continues to shape public discourse. Reproductive rights discussions have been solidly framed in the language of choice, or what Dorothy Roberts refers to as "the dominant meaning of reproductive liberty."[42] A rhetoric of preferences is damaging when it obscures the legitimate needs and concerns of mothers who are essentially choiceless because they lack access to basic health services that privileged women take for granted. For example, abortion and contraception have been theorized widely as negative liberties (i.e. freedom from motherhood), and ARTs have been occasionally theorized as positive liberties (i.e. the freedom to be a mother). The liberty/choice-based framework reflects the class and race privileges of women with access to healthcare. Women of color continue to confront white supremacist definitions of maternity, which portrays them as reproductively irresponsible, unfit mothers, or welfare queens. So, the freedom to be a mother in these communities may be defined as freedom from sterilization and aggressive promotion of long-term contraception by health clinics in their communities, rather than access to ARTs and surrogacy services. This is why women of color's grassroots health organizations—such as Chicago's SisterSong and Asian Committees for Reproductive Justice—have shifted public conversations from a discourse on reproductive *rights* to one of reproductive *justice*. A justice-based framework not only recognizes the historical impact of poor healthcare and eugenic policies on communities of color, but also asks us to focus more broadly on the freedom to have children and to maintain families in the face of white supremacist population control policies. In addition, it directs activists and scholars to examine global trends in reproductive justice including the export of dangerous contraceptives to women in developing countries, forced contraception in maquiladoras, and more recently the globalization of surrogacy services. A justice-based framework makes room for the discussion of harms in a way that the choice/liberty-based framework does not. As members of the Asian Communities for Reproductive Justice explain:

> The existing discourse and focus of the reproductive health and rights agenda rarely includes an analysis of the effect of intersecting forms of oppression. When racial analysis has been inserted into mainstream discourse, it has often used a Black and White framework, without integrating the racial oppression experienced by Asian and Pacific Islander (API), Latina, Indigenous, or Arab American and Middle Eastern women. The focus on and orientation towards individual rights and individual responsibility, as they relate to articulation of reproductive health and women's choice, reinforce broader systems of political, economic, and cultural hegemony that privilege and maintain racial stratification in the United States, primarily through White supremacy.[43]

Unlike reproductive choice/rights-based frameworks, which point to individual rights solutions, the justice framework points to structural changes, and so begins by looking at reproductive justice intersectionally. Now, it may be the case that we need both a reproductive rights and a reproductive justice model. I'm open to the possibility that one might function more efficiently in some contexts (e.g. United Nations) better than in others (e.g. community health centers). However, avoiding white solipsism in feminist bioethics requires appealing to more than just the choice/liberty framework when considering these questions. White feminists must carefully examine the ways in which our topic choices, conceptual frameworks, and theoretical language reflect white supremacy.

Developing Interdisciplinary and Pluralist Accounts of White Supremacy

Feminist coalitions must also work collaboratively toward an interdisciplinary account of white supremacy. This requires pairing our talents with sociologists, activists, historians, and critical theory scholars to make visible the ways gender, heterosexuality, class, ability, and colonialism have shaped white supremacy.[44] About a decade ago Kim Hall observed "when white feminists remain silent while men of color and white men discuss race in ways that ignore gender and feminist insights, they are complicit in the erasure of women of color."[45] A few male philosophers of color have done very important and interesting work to expose the conceptual whiteness of academic philosophy. They have made white supremacy a legitimate topic of philosophical inquiry.[46] Intersections are acknowledged, but race and not plurality is at the heart of this approach. Following Francis Lee Ashley's general definition, for example, Charles Mills conceptualizes white supremacy as an interconnecting web of political, economic, legal, epistemological, ontological, social and cultural systems in which "whites overwhelmingly control power and material resources, conscious and unconscious ideas of white superiority and entitlement are widespread, and relations of white dominance and non-white subordination are daily reenacted across a broad array of institutions and social settings."[47] Mills *compares* white supremacy to patriarchy and capitalism and encourages philosophers to engage the systemic dimensions of racism with equal vigor, but he never addresses these intersectionally: that is, he never explores how white supremacy is maintained through the regulation of all women's domestic and reproductive labor and sexuality.[48] He rightly describes white supremacy as a multi-dimensional system of domination, but the dimensions shaping and sustaining white supremacy are characterized in economic, cultural, cognitive-evaluative, somatic, and metaphysical terms, but neglects to explore the role of sexuality, reproductive labor, and gender formation. His analysis foregrounds race by approaching white supremacy as an "overarching theoretical concept" that "enables us to pull together [these] different phenomenon" and to acknowledge that they are "interacting with one another in reality, jointly contributing to the reproductive dynamic that helps to perpetuate the system."[49] Mills's analysis proceeds as if gender and sexuality are categorically separate from race and that they can be temporarily bracketed, and brought into the discussion later once we understand how racial formation drives the historical production of white supremacy.[50] These approaches fall back into the problematic pop-bead metaphysics Elizabeth Spelman has warned us against.[51]

Thinking pluralistically about white supremacy requires paying strong attention to the roles gender, heterosexuality, ability, and colonialism play in maintaining white domination. Decolonial feminist scholarship in philosophy offers us one resource for beginning this conversation. In her recent article, "Heterosexualism and the Colonial/Modern Gender System" (2007) María Lugones draws on the work of postcolonial and decolonial theorists and historians to articulate a framework for understanding heterosexism as a crucial part of how gender fuses with race in the creation and maintenance of colonial power. The story she tells is much broader than Mill's account because it explains how white supremacy is held in place by more than just white domination (2007). Grounding her inquiry in the theoretical observations of Third World and U.S. women of color feminists, she carefully articulates what she calls the "colonial/modern gender system." Her description is simultaneously attentive to the broad macro-level systemic view of colonial projects and the micro-level attention to the impact these systems have on women's daily lives. Like race, she argues that gender (as we understand it in the modern sense) is a colonial introduction that has consistently been used to destroy peoples, cultures, cosmologies, and communities in ways that have allowed Europeans to expand Western "civilization." Colonialism did not simply export a ready-made pre-colonial European two-party gender system onto the peoples of Africa, Asia, Australia, and the Americas. It imposed a brand-new gender system that produced contrasting social arrangements for European males and females and the males and females they colonized. This makes sense: if gender is, in part, one way of organizing labor, and if one of the colonizer's goals is to extract labor, land, knowledge, and natural resources violently from the lands they colonize, then it makes sense that the sex/gender systems that colonizers used to organize labor in Europe would not work in colonial contexts. For instance, a modern sex/gender system that characterizes bourgeois white women as chaste, virtuous and domestic cannot be mapped onto Black women's bodies if colonial goals require an understanding of African women as property to be sexually exploited and forced to do hard manual labor. The result is that not all women have the same gender. Dividing sexual labor and its products into "a dark side" and "a light side" helps Lugones articulate how racialization and gendering are integral to the co-construction of the coloniality of power and the colonial/modern gender system. The "light side" of the colonial/modern gender system is marked by a strict sexual dimorphism which hegemonically constructs white bourgeois womanhood and manhood as paradigms of natural, divinely-sanctioned, human femininity and masculinity respectively: only white bourgeois females count as "women"; only white bourgeois males count as "men." Since white bourgeois women are valued for their ability to reproduce heirs to inherit the social status of the families of men that they marry, it makes sense to define white bourgeois female sexuality in terms of a compulsory heterosexuality, chastity, monogamy, sexual passivity, and moral purity. We need to understand the relational nature of these differences. That is, we need to recognize the ways that Black or Native women's so-called "deviant" sexuality makes white women's pure sexuality possible.[52] Since European, African and Native women are either expected/forced to make different sexual and reproductive contributions to capitalist colonizing projects, the light side of the colonial/modern gender system cannot be extended to colonized peoples. The dark side of the colonial/modern gender system is not marked by a strict sexual dimorphism. Sometimes the colonial gaze genders indigenous peoples as hermaphrodites or intersexed, or more generally as anomalies, monsters, and animals. Colonized females and males excluded from the light side were not just subordinate or inferior human forms; they were animals "in a sense that went further than the identification of white women with nature, infants and small animals. They were female flesh degendered.[53] They were animals in the deep sense of being 'without gender,' sexually marked as female but without the characteristics of femininity."[54] Pluralistic approaches then, clearly illustrate how gender and sexuality are integral to the rise and maintenance of white supremacy.[55] These discussions offer a promising alternative to earlier masculinist accounts that address white supremacy as if it were a phenomenon confined to a genderless public sphere.

Using Philosophical Skills to Clarify, Expand and Challenge Intersectionality

My earlier primer on intersectionality began on a cautionary note that now requires elaboration. From a philosophical perspective the scholarship on intersectionality is as expansive and popular as it is muddy and underdeveloped. Even today there is a great deal of slippage in the literature between the term's various usages and synonyms (i.e. plurality, complexity and multiplicity). The explanatory power of intersectional approaches is compromised immensely by the fact that scholars and policy makers have embraced its original insights with few revisions (and even fewer critiques).[56] There is no extended unified account of an intersectional methodology in the foundational literature. Neither Kimberlé Crenshaw (1991) nor Patricia Hill Collins (1990), two of the most respected practitioners of this approach, give readers more than a few sentences on what it means to work intersectionally. Both rely exclusively on examples to illustrate the virtues and necessity of approaching situations intersectionally rather than categorically. This is one case where the forefather's toolbox might come in handy. The philosopher in me is eager to clarify, expand and tidy up intersectionality's sketchy claims. This is what philosophers are supposed to do! For example, intersectional strategies seem to rely on the following premises[57]:

1. Categories (i.e. race, gender) and systems (i.e. patriarchy, colonialism) are neither separate nor competing frameworks.

2. The effects of categories and systems are multiplicative and cannot be derived additively or independently from the effects of these individual systems or categories. They cannot be cleanly separated. Race and gender should be conceptualized not as "race+gender," instead they should be discussed as "gendered racism" or how "gender is racialized." It makes sense to talk about capitalist patriarchies rather that capitalism and patriarchy. [58]

3. Categories and systems cannot be ranked in terms of importance or influence. For example, we should not think in terms of race having a greater influence than gender or sexuality on Latina's lives because these influences are inseparable, imbricated, and mutually coexist.

4. Categories and systems are neither reducible to nor interchangeable with one another. That is, we cannot simply reduce questions of racism or white privilege to matters of class.

5. All social frameworks and categories permeate, influence, align, and intermingle in all social relations (e.g. reproductive rights, cancer research, family structure, job discrimination).

I realize that my impulse to tidy up this approach might be problematic in some cases. Susan Bordo summarizes my ambivalence:

> [The Cartesian model], although under attack, is still largely with analytic philosophy today, and it still revolves around the image of *purity*. Locke spoke of philosophy as removing the "rubblish lying in the way of knowledge." Three centuries later, Quine wrote that the task of the philosopher was "clearing the ontological slums." The image of the philosopher as tidying the mess left by others is more subtly presented by Arthur Danto, who views the philosopher as "executing the tasks of conceptual housekeeping [the sciences and other disciplines] are too robustly busy to tend to themselves."[59]

Suggesting that feminists philosophers are best situated to rescue women of color's theoretical projects from muddiness smacks of paternalism. After all, one woman's clarification may be another woman's distortion. At the same time it's important to realize that there is a distinction between members of dominant groups entering into a different epistemic framework and motivating inquiry from that location in coalition with members of marginalized groups, as opposed to just borrowing useful methodologies generated from these locations and either making them intelligible in our own terms or in support of our own issues. White feminist philosophers must be mindful of this difference. Meaning making is always collective. And, in this spirit feminist philosophers might work with other scholars towards a more robust account of intersectionality while, at the same time, being aware that our urge to tidy can have both helpful and distorting effects.

Beginning inquiry in plurality reveals the complexity of women's experiences and works as a check on white solipsism, but we need to be open to the possibility that the methodology might not work in all locations and contexts. That is, intersectionality may only work to make some women of color's concerns visible on particular topics such as reproductive justice, the global economy, or sexual violence. Keeping this possibility in mind we might turn our attention to several projects.

First, we must recognize that intersectionality's explanatory scope is limited and that not all feminists of color treat it as a methodological panacea. As Andrea Smith reminds us, Crenshaw's crossroads metaphor has an additive ring: it sounds as if we can account for complexity by just running more roads through a designated intersection. If this is true, then the model is not flexible enough to address all women's experiences. That is, there may be cases where intersectionality makes visible one group's experiences with violence, while distorting or erasing another's. Crenshaw's structural account of sexual violence frames the discussion wrongly because it suggests that sexual and domestic violence are directed exclusively at women and not entire cultures. Running a "colonialism road" through the intersection will not correct this oversight. According to Smith, "If sexual violence is not simply a tool of patriarchy but also a tool of colonialism and racism, then entire communities of color are the victims of sexual violence" and entire Native cultures and their land become rapeable.[60] Crenshaw fails to see how, for Native peoples, sexual violence is not just a tool of patriarchy or white supremacy, but also a tool of genocide. So, we might have to come to terms with the limits of intersectionality, or consider whether other pluralist approaches offer us a more robust account of multiplicity.

Next, addressing the strengths and weaknesses of intersectionality also requires paying attention to its deeper metaphysical and epistemological claims. For example, over the past two years a few feminists in the social sciences have begun to challenge intersectionality's conceptual strength as a research paradigm arguing that a great deal of work remains to be done on exactly how to conceptualize and analyze the interactions between oppressive structures.[61] A few scholars have complicated foundational approaches by arguing that different intersectional constellations (additive, multiplicative and intersectional relations) make sense at different historical moments.[62]

Embrace Intellectual Traditions that Challenge and Enrich the Feminist Philosophical Canon

Finally, I would like to see feminists philosophers reach into other toolboxes—not for the purposes of colonizing what we find useful, but in order to begin our conversations anew from different locations. I worry that our reluctance to do so may be partially driven by a belief that non-European cultures and subjects produce inferior knowledges. If so, then countering white ignorance requires us to make a stronger effort to engage the philosophical dimensions of those texts, movements, and voices that simultaneously enrich and challenge our own. There is metaphysics being done in Audre Lorde's poetry. There are imaginative pluralist constructions of the self in Gloria Anzaldúa's narratives. We have much to learn from the moral psychology of Toni Morrison's characters. There are wonderfully resistant epistemologies in the works of Ralph Ellison and Fredrick Douglass.[63] Oyèrónké Oyewùmí's scholarship on Yorùbá ways of knowing challenges the dominance of visual metaphors characterizing western epistemology. Andrea Smith's observations about sexual violence and the U.S. government's orchestrated genocide of native peoples challenges traditional white feminist thinking about rape solely as a tool of patriarchy.

If feminist engagement with the work of the white forefathers remains a strong indicator of what it means to do philosophy, then Anglo-Eurocentric paradigms will continue to flourish and it will be difficult for people of color's insights, challenges and concerns to be taken seriously in the discipline. When people of color's voices and experiences are relegated to endnotes, not recognized as sites of discursive complexity, or dismissed as "not philosophy" (or, as mere politics) then the whiteness of the canon will continue to drive most feminist scholarship.[64] When white feminist philosophers fail to ground our work in plurality we risk having our resistance strategies reinforce the subordination and exclusion of people of color. To avoid this, feminist interdisciplinary coalitions need to de-center both white men's and white women's speech. This is a task requiring that we answer Anzaldúa's charge and bother "to learn other languages, which don't necessarily reflect our own culture and spirit."

Notes

1. This chapter has been deeply informed by conversations with Ann Garry, Sally Haslanger, Sarah Hoagland, María Lugones, Mariana Ortega, Gaile Polhaus, and Alexis Shotwell. I also received helpful feedback from discussions at *Breaking Boundaries: Forging Connections: Feminist Interdisciplinary Theory and Practice* conference at Mount St. Vincent University, Halifax, Nova Scotia, and at the *Building Coalitions Across Difference* conference at the University of Dayton.
2. Gloria E. Anzaldúa, "Speaking in Tongues: A Letter to Third World Women Writers," in *This Bridge Called My Back: Writings by Radical Women of Color*, ed. Gloria E. Anzaldúa and Cherrie Moraga. Second Edition (Berkeley, CA: Third Woman Press, 2002), 183.
3. María Lugones, *Pilgrimages/Peregrinajes: Theorizing Coalition against Multiple Oppressions* (Lanham: Roman and Littlefield, 2003), 74.
4. "We" and "our" are notoriously problematic. Although my remarks are directed primarily at white feminist philosophers, I also recognize that scholars of color, non-academic communities, and our allies are an integral part of this conversation. I also know that some white feminist philosopher's work defies my characterizations. So, I'll do my best to make it clear when I'm talking about white feminist philosophers, philosophers in general, and feminists in general, scholars of color who are not philosophers, non-academic communities of color, etc. I realize the instability of these categories can never be accurately captured by these collective nouns, and I really don't want them to be.
5. Naomi Zack, *Inclusive Feminism: A Third Wave Theory of Women's Commonality* (Lanham, MD: Rowman & Littlefield, 2005), 67.
6. Sandra Harding, *Whose Science? Whose Knowledge?: Thinking from Women's Lives* (Ithaca, NY: Cornell University Press, 1991), 191.
7. See Charles W. Mills, *Blackness Visible: Essays on Philosophy and Race* (Ithaca: Cornell University Press, 1998); Anna Stubblefield, "Meditations on Post Supremacist Philosophy" in *White on White, Black on Black*, ed. George Yancy (Lanham, MD: Rowman & Littlefield, 2005); and, George Yancy's Introduction in his *What White Looks Like: African American Philosophers on the Whiteness Question* (New York: Routledge, 2004).
8. See Mills, *Blackness Visible*; bell hooks, *Teaching to Transgress: Education as the Practice of Freedom* (New York: Routledge, 1994), 63; Uma Narayan, *Dis/locating Cultures/Identities, Traditions and Third Wave Feminism* (New York: Routledge, 1997); and, María Lugones "Heterosexualism and the Colonial/Modern Gender System," *Hypatia* 22, no. 1 (2007):186–209.
9. Mariana Ortega. "Being Lovingly, Knowingly Ignorant: White Feminism and Women of Color," *Hypatia*. 21, no. 3 (2006): 56–74.
10. This claim puts me on shaky ground. I'm not saying that our disciplinary toolbox is irreparably tainted and that we should abandon it. We need to recognize that philosophical tools have power and that many women of color in philosophy have found these tools immensely helpful. To suggest abandoning the patriarch's toolbox at the historical moment when women of color's interests in academic philosophy are increasing sounds suspicious to me.
11. Sarah Hoagland pointed this out to me. In conversation.

12. Feminist philosophers have not ignored this topic completely. Intersectional themes have been lurking in the background of feminist scholarship in philosophy of science, epistemology, and political theory. Harding's *Whose Science, Whose Knowledge* and Iris Marion Young's *Justice and the Politics of Difference* (Princeton, NJ: Princeton University Press, 1990) have strong intersectional dimensions. For more recent developments see Ann Garry "Essences, Intersections, and North American Feminist Philosophy" in the *Oxford Handbook of American Philosophy*, ed. Cheryl Misak (New York: Oxford University Press, 2008); Sarah Hoagland, "Heterosexualism and White Supremacy," *Hypatia* 22, no. 1 (2007): 166–185; Lugones, *Pilgrimages/ Peregrinajes* and her "Heterosexualism and the Colonial/Modern Gender System." At the time this chapter was written *The Philosopher's Index* listed only two articles addressing intersectionality.
13. This quotation is from a paper Crenshaw gave at the World Conference against Racism in 2001. The paper is no longer available online, but it is cited in Nira Yuval-Davism "Intersectionality and Feminist Politics," *European Journal of Women's Studies* 13, no.2 (2006): 196.
14. Ange-Marie Hancock, "When Multiplication Doesn't Equal Quick Addition: Examining Intersectionality as a Research Paradigm," *Perspectives on Politics* 5, no. 1 (March 2007): 63–64.
15. Charlotte Bunch, "Why the World Conference against Racism is Critical to Women's Human Rights Advocacy," Center for Women's Global Leadership, Rutgers, 2001. Available: http://www.cwgl.rutgers.edu/globalcenter/policy/csw01/csw01priority.html (Accessed: 16 February, 2008).
16. Kimberlé Crenshaw, "Mapping the Margins: Intersectionality, Identity Politics, and Violence against Women of Color," *Stanford Law Review* 43, no. 6 (1991): 1241–1299.
17. Most feminist philosophers will be reminded of socialist feminism's attempts during the 1980s to fashion a unified systems theory synthesizing Marxism's insights on class oppression with radical feminist's insights on gender oppression to develop a "capitalist patriarchy" or a "feminist historical materialism." See Alison Jaggar, *Feminist Politics and Human Nature* (Totowa, NJ: Rowman & Littlefield, 1983) and Iris Young, *Justice and the Politics of Difference*. Current discussions of structural intersectionality might be understood as an attempt to make good on the promise of a unified systems theory.
18. Patricia Hill Collins, *Black Feminist Thought: Knowledge, Consciousness, and the Politics of Empowerment* (Boston: Unwin Hyman, 1990), 222.
19. Crenshaw, "Mapping the Margins," 367.
20. Crenshaw, "Mapping the Margins," 360.
21. See Devon Abbot Mihesuah "Feminist, Tribalist, Activists?" in her *Indigenous American Women: Decolonization, Empowerment, Activism* (Lincoln: University of Nebraska Press, 2003): 166 and 168.
22. Crenshaw, "Mapping the Margins," 375.
23. Gloria Anzaldúa and Cherríe Moraga, "Entering the Lives of Others: Theory in the Flesh," in *This Bridge Called My Back: Writings by Radical Women of Color*, ed. Gloria E. Anzaldúa and Cherrie Moraga. Second Edition (Berkeley, CA: Third Woman Press, 2002), 21.
24. Gloria E. Anzaldúa, *Borderlands/la Frontera: The New Mestiza* (San Francisco: Spinsters/Aunt Lute Press, 1987), 20.
25. Evelyn Alsultany, "Los Intersticios: Recasting Moving Selves," in *This Bridge We Call Home: Radical Visions of Transformation*, eds. Gloria E. Anzaldúa and Analouise Keating (New York: Routledge, 2002), 107.

26. Naomi Zack, *Inclusive Feminism: A Third Wave Theory of Women's Commonality* (Lanham, MD: Rowman & Littlefield, 2005), 200.
27. See Stubblefield, "Meditations on Post Supremacist Philosophy."
28. For a complete account of arrogant perception see Marilyn Frye's "In and Out of Harm's Way," in her *The Politics of Reality* (Freedom, California: The Crossing Press).
29. Lugones, *Pilgrimages/ Peregrinajes*, 71–2.
30. Anzaldúa, "Speaking in Tongues," 192.
31. I'm not suggesting that feminist philosophy is completely insular: I know of many colleagues that move very comfortably between community and academic spaces.
32. On this point see Stubblefield, "Meditations on Post Supremacist Philosophy"; and, Shannon Sullivan. *Revealing Whiteness: The Unconscious Habits of White Privilege* (Bloomington, IN: Indiana University Press, 2006), 10.
33. Lugones, *Pilgrimages/Peregrinajes*, 73.
34. Ortega, "Being Lovingly, Knowingly Ignorant," 71.
35. Marilyn Frye wrote her essay "Oppression," (in *The Politics of Reality: Essays in Feminist Theory* [Trumansburg, NY: The Crossing Press, 1983], 1–16) in response to this phenomenon. In conversation.
36. Close examination of one's own privilege is not necessarily an unproductive starting point for addressing white supremacy. Working towards privilege-cognizance is a critical early step in anti-racist work. It requires white folks to momentarily and conceptually separate white privilege from other forms of oppression, so that we can focus on race privilege and not slide back into the more comfortable and familiar conversations on (hetero)sexism and classism.
37. There are promising signs of a demographic shift in philosophy. See Robin Wilson, "Black Women Seek a Role in Philosophy," *The Chronicle of Higher Education* (28 September 2007). Available: http://chronicle.com/article/Black-Women-Seek-a-Role-in/24971 (accessed August 27, 2009)
38. See Patricia Williams, *The Alchemy of Race and Rights: Diary of a Law Professor* (Cambridge, MA: Harvard University Press, 1991), 8–9.
39. See Sarah Hoagland's "Colonial Practices/Colonial Identities: Racial Formation and Epistemic Discipline in Feminist Discourse" in this volume.
40. For an overview of basic issues surrounding reproductive injustices to women of color see Dorothy Roberts, *Killing the Black Body: Race, Reproduction and the Meaning of Liberty* (New York: Vintage, 1998); Jennifer Nelson, *Women of Color and the Reproductive Rights Movement* (New York: New York University Press, 2003); Ricki Solinger, *Beggars and Choosers: How the Politics of Choice Shapes Adoption, Abortion, and Welfare in the United States* (New York: Hill and Wang, 2003); and Andrea Smith, *Conquest: Sexual Violence and American Indian Genocide* (Boston: South End Press, 2005). For an account of quinacrine sterilization see Tycie Young, "Quinacrine: Sterilizing the Poor," *Off Our Backs* 29, no. 9 (October 1999). Available: http://findarticles.com/p/articles/mi_qa3693/is_199910/ai_n8868843/?tag=content;col1 (Accessed: August 27, 2009)
41. For a brief overview of Indian surrogacy see Amelia Gentleman, "Foreign Couples turn to India for Surrogate Mothers," *International Herald Tribune* (4 March, 2008). Available: http://www.iht.com/articles/2008/03/04/asia/mother.php (Accessed: 30 March, 2008).
42. Roberts' term is used throughout *Killing the Black Body*.

43. Asian Communities for Reproductive Justice. A New Vision for Advancing our Movement for Reproductive Health, Reproductive Rights, and Reproductive Justice (2005): 2 Available: http://www.reproductivejustice.org/download/ACRJ_A_New_Vision.pdf (Accessed: 10 February, 2008).

44. Some feminist philosophers have begun to theorize white supremacy pluralistically. For example, Lugones, "Heterosexualism and the Colonial/Modern Gender System," and Hoagland, "Heterosexualism and White Supremacy," have argued for the strong connections between white supremacy and heterosexuality. Stubblefield's "Beyond the Pale: Tainted Whiteness, Cognitive Disability, and Eugenic Sterilization" (*Hypatia* 22, no. 2 [2007]: 162–181) makes connections between white supremacy and cognitive ability.

45. Kim Hall, "White Feminists Doing Critical Race Theory: Some Ethical and Political Considerations," *APA Newsletter on Philosophy, Law and the Black Experience* 98:2 (Spring 1999). Available: http://www.apa.udel.edu/apa/archive/newsletters/v98n2/lawblack/hall.asp (Accessed: 16 February, 2008).

46. See Charles Mills, *The Racial Contract* (Ithaca, NY: Cornell University Press, 1997); *Blackness Visible*; and "White Supremacy," in *A Companion to African-American Philosophy*, eds. Tommy L. Lott and John Pittman. Cambridge: Blackwell, 2003. See also George Yancy, ed. *What White Looks Like: African-American Philosophers on the Whiteness Question* (New York: Routledge, 2004); and his *Black Bodies, White Gazes: The Continuing Significance of Race* (Lanham, MD: Rowman & Littlefield, 2009), especially chapter two.

47. Mills, "White Supremacy," 269.

48. Mills, "White Supremacy," 271.

49. Mills, "White Supremacy," 48.

50. I don't mean to single out Mills for criticism. He and Carol Pateman do move conversations on patriarchy and white supremacy in decidedly intersectional directions in their new book *Contract and Domination* (Malden, MA: Polity Press, 2007). This earlier definition simply provides the clearest example of a trend that I believe is still prevalent. Many historical approaches ignore or bracket the role gender plays in the construction of white supremacy. For example, Theodore Allen's, *The Invention of the White Race* (London: Verso, 1994) and David Roediger's *The Wages of Whiteness* (London: Verso, 1991) both address the construction of whiteness through the lens of class, but focus almost exclusively on white male workers. George Lipsitz's *The Possessive Investment in Whiteness: How White People Profit from Identity Politics* (Philadelphia: Temple University Press, 2006) focuses on how white privilege shapes the public sphere (e.g. law, real estate, war, inheritance, and politics). These accounts are masculinist approaches because they rely almost exclusively on examples of public sphere activities to illustrate the magnitude of white supremacy.

51. Elizabeth Spelman, *The Inessential Woman: Problems of Exclusion in Feminist Thought* (Boston: Beacon, 1988), 15.

52. On this point see, Collins *Black Feminist Thought* (1990); Evelyn Hammond, "Toward a Genealogy of Black Female Sexuality," in *Feminist Theory and the Body: A Reader*, ed. Janet Price and Margaret Shidrick (New York: Routledge, 1997); Hoagland, "Heterosexualism and White Supremacy," and Chandra Talpade Mohanty, *Feminism without Borders; Decolonizing Theory, Practicing Solidarity* (Durham, NC: Duke University Press, 2003).

53. Hortense J. Spillers, "Mama's Baby, Papa's Maybe: An American Grammar Book," *Diacritics* 17, no. 2 (1987): 68.

54. Lugones, "Heterosexualism and the Colonial/Modern Gender System," 202–203.

55. Philosophers will find Andrea Smith particularly helpful on this point. See, "Heteropatriarchy and the Three Pillars of White Supremacy: Rethinking Women of Color Organizing," in *The Color of Violence: The Incite! Anthology*, ed. Incite! Women of Color against Violence (Cambridge, MA: South End Press, 2006).

56. Scholars in the social sciences have only recently moved critically beyond intersectionality's largely unargued premises to clarify the problematic and productive features of its many usages. See for example: Hancock, "When Multiplication Doesn't Equal Quick Addition"; Leslie McCall, "The Complexity of Intersectionality," *Signs: Journal of Women in Culture and Society* 30, no.3 (2005): 1771–1800, and Yural-Davis, "Intersectionality and Feminist Politics," *European Journal of Women's Studies* 13, no. 3 (2006): 193–209.

57. These premises support only what I call *foundational* accounts of intersectionality. I focus on these accounts because I want to bracket the complex metaphysical questions about how and when categories influence one another and how we make theoretical sense of this.

58. For example Philomena Essid refers to the intersections of "genderism" and "racism" as "gendered racism." See "Towards a Methodology to Identify Converging Forms of Everyday Discrimination." Available: http://www.un.org/womenwatch/daw/csw/essed45 (Accessed: 15 January, 2008).

59. Susan Bordo, *The Flight to Objectivity: Essays on Cartesianism and Culture* (Albany, NY: SUNY Press, 1987), 76.

60. Smith, *Conquest*, 8.

61. I have in mind here S. Laurel Weldon, "The Structure of Intersectionality: A Comparative Politics of Gender," *Politics and Gender* 2, no. 2 (2006): 235–248; and, Hancock, "When Multiplication Doesn't Equal Quick Addition."

62. What Weldon calls the *intersectionality-plus* approach, for instance, demonstrates that the effects of intersectionality need not be always multiplicative. There are times when intersections may also be thought of as additive. See her "The Structure of Intersectionality."

63. See in particular the two edited collections by Shannon Sullivan and Nancy Tuana: *Race and the Epistemologies of Ignorance* (Albany: State University of New York Press, 2007); and, their special issue on feminist epistemologies of ignorance: *Hypatia* 21, no. 2 (Summer 2006).

64. On the issue of women of color's work being dismissed as not philosophy see Andrea Nye's review essay "It's Not Philosophy," *Hypatia* 13, no. 2 (Spring 1998): 107–115.

4

The Man of Culture: The Civilized and the Barbarian in Western Philosophy

Lisa Heldke, Gustavus Adolphus College

> A blind man can form no notion of colors; a deaf man of sounds. Restore either of them that sense in which he is deficient; by opening this new inlet for his sensations, you also open an inlet for the ideas; and he finds no difficulty in conceiving these objects. The case is the same, if the object, proper for exciting any sensation, has never been applied to the organ. A Laplander or Negro has no notion of the relish of wine.
> —Hume, *An Enquiry Concerning Human Understanding*

> Sirs: You have the bad taste to say that soul food is tasteless. Your taste buds are so racist that they can't even deal with black food. Your comment that the "soul food fad" is going to be short-lived is dumb. But then your whole culture is made of short-lived fads. So you white folks just keep on eating that white foam rubber bread that sticks to the roof of your mouth, and keep on eating Minute Rice and instant potatoes, instant cereals and drinking instant milk and stick to your instant culture. And I will stick to the short-lived fad that brought my ancestors through four hundred years of oppression.
> —Vertamae Smart-Grosvenor, *Vibration Cooking*

The Man of Reason has a sidekick. Less well known than the MOR himself, the Man of Culture (as I'll call him) nevertheless plays a vital role in creating and advancing the projects of western philosophy. *He* it is who has the power to arbitrate matters of taste; his interests and pleasures define what it is to be a fully-enculturated human. Wine: yes; soul food: no.

Given the power and influence he exerts, I believe it is high time that we plumb the depths of the Man of Culture, study his nature, take his measure. In short, it is time we expose his identity. Once we do so, we will substantiate what we've known all along; that the Man of Culture is a white guy—an educated European white guy, to be exact. The world he valorizes (using the full array of western philosophical tools) is a European world of high Culture (singular), set apart by race and education ("breeding") from the grimy, inferior, and hopelessly *multiple* culture*s* (plural) that cover the rest of the globe. The standards he establishes for capital-t Taste may look universal, but they are, in fact, the preferences of people like himself, recast in a language that gives them both the aura of universality and a prescriptiveness that leaves no doubt about the superiority of those preferences.

I had suspected for some time that the Man of Reason was not acting alone—that, in fact, he possessed a confederate in the Man of Culture. Furthermore, I had a hunch that the MOC played a particularly powerful role in maintaining the white Eurocentrism—what I'll call the "Eurowhiteliness"—of philosophy. Reexamining David Hume's analysis of taste, as he develops it in "Of the Standard of Taste," and "Of the Delicacy of Taste and Passion," has confirmed my suspicions, convincing me of both the existence of the MOC and the magnitude of his role in keeping western philosophy Eurowhitely. His imprint on the projects of western philosophy, while perhaps not so all-pervasive as that of the Man of Reason, is nonetheless profound and significant.[1]

The MOC differs from the MOR in at least one crucial respect: while the Man of Reason has, in advertising his virtues, frequently tended to emphasize the *innateness* of his rational faculty (and then to sort humans according to the amount of this faculty each demographic group receives), the Man of Culture has generally made no bones about the fact that his special endowment is a matter *of* enculturation. He is a "cultured man" (like yogurt); one whose identity is deeply, inescapably a function *of* his having been cultured in a very particular kind of environment. As such, the Man of Culture is not only a man's man; he is also a *white* man's man, a man of "proper breeding."

The philosopher—who is not only a Man of Reason but also a Man of Culture—must also be (*or DBA, do business as*) a white man of privilege. If we would decenter whiteness in philosophy, we would thus do well to try to understand the Man of Culture. This chapter contributes to such an understanding. I draw inspiration for the effort from Genevieve Lloyd's essay, "The Man of Reason," as well as a book by the same name. In her essay, Lloyd specifically focuses on the concept of reason in the seventeenth century, and then considers the ramifications of that historical concept for the role of reason in our own era.[2] My effort follows a similar method, but focuses on just one figure—Hume—to show how his eighteenth-century notion of Taste also reveals something about the function of that capacity in our time.

One obvious way in which my project differs from Lloyd's is that, whereas she seeks to uncover the *maleness* of reason in western philosophy, my target is the whiteness (and also, not unrelatedly, the class-privilegedness) of culture. Where her paper's subtitle reads "'Male' and 'Female' in Western Philosophy," mine could read "'White' and 'Nonwhite' in Western Philosophy."

While Lloyd functions as the structural model for this chapter, the work of Monique Roelofs serves as its primary conceptual inspiration. Roelofs, in her essay "Racialization as an Aesthetic Production: What Does the Aesthetic Do for Whiteness and Blackness and Vice Versa," examines Hume's concept of Taste in great detail, revealing the ways in which that concept contributes to two projects: "racialized aestheticization," the term she coins to refer to "taste's racialized structure" or "the racial exclusiveness of taste";[3] and "aestheticized racialization," which refers to "civilization as structured and produced by way of taste."[4] Roelof writes, of Hume, that he "aestheticizes whiteness in the sense that he construes white civilization, in part, as an aesthetic achievement, a project to be attained through the operation of taste."[5] The present chapter revisits Roelofs' claim—a claim that, for her, is only part of a much larger project.

To begin this project of taking the measure of the Man of Culture, it will be useful to return, briefly, to Lloyd's Man of Reason, both to revisit her method of analysis and to remember just what's so manly about the Man of Reason. With his manliness before us as a model, the Eurowhiteness of the Man of Culture will spring into focus more readily.

Lloyd's Man of Reason

Thanks to Genevieve Lloyd, the MOR has been revealed as a "real man"—a deeply gendered being whose masculinist proclivities have shaped, molded and carved the contours of western philosophy. This has happened despite the MOR's periodic protestations that he is "just another rational agent, ma'am"— that "man" really means "human," and therefore (sometimes) includes women. Descartes, for instance, believed women were capable of exercising reason in the pursuit of certainty. As Lloyd notes, "In a letter written shortly after the publication of the *Discourse on Method,* [Descartes] commented that his thoughts on method seemed to him appropriate to put in a book where he wished that 'even women' might understand something." She offers several other passages as evidence of his "egalitarian intentions" toward women.[6] Such avowals of gender neutrality notwithstanding, "When the Man of Reason is extolled, philosophers are not talking about idealizations of human beings. They are talking about idealizations of manhood."[7] If women are indeed counted as less-hairy Reasoners, they are included only on terms established by a male paradigm.

Lloyd's profile of the Man of Reason identifies his chief character traits at various points in history, thereby enabling us to trace the influence of those traits on the historical projects of western epistemology, ethics and metaphysics. If we zero in on traits prevalent in the seventeenth century, we find Men of Reason who are able to formulate clear and distinct ideas, identify the "isomorphism between reason and reality," sharply distinguish their minds from their bodies, and sequester all non-rational faculties such as emotion and sensation.

There may not seem to be anything necessarily masculine about this characterization of reason and, as I've already noted, Descartes was more than willing to acknowledge the possibility that women could participate in the work of "making certain"—the work of reason. Nevertheless, Lloyd notes that this was the time at which the gendered nature of reason (gender being a feature of reason at least since the time of Aristotle) was given a powerful new undergirding, precisely in the form of that sharp distinction between mind and matter, and a correspondingly sharp distinction between reason and emotion. Ironically, despite Descartes's egalitarian impulses, his philosophy in fact shores up the maleness of reason, and does so in an entirely new way. Lloyd notes that "the claim that women are somehow lacking in rationality, that they are more impulsive, more emotional than men"[8] sets up a contrast that is no longer a contrast *within* reason. Now, the distinction is between a part of reason, and something altogether outside the rational.

The rub comes in the fact that learning to be rational—to restrain the emotional parts of oneself—requires training, training from which women are excluded. This means that women can be left behind in a pre-rational state, or, as Lloyd puts it, "this *makes* it true, in a way it need not have been before, that women are less rational than men."[9] After Descartes, women are quite literally *rendered less rational,* by virtue of their unequal educational opportunities. (Imagine that: if you don't educate women the way you educate men, they won't be educated enough to do the work men do. Thus they'll be less rationally capable. Q.E.D.)

To anticipate, for a moment, the case of culture, consider: Just as education ends up making it the case that men are more rational than women (given a certain definition of reason), so too does enculturation make it the case that members of nonwhite cultures are *less cultured* than Eurowhites. If you define Culture as that which Eurowhites possess, and then prohibit or otherwise limit nonwhites' access to said Culture (as was done, e.g, through any number of mechanisms of imperialist colonialism), then it should come as no surprise that "Negroes" make lousy wine tasters.

To illustrate the development of reason as a specifically *moral* tool (relevant for the present discussion, since Hume will cast the development of Taste as a moral enterprise as well), Lloyd turns to Spinoza. His Man of Reason must transform untamed passions into guided and guiding emotions through the mechanism of his reason; passions are passive, unclear and confused, while emotions are active, clear and rational. Emotions come to have moral weight because, in the process of cultivating his emotions, the MOR comes to understand the necessary causal chains that link all events together. With this understanding comes an increased detachment from particular objects of hate, love, etc., and also an increased capacity to treat all beings with calm equanimity—to act, instead of *re*acting. "The full picture is of a man detached from changeable objects of passion to the point where temporal transience, including the fact of death, is of no consequence."[10]

Lloyd points out that Spinoza's ideal is a masculine one; the "ultimate horror" for him is to be "'womanish,' which is associated with being under the sway of passions, untransformed by reason."[11] While Lloyd notes that there is much to be valued in Spinoza's account of reason—its capacity to transcend selfish, obsessive love, for instance—she nevertheless balks at a conception of reason that, in its effort to liberate us from the passions, throws out both "individuals as proper objects of love," and "'womanish' pity."[12]

Lloyd notes that seventeenth century rationalists like Descartes were already aware of some of the limits of their efforts to constrain reason within a fixed methodology. "Nonetheless, what has come down to us as our unmistakable inheritance from seventeenth century rationalism is the ideal of method, construed as expressing the true nature of the mind," where mind is understood to have nothing to do with intuition or with other "specifically female thought styles."[13] Whatever his inadequacies, the Man of Reason has thus managed to make his manly way down to the twenty-first century, with many of his faculties still intact. Given this fact, Lloyd calls for "a critique of [the Man of Reason's] standing as an ideal, whether as an object of male self-esteem or [as an object of] female envy."[14] In particular, she urges, we ought to pay attention to the ways in which the inherited ideal impoverishes both women *and* men; the degree to which it is limited "as a *human* ideal."[15]

How about the Man of Culture? What are *his* chief features? How does he function as an "object of self-esteem" for the white Europeans who identify with him; or an object of "envy" for people of color? How does his ideal make its way down to the twenty-first century? Does it—like the ideal of reason—impoverish those whom it privileges as well as those it degrades?

The Man of Culture: Counterpart to the Man of Reason

To uncover the whiteness (and the intellectual-economic privilege) of the Man of Culture is a project different in kind from Lloyd's uncovering of the maleness of the Man of Reason.[16] To claim that reason is gendered male was, when Lloyd first made the claim, to say something that seemed beyond wrong—even a bit kooky. Making that claim convincing (as it has now become) was a task of no small magnitude. In contrast, announcing that the MOC is *really* a privileged Eurowhite man seems to say nothing whatsoever—certainly nothing new. (High) Culture simply and unequivocally *is* European and upper class, and it is nothing more than a commonplace empirical observation to note its wealthy whiteness. To name it seems to say nothing philosophically illuminating—at least nothing illuminating about the whiteness of philosophy.

Culture is simply more transparent about its exclusivity than Reason. (Indeed, part of the allure of high culture is precisely its exclusivity.) While many philosophers, beginning with Plato, *have* in fact insisted that *anyone* can be a Man of Reason, most of those same figures have not questioned the fact that being a Man of Culture requires "culturing," an educational benefit not available to just anyone, and one usually reserved for only the most privileged members of any given society. Furthermore, some societies are simply outside of the reach of Culture altogether. The "Laplander or Negro" of whom Hume writes in the passage quoted at the beginning of this chapter, cannot appreciate the taste of wine precisely because neither has had the opportunity to savor it. Living as they do outside of wine country, they simply will not have the opportunity to be Cultured. Hume is not saying that they *couldn't*, by virtue of anatomy, develop a nose for New Zealand sauvignon blancs—quite the reverse, apparently, given his observation that their inability is entirely dependent upon their lack of access.[17] But in practical fact, they never will become knowledgeable, unless they move to a town with a decent wine store staffed by some sympathetic, knowledgeable and helpful clerks, none of which exists in either cultural milieu.[18]

Culture*s* (in the plural, and in contrast to Culture), are the provinces of people of color and also of the always-"colorful" laboring classes. (Capital-C Culture doesn't include *multi*culturalism in its scope.) To speak of culture*s* is to evoke *National Geographic* images of "the peoples and cultures of Africa/of South America/of the Pacific Islands" doing their "traditional dances" and eating their "traditional foods," while to speak of Culture is to call forth the hush of the art museum, the concert hall, the library—bastions of economic and racial privilege in Europe.[19]

Commonplace though they are, such observations as I am making here do in fact rest upon an important implicit philosophical prescription—a prescription about what can *count* as Culture. To state their importance another way, there is nothing accidental about the fact that the people who happen to *be* Cultured are white, wealthy and educated. On the contrary, to be in a position to be Cultured is to be possessed of certain crucial forms of privilege—racial, class. Furthermore and correlatively, what count as marks of Culture are *just those activities* that the possession of privilege makes possible. Just as Descartes's definition of reason, combined with the educational opportunities available to women at the time, effectively limit women's capacities for reason, so too does Hume's definition of taste, when coupled with the exclusionary nature of European society, effectively render all non-European, non-white persons Culturally deficient.

Western philosophy has worked to preserve the view that Eurowhite culture *equals* Culture, and it has attempted to do so by means of philosophical argument. To unseat this argument will require something more than an empirical solution; "adding people of color and stirring" will not resolve this problem, which is something more and other than a practical one. To challenge this philosophical prescription for culture is to contribute to the project of challenging philosophy's whiteness.

But does the matter of Culture *matter* very much to the project of revealing the whiteness of philosophy? Surely, whatever their philosophical underpinnings, we can address the white presuppositions of cultural institutions and practices without going through the rigmarole of constructing philosophical arguments about their whitely foundations, can't we? This can't be very important, can it?

In response, consider this: Hume suggests, in "Of the Delicacy of Taste and Passion," that, ultimately, the cultivation of one's taste is important not only for enjoying the finer things in life, but also in order that one might make better judgments in other human arenas, *including the arena of morality*. "And this is a new reason for cultivating a relish in the liberal arts. Our judgment will strengthen by this exercise. We shall form juster notions of life."[20] The Man of Culture is also the Moral Man; to understand the whiteness of the MOC is also to understand something about the whiteness of morality—no trivial matter.[21] Just as reason has a distinctively moral caste for Spinoza, so does taste for Hume. Lack of access to the realm of culture means, ultimately, lack of access to the moral sphere. To be disbarred from developing one's taste means one's moral development will likewise be arrested.

Hume's Man of Culture

Hume's Man of Culture emerges as the hero in the battle against the forces of aesthetic relativism. In "Of the Standard of Taste," Hume confronts the specter of relativism in aesthetic judgments, a specter that arises as a consequence of the fact that such judgments make no reference to "real matter of fact."[22] He then sets out to shore up these value judgments by observing, first of all, that *tremendous* agreement prevails among people regarding matters of taste. Contrary to the aesthetic chaos one might anticipate in the absence of "real matters of fact," and contrary to the superficial disagreement one does often find in the world of art, praise and criticism actually tend to cluster around the same paintings, poems and other works of art.

Hume goes on to analyze the basis for this agreement, locating it not in qualities found in the objects themselves, but rather in those who make judgments *about* those objects. The "standard of taste" lodges in the well-considered opinions of those whose "strong sense, united to delicate sentiment, improved by practice, perfected by comparison, and cleared of all prejudice"[23] qualifies them to be recognized as true judges.

Setting aside the obvious and important question of whether Hume's true judges could, in principle, win the battle against aesthetic relativism, I turn to a different sort of question, namely, how does Hume build whiteness into the very fabric of true judges' identity?

Actually, I wish to sharpen that question, by introducing into the discussion the concept of whiteliness, to which I have made passing reference thus far. How does Hume build *whiteliness,* specifically Eurowhiteliness, into the fabric of true judges' identity? The concept of "whiteliness" comes from Marilyn Frye, who distinguishes it from bare physical characteristics (whiteness) and explains it by analogy to masculinity:

> Being white-skinned (like being male) is a matter of physical traits presumed to be physically determined; being whitely (like being masculine) I conceive as a deeply ingrained way of being in the world. Following the analogy with masculinity, I assume that the connection between whiteliness and light-colored skin is a *contingent* connection; this character could be manifested by persons who are *not* "white;" it can be absent in persons who *are*.[24]

Frye is interested in whiteliness as a character trait—particularly a moral character trait—of individuals. I extend it to the realm of culture and taste, in order to describe a deeply ingrained way of determining and ascribing value to aesthetic objects. (As we've already seen, for Hume the aesthetic will also extend itself into the realm of the ethical.)

My claim is this: in the process of establishing the existence of, and qualifications for, true judges, Hume effectively creates a "Eurowhitely" aesthetic; a system for judging the aesthetic value of objects in which the only persons who can qualify as reliable judges of aesthetic questions are those who have had the opportunity to be enculturated as Europeans of a particular class—or enculturated *as if they were* members of that group.[25] To suggest that Hume's true judges are whitely is to say something about their aesthetic "being in the world." (Note that, for this claim to be true, it need not be the case that all true judges are white, or that all aesthetic objects accorded value are produced by people who check the "white, non-Hispanic" box on the census; as Frye notes, the connection between whiteness and whiteliness is contingent.)

There's something obvious, even banal, about my claim. After all, it's not news that western aesthetics privilege, say, the productions of Europeans. What I hope to add to the observation is an analysis of one way in which this privilege is made possible, legitimized, even valorized. Hume's system effectively *guarantees* that the only things deserving of the title of Culture are the productions of white Europeans, or the productions of those ethnic Others who have been properly "anointed" by white Europeans.[26] He knits Eurowhiteliness into the very fabric of his aesthetic system.[27] What happens if we attempt to unravel this whiteliness?

Hume begins "The Standard of Taste" with the observation that "The great variety of Taste, as well as of opinion, which prevails in the world, is too obvious not to have fallen under every one's observation."[28] This variety, he goes on to observe, may lead us to suspect that standards are in fact impossible, and that there really *is* no accounting for taste. To proponents of such a relativist view, our "natural" tendency to look for "a rule by which the various sentiments of men may be reconciled" is doomed to be left unsatisfied;[29] judgment and sentiment differ from each other, such that "all sentiment is right," whereas not "all determinations of the understanding are . . . right," a consequence of the fact that judgments "have a reference to something beyond themselves, to wit, real matter of fact...."[30]

While acknowledging the apparent truth of this distinction, Hume goes on to observe that, in point of fact, we find it ridiculous to suggest that all others' aesthetic judgments have equal merit; after all, when someone says Ogilby is as great a writer as Milton, do we not "pronounce... the sentiment of these pretended critics to be absurd and ridiculous?"[31] There exist, he concludes, "amidst all the variety and caprice of taste... certain general principles of approbation or blame, whose influence a careful eye may trace in all operations of the mind."[32] In short, while real matters of aesthetic fact are in desperately short supply, their absence does not leave us undone, nor force us to accept as legitimate the praise of velvet paintings of dogs playing poker. Instead of locating our aesthetic judgments in facts *contained in* aesthetic objects, Hume suggests that we turn our attention to *persons*, to the "true judges"; the decision lies (in a sense) within them.[33] And it is just in laying down the qualifications for these judges that Hume embeds whiteliness into the very fiber of his aesthetic system.

In an aesthetic system on which beauty is not a matter of something in *objects*, but rather a matter of something in *us*, we must pay attention to the process by which one becomes a member of the True Judges club. Hume identifies some capacities and activities that a would-be true judge must develop or undertake in order to cultivate their Taste to the point that its pronouncements deserve respect from others. Two of these, namely practice and the elimination of prejudice, deserve some attention. Examining them will enable us to see how Taste becomes not only a matter of having education and breeding but also (ultimately) a matter of whiteliness.

Practice

In identifying the characteristics that separate the Man of Culture from the rest of humanity, Hume notes first that a delicacy of taste is much to be desired. Such delicacy, he leads us to understand, is a *natural* asset in some individuals, whose "organs are so fine as to allow nothing to escape them, and at the same time so exact as to perceive every ingredient in the composition."[34] Important as this natural asset is, the advantage it bestows upon its possessor is vastly increased when it is given the opportunity to be exercised; as Hume puts it, "nothing tends further to increase and improve this talent, than *practice* in a particular art, and frequent survey or contemplation of a particular species of beauty."[35] Or, as Carolyn Korsmeyer observes, "L'homme de gout—the ideal man of Taste—is a product of careful cultivation."[36]

The Negro or Laplander of whom Hume speaks may or may not possess a tongue capable of detecting the minutest hint of a flavor; in the absence of opportunity to practice tasting wine, the presence of a natural faculty becomes frankly immaterial. He cannot become a wine expert.[37] Practice would play the same role for a would-be music expert; she may be possessed of perfect pitch and a marvelous memory for melody, but without the opportunity to listen to symphonic music frequently and carefully, she cannot become a true judge of music. Hume argues that the judgments of a practiced individual will come to be attended by a "clear and distinct sentiment," and that they will come to be made with a confidence that is borne of knowing that he can "pronounce, without danger of mistake, concerning the merits of each performance."[38]

At this stage of his account, Hume has already effectively stipulated that aesthetic taste can only develop in a cultural setting in which the would-be critic can experience art frequently. There's nothing surprising about this stipulation, of course; we wouldn't really expect him to argue that aesthetic appreciation is entirely a matter of raw talent.[39] Nor does such a claim seem, on the face of it at least, to shore up Eurowhiteliness; it doesn't explicitly suggest that there is anything better about cultivating one's taste for European symphonic music than, say, for West African drumming or Balinese gamelan music. The superiority of European cultural forms (and, by extension, of the critics who can appreciate them) emerges only as a result of the next stage of his account of the role of practice, the stage at which Hume asserts that practice is particularly necessary for seeing the "species and degrees" of excellence that various *kinds* of artwork possess.[40]

"One accustomed to see, and examine, and weigh the several performances, admired in different ages and nations, can *alone* rate the merits of a work."[41] Yes, even the "coarsest daubing," and the most "vulgar ballad" contain something of aesthetic value. But while such works will captivate the attention of "a peasant or Indian," they will not long fascinate the "person familiarized to superior beauties."[42] Here we begin to detect the outlines of a hierarchy within the hierarchy of beauty; it is not just that certain paintings are better than other paintings (and certain judges better able to detect their quality); it is that certain art *forms* are better than others, and only one who has had exposure to the entire range will be able to recognize this fact. Ballads are not arias; the aesthetic value of the former can never equal that of the latter, and only the individual who has *been accustomed to* see both will be able to ascertain this fact. The array of experience such a critic possesses will enable them to claim with authority that, intriguing and intricate though they may be, the performances of a West African drumming group, no matter how skilled, cannot, by virtue of their medium, be accorded the same aesthetic weight as a concerto, performed by an orchestra. Perhaps even a not-very-good orchestra!

Again, there is a level on which I wish to agree with Hume. Surely there are superior and inferior "musics," after all! A perfectly-tuned chorus of barking dogs performing Christmas carols, or even a virtuosic rendition of "O Solo Mio" performed on a wax-paper-covered comb probably cannot compete with the aesthetic merits of even a high school orchestra playing simple works by Tchaikovsky. But not all the discriminations this claim makes possible are equally unproblematic. If a "true judge" raised in the European symphonic tradition took it upon himself to study gamelan music at a later period in life, and if, on the basis of that study, he were to conclude that symphony is to gamelan as aria is to ballad, would we be equally comfortable with his judgment? Would he count as someone accustomed enough to seeing the performances admired in various nations to be a reliable judge on this front?

Hume is in a bit of a bind here; he can only say these paintings are better *because* of these judges. But what if we match judges head to head? A celebrity panel of Indians against one of Germans? Will the raga or the symphony emerge as superior? And to what can he appeal to claim that superiority?

In considering Hume's assertion that the true judge will be able to sort not just art *works* but also art *forms* into an aesthetic hierarchy, it is essential to remember that he cannot ground this judgment in anything like objective, independent standards, or innate qualities in a work. He has willingly forsaken all matters of fact, and asserted that the (*remarkable*) agreement obtaining among Men of Culture regarding the relative aesthetic merits of works of art cannot be based on any such external standards. Indeed, that is why he undertakes to identify the requisite capacities of true judges; their capacities *produce* or *enable* the uniformity our judgments possess. The true judge is the man who can say "this is good," and can know that his judgment will (generally) be validated by at least some other true judges.[43] He can also command the respect of those of the rest of us who lack the requisite delicacy of taste and practice and thus are literally in no position to judge.

But if agreement among experts is the only (substantial) thing supporting our assessment that African drumming is aesthetically less valuable than a concerto, it is difficult, in any given situation, not to ask, "who's doing the judging—on what cultural 'team' do they play? Have they had as much practice listening to drumming as to concerti? To what did they grow up listening? What else do they know about?" These questions matter because the "true judge" must be accustomed to experiencing (at least) *both* forms of music. And, given the power of these judges, it is absolutely fair to ask "what does accustomed look like?" or "would members of both audiences agree that this judge is *truly* accustomed to hearing this kind of music?"

Hume anticipates the suspicion I raise here—the suspicion that his judges will not in fact be culturally neutral, but will (wrongly) import their own racial, cultural, and class biases into the concert hall, rendering it impossible for the gamelan or the drumming group ever to get a fair hearing in a European venue. To address this suspicion, he introduces the second characteristic of the true judge; namely, the capacity to suspend one's prejudices.

Suspension of Prejudice

The critic, Hume tells us, should "allow nothing to enter into his consideration, but the very object which is submitted to his examination."[44] Expanding this idea, Hume goes on to say that the critic must learn how to "place himself in the same situation as the [originally intended] audience, in order to form a true judgment . . . ."[45] Hume offers some harsh words for the sort of person who views a work "addressed to persons of a different age or nation" and "rashly condemns what seemed admirable in the eyes of those for whom alone the discourse was calculated."[46] In short, Hume seems to have worried about the very matter about which I worried, and to have dealt with it admirably. If you're not the intended audience of the gamelan concert, then don't presume you are in position to judge its merits.

Not quite. Hume's proposal that the critic "preserve his mind free from all prejudice" creates a conceptual problem directly related to the matter of the Eurowhiteliness of his aesthetic model.[47] In revealing this problem, I will grant Hume the benefit of the doubt, and assume what actually seems to me quite unlikely; namely, that we *can* actually determine—as Hume stipulates we must—what a mind free from *all* prejudice would be like, and also how such a state would be achieved.

Hume seems to operate as if criteria exist by which we can separate the would-be critic's *prejudiced opinions* about the works of art of another culture from that person's *genuinely-aesthetic* and unprejudiced opinions. The body of knowledge that the critic has amassed through practice sorts itself into two piles: unprejudiced aesthetic principles he can carry into another context, and partisan preferences that he must leave at home. How can we make sense of such a view in the absence of independent criteria—features of the aesthetic objects themselves, perhaps, or intelligent Martian judges, unprejudiced toward any earthly cultures? As it stands, it is hard to see why we should believe the critic in question has assembled anything other than a set of regional prejudices, shared by those around him, and perhaps even by many people distant from him in time and place, but nevertheless still insufficient for his purposes when he sets off to investigate another time or place. Perhaps the critic even finds his regional preferences echoed in another region; this alone does not count as evidence that they are not "prejudices," but only that they are prejudices more widely held than others.[48]

My suspicion is this: judgments rooted in educated European aesthetic sensibilities will serve as the standard bearers against which others' judgments will be measured. As evidence supporting this suspicion, I would point to Hume's comments about the aesthetic capacities of Indians. Recall that he refers to them as the sorts of people who will appreciate the "coarsest daubings" on canvas, if such daubings display a "certain luster of colors and exactness of imitation."[49] Such a comment seems to assume, at the outset, the limitations of indigenous Indian aesthetics; in an aesthetic head to head between an Indian and a European critic, the Indian will tend to be wrong, as a matter of course, because of the general aesthetic sensibilities of their culture. One wants to ask where Hume stands to make such a claim; upon what grounds can he argue the relative aesthetic merits of the art forms of vastly disparate cultures? Has he, himself, preserved his mind "free from prejudice," as would be required of him? I suspect not—at least not in a world in which certain cultures are esteemed while others are denigrated. In a context in which there are cultural points to be scored in picking the right class of aesthetic objects to admire, the notion that would-be judges are not prejudiced toward them is hard to countenance. Indeed, acting whitely may give a member of an outsider race or culture some entrée, some cultural standing.

The second part of Hume's proposal—namely, that the "critic of a different age or nation" must try to "place himself in the same situation as the audience"—raises a separate, but related problem. Hume seems to suggest that, once one is free from *prejudice,* one will be able to experience a work of art as if one is a member of the intended audience of it. If we are to make "allowance for [the] peculiar views and prejudices" of persons from cultures other than our own in order to judge their artwork rightly, then it would seem that the proper aesthetic attitude (the attitude of an intended audience member) is not at all "freedom from prejudice," but rather a particular *kind of* prejudice or interest— specifically, the interest that comes from being an insider to the culture(s) for which an art work is intended.

If art is culturally situated, it becomes difficult to understand the grounds on which Hume can claim that there are "species of excellence," with some art forms simply higher than others. To repeat, where does a judge stand to make such a claim; outside of all audiences (the aesthetic view from nowhere)? Serially in several different audiences (the view from everywhere)? What does a mind "free from all prejudices" really look like—and how does such a mind *also* "make allowance for [the] views and prejudices" of people from a culture unlike his own, so that he can behave like an intended audience member and "form a true judgment" of the work of art?

Civilized nations, we are told do not disagree about their tragedians or epic poets, no matter how often they might squabble over philosophers.[50] In a "civilized nation," "prejudices . . . never unite in celebrating any rival to the true genius, but yield at last to the force of nature and just sentiment."[51] One wonders why the "civilized" caveat; is it really only in such nations that agreement is reached? Picking up the stick from the other end, is agreement about poetry meant to be taken as a measure *of* civilization, with "uncivilized" societies characterized by their inability to curb disagreement? Is such agreement intended to constitute evidence that they have properly suspended prejudice and adopted the attitude of intended audience members? What if opinion in your nation coalesces around a particular poet, while everyone in my nation agrees that she is the composer of doggerel? Does Hume's distinction also support the notion that certain (racial and cultural) audiences are simply more prejudiced than others, and thus culturally lower than white European ones? On what grounds can he press such a claim? To what standards can he appeal? When such disagreement occurs among people who are simply possessed of "different humors" in a way that "is entirely blameless on both sides," then "we seek in vain for a standard."[52] Why are the differences in "humors" among nations or cultures not the equivalent of such differences among persons of the same culture—that is, irreconcilable, the quintessence of "no accounting for . . . "?

The types of art Hume defines as most worthy of our attention are those of Europe—and of the cultures, past and present, that Europeans have anointed. In the end, only a Eurowhitely person can be a true judge; only they can be the mind "free from prejudice" that can evaluate and assess the cultural productions of other races—even (as in the case of a Black Eurowhitely person) one's own race.[53] Those who would be whitely have a clear task before them—a task of switching loyalties. More than a matter of passing, or "acting white," to be Eurowhitely requires one actually to come to embrace another aesthetic as superior to the aesthetic that prevails in one's own culture.

Vertamae Grosvenor is not interested in shifting loyalties. In the passage I quote from her at the beginning of this chapter, she makes clear her disdain for the white culture she sees surrounding her: whatever it may be at its more effete extremes, white culture is also foam rubber bread, potatoes and rice out of a box; instant cuisine and short-lived fads. Those *Time* magazine editors regard themselves as true judges, sitting in their lofty editorial perches passing judgment on the food that "brought my ancestors through four hundred years of oppression." Perhaps those magazine editors are eating something more interesting on their expense-account lunches, but back at the quotidian, white taste isn't much to brag about. Never mind the savor of wine; these people think Minute Rice tastes good!

Grosvenor echoes Hume, in a sense, by linking aesthetic value to ethical and social value. Soul food sustained the peoples of the African diaspora not only literally, but also figuratively. In contrast, the "instant" foods of white mainstream supermarket culture echo and perpetuate the "instant" faddishness she finds characteristic of that culture. Whatever may be true of the rarefied heights of European culture—heights at which food would still not be discussed seriously as an art form, though its aesthetic value would be recognized—the culture of our supermarkets is anything but aesthetically and ethically worthwhile.

Grosvenor, I'm suggesting, challenges Eurowhiteliness on at least two levels; explicitly, she disparages mainstream commodity culture as faddish and poor quality. There's also an implicit critique of high culture in her remarks, however. She is challenging *Time's* food reviewer, presumably a man whose tastes ran toward the high end. "I don't care what highbrow restaurant food you venerate; I know that *this* is what you people really eat."

I conclude this chapter with a snapshot of the contemporary Man of Culture—the Gastronomic Version.

The Man of Culture Today

Hume's prescription for the Man of Culture—a prescription for Eurowhiteliness—has not expired. There is something more than slightly paradoxical about my choosing to illustrate this fact by considering the matter of cuisine, however. Hume discusses tasting only as an *analogy* to true aesthetic taste, and cuisine has never been counted (by Europeans, at least) among the high arts. On a Eurowhitely scale in which "high" or "true" arts are set off against "low" arts or "crafts," there has been no question that cuisine, that deeply temporal, deeply bodily, deeply useful, deeply *subjective* body of knowledge, is nothing more than a minor art form, at best. Versions of this high/low distinction have also been responsible for ensuring that the artistic creations of the so-called traditional cultures of Africa, Asia and South America have tended to show up not in European or North American art museums, but in anthropology museums, or even museums of natural history. Europeans create art; Others create crafts, at most.

I submit that the tenuousness of cuisine's status is precisely what marks it as an interesting and revealing site from which to examine the role of the contemporary Man of Culture. In the "stump speeches" of those who would argue for cuisine as an art, we find distilled some of the clearest and most rigid definitions of art, taste, and Culture (Eurowhitely edition). This is because those who wish to argue cuisine into the fold must make the most unambiguous and conventional statements about what being "in the fold" looks like.

The work of Jean-François Revel marks a kind of attempt to legitimize cuisine as an art form. A political theorist by profession, Revel also set himself the somewhat unlikely task of writing a culinary history of (primarily European) cuisine. *Culture and Cuisine: A Journey Through the History of Food* is organized around what he takes to be a fundamental distinction between two forms of cuisine—a distinction he draws using criteria that sound not unlike what Hume prescribes for his true judges. Hume emphasizes the combination of inborn talent, practice and the suspension of prejudice he believes is necessary for the cultivation of true judges. Revel implicitly sets himself up as a kind of "true judge," able to draw the distinction between regional cuisines and truly universal international cuisine, the latter of which is an *art* worthy of more than "chauvinism and . . . parochialism."[54]

Revel commences his work by announcing that he will adopt "the tone of the critic," and "the role of the moralist rather than that of the historian." He does so because "cuisine is a normative art in which . . . description and prescription can scarcely be separated."[55] Here at the outset, Revel also lays out the distinction that serves as the backbone for his entire text, between "popular" (a.k.a. peasant, plebian, family, regional) cuisine and "erudite" (court, professional, international) cuisine. Popular cuisine Revel defines as a kind of natural, habitual and regional *craft*, one that draws upon the foods of a region and is "transmitted unconsciously by way of imitation and habit."[56] Regional cuisine belongs to the domain of "biology and ethnology" and is, he insists, "unexportable" from its locale.[57] Erudite cuisine, in contrast is eminently exportable, even universalizable. Based on "invention, renewal, experimentation," this cuisine is a genuine art.[58]

As Revel's history unfolds, it is gradually revealed that, of the two sorts of cuisines he outlines at the beginning of his account, the erudite cuisine really comes to flower on only one continent—and then, most fully only in one country, France. There, it emerges as an "international culinary art," a "body of methods, of principles amenable to variations, depending on different local and financial possibilities."[59] Elsewhere in the world, cultures may adopt this international art, or they may continue to produce their own (popular, peasant, regional) cuisines—cuisines which have their own rough-hewn beauty, not unlike Hume's ballads.

In one sense, there's no arguing with Revel on this point; the history of French cuisine, beginning in the seventeenth century, is the history of the development of a set of techniques and principles that came to be adopted worldwide by practitioners at the top of the culinary pyramid. But when we examine Revel's explanation for *why* this cuisine (and this cuisine only) ascended to the level of a culinary *art,* we find someone who sounds much like one of Hume's "true judges," with all the Eurowhitely presumptions that that identity entails.

Three-fourths of the way through his culinary history, Revel observes that "the reader has doubtless been struck by the fact that beginning with the middle of the seventeenth century [I seem] to have dealt exclusively with French cuisine," but that the reason for this is "not some sort of culinary nationalism."[60] Instead, it is because France is the birthplace of a genuine "international culinary art," rooted in a "body of methods, of principles amenable to variations . . . ."[61] Revel labels this Grand Cuisine, and notes that it "has the capacity to integrate, to adapt, to rethink . . . the recipes of all countries and all regions . . . ."[62]

Revel joins with the "true (culinary) judges" of history to pronounce (French) international cuisine a genuine art, a truly universal form whose appeal is not confined to a given time and place. Such a cuisine contrasts sharply with the regional cuisines that have predominated throughout history, and to which the bulk of Revel's text is devoted. He is at pains to explain how difficult it is for any contemporary eater even to imagine these regional tastes in ancient Greece or medieval Europe. Despite the difficulty of doing so, and despite his acknowledgement that many practices that now seem absurd to us would have been absolutely *de rigeur* in another era (mixing wine with sea water, e.g.), Revel nevertheless feels comfortable passing judgment upon such practices: "There were entire centuries, for example, in which every dish was bombarded with spices . . . . At other times and places, everything was drowned in cream or olive oil, two culinary adjuvants that have a particularly negative effect when used heavy-handedly."[63] In such passages, Revel sounds not unlike Hume, who cautions us about the importance of suspending prejudices, but cannot refrain from exercising his own.

(French) principles of international cuisine, in contrast to these regional missteps, have a kind of flexible universality that (we are led to understand) makes the products of this culinary art form always appealing, always desirable—at least to those true judges whose palates have been developed sufficiently to appreciate them. This (French) international cuisine can take the exportable aspects of regional cuisines and transform them into truly Grand works of genuine art.

Revel would likely not see himself as walking in the footsteps of Hume's true judges—men who have to pass their judgments without the benefit of "real matters of fact." Quite the contrary; Revel sometimes speaks of international culinary art in terms that suggest that he believes it is possessed of truths of an almost Platonic timelessness. Nevertheless, I submit that his pronouncements on the *theoretical reasons* that (French) international culinary art dominates the culinary world make him a strong contender for the title of contemporary Man of Culture.

94 Lisa Heldke

Notes

1. Monique Roelofs might argue that the impact is every bit as significant. She argues that aesthetic development plays a crucial role in the cultivation of individual and national identity. (Monique Roelofs, "Racialization as an Aesthetic Production: What Does the Aesthetic Do for Whiteness and Blackness and Vice Versa," in *White on White, Black on Black*, ed. George Yancy [Lanhan, MD: Rowman & Littlefield, 2005].)
2. Genevieve Lloyd, "The Man of Reason," in *Women, Knowledge, and Reality: Explorations in Feminist Philosophy*, ed. Ann Garry and Marilyn Pearsall. 2nd ed. (New York: Routledge, 1996), 149.
3. Roelofs, "Racialization as an Aesthetic Production," 90, 88.
4. Roelofs, "Racialization as an Aesthetic Production," 90.
5. Roelofs, "Racialization as an Aesthetic Production," 91.
6. Genevieve Lloyd, *The Man of Reason: "Male" and "Female" in Western Philosophy* (Minneapolis: University of Minnesota, 1984), 44.
7. Lloyd, "The Man of Reason," 149.
8. Lloyd, "The Man of Reason," 154.
9. Lloyd, "The Man of Reason," 154.
10. Lloyd, "The Man of Reason," 158.
11. Lloyd, "The Man of Reason," 158.
12. Lloyd, "The Man of Reason," 159.
13. Lloyd, "The Man of Reason," 161.
14. Lloyd, "The Man of Reason," 164.
15. Lloyd, "The Man of Reason," 164.
16. Lloyd does not discuss it, but the Man of Reason is also white; men of color are also excluded from its membership.
17. In interpreting Hume thus, I will seem to have ignored the important, and often-quoted passage in which he argues that Blacks are "naturally inferior" to whites. ("Of National Characters," in *Essays Moral, Political, Literary*, rev. ed. and with a Foreword, Notes, and Glossary by Eugene F. Miller, with an appendix of variant readings from the 1889 edition by T.H. Green and T.H. Grose [Indianapolis: Liberty Fund 1987, http://oll.libertyfund.org/title/704 accessed January 30, 2008].) This unvarnished racist claim has been discussed in several contemporary articles (as well as at least one blog). (Immanuel Eze, "Hume, Race and Human Nature," *Journal of the History of Ideas* 61, no.4 [2000]: 691–698; John Immerwahr, "Hume's Revised Racism," *Journal of the History of Ideas* 53, no.3 [1992]: 481–486; Eric Morton, "Race and Racism in the Philosophy of David Hume," *Journal of African Philosophy* 1, no.1 [2002]: http://www.africanphilosophy.com/vol1.1/morton.html.) Another interpretation of Hume's notions of race, grounded in an essay in which he denounces slavery in the United States, has also been discussed in print. (Hume, "Of the Populousness of Ancient Nations," in *Essays Moral, Political, Literary*. See comments from Vellas come from the entry "Hume and Racism," found in the blog "Philosophical Misadventures: The Thin Ice of Reason" [http://www.philosphicalmisadventures.com/?p=6], accessed January 28, 2008.) The question these contemporary texts debate is, "was Hume racist, and if so, on what basis does his racism rest?" Hume's claim in "Of National Characters," appears in a footnote that exists in two versions (one more blatant than the other). There, he asserts that blacks are inferior to whites *by nature:* "I am apt to suspect the negroes and in general all other species of men (for there are four or five different kinds) to be naturally inferior to the

whites" ("Of National Characters"). This may seem to settle the matter; contrary to what I have asserted about the wine passage, Hume in this passage *does* in fact assert that blacks are inferior by nature.

"Of the Populousness of Ancient Nations," on the other hand, argues that slavery is a heinous institution, one that harms the humanity of those who practice it, not just those who are enslaved: "The remains which are found of domestic slavery, in the American colonies, and among some European nations, would never surely create a desire of rendering it more universal. The little humanity, commonly observed in persons, accustomed, from their infancy, to exercise so great authority over their fellow-creatures, and to trample upon human nature, were sufficient alone to disgust us with that unbounded dominion" ("Populousness of Ancient Nations"). This passage certainly does not directly contradict the first, though it does complicate the picture of what Hume believes is due persons of African descent.

I am reluctant to regard either of these statements as constituting anything like the "true" or "definitive" picture of Hume's philosophical views on race. And in any case, I am not interested in exonerating Hume of the charge of racism. But instead of resting my interpretation entirely on individual, explicitly racist passages, I choose to understand his whiteliness as a more structural problem that pervades the system of his philosophical projects. In doing so, I follow Charles Mills, who observes that "[philosophers'] tacit reference when they write about 'people' is usually to whites, [so that] their theories are so structured as to exclude the distinctive and radically different experience of those, particularly blacks, who will *not* have been treated simply as people" (Charles W. Mills, *Blackness Visible* (Ithaca: Cornell, 1998), 206). Likewise, I wish to show how Hume's descriptions of seemingly-generic men of taste—"true judges," for instance—actually are structured in such a way as to exclude the experiences of anyone not of European descent.

In the end, my argument for the whiteliness of Hume's aesthetics does not stand or fall on the question of Hume believing in the inherent inferiority of Blacks or of any other group.

18. Apropos the discussion in the previous footnote, Roelofs argues that the matter is more than a practical problem; on the basis of the footnote in "Of National Characters," she argues that, in fact, "Hume excludes blacks thus not only from taste but also from the possibility of aesthetic education" ("Racialization as an Aesthetic Production," 87).

19. For a revealing look at the ways in which Euroamericans approach the images in *National Geographic*, see Catharine A. Lutz and Jane L. Collins, *Reading National Geographic* (Chicago: University of Chicago, 1993).

20. David Hume, "Of the Delicacy of Taste and Passions," in *Of the Standard of Taste and Other Essays*, ed. John W. Lenz (Indianapolis: Bobbs-Merrill, 1965), 27.

21. Roelofs addresses this question of the importance of taste in some detail. As she understands Hume, he "construes white civilization, in part, as an aesthetic achievement, a project to be attained through the operations of taste;" "Hume values taste in part on account of its civilizing labor" ("Racialization as an Aesthetic Production," 91).

22. David Hume, "Of the Standard of Taste," In *Standard of Taste*, 6.

23. Hume, "Of the Standard of Taste," 17.

24. Marilyn Frye, "White Woman Feminist," in *Willful Virgin: Essays in Feminism* (Freedom, CA: Crossing Press, 1992), 151–52.

25. Richard Shusterman has already thoroughly examined the matter of class in his essay "Of the Scandal of Taste: Social privilege as nature in the aesthetic theories of Hume and Kant." He writes, "Historically privileged subjective preferences (essentially those of the

historically socially privileged) are reified into an ahistorical ontological standard, a necessary standard for all subjects and all times" (In *Eighteenth-Century Aesthetics and the Reconstruction of Art,* ed. Paul Mattick, Jr. (Cambridge: Cambridge University, 1993), 98). The result, he argues, is that Hume (and Kant) "cannot get on without appealing to social privilege in an essential way and thus undermine their project of a foundational naturalistic, class-free aesthetics" (Shusterman, "Of the Scandal of Taste," 99).

26. I think, for instance, of the ways in which objects from African, Asian and South American cultures have been taken up by European artists—Picasso, for instance—and "made into" art objects. The European artist-viewer has the power to "make art" out of "mere artifact."

27. Following Shusterman, I would also argue that he knits it in in a way that effectively renders it invisible—or at least invisible to all those who are polite enough to agree that they don't see it. This is because Hume argues that the standard of taste is somehow grounded in the *natural.* So, perhaps what my account does is attempt, with Shusterman, to make it impossible for this claim of the naturalness of taste to go unremarked—to insist that the "polite" pretense of race- and class-neutrality be dropped.

28. Hume, "Of the Standard of Taste," 3.

29. Hume, "Of the Standard of Taste," 5.

30. Hume, "Of the Standard of Taste," 6.

31. Hume, "Of the Standard of Taste," 7.

32. Hume, "Of the Standard of Taste," 9.

33. Moniques Roelofs observes, on this point, that it would be incorrect to say that such judgments are *grounded* in these judges: "The true judges are certainly among the factors in which taste is grounded, but it seems to be possible that it is grounded in them derivatively, i.e., due to a more fundamental grounding in the five qualifications that make for what folks sometimes call 'art-appropriate' perception" (personal communication).

34. Hume, "Of the Standard of Taste," 11. Hume, in this passage, is speaking of taste in both the literal (tasting) and metaphorical (aesthetic Taste) senses. An aspect of Hume's essay that is often raised up for comment is his use of an extended analogy between these two senses of taste. The matter of the strength of the analogy is actually immaterial to my argument. Indeed, in choosing the passages with which I begin this chapter, I mean to suggest that the relation between these two forms of taste is *more* than simply that of analogy, and that food is *also* a proper matter of Taste. For an exploration of this matter, see Carolyn Korsmeyer, *Making Sense of Taste: Food and Philosophy* (Ithaca: Cornell, 1999).

35. Hume, "Of the Standard of Taste," 13.

36. Korsmeyer, *Making Sense of Taste,* 44.

37. If we take as definitive the evidence of the passage in "Of National Character" asserting that Blacks are naturally inferior to Europeans, then we must remove Africans from the list of those who could possess even the "raw material" to become a wine taster. But my point is that, whatever he claims regarding natural capacities, Hume has already independently guaranteed the whiteliness of Taste, with his insistence on practice of a certain sort.

While other writers have addressed the issue of Hume's racism by focusing on the footnote, the more important, and troubling, evidence of his racism comes precisely in these passages in which he discusses enculturation. While in at least some of these passages he insists that "Negroes" are incapable of some cultural activity *only* because of the accident of their residence, it turns out that this "accident" makes all the difference in the

world. Culture is a matter of enculturation, whatever else it might be—whether, that is, any element of inherent inferiority be present or not.
38. Hume, "Of the Standard of Taste," 13.
39. Shusterman points out, nevertheless, that such naturalism is, in a sense what Hume *ought* to claim, given his apparent adherence to the Enlightenment view that "if only we could see things naturally (free from disease and cultural prejudice) we would all see them aright..." ("Of the Scandal of Taste," 105).
40. Here, my "stealth agenda" about the significance of food as an art form merges with my explicit thesis about whiteness. In both arenas, my quarrel is with the way in which a Eurocentric "high culture" model is presented as the unquestionable model for what counts as a worthy art form.
41. Hume, "Of the Standard of Taste," 14, my emphasis.
42. Hume, "Of the Standard of Taste," 14.
43. If it is never so validated, then I think that the matter of his being a true judge ends up being called into question.
44. Hume, "Of the Standard of Taste," 15.
45. Hume, "Of the Standard of Taste," 15.
46. Hume, "Of the Standard of Taste," 15.
47. Hume, "Of the Standard of Taste," 14.
48. Shusterman puts the matter thus:

> "Hume begins by claiming that the critic 'must preserve his mind free from all prejudice....' But this clearly contradicts his demand that a good criticism requires the application of practice, good sense, and comparison, all of which take us beyond the object presently perceived to preconceptions of how such objects should be perceived...; such preconceptions are socially formed and modified and are culturally variant.... Good sense and practice in the refinements of art are (and surely were in Hume's day) inextricably bound with good breeding in a particular culture" ("Of the Scandal of Taste," 106). Hume "never faces up to the fact" that his "standard is culturally rather than naturally set, and as such reflects... the social authority of those who set the standard" ("Of the Scandal of Taste," 107).

49. Hume, "Of the Standard of Taste," 14.
50. Hume, "Of the Standard of Taste," 19.
51. Hume, "Of the Standard of Taste," 19.
52. Hume, "Of the Standard of Taste," 19, 20.
53. How can you be Black *and* Eurowhitely? As I noted in my discussion of Frye, the connection between whiteness and whiteliness is contingent; one can be whitely without being white.
54. Jean Jacques Revel, *Culture and Cuisine: A Journey through the History of Food*, trans. Helen R. Lane (Garden City, NY: Doubleday, 1979), 213.
55. Revel, *Culture and Cuisine*, 19.
56. Revel, *Culture and Cuisine*, 19.
57. Revel, *Culture and Cuisine*, 215, 19.
58. Revel, *Culture and Cuisine*, 19, 215.
59. Revel, *Culture and Cuisine*, 214.
60. Revel, *Culture and Cuisine*, 213.
61. Revel, *Culture and Cuisine*, 214.

62. Revel, *Culture and Cuisine*, 215.
63. Revel, *Culture and Cuisine*, 13–14.

5

Whiteness and Rationality: Feminist Dialogue on Race in Academic Institutional Spaces

Crista Lebens, University of Wisconsin-Whitewater

I am concerned with difficult conversations about race. Specifically, I am concerned about what happens and does not happen in conversation, dialogue and discussion at feminist philosophy conferences. Within feminist conversations, organizing, activism and theorizing in the past several decades there runs a thread of discussion about how race and gender coalesce to shape experience. Yet, white feminists as a group appear to have failed to understand and engage fully with the concerns of women of color feminists. I am concerned about how we discuss these failures, and how the failures indicate, to an extent, the way in which rationality is shaped by whiteness.

When I refer to "white feminists as a group," I have in mind a wide range of women I have encountered over the course of fifteen years of participation in feminist philosophy conferences, especially the Midwest Society for Women in Philosophy. Most, if not all, of the white feminists who have moved through that group at one time or another consider themselves, as I consider myself, committed to struggling against racism as well as against sexism and other forms of oppression. Many of these white feminists have made significant contributions toward articulating resistance to multiple oppressions.[1] This space has introduced me to many women who have been part of shaping my consciousness of and resistance to racism. Some of this learning takes place in formal sessions and the question and answer periods that follow. In the course of such discussions, periodically some misunderstandings arise that go deeply into what it means to resist racism. Sometimes this is between two white women, sometimes not. Sometimes I have understood the problem, but sometimes I have not. I am particularly interested in situations where white women, including myself, don't "get it" about race in some way. I am interested because I want to be as effective as I can in my resistance to racism. I do not want to act or think in ways that perpetuate harm to women of color. I hope that some women of color who are interested in such dialogues would also find this a productive space.

In my analysis of what goes wrong in the difficult conversations feminists have about race, I focus primarily on white feminists' role in these conflicts/failures. To situate this pattern of conflict and failure in a larger historical context, I offer an attenuated account of the history of white women and Black women in the United States during the suffrage and abolitionist movements. This background sets the stage for understanding the implications of the conflicts and breakdowns we face today. Next I describe several patterns of communication in academic spaces that I have observed over some time. Then I consider a particular type of racist move identified and articulated by Mariana Ortega, which she names "loving, knowing ignorance." Following Ortega, I situate this concept in a larger framework which includes Marilyn Frye's concept of "whiteliness" and María Lugones' concept of infantilization of judgment. I argue that whiteliness is a continuum, with infantilization on one end and arrogant knowing on the other end. When white feminists face uncertainty on matters of race, we need not retreat to either end of the whiteliness continuum. White feminists need to find ground that constitutes a resistance to whiteliness of either kind. We need to claim a space for genuine not-knowing, to accept uncertainty in the face of pressure to take a position of arrogance or infantilization. Finally, I build on some ideas suggested by many feminists of color and white feminists for navigating difficult conversations.

Betrayal, Solidarity

Contemporary relationships between women of color and white women in the United States must be placed in a historical context in order to understand the frustration and anger of women of color, and the incomprehension on the part of white women.[2] If we trace this history solely through the legacy of Black women and white women, it is a history that goes back centuries.[3] I shall focus on the actions of white women in the nineteenth century as abolition and women's rights movements took root. Drawing on the work of Angela Davis, it is a history of both widespread betrayal, and some solidarity.[4] Academic feminists, regardless of their home discipline, are likely to have a general familiarity with this history, but it is useful to explore some of the details, especially since white feminists seem to replicate some of the betrayals (and the solidarities) today.

Davis documents the brutality faced by slave women: beating a pregnant woman, inducing labor after which the woman died, whipping a nursing mother until blood and milk flowed together.[5] Consider the extent to which white women knew of such beatings. Some white women acted on that knowledge and spoke out. With respect to the abolition movement, white women played an integral role in its success. In response to white men's hostility toward their participation, white women learned political organizing skills and learned to articulate their experience of sexism.[6] Acts of solidarity were mirrored by acts of betrayal. In 1833, Prudence Crandall fought to allow a Black girl into her school. Though ultimately shut down, her act was a significant symbol of resistance to racism.[7] Yet other white abolitionist women succumbed to the racism in the movement, such as the woman who denied access to her school to Frederick Douglass' daughter in 1848.[8]

The Grimke sisters, Angelina and Sarah, two southern white women from a slave-holding family, stand as an example of white feminists who recognized the connections between the oppression of slave women and the subjugation of white women. Furthermore, as Davis points out, they were able to resist "the ideological snare of insisting that one struggle was absolutely more important than the other."[9] Yet the Grimkes were not in the mainstream of the women's movement. After the Civil War, when the issues at hand were reduced to the question of Black male suffrage or white women's suffrage, among the white women, Elizabeth Cady Stanton's position held sway. She considered the two issues to be in opposition to each other:

> Elizabeth Cady Stanton and others who believed that because, in their eyes, emancipation had rendered Black people "equal" to white women, the vote would render Black men superior, were absolutely opposed to Black male suffrage. Yet there were those who understood that the abolition of slavery had not abolished the economic oppression of Black people who therefore had a special and urgent need for political power.[10]

As Davis' analysis reveals, it is possible to support women's rights and support Black male suffrage without claiming that one takes absolute precedence over the other and at the same time recognize that the political realities reflect an urgent need to extend the vote to at least some Black people as soon as possible, then to all women following that. Frederick Douglass, and later Sojourner Truth and Frances E. W. Harper, took that position.[11]

The racism of white women sometimes reflected an incapacity to recognize their own role in directly exploiting another, such as the white feminist working in 1902 to improve working conditions for white female clerks. Until questioned she had no cognizance of the fact that she expected her maid, a Black woman, to work longer hours than that of the clerks whose situation she was petitioning against.[12] In a notable instance of déjà vu discourses,[13] this failure of self-awareness was challenged seventy-seven years later by Audre Lorde.[14]

Yet there is also the example of Myrtilla Miner, who faced great risks to create a school for Black women in 1851. Though her school was burned down, the inspiration continued in the form of Miner's Teachers College.[15] Davis ties the legacy of sisterhood between Black women and white women to the struggle for education:

> It could not have been a mere historical coincidence that so many of the white women who defended their Black sisters in the most dangerous of situations were involved in the struggle for education. They must have understood how urgently Black women needed to acquire knowledge....[16]

As white feminists we need to take seriously the history of colonized peoples. The connection between white supremacy and a kind of rationality which is coded white is forged historically in the treatment of non-white people by those who declared themselves white. White feminists need to recognize how our rationality is constructed by this dynamic.

White Privilege and Dialogue in Institutional Spaces: Some Recognizable Patterns[17]

What happens in institutional spaces such as professional feminist philosophy conferences (or conferences of feminists who practice philosophy professionally)?

Pattern #1

A white woman makes a statement that can be called racist. She is called on it, most likely by a woman of color. The white woman (anyone from a senior faculty member to a graduate student), who otherwise handles criticisms well, takes the criticism as a personal attack—she, not just her statement, is racist. Further discussion may ensue, the issue may be addressed, or it may be largely ignored. Both the white woman and the woman who called her on it (usually a woman of color) feel alienated. Frequently the white woman perceives the woman of color to be "angry."

Some Questions to Consider:[18]
- Who is harmed by being called racist?
- Who is harmed by taking the risk of calling a white woman on her racism?
- Who gets support and acknowledgement for this harm, and from whom?
- What does it mean to put the label "angry" on the action of identifying racism?
- In what ways, if any, is it appropriate for a white woman to question whether her actions are racist?[19]

Pattern #2

A white woman reads a paper on a topic in feminist philosophy. Though her paper addresses some dimension of gendered reality, it does not build in a consideration of the racial dimensions of gender. A woman of color attends the presentation, as well as numerous other sessions, and later comments that the only paper that addressed her experiences as a woman of color was the one read by another woman of color, the only paper read by a woman of color at the conference.

Variation on Pattern #2

The woman of color asks whether the author is speaking to white women only, or does she presume that all women are white. (See pattern #1).

Some Questions to Consider:
- Who in the audience notices the absence of other social identities besides gender?
- Who is likely to speak up about it? What does it cost her to do so?
- What does it cost the group, as a whole and individually, not to do so?

Pattern #3

A white woman presents a paper on a topic in feminist philosophy. It may or may not address issues of race, class, and sexuality, in addition to gender. The room is filled with white women (and perhaps a few white men). No people of color are present.

Some Questions to Consider:
- Who notices the absence of people of color?
- For whom is it a problem?

Pattern #4

A woman of color reads a paper at a feminist philosophy conference. The audience, predominantly women, is racially mixed. The lively discussion that follows engages the author's main points and deepens understanding of the topic. The rest of the papers, read by women of color and white women, have similarly dynamic discussions.

Some Questions to Consider:
- Is this a pattern? (Not likely.)
- Why not?

Anger and Frustration: A Call, but No Response

Whether calling or being called out, one feels it. The woman of color, I imagine, might wonder how many times she must say what Blanche Radford Curry calls "Déjà Vu Discourses," the idea that she (and many others) have said this many times before. She might be tired and cranky and fed up with this pattern, or well-rested, alert, and really pissed off. The white woman called out might be shocked by this charge of racism—so different from criticisms of the philosophical merits of the argument—as if the failure to consider racialized gender issues was not a philosophical issue. And she may be fed up, too. "Haven't we learned this already?" As if it is an individual topic-of-the moment from which we can (or should) move on. Or the white woman might simply be baffled. How is this racist?

Certainly these are examples of how white women reinscribe whiteness as a site of power. It is the white women who allow this to happen. It may not be as egregious as taking whiteness as universal, rather, it may be a use of race that is wrongly appropriated to make another point, a use of race that reinscribes a racist practice, or a use of race that (over)generalizes one kind of marginalization to account for all racialized experiences. In such cases, white women may have good intentions when they set out to "bring race into their papers," but do so in a way that causes harm rather than speaking to a multidimensional experience. Then when we fail, we react, still, in ways that make it difficult, still, for others to identify the harm done. This shuts down dialogue and squelches opportunities for learning and understanding. Whiteness prevails.

Whiteliness and Infantilization of Judgment

Marilyn Frye develops the concept of whiteliness as an analogy to masculinity. Men cannot cease to be male, but can challenge male supremacy by rejecting values predicated on masculinity. Similarly, white people cannot cease to be white, but can reject the values associated with being white, that is, whiteliness. Some elements of whiteliness are: denial of culpability, overwhelming belief in one's own goodness or good intentions, authorizing one's self or other white people to be the moral arbiters of the universe.[20]

María Lugones develops the concept of infantilization of judgment to account for the paralysis some white women exhibit when called on their racism. Some elements of infantilization of judgment are: claims of ignorance or good intentions by a white woman when called on her racism. She becomes paralyzed, unable to respond, and refuses to take responsibility for her actions. She becomes as if an infant, and so not responsible. But she is not an infant, as Lugones points out, she is an ethnocentric racist.[21]

I think there is a distinction between the two concepts on the "whiteliness" continuum. Arrogant whiteliness, I would argue, is that manifestation of whiteliness that claims the authority of the moral judge. This is "whitely" in Frye's construction. The arrogantly whitely person can brush aside questions of race, or presumes sufficient expert knowledge. Arrogance might be masked by what appears to be loving perception in the sense Mariana Ortega points out. To the extent that the focus is on achieving certainty or being right, morally or epistemically, I suspect the motivation is whiteliness. Feminists have worked so hard to claim a position as knowers that white feminists perhaps forget to recognize the limits of that knowledge as defined by our white privilege.

Infantilized whiteliness is infantilization of judgment as Lugones constructs it. This move is also whitely, however, because the one who practices it gets to decide she is not responsible for her racist actions, thereby setting herself, again, as moral arbiter of the universe. If a white woman can do work that either disregards race out of an arrogant or infantilized whiteliness, or appropriates race in white hegemonic ways, as in loving, knowing ignorance, and this work is deemed acceptable by other white feminists, then the harm becomes compounded. Acceptance of that work deems such work rational, and thus, rationality is defined as that which is meaningful to white people. Rationality is coded white.

Loving, Knowing Ignorance

Mariana Ortega introduced a concept she calls "loving, knowing ignorance" to describe the racist actions of well-intentioned white feminists.[22] Ortega references Marilyn Frye's concepts of arrogant perception and loving perception, and María Lugones' appropriation of the concept to include white women's arrogant perception of women of color. Ortega's analysis of this move identifies it as arising out of something like loving perception with elements of arrogant perception as well. Ortega's analysis draws on the work of Paula Moya,[23] who criticizes Donna Haraway's concept of the cyborg and Judith Butler's early work on deconstructing the category "woman." Each of these theorists uses the work of women of color in their own theoretical projects. Based on Moya's criticism, Ortega calls their appropriations examples of loving, knowing ignorance:

> Those guilty of this kind of loving, knowing ignorance have learned the main sayings of such well-known feminists of color as hooks, Lorde, and Lugones, and are aware of Spelman's claims about the problems of exclusion in feminist thought. They theorize and make claims about women of color. However, they do not check whether in fact their claims about the experience of women of color are being described with attention to detail and with understanding of its subtleties. In other words, this ignorance goes hand in hand with the production of knowledge about the experience of women of color. The result of this ignorance is that women of color continue to be misunderstood, underrepresented, homogenized, disrespected, or subsumed under the experience of "universal sisterhood" while "knowledge" about them is being encouraged and disseminated and while feminism claims to be more concerned and more enlightened about the relations between white women and women of color.[24]

Ortega's analysis highlights several key issues. First, the white feminist in her account believes herself to be doing antiracist work. She is well-intentioned, i.e., "loving," and informed about the work of feminists of color, i.e., "knowing." Second, other white feminists can point to her work as proof that white feminists do address issues of race. Third, the white feminist is producing a kind of knowledge, but this is a knowledge characterized by an important kind of ignorance. Ortega frames this kind of knowledge production within the context of epistemologies of ignorance where misrepresentations and misunderstandings of women of color are produced and reproduced. This in itself is harmful to women of color. The harm is compounded by an additional issue, namely, that this method of generating knowledge seems to be accepted by white feminists until it is challenged by a woman of color, and then, the initial account is far better known than the criticism. So what counts for knowledge is a method of production that directly supports a kind of institutional white supremacy. This codes rationality as white.

Genuine Knowing and Not-Knowing

There are things white folks cannot know about the experience of folks of color. All the reading, all the conversations, all the imaginings cannot replace lived experience, though they can go a long, long way toward fostering better understanding. So white folks need to be very aware of what is knowledge, what is whitely arrogance masked as knowledge, and conversely what is genuine lack of knowledge, and what is whitely infantilization masked as lack of knowledge.

In a sense, arrogance and infantilization are at opposite ends of the whitely spectrum. The former is a claim to knowledge and authority that is unjustified and serves to maintain white hegemonic power. The latter is a claim to ignorance or innocence and serves to maintain white hegemonic power. Both of these are claims about knowledge. Resistance to whiteliness is resistance to both arrogance and infantilization. When we consider the conflict that can arise when a white feminist philosopher is called on perceived racism, how can we navigate these channels of knowledge? Whose knowledge is authorized, and whose should be?

Many feminists of color have called, repeatedly, for white feminists to engage the work of women of color. This call raises some epistemological questions for white women. How can we engage such work without being whitely and arrogant about authority? And when we recognize our lack of knowledge, how do we ensure that it is not a case of infantilization? Again, I return to the problem of confrontation/response as work that women of color and white women do, and that white women must engage, and do so in non-whitely, non-infantile ways. For example, Gloria Anzaldúa describes mestiza consciousness as, among other things, a tolerance for ambiguity, a breaking down of the subject/object dichotomy.[25] Though white feminists should not appropriate mestiza consciousness for our own, we can recognize that epistemology as one that challenges the epistemology of whiteliness, that is, mestiza consciousness challenges the need for certainty and the commitment to dualism.

Inspired by Gloria Anzaldúa's work, María Lugones calls for loving perception, "world"-traveling, and curdled consciousness, which is a form of consciousness that need not be located in mestiza culture.[26] And Mariana Ortega, in calling for white feminists to engage flesh and blood women of color, asks white feminists, "What is 'world'-traveling to you?"[27]

I offer the following response to Ortega's question. It means trying to bring a curdled consciousness into my everyday experience of the world, so that I am not just being attentive to race, but to class, ability and other areas in which I am privileged, not to mention gender, sexuality and other ways I am marginalized. It means noticing, with respect to race, when I am in a room, on the street, in a bus, who is present and who is absent, and why?[28] It means considering my life choices and how they reflect my politics—specifically, what city do I live in— what neighborhood do I live in—who are my friends. It means learning about people and cultures and economics. Who makes the things I consume? It means considering how my *life* has to change if this work really matters to me:

> [When read from an engaged position, the work of people color] can help the white/Angla become self-consciously white/Anglo in the racial and ethnic senses of the words: they can help her unravel the connections between racism, ethnocentrism, white/Anglo self-esteem, polite arrogance, polite condescension, and a troubled sense of responsibility in the face of people of color. [29]

Engagement must also mean that white/Angla women bring this consciousness out of the work space and into the rest of one's life.

In following these calls, I suggest that white women need to consider how to assess a claim that one's actions are racist. Why am I interested in such a project? That sounds like a problematic aspiration. What I really want to be able to do, as a white feminist, is have open, honest dialogue with women of color. That means, among other things, the ability to assess whether my work, the knowledge I produce, is harmful to women of color. Such a suggestion comes with risk—the risk of setting myself up as the judge, and if I judge my actions to be acceptable, I risk discounting women of color yet again. Perhaps the result might be that white women cannot usually make this call. I fear that wanting to be able to disagree when an action is called racist is to authorize the loving, knowing ignorant white people of the world to wreak havoc with people of color. Few people *intend* to be racist. Open season on women of color is not what I seek, and I understand how my call could lead to that.

For white feminists to be able to respond to a criticism that her work is racist in some way, it seems to me that she needs to be able to disagree without her disagreement coming out of denial, hostility, arrogance, whiteliness, infantilization, or loving, knowing ignorance. But the work of women of color in feminist epistemology teaches us that the privileged group frequently cannot (or will not?) assess its own actions in the way the marginalized group does. So, white feminists are left with a criticism and few tools to assess the criticism or respond, except to learn. This feels disempowering to us as knowers because it points out something we cannot know. That can trigger the whiteliness response—perhaps to go theoretical. We want to have knowledge some way.

Speaking Some Truth

Of course women of color want open, honest dialogue as well. Consider the value of "speaking one's truth" that African-Americans hold dear. Jackie Anderson said that if she didn't speak her truth her way, including doing so in discussions with white feminists, the result might be that what she said turned out to be not her truth. That would be a serious loss. Dianne Riley put it this way, that people of color appreciate it when one speaks the truth, because part of struggling with oppression is fighting through many, many layers of deception. Speaking the truth is a way of cutting through the obfuscation that can mask white supremacy.

Riley also led me to realize that one cannot simultaneously tell one's truth *and* take care of the other person.[30] Speaking the truth, in the heat of the moment, in a public setting, is a fraught situation. I have doubts about the extent to which truth about white supremacy can be told in academic settings, which are intrinsically structured by the logic of whiteliness. Much militates against it. But to the extent that we are committed to dismantling institutional oppression, we must take risks.

Tamara K. Nopper tells some hard truths about the hypocrisy of white antiracists. I suggest every white person who wants to do this work read her open letter with an open mind. It would be easy to dismiss her work as counterproductive, or to conclude that she thinks white antiracist action is futile. I disagree. White people who work to resist racism need some way to call out our ignorance and our mistakes, no matter how painful it is to hear it. Nopper does just that:

> White people at meetings will often discuss how they feel "silenced" by nonwhites, or that they are being "put in their place." Let me make one thing clear: it is impossible for a non-white person to put a white person in her place . . . because that is a part of whiteness, the ability to take up space and feel a prerogative to do so. . . .[31]

Nopper draws on a structural analysis of oppression to argue that a white person always has the institutional power of whiteness with respect to a person of color. Any perception of silencing between two individuals ignores the larger context of such institutional power. Therefore, she concludes, a white person cannot be "put in her place" by a person of color.

The phenomenon Nopper refers to, that of a white person taking up space and claiming the authority to do, and calling any challenge to that taking up space "silencing," is the essence of whiteliness. And to claim that one is silenced in such a context is what Mary Daly would call a reversal.[32] A white woman who claims to be silenced is ignoring the privilege she draws on by simply having a choice about whether to be in attendance, by assuming others will take her seriously when she speaks, and by assuming she has something to contribute to the conversation. On the other hand, she may argue that women in general, and she in particular, have been barred entry, ignored, and dismissed from the "the discussion." Both claims are true. It is also true that a white woman may *inadvertently*, but nevertheless *actually* exercise white privilege in a feminist space where her authority to speak is not challenged.

Another response that follows the line of reasoning regarding silencing is that of the white woman claiming to be bullied into silence by the woman of color. Certainly there are bullies in every group—no one has the moral high ground without qualification. If the woman of color is being a bully, she should be called on it. But how can the white woman make that call? Certainly we must recognize that the default position is likely to be one of whiteliness and perhaps infantilization. The well-meaning white woman may be demonstrating loving, knowing ignorance. How can she know that about herself? At the very least, she ought to take seriously the concern that she is being whitely. This consideration takes time. It may take a year (or several) to grasp fully the possibility that one's own actions demonstrate whitely arrogance. In the mean time she must act. The best one can do is respond to the situation—raise the question of bullying, but keep open the examination of one's own behavior. Likely she will never be able to settle the question definitively. Challenging one's own whiteness requires that we relinquish the quest for certainty on this matter. Yet, such recognition should never be used as an excuse not to try to discern how whiteliness functions with regard to women of color.

I speak from direct experience of this dynamic. I have been in a situation where I felt silenced by a woman of color. I thought a great deal about my interpretation of the interaction, and I continue to think about it. Days later, I told her how I read the situation; I felt I had been shut down. She communicated her concerns, that her experiences had been erased by my actions. Neither of us intended to do what we had done. Who is right about what happened? There is no settling the matter. Nevertheless, one draws conclusions about such interactions, conclusions which may or may not be well-founded. Dialogue holds the prospect that these conclusions might be shared. In pursuing my concern about being "shut down," I risked being the racist anti-racist white woman that Nopper describes. I was aware of that risk. I also knew it was important to me to continue dialogue about what happened. Because of that, I learned more about the consequences of my actions for the other woman, and she had a chance to respond to my concerns—the consequences of her actions. I don't think it was a mistake to seek that dialogue.

Tamara Nopper criticizes what she calls an economy of gratitude among white antiracists:

> Additionally, white activism, especially white anti-racism, is predicated on an economy of gratitude. We are supposed to be grateful that a white person is willing to work with non-white people. We are supposed to be grateful that you actually want to work with us and that you give us your resources. I would like to know why you have those resources and others do not? And don't assume that just because I have to ask you for resources that it does not hurt me, pain me even. Don't assume that when you come into the space, that doesn't bother

me. Don't assume that when you talk first, talk the most, and talk the most often, that this doesn't hurt me. Don't assume that when I see you get the attention and accolades and the book deals and the speaking engagements that this does not hurt me (because you profit off of pain). And don't assume that when I see how grateful non-white people are to you for being there, for being a "good white" person that this doesn't hurt me. And don't assume that when I get chastised by non-white people because I think your presence is unnecessary that it does not hurt me. Because all of these things remind me of how powerless non-white people are (albeit differently) in relation to white people. All of these gestures that you do reminds me of how grateful I am supposed to be towards you because you actually (or supposedly) care about what is happening to me. I am a bit resentful of economies of gratitude....[33]

Any white person doing work that could be called antiracist, whether it is activism or scholarship, ought to question, from time to time, why she is doing it. I know from doing feminist work in non-feminist classrooms how much easier it is for me, a white person, to challenge racism than it is for me, a person who is a woman, to challenge sexism, patriarchy, misogyny. In the former I have the appearance of objectivity in naming injustice. In the latter, I have the appearance of acting out of self-interest.

My scholarship has centered on intersections of social identities, and therefore considerations of race are central. I do this work in part because I believe that is what feminist theory should be doing and in part for personal reasons. But I have advanced professionally because of my work, including getting tenure. While Tamara Nopper's words may seem harsh, or overgeneralized, I recognize the truth in them. I'd like to think that being white didn't help me get a job, or get published, but I'd be fooling myself. And, it's been said before by people of color, white people do have a choice about whether or not to work on race. People of color are doing it for their survival.

I was involved in an action around *Día De Los Muertos* (Day of the Dead—November 1). The march, organized by MECHA (*Moviemiento Estudiantes Chicanos de Azatlán*) was largely composed of Latinas and Latinos and included people of other races including white folks. At one point the marchers came across a (white) sorority that was collecting clothing to distribute to low-income families. There was some criticism of the "do-gooders" by the marchers and some hurt and puzzlement on the part of the sorority members. One guy spoke to me, as a fellow protester, in anger and frustration: "Yeah, they want us to be grateful when they say 'here's my old coat, you piece of shit.'" I wasn't able to completely conceal my surprise. He turned away from me and walked off. I wished that I could have stood with him in solidarity with his anger at being treated like shit and the expectation that he should be grateful for cast-offs. But the truth is, though I understood his frustration, I hadn't considered how it would feel to be in that situation until that moment. Though I got it immediately, my understanding came a moment too late to stand with him. I understand what Tamara Nopper means by an economy of gratitude.

Whiteness and Rationality   *111*

> But white people need to think of how their activism reproduces the actual structure of white supremacy some—not all whites activists—profess to be about. This structure of white supremacy is not just in an activist space, it actually touches upon and impinges on the lives of non-white people who may not be activists (in your sense) or who do not interact with you in activist worlds. [34]

Food drives, clothing drives and so on might alleviate the immediate need of some individuals, which is significant, but such actions leave intact structural power imbalances that result in poverty and hunger. Failing to recognize the larger context in which their help was perceived, the sorority members could not understand the anger directed at them. But this could perhaps be an example of infantilization of judgment. What can be said of white feminist philosophy of race? We certainly need to consider the ways in which our work supports white supremacy. Is that a reason to stop doing antiracist work? I don't think so. Purity is a fiction.[35]

Nopper does not try to solve the white antiracist's oxymoronic dilemma. She does offer some suggestions to those of us who want to be more effective in our antiracist efforts:

> But consider what your presence means in a community that you decide to set up your community garden in, or your bookstore in, or your meeting space in, or have your march in. What does it mean when you decide that you want to be "with" the oppressed and you end up displacing them? Just because you walk around with your dreadlocks, or decide that you will not wear expensive clothes does not mean that your whiteness does not displace people in the spaces you decide to put yourself in. How do you help to bring more forms of authority and control in a neighborhood, whether through increased rent and housing costs, more policing, or just the ways in which your white bodies can make people feel, as a brilliant friend of mine once asked, "squatters in somebody else's project"?[36]

Part of what it means to function in a racist, ethnocentric culture is that one is maintaining that structure. Life as a white anti-racist *is* a contradiction. The best we can do is to try to make choices in resistance to whiteliness, that is resistance to the desire for knowledge and certainty that set one's self up as *the Knower*, and resistance to the temptation to mask as ignorance or innocence a failure to engage.

To return to the example above where I perceived that I had been shut down by a woman of color, my engaging her in dialogue afterwards was everything Tamara Nopper says is wrong about white antiracists: I claimed to be silenced, I claimed to be doing something that was antiracist yet also had the effect of shutting out a woman of color, and I was taking up space in an academic setting in a presentation pertaining to race. In some ways I had done everything wrong. But I have struggled to consider this situation in ways that are not whitely, that are not lovingly, knowingly ignorant, and that are not infantilized, and I continue to strive for awareness of my ignorance.

Conclusion:
Some thoughts about the discipline of Philosophy

To return to the original question, how can white feminists more fully engage with the concerns of women of color? We can build on the work of philosophers of color who connect our present concepts of rationality with the history of colonialism, and we can continue to de-center forms and practices of rationality that enforce whiteliness and white supremacy. For example, we can articulate the way in which analytic philosophy teaches us to think ahistorically, and consider how that isolates white people from a history that would reveal our connections to the legacy of white supremacy. White people made philosophy a whitely endeavor. But an uncritical study of philosophy can make white people even more whitely. White feminist philosophers know how to interrupt the construction of rationality as masculine. As white feminist philosophers, we need to continue the process of interrupting ourselves.[37]

Notes

1. I am grateful to the women of Midwest SWIP, past and present who have contributed enormously to my development as a feminist.
2. Shireen Roshanravan helped me recognize the importance of placing this topic in a historical context.
3. To be complete, such a consideration should take into account the experience of the Indigeneous peoples of the Western Hemisphere and Asian immigrants, and the legacy of colonialism and violence, including sexual violence. For example, Andrea Smith, *Conquest: Sexual Violence and American Indian Genocide* (Boston: South End Press, 2004) and Thomas Almaguer, *Racial Faultlines* (Berkeley: University of California Press, 1994).
4. For this brief foray into history, I use Angela Davis's work, *Women, Race, & Class* (New York: Random House, 1981). Davis presents an invaluable argument that nineteenth century racial and class tensions between Black women and white women, and among white women in the North, account for the divisions in the Women's Movement of the late twentieth century.
5. Davis, *Women, Race, & Class*, 9–10.
6. Davis, *Women, Race, & Class*, 39–45.
7. Davis, *Women, Race, & Class*, 34–35.
8. Davis, *Women, Race, & Class*, 59.
9. Davis, *Women, Race, & Class*, 44.
10. Davis, *Women, Race, & Class*, 72–73. At this writing, the 2008 Democratic Primary season is still in progress. The decision appears to be between Hillary Clinton, a white woman, and Barack Obama, a Black man. Ironically, Gloria Steinem, in her endorsement of Hillary Clinton, invoked reasoning similar to Elizabeth Cady Stanton. "Women are Never the Frontrunners," *NY Times* Op/Ed, January 8, 2008. In response to a post referring to the editorial, I posted the following response on the FEAST listserv:

> I think it is important to bring discussions of sexism into the public, however, I was quite angered by Gloria Steinem's op-ed piece. The example she used, that "Achola" Obama wouldn't have a chance as a presidential candidate, implies that this is because of sexism. She does not identify the effect that gender and race together would have on a woman of color. Indeed, she claims that "Gender is probably the most restricting force in American life . . . . " The example and that statement erase Hillary Clinton's race. One could say it is because HRC is white that she is a viable candidate. And that wouldn't tell the whole story either. In setting racism against sexism, Steinem missed an opportunity to define feminist concerns as inclusive of racial issues. And she causes real harm by erasing and excluding women of color. When we set racism and sexism against each other, it's the white men who win. I think we as feminists need to call out the sexism, but not claim it as worse, better than, or even completely separate from racism. Rather, we need a more nuanced articulation that recognizes the different ways each is manifested.

I regret that I did not also criticize Steinem's distortion of history. At the time I wrote the post, I was not completely certain I had my historical facts right. An opportunity missed.
11. Davis, *Women, Race, & Class*, 83–84.
12. Davis, *Women, Race, & Class*, 96–97.

13. Blanche Radford Curry, "Whiteness and Feminism: Déjà Vu Discourses, What's Next?" in *What White Looks Like: African-American Philosophers on the Whiteness Question*, ed. George Yancy (New York: Routledge, 2004), 243–262.
14. Audre Lorde, "The Master's Tools Will Never Dismantle the Master's House," *Sister/Outsider* (Freedom, CA: The Crossing Press, 1984).
15. Davis, *Women, Race, & Class*, 102–104.
16. Davis, *Women, Race, & Class*, 104–105.
17. Of course it is not as simple as these examples suggest. Personalities (egos) are involved. We all fluctuate in our ability to respond effectively and attentively to a criticism or to communicate a criticism clearly. Nevertheless, these are patterns I have observed (or that have been pointed out to me) over a period of time. And I'm as guilty as anyone of a failure to respond effectively at times, including a failure to consider multidimensional aspects of identity, even when directly addressing issues of race. I am the antiracist racist white woman.
18. These questions, and my thoughts on these issues, emerge out of conversations, some over the course of many years, with the following compañer@s: Jackie Anderson, Jennifer Benson, Suparna Bhaskaran, Anne Courtney, Barry DeCoster, Marilyn Frye, Sarah Hoagland, Seth Jensen, María Lugones, Tari Muñiz, Dianne Riley, Shireen Roshanravan, Lisa Sayles, and Allison Wolf.
19. We may not be at the place where white people can be trusted to judge whether something is racist or not. Even if the practical answer to "when is it appropriate" is "never," we still need to articulate why that is the case, and consider what that means, especially how it acts as a block to honest engagement of racial dynamics.
20. Marilyn Frye, "White Woman Feminist," in *Willful Virgin: Essays in Feminism, 1976-1992* (Freedom, CA: Crossing Press, 1992), 152–157.
21. María Lugones, *"Hablando Cara a Cara/*Speaking Face to Face" in *Pilgrimages/Perigrinajes: Theorizing Coalition Against Multiple Oppressions* (Lanham, MD: Rowman & Littlefield, 2003), 48–49.
22. Mariana Ortega, "Being Lovingly, Knowingly Ignorant: White Feminism and Women of Color," *Hypatia* 21, no. 3 (Summer 2006): 56–74.
23. Paula Moya, *Learning from Experience: Minority Identities, Multicultural Struggles* (Berkeley, CA: Univ. of California Press, 2002), 32–35.
24. Ortega, "Being Lovingly, Knowingly Ignorant," 62.
25. Gloria Anzaldúa, *Borderlands/*La Frontera: *The New Mestiza* (San Francisco, CA: Spinsters/Aunt Lute, 1987), especially 77–80.
26. María Lugones, "Purity, Impurity and Separation." in *Pilgrimages/*Perigrinajes: *Theorizing Coalition Against Multiple Oppressions* (Lanham, MD: Rowman & Littlefield, 2003), 144–146.
27. Ortega, "Being Lovingly, Knowingly Ignorant," 69.
28. I first learned to ask these questions in a Women's Studies class taught by Marilyn Frye.
29. Lugones, *"Hablando Cara a Cara,"* 46.
30. "Care" must be defined further. I read an earlier version of this paper at the meeting of the North American Society for Social Philosophy held in conjunction with the American Philosophical Association, Eastern Division Conference held in Baltimore, Dec. 2007. At that presentation, an African-American woman pointed out that telling the truth can be a very caring gesture. One tells the truth to someone one has some care for, rather than dismissing them as not worth the trouble. I completely agree with this reading. The idea I mean to convey is that one cannot shield the other from hurt feelings and simultaneously tell them a painful truth. I hope to learn her name in the future.

31. Tamara K. Nopper, "The White Anti-Racist Is an Oxymoron: An Open Letter to 'White Anti-Racists'" in *Race Traitor*, archived at the following site: http://racetraitor.org/ (accessed February, 2008).
32. Mary Daly analyzes the reversals of word meanings in ways that disempower women in patriarchy. For example, Adam gives birth to Eve; Zeus gives birth to Athena. Mary Daly, *Gyn/Ecology: The Metaethics of Radical Feminism* (Boston: Beacon Press, 1978, 1990), 8.
33. Nopper, "The White Anti-Racist is an Oxymoron."
34. Nopper, "The White Anti-Racist is an Oxymoron."
35. Lugones, "Purity, Impurity and Separation," 126–133.
36. Nopper, "The White Anti-Racist is an Oxymoron."
37. I am grateful to Jennifer Benson, Annie Courtney, Dianne Riley, Shireen Roshanravan, and George Yancy for comments on earlier drafts of this chapter.

6

Appropriate Subjects: Whiteness and the Discipline of Philosophy

Alexis Shotwell, Laurentian University

When I decided to do an interdisciplinary Ph.D., I knew that it was unlikely that I would ever work in a philosophy department. Even the degreed philosophers with whom I studied in grad school—Angela Davis and David Hoy—were heterodox in their approach and focus, particularly from the point of view of that mythical-yet-real beast, the Anglo-American analytic philosopher. When I went on the market, then, I was surprised to get a number of interviews in Philosophy departments, albeit unusual departments, willing to entertain a candidate who listed her research interests as including "unspeakable and unspoken knowledge" and "critical race studies." At an APA conference interview, I remember one interviewer saying in relation to my research: "I see why this is an interesting project; I just don't see how it is philosophy." Anecdotal reports suggest that the experience of variations of this response is common for people who attempt to do work in philosophy while departing in archive and method from accepted norms. In 1964, Justice Potter Stewart famously declared that he couldn't define pornography, but that he knew it when he saw it. Many philosophers are similarly unable to define philosophy, but most seem to be able to identify quite clearly what it is not when they see it.

In this chapter, I argue that the constitution of appropriate subjects for attention within philosophy (the formation of the discipline) is connected to being appropriate subjects of philosophy (being disciplined). I begin with a discussion of disciplining and the formation of academic disciplines, drawing on theories of interdisciplinarity. Following this, I chart some analogies between intersectionality and interdisciplinarity. I next consider subjects understood as appropriate for philosophical study and the associated canon formation, and suggest that one of the cause-effect pairs that defines philosophy as a discipline is its refusal to consider race a properly philosophical subject. I am particularly interested in what questions it is possible to ask and what methods it is possible to deploy, while still "counting" as properly philosophical. Finally, I reflect on how philosophical methods relate to the subjects who practice academic philosophy. Throughout, I am interested in investigating the connections between method and subjectivity.

The Discipline and Boundary Maintenance

Work on interdisciplinarity highlights a number of features of the production of disciplinarity. Consider three common defining traits of disciplinary formation, against which interdisciplinarity is often defined. First, disciplines mark discursive histories, tracing practices as a means to define the boundaries of disciplines. Salter and Hearn thus describe disciplines as "recognizable communities of scholars that develop conventions governing the conduct of research and its adjudication . . . [that] rely upon technical language and particular methods of analysis . . . [and that] develop standards of evaluation specifically suited to their methodology and objects of analysis."[1] On this account, disciplines are determined by the kind of intellectual work undertaken: one could tell whether someone was a philosopher by his/her (historically embedded) language, methods, and objects of analysis. Second, disciplines are sometimes understood as social organizations, producing standards of membership that are simultaneously epistemological and political.[2] Finally, disciplines are framed as systems through which subjects are shaped. Janet Parker argues that "to be engaged in a discipline is to shape, and be shaped by, the subject, to be part of a scholarly community, to engage with fellow students—to become 'disciplined.'"[3] Readers of Michel Foucault will recognize the notion of how border maintenance can seem repressive while in fact being productive, and how the policing of borders might function as a means to create the "insides" which are bounded. Of course, all of these definitions of disciplinarity fail to map fully the practices through which disciplines form themselves. By extension, if interdisciplinarity relies on some conception of disciplinarity, it will be difficult to define, as well.[4]

Although I frequently hear philosophers characterize the discipline of philosophy as the mother of all interdisciplinary work, I believe that in fact the discipline bears all three of the general tendencies I've outlined above: discursive histories that delineate "insides" and "outsides," social formations structuring and structured by standards of power-inflected knowledge-making, and rigorous boundary-maintenance enacted through forming appropriately disciplined subjects. To the extent that boundary-protecting practices are important to certain forms of philosophical work, "philosophy" as a discipline defines who counts as "in" in part through refusing particular forms and subjects that identify as multi- or interdisciplinary. Logical analysis is philosophical; poetry or qualitative sociological data collection are not. Philosophy's refusal of certain forms of interdisciplinary pollination has the twined result of limiting the subjects of philosophy (who does it and what they do) while producing what I will argue is "whiteness as method." We end up with a depressingly flat, homogenous, limited field of study dominated by white men and those who—somehow—win enough recognition to survive. I care about this because I believe that philosophers and philosophy ought (and therefore can!) do more than reproduce a moribund, irrelevant, systemically racist discipline.

Of course, only *some* forms of interdisciplinarity are refused or disciplined out of the discipline. There are significant interdisciplinary projects that "count" as properly philosophical: the X-Phi/experimental philosophy approach, or work at the intersection of philosophy of mind and cognitive science, for example. Though I don't have real data to back either of the following claims up, it seems to me that interdisciplinary work is relatively easily accepted that crosses the "hard" science/philosophy boundary, often with reference to quantitative experiments, as well as work along the border with linguistics.[5] Interdisciplinary approaches promising "empirical grounding" through experimental data gathered using methods from the social (and non-social) sciences are held out as offering real-world confirmation of moral intuitions. It thus seems that only some sorts of interdisciplinarity cause a theoretical work to fall outside the bounds of philosophy as conventionally defined. Attention to gender has often done this (though perhaps this tide is turning); attention to race even more often. Methods can have a similar boundary-defining effect: literary analysis or critical historiography tend to move one "out of bounds." Perhaps it is mere coincidence that these bounds enclose and endorse philosophical objects and methods that do not challenge the racialized hierarchies of attention prevalent in much of the discipline: I don't think so.

Angela Davis has argued for a connection between the object and method arising out of women of color feminisms. She posits that the practice of theorizing across social and political difference in activist anti-racist spaces produces not only new objects of study and knowledge, but new methods.[6] An activist collective in California, the LA Crew, reframes intersectionality as "unbreakapartability," or the idea that "oppressions (racism, sexism, homophobia, class oppression, able-ism, etc.) are intertwined and, when they intersect with each other, they actually create a different experience than the sum of their parts."[7] In order to study these intertwined experiences adequately, one would need to draw on many disciplinary frameworks, as well as on frameworks outside of existing disciplines. There are thus important historical reasons why conceptions of interdisciplinarity emerged from the situated, subjective experience of people who experienced multiple forms of mutually-constituting oppressions. Their theoretical understanding of any given measure of the socially-produced suffering associated with class, gender, sexuality, or race was inextricably inflected by the other categories. Intersectional analysis would then have a more-than-accidental connection with interdisciplinarity.

Since we are all in fact thoroughly entangled in webs of social relations, even when some of us move through them with the greatest of ease, it is not only people subjected to multiple forms of oppression who will need to take up this sort of analysis if they want to think about the (always-social) human world. Whether someone benefits from oppressive social relations without understanding their own complicity in them or whether they actively promulgate racist social relations (for example), we would need an intersectional analysis to think about their experience well. Of course, only people who hold particular sorts of politics will pursue intersectional analysis, and the interdisciplinary approach I believe goes along with it. Only very particular philosophers are interested in either—and perhaps even fewer still work in philosophy.

Davis's gesture toward the connection between unbreakapartability or intersectionality and interdisciplinarity is borne out in non-philosophical works trying to be adequate to a topic like "sexual violence and colonization." Consider Andrea Smith's book *Conquest: Sexual Violence and American Indian Genocide*.[8] It may not be possible to talk about how sexual and colonial violence are connected without, as Smith does, drawing on disciplines from Literature to Sociology to History to Economics to Religious Studies and more. Methods appropriate to works in each discipline come along with the inquiry. When Smith discusses the sexualization of knowledge in academic appropriations of Native American spirituality, she uses hermeneutic Biblical analysis. When she analyses the effects of boarding schools on indigenous people and communities, she uses interview findings and fine-grained historical methods along with readings of pertinent legal precedents for the possibility of reparations. Smith's work is a good example of the use of a commitment to intersectional methods, which can make palpable disallowed or marginalized knowledges. Experiences like those of many indigenous women on Turtle Island have been culturally, historically, and epistemologically erased in the process of colonization. Doing justice to these histories and experiences may require finding evidence that the very methods used in disciplines like philosophy obscure, erase, or distort.[9] I believe that much writing that attempts to take intersectionality or unbreakapartability seriously also ends up being interdisciplinary in approach.

The reverse is not true. Interdisciplinary writing is not always or even usually intersectional—interdisciplinary writing can and does ignore all sorts of social relations. Theorists of interdisciplinarity suggest ways of thinking about disciplinarity that might illuminate the connections between whiteness and some, canonical, philosophical method. The boundary-maintenance work so necessary to discipline formation is grounded on practical matters: academic departments work hard to maintain a sense of "turf," protecting tenure-lines, securing funding, and producing a departmental profile in order to attract students. The more interesting and less visible boundary-maintenance work is conceptual: through systems of certification and validation, professionalization, habitus-creation, and classification, some things stand as "proper" to the discipline. The work of delineating what is within and what without a given discipline thus calls for a concern with boundaries, purity, and markers of belonging defined by some measure of sufficient rigor.

Notice a few salient analogies with the work of policing and producing whiteness. Just as certain core forms of philosophy are concerned with conceptual purity, by means of which we might tell what's not philosophy, whiteness is consistently defined against what is not white. The logic of purity is at once central to philosophy and whiteness; the connection between these is both historical and structural. Whiteness names an operation through which some things are defined as good, proper, pure, and other things are framed as dirty, spoiled, impure, muddy, and category-busting. Thus, whiteness produces people as within or outside bounds through methodological parsing, clarifying, classifying. The classificatory obsessions through which colonial administrations, in particular, worked to define whiteness against contamination by racialized others [10] were grounded on deeper and more philosophical classificatory work.[11] Fear of "miscegenation" in particular has structured the classificatory operations through which whiteness defends its boundaries.

María Lugones has compellingly articulated the importance of theorizing ambiguity and *mestizaje* in these terms. Drawing on the image of separating egg whites from egg yolks in order to make mayonnaise, she writes:

> When I think of *mestizaje*, I think both of separation as curdling, an exercise in impurity, of separation as splitting, an exercise in purity. I think of the attempt at control exercised by those who possess both power and the categorical eye and who attempt to split everything impure (as in egg white and egg yolk) for the purposes of control .... *Mestizaje* defies control through simultaneously asserting the impure, curdled multiple state and rejecting fragmentation into pure parts. In this play of assertions and rejection, the mestiza is unclassifiable, unmanageable.[12]

Extending this analysis, I want to suggest that the disciplining of philosophical boundaries has come out of a fear of monstrous or unpredictable mixing. Lugones makes an historical connection between the logic of purity and the logic of colonization; modern philosophy and European colonization emerge at the same time and to some significant extent constitute and support one another. As whiteness must defend itself against miscegenation, philosophy must defend itself against mixed subjects and their associated loss of control. One way disciplinary purity has been maintained, to the extent that it has, is by delimiting the methods deemed appropriate for philosophical work. Another is by restricting subjects to which one might attend.

"Appropriate Subjects for Philosophical Inquiry"

I take the title for this chapter from a conversation between George Yancy and Angela Davis. In it, Yancy asks Davis how African-American philosophers can "come to see their departments as sites for struggle." Davis answers: "I think that is an important question in the US, particularly in philosophy departments where race is not always considered an appropriate subject for philosophical inquiry, especially given the popular philosophical emphasis on color blindness in contemporary US society."[13] Not only might some methods fall outside conventional conceptions of proper philosophical approaches, then, some topics might be beyond the pale.[14] I have only anecdotal evidence for my sense that race is implicitly understood as an especially inappropriate subject for philosophical inquiry, but I believe that Davis is correct in her observation about this question. Further, to the extent that some objects call for currently illegible or unsanctioned methods, color blindness might be a philosophical as well as sociological problem. It is notable that when philosophers of the past have considered what we now call "race," such work is considered historically-situated, non-philosophical, and a product of their times. Often this happens simultaneously with a conceptualization of their non-racializing work as foundational philosophy as we practice it today.[15] In other words: racializing and racist work by philosophers is seen as non-philosophical, while work that does not discuss race is (sometimes) philosophical.

Consider Charles Mills's generative discussion of philosophy as a dynamic system that reproduces its own whiteness. Mills specifies that this dynamic in philosophy is structured not primarily by "the uncontroversial whiteness of the skin of most of its practitioners but what could be called, more contestably, the *conceptual* or *theoretical* whiteness of the discipline."[16] Some things that are taken to have nothing at all to do with racial formation, things that are seen as appropriate subjects for philosophical inquiry, turn out to be very much implicated in this dynamic system of racial exclusion. Two aspects of Mills's discussion are important to my thinking here: first, his discussion of the production of generality and abstraction, and second, his understanding of social ontologies as significant for philosophical work.

Generality and abstraction can be useful philosophical tools. After all, saying anything about what sorts of ethical or political systems we ought to aim for, standards for justification, or other "normal" philosophical concerns can involve abstracting from particulars toward something that can apply to any relevant subject.[17] Philosophers concerned with racial injustice, among others, will want to call on such standards. Mills is not disputing the use of these tools altogether. Rather, he highlights the actual particularism of ostensibly generic claims in the practice of philosophy. In moral philosophy, for example, founding fathers described moral ideals of individual liberty while ignoring the fact of slavery and stipulating that women, indigenous peoples, and others were ineligible for citizenship. In the US today, these classificatory recognitions of personhood under the state continue: there is a significant part of the population subject to what Angela Davis calls "civil death," such as people convicted with felonies who are permanently barred from voting, for example. Mills argues that it is "not merely that the ideal was not always attained but that, more fundamentally, *this was never actually the ideal in the first place. A lot of moral* philosophy will then seem to be based on pretense, the claim that these were the principles that people strove to uphold, when in fact the real principles were the racially exclusivist ones."[18] In political philosophy, similarly, Mills discusses the production of presumed commonality and generalism:

The only slavery Rawls mentions is that of antiquity, while Nozick's thoughts on the possible need to rectificatory reparations occupy a few sentences and an endnote reference. So the focus on "ideal theory" (Rawls) here will seem in part ideological, a steering away from disquieting questions and unresolved issues. It is a generalism, and abstractness, which is covertly particularistic and concrete, in that it is really based on a white experience for which these realities were not central, not that important.[19]

The issue, then, is what to do with pretentions to a general, ideal theory that in fact is deeply partial. A broader question, more fully fleshed out in the work of theorists like Donna Haraway and Sandra Harding, would concern the degree to which knowledge will always be partial and situated. Mills argues that: "One can no longer speak with quite such assurance of *the* problems of philosophy; rather these are problems for *particular* groups of human beings, and for others there will be different kinds of problems that are far more urgent."[20] And if the particular group of people one belongs to is socially situated as white, disciplinary boundaries might well express or even define the concerns of white worldviews.

Starting philosophical work from a situated perspective would transform how and what we do within the discipline. Mills illustrates this point with a conception of social ontologies, attending particularly to what he calls "non-Cartesian *sums*." The Cartesian *sum* is familiar: that isolated, only-temporarily self-doubting knower from whom spring whole systems of knowledge validation, theology, and conceptions of the body and mind. This way of being is, Mills argues, "represented as a allegedly universal predicament." But if we consider a non-Cartesian *sum*, such as the narrator of Ralph Ellison's *Invisible Man*, a very different set of concerns and philosophical issues arise. Centrally, his philosophical problems will begin not from the point of view of attempting to first doubt and then prove his existence, but from the point of view of being socially created as subhuman—he is ontologically subject to the power of a gaze that denies his existence while also holding social power.[21] The *sum* in question here, then, "will be a *sum* that is metaphysical not in the Cartesian sense but in the sense of challenging a *social* ontology; not the consequent of a proof but the beginning of an affirmation of one's self-worth, one's reality as a person, and one's militant insistence that others recognize it also."[22] Understanding racial formations in terms of the social ontologies they encode would create a situation in which "the kind of problems with which you must grapple, the existential plight, the array of concepts found useful, the set of paradigmatic dilemmas, the range of concerns, is going to be significantly different from that of the mainstream white philosopher."[23]

Significant occlusions structure philosophy as a discipline. They are not limited to racialized abstractions; partitioned social ontologies have also to do with ability and disability, heteronormativity, and gender formation—among others. But all of these categories are racialized, and in ways that bear the marks of the reproduction of whiteness specifically. Given the operations through which the specificity of white racial formation is made to stand in for general, universal experience, it is no surprise that work on race is rarely considered properly philosophical. Nor is it a surprise that it is so very possible to do work on subjects that are in fact deeply racialized—like individual liberty or citizenship—as though race had nothing to do with the question. This topical racialization extends, I would argue, into more structural characteristics of the whiteness of philosophy: only some questions will be possible to ask and only some methods understood as legitimate ways forward.[24] And all of this will help to determine who ends up practicing philosophy—which subjects subsist in the discipline as philosophers.

Method and the Philosopher

Some significant work has been done to make sense of the current dismal statistics on the status of women in philosophy. For example, the American Philosophical Association recently issued a report detailing the gender distribution of hires into philosophy departments in the US.[25] I, and a number of my fellow white women junior philosophy colleagues, found this piece a useful mirror to our experience in struggling to find our footing in the discipline.[26] I want to focus more closely on what this resonance occludes. In many of the blogs, emails, and conversations I've encountered about the APA report, people tend to slide between the locutions "women in philosophy" and "women and minorities in philosophy." It's crucial to explicate how women's experience around things like potential childbearing and rearing structure our experience of academe as a chilly clime in gendered ways. However, a focus on womanhood as a racially unmarked category may reinforce a distinction between white womanhood and racialization, thereby reinscribing whiteness as a philosophical norm at precisely the site of contesting gendered norms within the discipline. "Minority" seems to signal racialized otherness (though perhaps also along forms of disability, class position, and sexuality). Thus the slide from "women in philosophy" to "women and minorities in philosophy" (even while marking that there are other kinds of minority experience in the discipline) elides both the existence of racialized women in philosophy and racialized men in the discipline. This tells us something important about white womanhood and philosophy and about the whiteness of feminist philosophy. Failing to attend to the real differences between white women, racialized women, racialized men, and other people who fall into the category of the philosophical minority replicates implicitly the effects of more explicit decisions to focus attention on winning a place at the table for white women in particular.[27]

Philosophical classificatory methods in works such as Kant's *Anthropology* have delineated the rational potentials present in different sorts of people. Though these classifications have distinguished—and still do distinguish (consider work on the permissibility of killing severely disabled infants[28])— between different sorts of beings based on whether they can attain full rationality based on disability or sex, a persistent theme has been to decide whether someone can attain standards of rationality based on racial classification. Women, on these schemes, as Genevieve Lloyd and others discuss, were variously considered as (potentially) able to reach the status of reason.

As Charles Mills observes, while the position of women was debated and theorized, many philosophers in the Anglo-American canon simply ignored questions of race. This epistemology of ignorance constitutes what Mills describes as the conceptual or theoretical whiteness of philosophy, with practical outcomes. What Mills calls the "likely feeling of alienness, strangeness, of not being entirely at home in this conceptual world"[29] results in actual people leaving or being forced out of philosophy as a discipline.

Such expulsions may take the shape of conceptual impossibilities ("how is this philosophy?") or be the more quotidian result of disciplining ("this candidate is very interesting, but what she's doing simply doesn't cover the traditional teaching needs of our department"). Either way, the maintenance of philosophical whiteness comes down to questions of method: how do "we" do what we do, and what does that have to do with who we are? A too-simple answer to this question might be: white men like to argue with each other *in a particular way*; white men have power in the discipline of philosophy; they define philosophy as arguing with each other *in a particular way*.[30] Let me flip this progression in order to argue something related but different: our methods constitute us as intellectuals; to the extent that methodological commitments structure our approach to the work we do, they shape the kind of intellectual subjectivity we can inhabit. Thus, restricting what "counts" as philosophical method to very particular approaches will either torque the subjectivities it is possible to inhabit or cause people who take up unsanctioned methods to leave the discipline. It is thus important to ask some interlinked questions: What counts as method? Who has the power to bestow recognition of what counts? How does methodogical orthodoxy shift? Standards of justification, questions of "fit," and assessments of rigor are always also methodological questions.

In philosophy as a discipline, the general indicators of characterizing boundary-maintenance work as discipline-formation are sharpened. Because philosophical method itself is often understood as reducible to the pursuit of conceptual clarity and rigor, the disciplining of philosophy may itself tend toward the purist form of disciplinarity. Where other disciplines have methods like "quantitative analysis," many forms of philosophy aim to state things clearly, determine the logical connections among terms in arguments, and frame arguments such that their truth might suggest reasons for belief. Of course, part of the problem here is that this method really only describes some philosophy—but I would argue that it is the practitioner of those methods beyond this style of work who is most often asked how her project is philosophical. Dominant analytic philosophical method shares a lot with methods through which disciplines are made: clearly classify insides and outsides, pare away ambiguity, trace lines of descent. The difficulty in making claims about any of this, of course, is that to define "philosophical method" in these ways performs precisely the type of operation I am critiquing here.[31]

If the category of "philosophy" is at heart normative, I see the current conditions for successful instantiation of philosophical subjectivity to be threefold: first, philosophy proper often signals an intellectual heritage, second, it signals particular objects, third, it is often expressed using particular analytical skills. First, then, is an allegiance to purist lineages of philosophy, marked by familial-like lines of intellectual descent legitimated through institutional structures: philosophy departments hire almost exclusively people who have completed graduate training in philosophy departments taught by people who themselves underwent such training. Insofar as our methods arise from our training, these lineages will prepare philosophers to do philosophy in line with accepted philosophical methods. I regard this as a non-contentious claim; indeed, even the most wild-eyed reformer of philosophical orthodoxies might argue for the benefits attached to systems of institutional validation and credentialing. I think we should contest allegiances to philosophical lineages in this mode to the degree they result in not only the reproduction of particular bodies in philosophical departments—disproportionately white men, in North American contexts—but to the degree that they produce politically conservative restrictions in philosophy in its objects and methods.

Second, consider the extent to which only some objects are considered properly philosophical: objects that cannot be investigated using reason alone, that are mixed or contradictory, or that in other ways resist specific boundaries may cause the people examining those objects to not "count" as real philosophers. If I am right that many of the most interesting questions in current social and political philosophy are intersectional, they will be improper objects of analysis: it will be difficult at the very least to do justice to them within the bounds of accepted philosophical practices. I think this is one reason that even within feminist philosophy there is so little instantiation of the call to take multiple forms of oppression into account when theorizing the social relations we call "gender," for example. Finally, to the extent that philosophical methods tend toward analytical skills that give priority to conceptual purity, clearly defined categories, fungability, and universalizability, we ought to worry about whether these methods have more content than they purport. Since there is real resonance between the methods defining much "proper" philosophy and the methods through which whiteness is discerned and defined, we ought specifically worry about the degree to which the method of philosophy in effect produces whiteness as method.

Given the racialized effects of boundary-maintenance in defining the discipline of philosophy, how ought white women philosophers, admittedly embattled within the discipline, understand our own capacity to stay "in" this fight? A further question: if our (my) capacity to create space for feminist philosophy, for women in the discipline, and for philosophy on racial formation is predicated on systemic racism, as I believe it is, what is to be done?

I am not Lenin, and so I don't have a firm answer to this question. But since firm answers and an associated "hardening of the categories"[32] are precisely some of the problems with philosophy I am trying to lay out, I turn instead to starting points. A useful starting point is George Yancy's conception of the *philosopher as troublemaker*:

> The philosopher as troublemaker, inflected through my own current philosophical projects and sense of mission, suggests one who is *not* content with the philosophical status quo, the strict policing of philosophical borders, the rigidity of historical and philosophical nostalgia, the encouragement of curricular calcification through the stipulation of myopic criteria for what constitutes philosophy and who its key players are. . . .[33]

I would like those of us who worry hard about whiteness and the discipline of philosophy to become troublemakers in this sense. I would like us to claim what we do as philosophy. I would like us to work practically and conceptually to transform the terrain on which we struggle. I think of a third-hand story I have of Gayatri Spivak, one of the philosophical troublemakers who inspire me.[34] Apparently a student once asked her that old question: "I'm just a white guy, what can I do?" and she answered: "*Rage against the script history has dealt you.*" I would like to pair that statement in all its ambiguity and all its affective charge with a still-useful chestnut from Marx, who observed that we "make history, but not in circumstances of [our] own choosing." Given the circumstances we find ourselves in, changing the discipline of philosophy will require those of us who care, to try to be and to think about and nurture inappropriate subjects.

Notes

1. Quoted in Kathryn Shailer, "Interdisciplinarity in a Disciplinary Universe: A Review of Key Issues," Faculty of Liberal Studies, Ontario College of Art & Design http://www.brocku.ca/secretariat/senate/agendae/2005-05-18/528-2c.pdf, 3 (accessed May 5, 2009).
2. See Liora Salter and Alison Hearn, *Outside the Lines: Issues in Interdisciplinary Research* (Montreal: McGill-Queen's University Press, 1996) and John D. Aram, "Concepts of Interdisciplinarity: Configurations of Knowledge and Action," *Human Relations* 57, no. 4 (2004): 379–412.
3. Jan Parker, "A New Disciplinarity: Communities of Knowledge, Learning and Practice," *Teaching in Higher Education* 4 (2002): 373–386, quotation on 374.
4. Although I will not here give more discussion of theories on interdisciplinarity, my thinking about it has been shaped by John D. Aram, "Concepts of Interdisciplinarity" and Angelique Chettiparamb, *Interdisciplinarity: A literature review*. http://www.llas.ac.uk/resourcdownloads.aspx?resourceid=2892&filename=interdisciplinarity_literature_review.pdf (accessed May 5, 2009); Kathryn Shailer, "Interdisciplinarity in a Disciplinary Universe"; Julie Klein Thomson, *Interdisciplinarity: History, Theory, and Practice* (Detroit: Wayne State University Press, 1990); William Newell and William J. Green "Defining and Teaching Interdisciplinary Studies" from *Interdisciplinarity: Essays from the Literature* (New York: College Entrance Examination Board, 1998); P. Weingart and N. Stehr, eds., *Practising Interdisciplinarity* (London: University of Toronto Press, 2000); Susan Sherwin, "Introduction" and "Relational Approaches to Autonomy" from *The Politics of Women's Health: Exploring Agency and Autonomy* (Philadelphia: Temple University Press, 1998); Marilyn Strathern, *Commons and Borderlands: Working Papers on Interdisciplinarity, Accountability and the Flow of Knowledge* (Oxford: Sean Kingston Publishing, 2004); and Liora Salter and Alison Hearn, *Outside the Lines*, among others.
5. I am thinking of Shaun Gallagher's, Alva Noë's, or Jason Stanley's work, among others. See, for example, Shaun Gallagher, *How the Body Shapes the Mind* (Oxford: Oxford University Press, 2005); Alva Noë, *Perception as Action* (Cambridge: MIT Press, 2004); Jason Stanley (with Timothy Williamson), "Knowing How," *The Journal of Philosophy* 98.8 (2001): 411–44.
6. Angela Y. Davis, "Legacies of Women of Color Feminisms." Paper presented at the Center for Cultural Studies Colloquium Series, University of California, Santa Cruz, October 6, 2004.
7. LA Crew, "Ideas in Action: An LA Story," *Left Turn* no. 31 (Jan/Feb 2009): 50–54, quotation on 54.
8. Andrea Smith, *Conquest: Sexual Violence and American Indian Genocide* (Cambridge, MA: South End Press, 2005).
9. Thanks to Alison Bailey for comments on this point.
10. See: Sander L. Gilman, *Difference and Pathology: Stereotypes of Sexuality, Race, and Madness* (Ithaca: Cornell University Press, 1985); Virginia Dominguez, *White by Definition: Social Classification in Creole Louisiana* (New Brunswick, NJ: Rutgers University Press, 1994); Anne McClintock, *Imperial Leather: Race, Gender, and Sexuality in the Colonial Contest* (New York: Routledge, 1995); Ann Laura Stoler, *Race and the Education of Desire: Foucault's History of Sexuality and the Colonial Order of Things* (Durham, NC: Duke University Press, 1995); Robert J. C. Young, *Colonial*

Desire: Hybridity in Theory, Culture and Race (New York: Routledge, 1995); Siobhan Somerville, *Queering the Color Line: Race and the Invention of Homosexuality in American Culture* (Durham, NC: Duke University Press, 2000).

11. See Robert Bernasconi and Tommy Lee Lott, eds., *The Idea of Race* (Indianapolis, Indiana: Hackett Publishing, 2000); Robert Bernasconi, "Will the Real Kant Please Stand Up: The Challenge of Enlightenment Racism to the Study of the History of Philosophy," *Radical Philosophy* 117 (2003): 13–22 and "Who Invented the Concept of Race? Kant's Role in the Enlightenment Construction of Race," in *Race* ed. Robert Bernasconi (Malden, MA: Blackwell Publishers, 2001), 11–36; Emmanuel Chukwudi Eze, *Race and the Enlightenment: A Reader* (Cambridge, MA: Wiley-Blackwell, 1997), among others.

12. María Lugones, *Pilgrimages/Peregrinajes: Theorizing Coalition against Multiple Oppressions* (Lanham, MD: Rowman & Littlefield, 2003), 123.

13. George Yancy, "Interview with Angela Davis" in *Women of Color and Philosophy: A Critical Reader*, ed. Naomi Zack (Malden, MA: Wiley-Blackwell, 2000), 144.

14. I reference the genealogy of "pales" and what it is to be beyond the pale intentionally—the concept names the stakes used to mark boundaries, places that have been historically defended, like the 15th century Pale the English defended near Dublin, and also situations in which people are restricted to certain domains, such as the Pale of Settlement for Jews in Tsarist Russia. Boundaries can enable; usually they restrict.

15. I am thinking of discussions I've participated in about Hegel and phrenology or Kant and "physical geography." Thanks also to Adam Hefty and Surya Parekh for their thinking on these issues.

16. Charles W. Mills, *Blackness Visible: Essays on Philosophy and Race* (Ithaca, NY: Cornell University Press, 1998), 2.

17. See Charles Mills, "'Ideal Theory' as Ideology," *Hypatia* 20, no. 3 (Summer 2005): 165–84; Sophia Isako Wong "The Moral Personhood of Individuals Labeled 'Mentally Retarded': A Rawlsian Response to Nussbaum," *Social Theory and Practice: An International and Interdisciplinary Journal of Social Philosophy* 33, no. 4 (October 2007): 579–94; Lisa Tessman, ed., *Feminist Ethics and Social and Political Philosophy: Theorizing the Non-Ideal* (Dordrecht: Kluwer/Springer, 2009).

18. Mills, *Blackness Visible*, 4.

19. Mills, *Blackness Visible*, 5.

20. Mills, *Blackness Visible*, 10.

21. Thanks to George Yancy for clarifying this idea.

22. Mills, *Blackness Visible*, 9.

23. Mills, *Blackness Visible*, 7.

24. Another way to think about the picture I'm sketching of the work of whiteness in philosophy is in terms of a different sort of algorithm, suggested to me by Scott Neigh: a broader claim we can read Mills making here is that much philosophical work is built on abstracting away from the really existing social world, even in areas of philosophy (social and political, say) that aim to explain or work with the "real" world. To the extent that this approach structures philosophical worldviews, doing philosophy as if the world mattered might also cause one to fall outside the boundary.

25. http://www.apaonline.org/governance/committees/women/0708EmploymentStudy.aspx (accessed May 5, 2009).

26. See http://www.apaonline.org/governance/committees/women/0708Employment Study.aspx (accessed May 4, 2009). Also significant is Sally Haslanger's piece on gender and philosophy publications. Sally Haslanger, "Changing the Ideology and Culture of Philosophy: Not by Reason Alone," *Hypatia* 23, no. 2, (2008): 210–223.

27. Recall, for comparison, how white suffragists in the U.S. mobilized white womanhood in their pursuit of the vote. Angela Davis lays out how at key junctures the pursuit of the vote for white women was given priority over abolitionist aspirations, for either explicitly racist reasons (white women were conceptualized as useful in pro-slavery states because they were educated and would "vote with their race") or on "grounds of expediency" (it was too much, politically, to strive for emancipation for women, slaves, and immigrants all together) (Angela Davis, *Women, Race, and Class* [New York: Vintage, 1983] 112 & passim). There is nothing like this in the current discourse about improving the numbers of women in philosophy—among other things, the stakes are much lower. However, to the extent that we focus on the plight of "women" while rendering that category as racially unmarked, I believe we white women repeat the mistakes of our white foremothers. This operation may happen without explicit discussion.

28. Perhaps the most widely cited philosopher on this question is Peter Singer, who has argued for the moral permissibility of killing disabled people. See, for example, *Practical Ethics* (Cambridge: Cambridge University Press, 1993).

29. Mills, *Blackness Visible*, 3.

30. A less-simple reflection on masculinism and philosophy can be found in Norman Swartz's "Philosophy as Blood Sport" 1994 (http://www.sfu.ca/philosophy/swartz/blood _sport.htm) (accessed May 4, 2009). Janice Moulton offers a parallel consideration in "A Paradigm of Philosophy: The Adversary Method" in *Women, Knowledge, and Reality: Explorations in Feminist Philosophy*, ed. Ann Garry and Marilyn Pearsall (New York: Routledge, 1992), 5–20.

31. Susan Sherwin's important reflections on methodology are instructive here: "Philosophical Methodology and Feminist Methodology: Are They Compatible?" in *Women, Knowledge, and Reality: Explorations in Feminist Philosophy*, ed. Ann Garry & Marilyn Pearsall (New York: Routledge, 1992), 20–35.

32. I take this phrase from Donna Haraway, an inveterate resistor of over-calcified categorical work, in conversation.

33. George Yancy, "Introduction," in *Philosophy in Multiple Voices*, ed. George Yancy (Lanham, MD: Rowman & Littlefield, 2007), 5.

34. Adam Hefty related this story to me, in conversation.

7

Color in the Theory of Colors?
Or: Are Philosophers' Colors all White?

Berit Brogaard, University of Missouri, St. Louis

Introduction: White Theories of Color

Let's say that a philosophical theory is white just in case it treats the perspective of the white (perhaps Western male) as objective.[1] The potential dangers of proposing or defending white theories are two-fold. First, if not all of reality is objective, a fact which I take to be established beyond doubt,[2] then white theories could well turn out to be false.[3] A white theory is unwarranted (and indeed false) when it treats non-objective reality as objective. Second, by proposing or defending unwarranted white theories one thereby treats the perspective of the non-white as faulty, and this in turn serves to perpetuate the distorted representation of whites as superior to non-whites. As David Owen puts it:

> [whiteness] serves to underwrite perceptions, understandings, justifications and explanations of the social order that perpetuate distortions in the social system that are a legacy of our nation's history . . . what is associated with whiteness becomes defined as natural, normal or mainstream.[4]

In this chapter I will focus on a particular class of philosophical theories, viz. philosophical theories of color. I argue that realist theories of the objectivist variety (and indeed some non-realist theories) are unjustifiably white: They aim at explaining away cross-ethnic (and cross-gender) variation in color perception and cognition by attributing unwarranted and oppressive color vision deficiencies to people of color and women.

The first part of the chapter is concerned with showing that objectivists must subscribe to the following three hypotheses: (i) there is a perceptual norm, (ii) perceivers who do not satisfy the perceptual norm suffer from color vision deficiencies, and (iii) non-whites and females suffer from color vision deficiencies. The second part of the chapter is concerned with showing that these hypotheses are unwarranted. At the end of the chapter I draw some conclusions as to how whiteness is embedded within the conceptual tools of theories of perception more generally.

My argument runs as follows. Objectivists hold that there is a perceptual norm. The perceptual norm is satisfied only by those who do not suffer from color vision deficiencies. Some perceivers plausibly suffer from color vision deficiencies. Blind people might fall into this category.[5] But matters a bit more complicated than this. As we will see below, evidence indicates that whites and people of color perceive colors differently. But if this is so, and objectivism is right, then perceivers in at least one of the two groups fail to satisfy the perceptual norm. But if people who do not satisfy the perceptual norm suffer from color vision deficiencies, then either people of color or whites suffer from color vision deficiencies. Some color scientists hypothesize that chronic exposure to UV-light causes the eye to age. If these UV-caused changes in the eye are passed down through the generations, and if people of color descend from perceivers living in areas close to the equator, then people of color are likely to have an "aged" eye. As far as the aforementioned color scientists are concerned, an "aged" eye is a deficient eye. So, it is concluded that people of color suffer from color vision deficiencies. It is not difficult to conjure up similar arguments in support of attributing color vision deficiencies to women. So, it is tempting to conclude that the perceptual norm is satisfied only by white males. However, for reasons I will get into below, these lines of argument are unsound. Hence, attributions of color vision deficiencies to people of color and women are unwarranted.

Attributions of color vision deficiencies to people of color and women are also oppressive because, by taking white males to constitute the perceptual norm, one thereby implicitly endorses a distorted world view associating the natural, normal and well-functioning with whiteness and maleness. As George Yancy puts it for the case of whiteness, "Whiteness is that according to which what is nonwhite is rendered Other, marginal, ersatz, strange, native, inferior, uncivilized, ugly."[6] Objectivists inadvertently attribute unwarranted and oppressive color vision deficiencies to people of color vis-à-vis those (white males) who constitute the perceptual norm. I say "inadvertently," because it is not normally the case that objectivists intend to endorse a distorted world view associating the natural, normal and well-functioning with whiteness and maleness. In many cases objectivists do not even recognize that these sorts of attributions follow from their view. Despite being inadvertent, however, the implicit division of human beings into perceptually superior white males and perceptually inferior people of color and females is still highly problematic philosophically, ethically and socially. Just as the inadvertence of the sort of male favouritism that is common practice in our profession does not make male favouritism reasonable or just, so the inadvertence of attributions of color vision deficiencies to people of color and women does not render these kinds of attributions unproblematic.

The consequences of endorsing a distorted world view associating naturalness, normality, and optimality with whiteness and maleness are far-reaching. The consequences needn't just amount to inequalities in the distribution of social and economic goods but can also amount to differences in how women and people of color are perceived, approached and evaluated in terms of intelligence or moral character. George Yancy, for example, describes how his skin color gives rise to inadvertent misperceptions of his moral character.[7] Due to the negative value associated with the color of his skin whites sometimes inadvertently respond to him as if he were threatening or wicket. As Yancy puts it, "whiteness comes replete with its assumptions for what to expect of a Black body (or nonwhite body), how dangerous and unruly it is, how unlawful, criminal and hypersexual it is."[8] Associating the white body or, what is more relevant to the topic of this chapter, the white visual system with the normal, superior and well-functioning is perhaps rarely intentional but may have deeply regrettable consequences nonetheless.

Color Objectivism

Before stating my argument to the conclusion that positing a perceptual norm has unwarranted consequences I shall begin with a quick overview of the philosophical commitments of objectivist theories of color. Objectivism is committed to the view that, relative to the world as a whole and the human species as a whole, there is a fact of the matter as to which perceivers and viewing conditions are normal. Given objectivism, then, there is a perceptual norm, and there are human perceivers that satisfy the norm, and human perceivers who don't. Those who don't are often mistaken about the colors of objects.

Here are three examples of objectivist theories: objectivist reflectance physicalism, objectivist dispositionalism, and objectivist primitivism. Objectivist reflectance physicalism takes the colors to be dispositions to reflect certain proportions of the incident light or, more plausibly, equivalence classes of these, for instance, disjunctions of those reflectances that give rise to certain phenomenal effects in normal human perceivers in normal viewing conditions.[9] Objectivist dispositionalism takes the colors to be dispositions to give rise to certain phenomenal effects in normal human perceivers in normal viewing conditions.[10] And objectivist primitivism takes the colors to be primitive non-relational and non-disjunctive color properties that are possessed by objects and revealed directly in the color perception of normal perceivers in normal viewing conditions. When revealed they are the representational equivalents of phenomenal color properties.[11]

Even setting aside the evidence for variation in color perception across different groups of perceivers, difficulties arise when we attempt to get clear on what the perceptual norm is. What exactly is a normal perceiver? Some cases are perhaps clear enough. If you can't see, you don't satisfy the perceptual norm. A tree doesn't satisfy the perceptual norm. A blind person might not satisfy it either. However, beyond the more obvious cases, it is hard to say what it takes to satisfy or fail to satisfy the norm. A normal perceiver presumably is not one who is sufficiently similar to perceivers in a uniform majority group. First off, it is highly doubtful that there is a uniform majority group. Supposing that there is seems to evade the question to some extent. Second, even if there is a uniform majority group, it is doubtful that one satisfies the perceptual norm in virtue of being a member of that group. Suppose that due to a nuclear event only 5% of the global population survives, including the 8% of the male population who are color blind. Despite the fact that the number of color blinds would exceed that of non-color blinds in this scenario I suppose objectivists would not want to say that a normal perceiver in the envisaged scenario is a color blind perceiver.

Rather, normality is somehow linked to non-defectiveness in humans. To a first approximation, a normal perceiver is a perceiver whose color vision works optimally for a human. The color vision of color blinds, for example, does not work optimally for humans, so they do not count as normal perceivers. This is a first approximation only. As we will see below, it is not at all clear that there are any optimal perceptual systems. There is too much variation in color perception for that to be the case.

In the next section I will review some of the evidence for variation in color perception. I will then move onto the question of how objectivists might attempt to accommodate this evidence.

The Objection from Color Variability

Variations in Color Perception

It would be rather surprising if there were no variation in the color experiences of individuals who pass tests for color vision normality. The number of cones (photoreceptors) in the human retina is not constant.[12] Sometimes they are present in large numbers, and sometimes they are barely present. And this difference occurs in so-called normal individuals who react in the same way to color stimuli. This suggests that there are mechanisms in the brain which somehow automatically adjust the input from the retina, and hence that variations in color perception are not purely a matter of the nature and number of the cones in the retina. It is not hard to imagine that the automatic calibration of input from the retina is not constant among different individuals, thus giving rise to different color experiences relative to the same input.

One approach to test for variation in color vision is to test for variations in color judgments and color discrimination abilities. Such tests have demonstrated vast variation in color vision across perceivers exposed to the same stimulus. Gokhan Malkoc, Paul Kay and Michael Webster,[13] for example, report vast individual differences in which stimuli are chosen as the individuals' best examples of a unique hue (e.g. red) or a binary hue (e.g. orange). One stimulus chosen as one individual's best example of orange, for example, was chosen by other individuals as their best example of red.

Malkoc et al tested only for individual differences in hue settings and not for how hue settings line up with gender, national origin, or ethnicity. But others have conducted experiments showing variations across gender, national origin, and ethnicity. I. G. H. Ishak, M. L. Daley and others and N. Louanna Furbee and others, for example, report a difference in spectral sensitivity in the short-wavelength (blue) regions of the color spectrum between Africans and Caucasians.[14] As we will see below, these differences happen to correlate with differences in the lexical entries of languages spoken by the individuals' ancestors.

Sex differences in color vision have been demonstrated on several occasions.[15] Recent studies indicate significant variance in a gene located on the X chromosome which codes for a protein that detects light in the long-wavelength (red/orange) regions of the color spectrum.[16] As women have two copies of the X-chromosome, it is possible for them to have two different versions of this gene, and hence it is possible for them to have a more fine-grained ability to discriminate light in the long-wavelength regions of the color spectrum. Women are thus potentially in a position to perceive a broader spectrum of colors in the long-wavelength regions than men.

Kimberly Jameson and her colleagues have taken the hypothesis that there are sex-differences in color vision one step further.[17] They speculate that up to 40% of women have tetrachromatic color vision. The line of argument runs as follows. Most humans have three cone types, which absorb maximally in different regions of the spectrum. So, most humans are trichromats. However, 8% males (and an insignificant number of females) have only two cone types. They are dichromats (color blind). Dichromacy results when a genetically mutant red or green photopigment gene on the X-chromosome fails to express retinal photopigment. Women who carry a deviant photopigment gene needn't be color blind but if she has a male offspring he is highly likely to have some degree of color blindness. Now, the mothers and daughters of dichromats and the mothers and daughters of males with deviant red/green photopigment genes may have a typical X chromosome and an X chromosome that carries one of the deviant red or green photopigment genes. If the normal red and green photopigments and a highly altered variant are all expressed, together with the blue photopigment (from chromosome 7), then the woman could have tetrachromatic color vision. Of course, for tetrachromacy to be present, the variant photopigment must constitute a distinct cone type, and the brain must be able to process the color signal coming from the variant photopigment.

Jameson argues that evidence for the possibility of female human tetrachromacy can be found in the animal kingdom. Female spider monkeys are normally dichromats but females possessing extra photopigment gene variants are trichromats. The gene variants allow some female monkeys to experience shades of color which others can't experience.[18] Experiments that test for tetrachromacy in women with dichromatic offspring have also been conducted.[19]

Though still preliminary, the results indicate that women who are genetically capable of expressing more than three kinds of photopigments tend to perform differently on tests involving color categorization, color naming, and color similarity judgments, thus suggesting that some women do have tetrachromatic color vision.

Variation in Color Categories across Languages

Variation in color categories across languages is another indicator of variation in color vision. Many languages are so-called "grue languages." They do not lexically discriminate blue from green but have only one basic color term that names stimuli with dominant wavelengths in the middle- and short-wavelength (blue/green) regions of the color spectrum. These include Vietnamese, Kuku-Yalanji (an aboriginal language), Tswana (a South-African language), and Zulu (a South-African language). Other languages do distinguish between blue and green but also have "mixed" color terms that name stimuli with dominant wavelengths in the middle- and short wavelength regions of the spectrum. These include Chinese, Korean, and Japanese.

Some languages are so-called "dark languages," they do not lexically discriminate blue from gray or black (e.g. Tswana), and some languages only have two words, one for dark and one for light (e.g. Dani, a New Guinean language and Lani, the Indonesian language). There are also languages that have more color terms than English. For example, Russian has a term for light blue ("goluboy") and a different term ("siniy") for medium and dark blue. Furthermore, the lexical category boundaries between the colors shift as we move across linguistic communities, for example, in Chinese light blue and green fall in the same category as do dark blue and black.

Now, linguistic variability by itself does not demonstrate variation in color perception. But it does indicate it. On the assumption that when things go right, color discourse reflects the content of color perception, differences in color discourse ought to correspond to differences in the content of color perception. Of course, differences in the color lexicon needn't indicate differences in the content of current color perception. But at least one should think that it might have done so at stages at which the language developed. If the differences in color perception are linked to differences in the visual system, and these differences are passed down through the generations, then differences in the color lexicon suggest variations in color perception.

We thus have evidence for variation in color perception from two sources: Evidence from tests for variations in color judgments and color discrimination abilities and evidence from differences in the lexical entries for color terms in different languages.

The Objection from Color Variability

Variation in color perception presents a challenge to objectivism. Objectivism presupposes that normal individuals detect the same color properties when exposed to the same stimulus in the same viewing conditions. But the empirical evidence indicates that this is false. If we take the empirical evidence at face value, individuals who pass standardized tests for normality detect different color properties when exposed to the same stimulus in the same viewing conditions. Call this *the objection from color variability*.

There are several ways for objectivists to respond to the objection from color variability. One is to insist that normal individuals are individuals whose color vision operates the way Mother Nature originally designed human color vision to work. Michael Tye entertains this line in the following excerpt:[20]

> many of today's human perceivers are not Normal. Their colour detection systems are not operating as Mother Nature originally designed. Genetic mutations have resulted in a shift in such humans' colour experiences. So, where some stimulus looks red to me and orange to you, for example, one of us is subject to a normal error or misperception, that is, an error or misperception occurring under everyday viewing conditions in a human perceiver who passes the usual perceptual tests for normality.[21]

The color vision of a colorblind male, for example, is not operating as Mother Nature originally designed human vision to operate. So, on the envisaged view, colorblind males are not normal. Hence, the deviant color experiences of colorblind males are falsidical.

There are two problems with this way of dividing humans into normal and deviant perceivers. First, there are differences in the color vision of individuals who pass standardized tests of normality. These differences suggest, not that the color vision of some of these individuals is not as Mother Nature designed it to be, but rather that Mother Nature did not design human color vision to operate in just one way. Second, the envisaged view cannot easily account for cognitive development. Suppose humans develop tetrachromatic color vision. Modern humans then can distinguish colors in, say, the red region of the visible spectrum, which their ancestors could not distinguish. But Mother Nature originally designed humans to be trichromats. So, when human tetrachromats experience two ripe tomatoes that have different reflectance tokens as having different colors, and trichromats experience them as having the same color, the experiences of the tetrachromats are falsidical. But that is odd. After all, the color vision of tetrachromats is, by all important measures, better than the color vision of trichromats.

A different way to justify classifying some individuals who pass standardized tests of normality as normal and others as deviant is to insist hardheadedly that there is a fact of the matter about normality and hence about the colors of objects. Byrne expresses the view as follows (in response to Jonathan Cohen):

> Suppose that normal human observers S1 and S2 are viewing a chip C . . . C looks unique green to S1, and bluish green to S2. The problem, as Cohen has it, is to explain "what would (metaphysically) make it the case" that S1, say and not S2, is perceiving C correctly. He purports to find the explanation "extremely hard to imagine," and so concludes that *both* S1 and S2 are perceiving C correctly . . . what "makes it the case" that S1, not S2, is perceiving C correctly, is that S1 is representing C as being unique green, S2 is representing C as being bluish green (no problem so far), and C *is* unique green, not bluish green (likewise no problem).[22]

On Byrne's view, whenever two individuals disagree about what the color of an object is or whether two objects have the same color, at least one of them is wrong. One apparent problem for this view is that it entails that there are unknowable color facts.[23] For any colored object, there are bound to be individuals who pass standardized tests of normality yet disagree about color attributions. But if there is possible disagreement among normal individuals about all questions of the form "what is the color of that object?", then answers to all such questions are unknowable. So, radical color epistemicism is true. We will return to the problems with this thesis below.

Probably the best strategy for color objectivists is to borrow from defenders of a currently popular thesis in cognitive science, known as "color universalism." According to color universalism—a thesis originally made famous by Berlin and Kay in the late 60s—despite cultural variation in color perception and cognition there are a fixed number of basic color categories.[24] Berlin and Kay suggested that there are eleven basic color concepts corresponding to the white American English color lexicon (red, orange, yellow, green, blue, purple, pink, brown, grey, black, and white). This correspondence between the basic color concepts and the basic color terms in white American English is no coincidence, according to them, for, as they argue, color concepts like other language universals are innate and biologically constrained, where the biological constraints may, as Furbee et al put it, "be extended or restricted by cultural processes."[25]

The universality thesis started out as a response to the so-called linguistic relativity thesis, originally set forth by Edward Sapir and Benjamin Whorf.[26] Linguistic relativity is the thesis that color naming is a relatively arbitrary linguistic convention, and that linguistic differences affect how people perceive colors. However, we are familiar with the challenges to this view. First, it cannot account for similarities in color categorization in radically diverse communities. Second, it seems to be undermined by the fact that speakers of languages with very few color words sometimes perform as well as (or better than) English speakers on prototype categorization tests.[27]

The universality thesis offers a way of accommodating the obvious cultural differences in color categorization while maintaining the idea that there are color universals. But it does so only by classifying some perceivers who pass standardized tests of normality as suffering from color vision deficiencies. In a nutshell, the idea underlying universalism is that while some languages do not possess separate lexical entries for blue and green or for blue and black, people who do not suffer from color vision deficiencies have the innate ability to discriminate between the two. Those who don't have this discriminatory ability are those who suffer from color vision deficiencies.

Universalism does not offer a complete explanation of color variation. For example, it does not offer an account of why some languages lack the universals that universalists claim exist. However, the lack of certain color terms in Asian and African languages has recently been argued to be due to phototoxic effects of sunlight on the eye. The story, which is due to Delwin Lindsey and Angela Brown, runs as follows.[28] Variations in the lexical entries for color terms result from differences in color perception due to an accelerated aging of the eye in populations who have had chronic exposure to ultraviolet light (UV-B). Languages that have developed in low-UV linguistic communities generally have the word "blue." Languages that have developed in high-UV areas tend not to have the word "blue." Instead they call short-wavelength stimuli "green" or "dark." As Lindsey and Brown point out, their hypothesis does not presuppose that all members of a linguistic community are or were at some point visually impaired, but only that sufficiently many members of the population suffer or suffered from color vision deficiency. If sufficiently many speakers have difficulties distinguishing two basic colors, then there will be no need for separate lexical entries for the corresponding color terms, the reason being that "communication of color information requires color competence in both speakers and listeners."[29]

Lindsey and Brown's UV-light hypothesis, if correct, explains why many Asian and African languages having developed in high-UV areas do not or did not originally have separate lexical entries for blue and green. It furthermore explains why people from populations farther from the equator make more discriminations in the blue range of the color spectrum.

Moreover, the Lindsey/Brown UV hypothesis underwrites the universalist claim that color variability is partially due to color vision deficiencies. Color variability at the level of lexical entries may or may not correspond to underlying variations in color perception. But the two phenomena are at least weakly connected. Languages that lack color terms lack them because a sufficiently large proportion of the original population had a color vision deficiency. Current variations in color perception can likewise be understood in terms of degrees of separation from perceivers with color vision deficiencies perhaps partially caused by the phototoxic effects of sunlight.

According to one version of color universalism, then, brown eyes and non-white skin are not the cause of color vision deficiencies. Rather, brown eyes, non-white skin, and color vision deficiencies have a common cause: high, chronic exposure to high UV-light.

The Lindsey/Brown UV hypothesis does not explain variations in color vision that are not linked to variations in UV exposure. But their explanation suggests the beginning of a general story. Variations are due to color vision deficiencies: some are linked to high UV exposure, others might be linked to genuine aging of the eye, yet others might be linked to gene mutations normally responsible for color blindness in males, etc.

One way for color objectivists to respond to the color variability objection then is to say that perceivers in high-UV localities, aging perceivers, and a large number of females fall outside of the range of normal perceivers/cognizers. Variations in color perception are due to mutations, aging, and so on, hence color objectivism is true.

However, this sort of reply, though less incomplete than the original objectivist replies, is far-fetched.

Let it be granted, at least for argument's sake, that sufficiently large proportions of populations in high-UV localities are negatively affected by high, chronic exposure to UV light. The lack of certain abilities to detect certain color differences which individuals in low-UV localities can detect can be understood as a deficiency only relative to individuals in low-UV localities. But what are we to say about individuals in low-UV localities? Individuals in low-UV localities can perceptually and cognitively discriminate blue from green. But unlike some non-human animals, they cannot perceptually or cognitively discriminate violet from ultra-violet. Lizards, goldfish, and ducks, among many other animals, have tetrachromatic color vision, and so can detect colors which most humans cannot detect, including in some cases ultraviolet. So, relative to such extra-human perceivers, the color vision of human individuals in low-UV-localities is deficient. Furthermore, in humans ultraviolet light is normally blocked by the lens. But humans with aphakia, a condition where the eye lacks a lens, sometimes appear to have the ability to detect ultraviolet.[30] So, relative to people with aphakia, people who don't suffer from aphakia might turn out to suffer from color-vision deficiencies.

The standard response to the argument from tetrachromatism or enhanced color vision in other species is to insist on that when we offer an analysis of The Colors, we are interested only in the human colors—the colors humans can detect. But this sort of response gives non-objectivists a way of responding to the objectivists. Just as it might make sense to distinguish among human colors, fish colors and monkey colors, we ought to be able to distinguish between low-UV colors and high-UV colors, aphakia and non-aphakia-colors, female and male colors, and so on. To put the point differently: Just as one might insist that it doesn't make sense to say that human color vision is deficient compared to the color vision of fish, so one might insist that it doesn't make sense to say that the color vision of high-UV individuals is deficient compared to that of low-UV individuals or that the color vision of people who don't suffer from aphakia is deficient compared to that of people who suffer from aphakia.

There is a further reason to think that the color vision deficiency hypothesis cannot be correct: If individuals who deviate from The Normal suffer from color vision deficiencies, then tetrachromatic women who are tetrachromats in virtue of gene mutations presumably would classify as deviant. They would fail to satisfy the perceptual norm, which would be satisfied only by trichromatic perceivers. And this would be so even though tetrachromats are in a position to perceive a broader spectrum of colors in the long-wavelengths (red/orange) regions of the color spectrum. But this conclusion is absurd on its face. If, on the other hand, the color objectivists were to admit that women with tetrachromatic color vision and others who have improved abilities to detect differences in the visible spectrum are normal, and that individuals with standard trichromatic color vision are deviant, then the objectivists might have to accept that the majority of the human population are systematically mistaken when they make color comparison judgments (e.g. "these two objects have exactly the same color"). This conclusion too is absurd on its face (at least, given realism about colors).

The upshot is that color objectivism does not offer a plausible account of variations in color perception. Color objectivism aims at explaining away variations by attributing unwarranted color vision deficiencies to people of color, women and others who pass standardized tests of normality.

The attributions of color vision deficiencies to people of color and women are not only unwarranted but also oppressive. They implicitly encourage a distorted world view associating the normal and well-functioning with whiteness and maleness. The white male's visual system is that according to which the perceptual norm is defined. Of course, the objectivist's implicit treatment of the non-white or female visual system as deficient is not normally recognized as being oppressive, in most cases it is not even recognized as a consequence of the view, but the inadvertence of an unwarranted and oppressive act does not make the act significantly less problematic.

Linguistic and Perceptual Relativity

Objectivism, it seems, attributes unwarranted and oppressive color vision deficiencies to people of color vis-a-vis those (white males) who constitute the perceptual norm. This gives us good reason to reject the view. What should we adopt in its place? Should we resort to linguistic or perceptual relativity? Should we say that color categorization is the result of arbitrary convention, and that color vision is affected by this convention? I think not. Linguistic relativity is not a viable thesis. The fact that English has the lexical entries "blue," "green," and "black" indicates that English speakers have or have had the ability to perceptually and cognitively discriminate between stimuli in the blue and green range of the visible spectrum; it doesn't show that speakers of other languages sometimes do not make the same discriminations as English speakers because they possess a different set of color concepts. Perception probably doesn't require the *possession* of concepts, though it may require recognitional or discriminatory abilities. So, possessing different concepts probably doesn't entail perceiving differently. Which beliefs, thoughts and ideas we have about the world and which judgments we are able to make on the basis of perceptual experience, on the other hand, plausibly are affected by which concepts we possess. And, I believe that it is this latter thesis concerning our conceptual inner life, together with popular myths, which underlies the initial plausibility of the early linguistic relativity thesis.[31]

This is not to say that no version of the linguistic relativity thesis has any degree of plausibility. Color-emotion relativity is highly plausible. Color-emotion relativity, as I will construe it, is the thesis that different cultural attachments of value to color and traditional use of color can affect which emotional experiences exposure to color stimuli produces. There are familiarly great cultural variation not only in color categorization but also in color use and the attachment of value to colors. In most North-Western countries wedding dresses are traditionally white or green, in India they are traditionally red. In most North Western countries one wears black to funerals, in South Africa red is the color of mourning. So, a Dane or an Indian might experience joy when exposed to a white or a red dress, whereas a person from South Africa might experience sadness when exposed to the same article of clothing. In Northern countries (in America, in particular) the perception of dark skin produces negative emotions in white perceivers. As an illustration, George Yancy offers the following elevator case in which he, despite being well-dressed and non-threatening, is negatively seized by a white woman:

> Well-dressed, I enter an elevator where a white woman waits to reach her floor. She "sees" my Black body, though not the same one I have seen reflected back to me from the mirror on any number of occasions . . . . Her body language signifies, "Look, *the* Black!" . . . her body language functions as an insult. Over and above how my body is clothed, she "sees" a criminal, she sees me as a threat . . . . It is not necessary that I first perform a threatening action. The question of *deeds* is irrelevant. I need not *do* anything . . . . It is as if my Black body has always already committed a criminal *deed* . . . . My dark body occludes the presumption of innocence. It is as if one's Blackness is a congenital defect, one that burdens the body with tremendous inherited guilt. On this reading, one might say that Blackness functions metaphorically as original sin. There is not anything as such that a Black body needs *to do* in order to be found blameworthy.[32]

Based on first-person experiences Yancy reports that his dark skin signifies to white people the original sin, and that this contingent fact about his skin color produces fear and other negative emotions towards him.

Color-emotion relativity is highly plausible. But color-emotion relativity, of course, is not a thesis about basic color vision. It is a thesis about how the link between color perception and emotion is differentially affected by social factors.

As for variations in color vision, I think we should opt for perceptual and linguistic relativity but not of the old-fashioned kind. Rather, we should reject the thesis that colors are objective. I propose that we treat the colors as centered properties—properties objects can posses only relative to a perceptual perspective.[33] Call this view "color perspectivalism." On this view, ripe tomatoes will possess the property red only relative to a perceptual perspective. This view may seem radical. However, most objectivists are already committed to a weak form of perceptual relativity. Objectivists who believe that there is a plurality of possible worlds, for example ersatz worlds, must deny that objects simply possess properties. They possess properties only relative to a possible world. A ripe tomato does not simply have the property of being red. It has the property of being red relative to the actual world but relative to a different world it has the property of being blue. What I suggest is that some properties, including the colors, can be possessed not relative to a possible world but only relative to a possible world and a perceptual perspective. Or more simply put: I suggest that some properties can be had by objects only relative to centered worlds; they are centered properties.

Though there are various different ways in which the colors can be treated as centered properties, I prefer a centered version of realist primitivism. I have defended this view elsewhere.[34] Here I will just note that the view avoids attributing color vision deficiencies to females and people of color. The perspectives of females and people of color are just as valid as the perspectives of males and whites. Unlike color universalism and color objectivism, perspectivalism thus does not sanction white supremacism, androcentrism or Eurocentrism.[35]

Color Non-Realism

Unlike standard realist views of colors, perspectival theories of color are not white; they do not assume a white perspective as objective. Objectivist forms of physicalism, dispositionalism, and primitivism, on the other hand, are unjustifiably white. They are committed to the view that there is a particular white perspective which is natural, normal and mainstream and which should be considered superior to other perceptual perspectives. The perspective is that of the white male.

How do non-realist theories fare compared to realist theories? Are non-realist theories of colors white? Non-realist theories are committed to an error-theory about colors. Strictly speaking, objects are not colored.[36] Non-realist theories would thus seem to agree with the centered view of the colors that no single property is detected by normal humans exposed to the same color stimulus in appropriate viewing conditions. Non-realist theories, however, can be just as white as their realist counterparts.

Non-realists hold that objects do not instantiate colors. They grant that colors partially constitute the content of color perception (Chalmers),[37] or that colors are instantiated in a visual array (Velleman and Boghossian).[38] But the colors that constitute the content of color perception or are instantiated in a visual array are not instantiated by the objects of experience. However, even though non-realists reject the idea that human color vision detects colors instantiated by external objects, they could grant that human color vision detects *some properties or other* which are instantiated by external objects. It's just that these properties are not to be equated with the colors. In fact, non-realists probably should grant that this is so. Otherwise, they cannot account for the difference between cases in which perception is falsidical yet normal and cases where perception is falsidical yet deviant. For example, they need to account for the difference between a scenario in which a perceiver is looking at a piece of regular printer paper illuminated by red light and comes to believe on that basis that the paper is red and a scenario in which a perceiver is looking at a piece of regular printer paper in standard lighting conditions and comes to believe on that basis that the paper is white. The experience in the first scenario is faulty in a way that the experience in the second scenario is not. One way to account for the difference is to allow for experiences to be falsidical yet imperfectly veridical.[39]

There are several ways to cash out the notion of imperfect veridicality. One could follow the objectivist's lead and take a color experience to be imperfectly veridical just in case the experience is of a kind that a normal perceiver would have when looking at the object in question in normal viewing conditions. One could then justifiably say that the perceiver who views a piece of paper in normal lighting conditions and comes to believe on this basis that the paper is white has an imperfectly veridical experience. The experience is imperfectly veridical because it is the kind of experience which a normal perceiver looking at the piece of paper in normal viewing conditions would have. The perceiver who views a piece of paper illuminated by red light and who comes to believe on that basis that the paper is red, on the other hand, does not have an imperfectly veridical experience. Her experience is falsidical through and through. But now the non-realist is no better off than the realist of the objectivist variety. She is forced to single out a type of perceiver as normal. Non-realism by itself, it seems, does not solve the problem of color variation.[40]

Whiteness and the Conceptual Tools of Theories of Perception

Philosophical theories of perception, like many other philosophical theories, aim at objectivity. Naïve realists treat veridical experience as a relation to an external fact or object. Representationalists treat the content of experience as composed of objects and properties and standardly treat properties as something an object can possess relative to the world as a whole. But arguably objects are experienced as having lots of features that cannot be possessed by objects relative to the world as a whole but which can be possessed only relative to a particular experiential perspective. I experience strawberries as sweet, Indian curry as pungent, my best friend as gracious, my place in the social world as auspicious, my happiness as pleasant and my longing as painful. But strawberries are not sweet, relative to the world as a whole. Strawberries taste sweet to me, but not to my cats. Indian curry is not pungent, relative to the world as a whole. It is pungent to me, but not to someone who suffers from ageusia. Still, I experience strawberries as sweet, and not necessarily as sweet-relative-to-me, and I experience my longing as painful, and not necessarily as painful-relative-to-me. The properties which things are perceived to have are not normally phenomenologically relational, they are phenomenologically non-relational. Yet non-relational pains, pleasures, sweetnesses and so on are not the sorts of entities that are instantiated by objects relative to the world as a whole. They are the sorts of entities that are instantiated relative to centered worlds in which (varying) experiential perspectives are marked.

Perceptual theories that ignore the centeredness of experience either treat the properties which objects are experienced as having as intrinsically relational, thus getting the phenomenology of experience wrong, or they treat the properties which objects are experienced as having as non-relational and objective. It's the latter kind of theories that risk giving privilege to the perspective of the white (perhaps Western male). The latter kinds of theories give privilege to the perspective of the white by mistakenly treating the perceptual systems of white perceivers as normal and that of non-whites as deficient.

A philosophical theory can, of course, be objective without being white. For example, an objectivist theory of color needn't treat tetrachromatic color vision or a failure to perceptually discriminate between certain reflectance types in the middle- and short-wavelength regions of the color spectrum as a deficiency and hence as something bad. It is a contingent fact that color vision that deviates from that of the white Western male comes to be associated with negative value by virtue of being treated as deficient and abnormal, and as the manufacturer of falsidical experience.

Nonetheless objective theories by their very nature need to treat *some kinds* of color vision as deficient. They could in principle treat trichromatic color vision as deficient and abilities to distinguish a vast variety of reflectances in the middle- and short-wavelength regions of the visible spectrum as deficiencies. It is, however, unlikely that anyone would defend such a theory, and it is unclear what its motivation would be.[41]

The objectivist carries the burden of proof to refute the allegation that it sanctions white supremacism, androcentrism and Eurocentrism. The objectivist could, of course, take the epistemicist route and remain silent on the issue of which perceivers suffer from deficiencies. He can then defend his corner without sanctioning white supremacism, androcentrism or Eurocentrism.

For example, the color objectivist might with Byrne just note that whenever the color experiences of two normal individuals exposed to same stimulus differ, then at least one individual is wrong, and then add that it is not discoverable by us who is right (if any) and who is wrong.

In the case of colors, the problem with the epistemicist line is that it entails that there is no knowable fact of the matter as to what an object's color is. Realists at least should be puzzled by this consequence. Someone who takes an epistemicist line with respect to ordinary vagueness can say that, in addition to the borderline cases in which it is unknowable whether or not the term applies, there are definite cases in which we know whether the term applies.[42] For example, even if we don't know (and couldn't come to know) whether a person who is 5 feet 9 is tall for an American male, we do know that a person who is 7 feet is tall for an American male. Likewise, even if we don't know (and couldn't come to know) whether someone whose great grandfather is Greenlandic is Greenlandic, we do know that a person both of whose parents are Greenlandic is Greenlandic.[43] So the epistemicist with respect to vague terms like "tall" or "Greenlandic" can say that we come to know the meaning of the term by being exposed to definite cases. But this is not so if one is a radical epistemicist with respect to color facts. If one is a radical epistemicist with respect to color facts, then there are no definite cases, that is, there are no cases in which one can say with justified certainty what the color of an object is. So, whereas the standard epistemicist can say that one comes to know the meaning of vague terms by being exposed to definite cases, the objectivist has no way of accounting for how one comes to know the meaning of color terms. The objectivist is forced to say that the meaning of color terms has no bearing on color facts, or worse: that meanings too are unknowable. And the same sort of problem, of course, is likely to arise also for radical epistemicism about other experiential terms.

There are further problems: even assuming an epistemicist line, we are left with an aim of inquiry problem. Even if it is not currently (or ever) discoverable who is right and who is wrong about the properties of objects, it would be nice if we had some guidance when forming beliefs about these matters. Yet it seems that there is none to be had.

A related worry is that until we discover who is right and who is wrong (if ever), the epistemicist position entitles us to continue believing that people of color, women, etc., are abnormal and inferior. Of course, it is open to appeal to pragmatic factors when deciding what to believe. Pragmatic factors might give preference to beliefs that reflect a treatment of otherwise privileged individuals as non-privileged. Western moral codes arguably include the following deontic rule: "You should not commit burglary but if you do, at least leave behind the sentimental items." Likewise, our list of rules for belief formation could include retribution or epistemic-affirmative-action rules of the following kind: "You shouldn't form beliefs about the colors of objects (as answers to questions of the form 'what is the color of that object?' are unknowable), but if you do, at least give less weight to the judgments of those who are normally treated as privileged and supreme in modern society." But one could, however, also treat the fact that the objectivist has to resort to epistemic affirmative action as a reductio on the view.[44]

In conclusion: objectivism aims at explaining away cross-ethnic and cross-gender variation in perception and cognition by attributing deficiencies to people of color and others who pass standardized tests for normality. But not only are these attributions unwarranted, they also serve to perpetuate the distorted representation of whites as superior to non-whites, males as superior to females, and Westerners as superior to non-Westerners.[45]

Notes

1. This definition is roughly parallel to the standard characterization of androcentric theories. A theory is androcentric if it, as Sally Haslanger puts it, "takes males or masculinity to be the norm against which females and femininity are considered deviant, or if it considers its subject matter from the point of view of men and simply ignores women and women's perspective" (109). See, Sally Haslanger, "Feminism in Metaphysics: Negotiating the Natural," in *The Cambridge Companion to Feminism in Philosophy*, ed. Jennifer Hornsby and Miranda Fricker (Cambridge: Cambridge University Press, 2000), 107–126.
2. Certainly, there is no one objective answer to the question of whether this water park is fun or this chili is tasty.
3. Of course, white theories, thus understood, needn't be false. A linguistic analysis of "bachelor" may well be white in that it implicitly treats the white person's linguistic analysis as objective. But if there is an objective fact of the matter as to how to analyse "bachelor," then I suppose there is no inherent danger or flaw in treating the analysis as objective.
4. David S. Owen, "Towards a Critical Theory of Whiteness," *Philosophy & Social Criticism* 33 (2007): 203–222, quotation on 203, 206.
5. I hesitate here because some people with blindsight can reliably track movement and attribute properties to objects. Moreover, it is not obvious that blind people suffer from color vision deficiencies. Even if they cannot see, some blind people report that they are able to experience phosphenes and after-images. But one could hold a view to the effect that, as long as blind people experience color, they do not suffer from color vision deficiencies.
6. George Yancy, "Elevators, Social Spaces and Racism: A Philosophical Analysis," *Philosophy & Social Criticism* 34 (2008): 843–76, quotation on 846.
7. See Yancy, "Elevators, Social Spaces and Racism."
8. Yancy, "Elevators, Social Spaces and Racism," 846.
9. For a defense of reflectance physicalism, see for example, Michael Tye, *Consciousness, Color, and Content* (Cambridge, MA: MIT Press, 2000) and Alex Byrne and David R. Hilbert, "Color Realism and Color Science," *Behavioral and Brain Sciences* 26 (2003): 3–21.
10. Classical dispositional theories, going back to John Locke, are objectivist. Contemporary defenses of objectivist and non-objectivist versions of dispositionalism include Colin McGinn, *The Subjective View: Secondary Qualities and Indexical Thoughts* (Oxford: Oxford University Press, 1983); John McDowell, "Values and Secondary Qualities," in *Morality and Objectivity*, ed. Ted Honderich (London: Routledge and Kegan Paul, 1985), 100–29; A. D. Smith, "Of Primary and Secondary Qualities," *The Philosophical Review* 99 (1990): 221–54; Mark Johnston, "How to Speak of the Colors," *Philosophical Studies* 68 (1992): 221–63. Evan Thompson, *Colour Vision* (New York: Routledge, 1995) and Alva Noë *Action in Perception* (Cambridge, MA: MIT Press, 2005) defend the view that the colors are ecological dispositions. For a defense of the view that the colors are the categorical grounds of dispositions, see, for example, Frank Jackson, "The Primary Quality View of Color," *Philosophical Perspectives* 10 (1996): 199–219, and Brian P. McLaughlin, "The Place of Color in Nature," *Colour Perception: Mind and the Physical World*, ed. Rainer Mausfeld and Dieter Heyer (Oxford: Oxford University Press, 2003), 475–505.

11. Various objectivist and non-objectivist versions of primitivism have been defended by e.g. J. Campbell, "A Simple View of Colour," *Reality Representation, Projection*, ed. John Haldane and Crispin Wright (Oxford: Oxford University Press, 1993), 257–68; Stephen Yablo, "Singling Out Properties," *Philosophical Perspectives* 9 (1995): 477–502; Berit Brogaard, "Perspectival Truth and Color Primitivism," *New Waves in Truth*, ed. C. Wright and N. Pedersen, (forthcoming); and, Berit Brogaard, "R-Primitivism Defended," (manuscript). The view is discussed in Alex Byrne and David R. Hilbert, "Color Primitivism," *Erkenntnis* 66 (2007): 73–105. David J. Chalmers ("Perception and the Fall from Eden," in *Perceptual Experience*, ed. Tamar S. Gendler and John Hawthorne [Oxford: Clarendon Press, 2006], 49–125) defends the view that the content of color perception contains perfect primitive color properties but on his view, these properties are not instantiated by objects.

12. Heidi Hofer, Joseph Carroll, Jay Neitz, Maureen Neitz, and David R. Williams, "Organization of the Human Trichromatic Cone Mosaic," *Journal of Neuroscience* 25, no. 42 (2005): 9669–9679.

13. Gokhan Malkoc, Paul Kay, and Michael A. Webster, "Variations in Normal Color Vision. IV. Binary Hues and Hue Scaling," *Journal of the Optical Society of America A* 22, no. 10 (2005): 2154–2168.

14. I. G. H. Ishak, "The Spectral Chromaticity Coordinates for one British and Eight Egyptian Trichromats," *Journal of the Optical Society of America* 42, no. 8 (1952): 534–539; M. L. Daley, G. A. Burghen, D. Meyer, and P. Malsky, "Differences in Color Vision Between Racial Groups," *Engineering in Medicine and Biology* 13 (1991): 1913–1914; and, N. Louanna Furbee, Kelly Maynard, J. Jerome Smith, Robert A. Benfer Jr., Sarah Quick, and Larry Ross, "The Emergence of Color Cognition from Color Perception," *Journal of Linguistic Anthropology* 6, no. 2 (1996): 223–40. See also Ned Block, "Sexism, Racism, Ageism, and the Nature of Consciousness," *Philosophical Topics* 26, no. 1&2 (1999): 39–70 for discussion.

15. See, for example, David Bimler and John Kirkland, "Sex Differences in Color vision and the Salience of Color-Space Axes," *Journal of Vision* 2, no. 10 (2002): 28a.

16. Brian C. Verrelli and Sarah A. Tishkoff, "Signatures of Selection and Gene Conversion Associated with Human Color Vision Variation," *The American Journal of Human Genetics* 75, no. 3 (2004): 363–75, cf. John D. Mollon, "Worlds of Difference," *Nature* 356 (1992): 378–379.

17. Kimberly A. Jameson, "Tetrachromatic Color Vision," in *The Oxford Companion to Consciousness*, ed. Tim Bayne, Axel Cleeremans, and Patrick Wilken (Oxford: Oxford University Press, 2007).

18. Cf. G. Jordan and John. D. Mollon, "A Study of Women Hererozygous for Colour Deficiencies," *Vision Research* 33 (1993): 1495–1508.

19. Kimberly A. Jameson, Susan M. Highnote, and Linda M. Wasserman, "Richer Color Experience in Observers with Multiple Photopigment Opsin Genes," *Psychonomic Bulletin & Review* 8, no. 2 (2001): 244–61; Kimberly A. Jameson, David Bimler, and Linda M. Wasserman, "Re-assessing Perceptual Diagnostics for Observers with Diverse Retinal Photopigment Genotypes," in *Progress in Colour Studies 2: Cognition*, ed. Nicola J. Pitchford and Carole P. Biggam (Amsterdam: John Benjamins Publishing Co., 2006), 13–33.

20. Tye's own view is captured in the following excerpt from his "The Truth about True Blue," *Analysis* 66 (2006): 340–44:

The upshot is that there is nothing in the Malkoc results that requires the admission that there is error at the level of coarse-grained colour experience for *Normal* perceivers under design conditions. Error arises, (as noted in Tye 2006), at the level of very fine-grained hue experiences such as that of true blue. Where at least one of John and Jane *must* be wrong is at the level of their experiences of different, determinate, finegrained hues; for S cannot have both the determinate, fine-grained hue John experiences it as having and the determinate finegrained hue Jane experiences.

The truth about true blue and other determinate hues at its level of grain is that Mother Nature did not bother to design us so as to detect *them*. There was no point in Her doing so. No selectional advantage would have accrued. Thus, even when everything is working as it should, still sometimes a surface can look true blue and not be. This did not worry Mother Nature; and it should not worry us either. (344)

There is something to be said for this line of argument. However, I think that the considerations I set out below should raise a worry even for Tye's view. For example, if the evidence commits the objectivist to the view that tetrachromatic females are systematically wrong about finegraned hues, then this is a genuine worry.

21. Tye, "The Truth about True Blue," 342–43.
22. A. Byrne, "Comments on Cohen, Mizrahi, Maund, and Levine," *Dialectica* 60 (2006): 337–40, quotation on 337.
23. Byrne and Hilbert, "Color Realism and Color Science," n50, 21.
24. Brent Berlin and Paul Kay, *Basic Color Terms: Their Universality and Evolution* (Berkley: University of California Press, 1996).
25. Furbee, Maynard, Smith, Benfer Jr., Quick, and Ross, "The Emergence of Color Cognition from Color Perception," 224.
26. Edward Sapir, *Language: An Introduction to the Study of Speech* (New York: Harcourt Brace, 1921) and Benjamin Lee Whorf, *Language, Thought, and Reality*, ed. John B. Carroll (Cambridge, MA: MIT Press, 1956).
27. Eleanor Rosch, "Principles of Categorization," in *Cognition and Categorization*, ed. Eleanor Rosch and Barbara L. Lloyd (Hillsdale, NJ: Lawrence Erlbaum, 1978), 27–48.
28. Delwin T. Lindsey and Angela M. Brown, "Color Naming and the Phototoxic Effects of Sunlight on the Eye," *Psychological Science* 13 (2002): 506–12, cf. Marc H. Bornstein, "Color Vision and Color Naming: a Psychophysiological Hypothesis of Cultural Difference," *Psychological Bulletin* 80 (1973): 257–87.
29. Lindsey and Brown, "Color Naming and the Phototoxic Effects of Sunlight on the Eye," 511.
30. Austin Roorda and David R. Williams, "The Arrangement of the Three Cone Classes in the Living Human Eye," *Nature* 397 (1999): 520–22.
31. One popular myth supporting linguistic relativity is the claim that Greenlandic Inuits have more words for snow than do speakers of English and accordingly perceive snow differently than do monolingual English (or Danish) speakers. Peter Hoeg's novel *Smilla's Sense of Snow*, for example, mentions that Inuits have dozens of words for snow and represents the main character Smilla (who is half-Danish and half-Inuit) as having an increased sense of snow.
32. Yancy, "Elevators, Social Spaces and Racism," 846–847.

33. Alternatively one could treat the colors as subjective relational properties as proposed by Jonathan Cohen. See, "Color Properties and Color Ascriptions: A Relationalist Manifesto," *The Philosophical Review* 113 (2004): 451–506.
34. The view is defended at greater length in Brogaard, "Perspectival Truth and Color Primitivism" and "R-Primitivism Defended."
35. I take "Eurocentrism" to apply to theories and worldviews that privilege the perspectives of Europeans and people of European descent.
36. Chalmers, "Perception and the Fall from Eden," argues that the color terms might pick out imperfect colors, that is, the properties which normally cause the corresponding perfect phenomenal experiences.
37. David J. Chalmers, "The Representational Character of Experience," in *The Future for Philosophy*, ed. Brian Leiter (Oxford: Oxford University Press, 2004), 153–81; and, Chalmers, "Perception and the Fall from Eden."
38. Paul Boghossian and David Velleman, "Colour as a Secondary Quality," *Mind* 98 (1989): 81–103.
39. Chalmers, "Perception and the Fall from Eden."
40. Chalmers, "The Representational Character of Experience," allows that different normal perceivers exposed to the same stimulus can have different non-faulty experiences. But he avoids the objection from color variability not because of his non-realism about perfect colors but because he takes the physical properties in the content of perception to be picked out under different centered modes of presentation. *The property that normally causes red experiences* may pick out one reflectance type relative to me and a different reflectance type relative to you. In his "Perception and the Fall from Eden," Chalmers argues that color experiences have edenic content which consists of perfect properties. These properties are not instantiated in the world, but stand in a matching relation to physical properties which are instantiated in the world. Different edenic or perfect properties can match the same physical property in different perceivers. For example, relative to inverts perfect green matches the physical property which perfect red matches in nonverts. This view can thus account for differences in the edenic content of the color experiences of different perceivers exposed to the same stimulus.
41. Of course, it could be motivated by anti-white-supremacy or feminist/anti-androcentric standpoint-theoretic considerations. Standpoint theories take the standpoint of the oppressed to provide valuable insight into the nature of the natural and social world. For a defense of feminist standpoint theory, see Sandra Harding, *The Feminist Standpoint Theory Reader, Intellectual and Political Controversies* (New York and London: Routledge, 2003).
42. Cf. Timothy Williamson, *Vagueness* (London: Routledge, 1994).
43. Of course, someone both of whose parents are Greenlandic needn't be Greenlandic in the social sense of the term but arguably she would be in the ancestral sense.
44. See, however, Louise Antony, "Sisters, Please, I'd Rather Do It Myself," *Philosophical Topics* 23 (1995): 59–94, quotation on 89, for a defense of epistemic affirmative action as a way of removing biases towards females-qua-individuals-in-possession-of-knowledge.
45. I am grateful to David Chalmers, Dimitria Gatzia, Susanna Schellenberg and George Yancy for helpful comments and discussion.

8

The Secularity of Philosophy: Race, Religion and the Silence of Exclusion

Shannon Sullivan, Penn State University

The shift from *de jure* to *de facto* white domination and privilege in the United States has meant that whiteness increasingly operates in hidden, covert ways. In the days of lynching and Jim Crow, for example, whiteness used to stomp around in big-booted strides of oppression. Nowadays it tends to tiptoe, but its soft pattering can be deceptive.[1] The fact that white privilege and domination are more difficult to detect does not mean that they have disappeared. Today white privilege often functions unconsciously and "invisibly" (at least to most white people) and is all the more effective and difficult to eliminate because of its hidden modes of operation.[2]

Within the academic discipline of contemporary philosophy, whiteness also tends to function in unseen ways. As I will argue in this chapter, one of those ways is through contemporary philosophy's secularity. Given that religion and spirituality often are important components of the lives of people of color, a philosophy that is hostile to religion tends to produce a chilly climate for them. That chilly climate helps ensure the ongoing whiteness of philosophy by implicitly discouraging people of color to enter and remain in the academic discipline of philosophy. This process is especially effective because it functions without explicit mention of the topic of race. Whether the discipline is friendly or hostile to religion would seem to have nothing to do with the whiteness of philosophy, and this seeming lack of connection makes the whiteness of philosophy all the more powerful because it enables philosophy's whiteness to perpetuate itself in hidden, invisible ways.

I will begin with support for my claim that contemporary mainstream (read: white) philosophy in the United States tends to be secular. In a variety of ways that have similar effects, contemporary philosophy in the United States (and the North Atlantic more generally) tends to be unconcerned with religious or spiritual matters, and this is true across different approaches to philosophy, e.g., continental, analytic, pragmatist, and feminist. I then will discuss the importance of religion and spirituality to people of color broadly considered, which is not to claim that every person of color is religious, but that religion often is a part of the life-world of people who historically have been oppressed, such as African American and Latino/a people. The exclusion of religious concerns from philosophy thus effectively excludes the interests of many people of color. The solution to this problem is not necessarily for philosophy of religion to become central to the discipline of philosophy. For the overbearing whiteness of philosophy to be eliminated, the culture, society, and lived concerns of people of color must be part of the discipline's center, and this change in the center requires that religious concerns and worldviews no longer be marginalized by mainstream philosophy.

Philosophy's Secularity

When I say that contemporary philosophy in the United States is secular, I mean that it generally is exclusionary of and sometimes also hostile to religion as a meaningful component of a person's lived experience. This is a slightly different usage than that found in most dictionaries, where "secular" does not necessarily entail explicit rejection of religious matters. (Think here of "secular clergy.") In practice, however, the term "secular" today tends to connote opposition, or at least indifference to religious matters. Analyzing the secular age in which the Western world currently lives, Charles Taylor describes secularity as a "falling off of religious belief and practice" that makes belief in God merely one option among many, and "an embattled option" at that.[3] Our current age (in the North Atlantic world) is secular in that it presumes most people do not believe in a higher being and, moreover, it finds it difficult to fathom those who do profess such belief. Religious believers do still exist in the Western world, of course, but "the presumption of unbelief has become dominant in more and more . . . milieux; and [it] has achieved hegemony in certain crucial ones, in the academic and intellectual life, for instance."[4]

Perhaps nowhere is this truer than in the academic discipline of philosophy. In the United States, the mood of philosophy is decidedly secular: sometimes its secularity means that it is openly hostile to religious interests and concerns, and other times its hostility is veiled. As with any mood, it can be difficult to point to a tangible thing or definitive event that conclusively proves its existence. The situation is more fuzzy and indeterminate than this, often the result of a number of small things each of which are relatively inconsequential but that can add up to something significant and formidable. For example, in its more veiled form, philosophy's hostility to religion often takes the form of "strain[ing] metaphysics out of politics," as William Connolly argues.[5] How, political philosophers ask, can political and cultural conflict be eliminated when different groups have different understandings of moral truth? The secular answer tends to be "to dredge out of public life as much cultural density and depth as possible so that muddy 'metaphysical' and 'religious' differences don't flow into the pure water of public reason, procedure, and justice."[6] Contemporary political philosophy tends to relegate anything smacking of the transcendental or metaphysical, including belief in God, to the private sphere where it cannot and should not interfere with public discussion.

In its more open form, contemporary philosophy's hostility to religion still can be difficult to detect, at least in official publications or pronouncements. Anecdotally, one instance of this hostility that I have witnessed is the dismissive attitude of some graduate students to other graduate students who hint at their belief in God. "You still believe in God? Well, you must not have read any Heidegger yet." Heidegger's name could be replaced with that of Nietzsche or Sartre or some other important historical figure in philosophy. The effect is the same: in many philosophical circles, belief in God tends to be seen as proof of childlike naiveté and lack of sophistication. "Real" philosophers—which many graduate students often fear that they are not and so anxiously seek to demonstrate that they are[7]—know better and have abandoned belief in God.

This explains another event that I recently witnessed, a passing comment that did not receive much notice and yet that said volumes about the rightful place (or lack thereof) of religious interests in a formal philosophical setting. When Charles Taliaferro, a prominent analytic philosopher who is a self-described theist, recently was at my home institution presenting a Shakespearean concept of redemption, he briefly apologized to his audience with an embarrassed smile for being a "philosophical Neanderthal" when appealing to the concept of faith in connection with redemption.[8] This tiny two-word phrase does not just concern Taliaferro and how he presents or perceives himself within philosophy. It reveals an enormous amount about the discipline at large. In many philosophical circles, to be a person of faith is to be perceived as ignorant, backward, and primitive. It is to be seen as incapable of the intellectual abilities and sophistications that are expected of successful philosophers. While said in a half-joking way, Taliaferro's apology was a meaningful confession that simultaneously acknowledged and partially confronted the bias against religious believers that exists in academic philosophy.

Taliaferro's confession complements what one SWIP-list (Society for Women in Philosophy) contributor recently argued online concerning philosophy and religion. After questioning another feminist's claim that "professional philosophy lends support to all patriarchal religions," the contributor explained why she thought a religious person "would not be very comfortable in philosophy":

> Almost every philosopher I know is an atheist, although most don't like to say it out loud since over a third of the country is evangelical and well armed. (Only sort of kidding.) When we teach the philosophy of religion, the focus is on the three major proofs for the existence of God and how they fail, and the problem of evil and how it is insurmountable. Maybe you do Pascal's Wager and then demolish that. Then, just in case we haven't made our point, we use Deborah Mathieu's piece on male chauvinist religion. You can always go empirical and talk about the relationship between religion and violence .... Yes,

you can get a few philosophers to say they believe in God. But then it's qualified: "It depends on what you mean by God," and then it turns out that God is some force more powerful than "us" (i.e., humans), which turns out to be something all atheists accept, so there you are.[9]

The jagged wit that the contributor uses to describe the situation in contemporary philosophy makes it difficult to discern if she regrets philosophy's aversion to religion. What is clear, however, is that such aversion exists and that it tends to operate somewhat covertly: allegedly not through personal bias but through "objective" reason and philosophical argumentation.

Indeed, unlike the work of historical figures such as Nietzsche, the texts written by contemporary philosophers usually are silent about, rather than openly hostile to religion. But explicit opposition to religion in published philosophical works occasionally occurs nowadays too. Richard Rorty's work offers a prominent example of such opposition, although, in his case, an "allergic reaction" might be the more accurate term. While sometimes it tries to do so, Rorty's pragmatist philosophy cannot accommodate more than the smallest amount of religion without having an aversive reaction to it. Reviewing Cornel West's monumental *The Evasion of American Philosophy*, for example, Rorty tries to separate his leftist secularism from that of "most white leftists," who are embarrassed by the religious affiliations of Martin Luther King, Malcom X, and Jesse Jackson and "wish that African Americans would grow up, would find some firmly secularist leaders." As Rorty remarks, "so much the worse, in my view, for that Left."[10] But his claim that he is not dismissive of religion rings hollow, especially when he continues to insist that religion and politics be sharply separated into private and public spheres. A decade later after reviewing West's book, Rorty says, "we secularists have come to think that the best society would be one in which political action conducted in the name of religious beliefs is treated as a ladder up which our ancestors climbed, but one that now should be thrown away."[11] For Rorty, religious belief has no rightful place other than the individual, personal space of one's private belief (and understanding those beliefs as having no impact on anything political or public outside themselves). They are similar to children's belief in Santa Claus: something that might be tolerated in only a supposedly inconsequential area of human life, such as childhood, where it allegedly can do no harm. A society that allows religion any more weight than this is a primitive society that has yet to grow up.[12]

Rorty's allergy to religion is fairly obvious, but in the case of other philosophers who are hostile to religion, their hostility occurs in the margins of their work, making it easy to ignore. For example, in the introduction to *The Politics of Reality*, Marilyn Frye explains her occasionally idiosyncratic grammar. As she does so, she briefly remarks that "though my use of upper case letters is normal for the most part, I do not dignify names of religions and religious institutions with upper case letters. Hence the word 'christian,' used either as noun or adjective, is not capitalized, nor is the word 'church' or 'catholic,' etc."[13] The topic of religion does not appear anywhere else in the book, except in Frye's biographical statement, which is on the last page and falls outside of the book proper. Frye mentions there, among other things, that she was reared in a "devoutly christian family."[14] It is striking that Frye makes a point of explaining her treatment of religious names when they virtually never appear in her book and certainly play no significant role in its creative vision. While the alleged goal of her grammatical explanation is just that—explanation—the effect of her remark, if not also its ultimate goal, is to let readers know that religion has no place in the women-friendly and anti-sexist world that Frye imagines. The implication of her brief comments is that religion has been complicit with, perhaps even a major source of male domination, and thus feminists who wish to challenge that domination effectively must condemn any and all forms of religion as sexist.[15]

Like Richard Rorty's work, Marilyn Frye's philosophy is distinctive not because it dismisses religion as a meaningful part of a (feminist) philosopher's worldview, but because it so blatantly dismisses it. In general, most contemporary feminist philosophy is not so much overtly hostile to religion as it is generative of a chilly atmosphere for religious concerns through its silence about them. Feminist philosophy of religion exists as a small sub-field, and important philosophical work has been done on the intersections of religion, women's lives, and male domination.[16] But religion only occasionally is at the center of contemporary feminist philosophy, and often when it is focused on, the focus is critical rather than constructive. Catherine MacKinnon's feminist legal philosophy, which focuses on sexual harassment and pornography as forms of sexual discrimination and more recently on rape as an act of genocide in international conflicts, is a typical example of this point.[17] Religion rarely is mentioned in her work, and when it is discussed, it tends to be treated solely as a conservative and thus problematic support for laws that give women fewer rights than men.[18]

The broader field of philosophy of religion might appear to be an exception to the claim that philosophy is hostile to religion. After all, philosophy of religion focuses precisely on religious questions about God's (or some such Transcendent Being's) existence and nature, the problem of evil, reasons for (dis)believing in miracles, the relationship of faith and reason, and the relationship between religion and morality. Philosophy of religion thus makes room for religious beliefs and believers. Even so, the field is symptomatic of philosophy's disdain for religion. It is a small field in which analytic philosophy has ghettoized issues of religion and appears to receive little respect from other analytic philosophers. (This certainly seems true based on my experience on the program committee of the Eastern Division of the American Philosophical Association [APA].) As the contributor to SWIP-list quoted above attests, philosophy of religion often is not very open to religion at all and instead turns out to be a primary philosophical site for dismissing religious claims. This has not always been the case. According to Cornel West, from roughly 1910 to 1940—the "Golden Age of philosophy of religion in modern Euro-American thought" in which American pragmatism thrived in the United States—religious beliefs were treated by philosophers as beliefs linked to experience, not as scholarly puzzles for philosophers to solve.[19] The rise of logical positivism soon after World War II, however, led to "the near collapse of [philosophy of religion] as a serious academic discipline," leaving the subfield with "little or no academic legitimacy."[20] Those with interest in philosophy of religion turned to seminar or divinity schools, and professional philosophers had little to say about religion except to debunk it.

However contemporary philosophy of religion came to have the particular character that it has today, the problem is that its style tends to be alienating to many people of color. Even if the field of philosophy of religion were well-respected, in other words, it would not be an area that generally would attract many philosophers of color. This is largely because philosophy of religion primarily is characterized by arguments surrounding the epistemology and metaphysics of God: how can we know if God exists, and what would God be like if He, She, or It did exist? But what if these are not the important questions for many believers, especially those who are people of color? What if proving with certainty or at least establishing with justifiable warrant that (a benevolent) God exists is considered fairly irrelevant to religion? Within the framework of contemporary philosophy of religion, such a question almost sounds ridiculous. It can be difficult to think within that framework what religion might mean absent the question of knowledge of and belief in God. But if, in Charles Taylor's words, "belief and unbelief [are not] rival *theories* . . . [but more like] different kinds of lived experience involved in understanding your life in one way or the other," then the epistemology of God business that goes on in most contemporary philosophy of religion will seem rather pointless.[21] And this, as I will explore below, tends to be the case for many people of color. While people of color can and have responded to racial oppression in non-religious ways,[22] religion and spirituality have tended to play an important role in generating non-white resistance to racism and white domination.

Religion in the Lives of People of Color

Cornel West has argued that "the culture of the wretched of the earth is deeply religious," and since many of those wretched worldwide are people of color, this means that the culture of many people of color is religious. Continuing his point, West urges "to be in solidarity with them requires not only an acknowledgement of what they are up against but also an appreciation of how they cope with their situation," which includes appreciation of the place of religion in their lives.[23] I will discuss the positive role of religion in West's prophetic pragmatism shortly. But first, let me turn to other African American and Hispanic/Latino scholars who attest to the importance of religion to the lives of people of color. My claim is not that all African Americans or Hispanics/Latinos are religious nor that wretchedness sums up either group's lived experience. And I recognize that some philosophers of color explicitly reject religion because they are concerned, for example, about "the morally questionable record of religion" and the fact that religion seems "always [to be] on the side of those who [are] in power."[24] Avoiding stereotypes of African Americans and Hispanics/Latinos should not mean, however, ignoring broad patterns of meaning and experience in their lives. One of those crucial patterns is that religion tends to play an important role in the lives of many Hispanics/Latinos and African Americans.

According to a 1989 longitudinal and cross-national survey, African Americans are more religious than any other people in the world. They rank God's importance in their lives higher than any other ethnic or national group, and compared to 57% of the general population, 75% of them believe that religion can solve most of the world's problems today.[25] Those problems include racism and white supremacy. The black church in particular has a long history of nurturing black political struggle against white domination and stimulating African Americans' involvement in political activism, such as the Civil Rights Movement.[26]

The close relationship between the spiritual and the political in African American experience explains some black scholars' frustration with the mainstream's privatization of the spiritual. For example, Jacqui Alexander worries that secular (read: white) feminism has assisted in this privatization by separating religion from organized political work. While religion is sometimes thought to lead to disengagement from politics, Alexander argues "that suspicion is simply not borne out in practice." Citing examples from liberation movements in Latin America to the anti-colonial struggles that Gandhi's prayer life motivated in India, Alexander insists that "we [who are oppressed] were political *because* we were spiritual," not in spite of that fact.[27] In contrast to most feminist movements, womanism is rooted in black and other women of color's experiences and is marked by its inclusion of a spiritual realm in which human life and the broader environment are intertwined.[28]

In a similar fashion, Michele Moody-Adams sharply criticizes Richard Rorty's attempts to understand civil disobedience as practiced in the Civil Rights Movement apart from its connection with the black church. According to Moody-Adams, "these were people who were rooted in the Black church who believed in a higher purpose for which they were living and acting and Rorty seems not to have understood this as a psychological phenomenon at all," especially when he argues that the concept of solidarity can serve in place of the concept of objective truth in political struggle.[29] Howard Thurman sums up the point in his classic *Jesus and the Disinherited*: "Christianity as it was born in the mind of [Jesus] . . . appears as a technique of survival for the oppressed . . . . Wherever his spirit appears, the oppressed gather fresh courage."[30] For many African Americans, belief in God and membership in the Christian church are the main sources, techniques, and motivations for political and personal struggle against racial oppression.

The Christian tradition and church also play a significant role in the lives of many Hispanics and Latinos in the United States. Charting the importance of community to U.S. Hispanic identity and culture, anthropologist Roberto Goizueta explains that the historical, cultural, and anthropological reality of that community is *mestizaje*: a blending of Native American, African and European cultures that produces a subjectivity different from and marginal to its original roots. And according to Goizueta, "*mestizaje* is characterized by suffering . . . ; it is an experience of the cross."[31] The confluence of cultures that produces U.S. Hispanics is conflictual and violent, resulting in alienation, marginalization, and oppression for many U.S. Hispanics. That experience is akin to what Jesus Christ experienced when crucified on the cross: profound suffering, but also a transformation in which a new kind of existence is possible. *Mestizaje* thus simultaneously brings Hispanic people closer to the crucified Jesus and makes Christianity an important tool for understanding their everyday experiences. As Goizueta argues, being faithful to one's experience as a U.S. Hispanic often means being faithful to the role of spirituality and religion in that experience.

This message is confirmed by Ada María Isasi-Díaz's account of *mujerista* theology. "Why?" she asks emphatically, responding with and to frustration about the neglect of religion in academic perspectives on Hispanas/Latinas lives:

> Why continue to insist on the importance of the religious understandings and practices of grassroots Hispanas/Latinas? . . . Why continue to see our theological elaborations as a praxis of liberation even when "liberation" has stopped being fashionable? Why? Because justice is a constitutive element of the Gospel message. Because without the participation of those who suffer injustice in the institutions, norms, and practices that affect our lives, justice will not be accomplished.[32]

The grassroots experiences of Hispanic and Latino women in particular, Isasi-Díaz argues, involve personal and political struggle for dignity and liberation from oppression that cannot be separated from a spiritual understanding of the world. Justice requires the liberatory work of Hispanas, Latinas, and other oppressed peoples, and since that work often is grounded in religious practices, justice must welcome spirituality as a partner in struggle. The picket line has its own kind of spirituality, for example, and it can be just as much of a religious site as is the sanctuary of a church.[33]

What these accounts demonstrate is that for many Hispanic/Latino and African Americans, religion primarily centers on concrete struggle for social-political justice and personal meaning, not abstract metaphysical debates about God's existence. The burning questions posed by religion, the questions that a believer feels compelled to answer, are how to make sense of and to try to change a world that systematically has oppressed people of color, not questions about, for example, the compatibility of God's benevolent nature with the existence of evil. Oppressed groups might cry "Why, Lord?" when faced with racist evil, but their cry tends to be one of anguish and even anger, not a demand for logical consistency on God's part. The latter way of understanding the question "Why, Lord?" misses the point of most people of color's engagement with God. As Cornel West insists, "I don't believe that any arguments for or against the existence of God have much weight one way or other. Not at all. I think that particular way of couching the question is already impoverished, and it reflects a certain ahistorical way of understanding God-talk of which I am highly suspicious."[34]

West perhaps is the best known contemporary philosopher to incorporate religion into philosophy without reducing religion to ahistorical God-talk. Before explaining how he does so, however, it is important to note that his prophetic pragmatism does not mandate Christianity or any other form of religion. As West remarks, prophetic pragmatism "neither requires a religious foundation nor entails a religions perspective," and it "is possible to subscribe to prophetic pragmatism and belong to different religious and/or secular traditions."[35] As West develops it, prophetic pragmatism is cultural criticism that filters a utopian vision for the future through a Deweyan conception of democracy (as a way of life, not merely a form of government) and a DuBoisian analysis of the limits of capitalist democracy in particular.[36] Combining critical intelligence with social action, prophetic pragmatism emphasizes the possibility and importance of human agency: change can occur through the actions of human beings. But West's emphasis on agency is not Pollyannish. It is tempered with "a profound sense of the tragic character of life and history."[37] It confronts evil as one of the results of human choice and action, and while it insists that evil can be fought, prophetic pragmatism has no expectation of eliminating all evil in the world once and for all.[38]

While secular traditions also might grapple with cultural criticism, human agency, and the reality of tragedy, all of this makes the most sense, according to West, when interpreted through the Christian tradition and biblical focus on the plight of the wretched of the earth. The term "prophetic" in prophetic pragmatism is revealing on this issue. A colloquial understanding of the function of a prophet is that she or he sees into the future, discerning distinctive events that are likely to occur, and then tries to tell people about that future so that they can either encourage or avoid it, depending on the good or bad nature of the events foreseen. But the actual definition of "prophet" and, perhaps more importantly, the role of the prophet in Jewish and Christian traditions has little to do with foretelling the future. The Judeo-Christian prophet was and is one who speaks about the present, more specifically the pressing problems that she sees in the world around her. Prophets bring "urgent and compassionate critique to bear on the evils of their day . . . speak[ing] the truth in love with courage—come what may."[39] True to the pragmatist side of his prophetic pragmatism, West insists that prophecy does not concern itself with a ready-made future. Prophetic vision is not seeing a future that already exists, but seeing present problems that can and should be corrected so that human beings might bring about a better future.

For West, the Judeo-Christian tradition of prophecy provides a meaningful context for struggle against the evils that plague oppressed and downtrodden people throughout the world. Because they lack the richness and maturity of older, religious traditions such as Christianity, secular traditions generally cannot match religious traditions in social analysis and cultural criticism. In West's view, the issue at hand when a person decides to embrace Christianity thus is not a matter of rationally and logically proving that Christianity is true and deciding that it therefore can help struggle against evil. This approach is wrong-headed because it makes epistemological questions primary and delays moral and political action until those questions can be answered with some degree of certainty. Here is where epistemology should be evaded, West would insist. The need that West's prophetic pragmatism addresses is not epistemological, but onto-existential: religion is not a matter of knowing if Christianity is true, but a matter of staying sane in an absurd world. The question is whether Christianity is an enabling tradition, that is, a tradition that promotes survival through solidarity and struggle. And the risk taken in embracing Christianity is not logical, but psycho-ontological: "one risks not logical inconsistency but actual insanity; the issue is not reason or irrationality but life or death."[40]

Another reason that a religious version of prophetic pragmatism makes the most sense according to West is the deeply religious nature of the culture of the wretched of the earth. Solidarity with the wretched means appreciating the specific challenges in their lives and how they cope with them. Religion gives better, broader access to the life-worlds of the wretched and thus best enables this appreciation. Prophetic pragmatism does not mean uncritically accepting religion or the oppressive consequences that, West admits, it sometimes has had, especially for the wretched. But as others also have argued, examples such as the church-based civil rights movement show that Christianity can be something other than an opiate of the masses.[41] The black church in particular is not escapist. It instead, West explains, emphasizes "marshaling and garnering resources from fellowship, community, and personal strength (meditation, prayer) to cope with overwhelming limited options dictated by institutional and personal evil."[42] In fact, West goes so far as to claim that the black church has been central to many black people's lives not because they go there to find God, but because they go there to find shared heritage and community in the midst of an anti-black world.[43]

The Racialized Effects of Secularity

Given the importance of religion to the lives of many people of color, the effect of philosophy's silence on the subject is similar to that which Charles Mills has called the silence of exclusion.[44] Mills explains how the silence about race and racism in most of mainstream Western philosophy implicitly excludes people of color from participating in the field. The message sent by this exclusion is that the lives of people of color do not matter enough even to be acknowledged in philosophical discourse. Likewise, philosophy's silence about religion is not neutral. It sends a message that religion has no positive role to play in sophisticated, up-to-date philosophical discussion.[45]

This message, in turn, sends another: that the concerns of people of color are not the concerns of philosophy. Excluding religious concerns from philosophy has racialized effects for the discipline, in other words, indirectly but effectively saying to people of color that they have no place in philosophy—at least, not *as* people of color. Generally speaking, only if people of color have been willing to check their race at the door when they enter the whitewashed halls of philosophy could they enter at all. The result was and is the demographic and conceptual whiteness of philosophy.[46] Philosophy in the northern and western hemispheres tends to be populated by white people who then take up their concerns as if they were universal, without acknowledging or even seeing their false universalization. Without mentioning the word "race" at all, the very framework of philosophy as exclusive of religion can estrange people of color from the discipline.[47] No wonder then that philosophy often does not appeal to students of color, who then would never consider continuing their graduate studies in philosophy so they could enter the profession. The failure of philosophy to appreciate religious life as a meaningful form of lived experience is not the only reason that people of color sometimes avoid the field, but it is an important one.[48]

My point is not that philosophers must at all times be analyzing philosophical problems concerning the existence of God and similar issues for philosophy to be more inclusive of the concerns of people of color. Neither, echoing West, is my claim "that [all] . . . philosophers [should] become religious, but rather that they [should] once again take religion seriously, which also means taking culture and society seriously."[49] And this in turn means insisting that it not be only the culture and society of white people that is taken seriously by philosophy. The cultures and societies of people of color also should be at the center of what concerns academic philosophy.

The general dismissal of religion in academic philosophy is alienating not just to many people of color, but also to some white people. People of color are not the only ones negatively affected by philosophy's hostility toward religion. And some mainstream white philosophers, such as Charles Taylor, characterize religion in ways that are at least indirectly sympathetic to the interests and concerns of people of color. Pockets of philosophical friendliness to richly existential rather than narrowly epistemological conceptions of religion do exist. Finally, there are many instances of the conceptual whiteness of philosophy other than its dismissal of religion that can be off-putting to people of color. Philosophical hostility to religion is not the only, or perhaps even the primary reason that many people of color often find the discipline of philosophy unappealing. But, as I have argued, it is one factor in the overwhelming demographical whiteness of philosophy, one that might be more important than has been acknowledged to date. When one adds that factor to others such as philosophy's strong tendency toward exclusionary silence about specific issues of race and racism, the combination can become truly formidable for people of color.

Philosophy's secularism tends to interfere with the diversification of the discipline. This is somewhat ironic since at least some forms of secularism, such as that found in John Rawls's political conception of justice, propose secular strategies for dealing with public conflict so that inclusive forms of consensus might emerge. But the effect of those strategies can be the opposite of what is intended. As William Connolly explains, "secular models of thinking, discourse, and ethics are too constipated to sustain the diversity they seek to admire."[50] Philosophy needs to clear away the many obstacles to participation in the discipline that it presents to people of color, and secularism is one of those "invisible," largely unrecognized obstacles. Addressing philosophy's dismissive attitude toward religious ways of life will not by itself solve the problem of the dominant whiteness of philosophy, but it can and should be part of the solution. If philosophy is to concern itself with the interests, needs, and lives of more than just white people, it needs to better open itself to religion as a meaningful way of life.

Notes

My thanks go to Mariana Alessandri for first drawing my attention to the effect of philosophy's hostility to religion on people of color, and to George Yancy for his helpful comments on an earlier draft of this chapter.

1. Patricia Williams uses the metaphor of big-booted stomping versus tiptoeing in *Seeing a Color-Blind Future: The Paradox of Race* (New York: Farrar, Strauss, and Giroux, 1997), 61.
2. Shannon Sullivan, *Revealing Whiteness: The Unconscious Habits of Racial Privilege* (Bloomington, IN: Indiana University Press, 2006).
3. Charles Taylor, *A Secular Age* (Cambridge, MA: Harvard University Press, 2007), 2–3.
4. Taylor, *A Secular Age*, 13.
5. William E. Connolly, *Why I Am Not a Secularist* (Minneapolis, MN: University of Minnesota Press, 1999), 22.
6. Connolly, *Why I Am Not a Secularist*, 23.
7. This has as much, if not more to do with graduate school as a breeding ground for insecurity and inferiority complexes than with graduate students' personal character, but that's a story for another time.
8. Charles Taliaferro, "A Shakespearean Account of Redemption," Penn State University, March 23, 2007.
9. Ruth Sample, posting on swip-l@listserv.uh.edu, December 16, 2007.
10. Richard Rorty, "The Professor and the Prophet," *Transition* 52 (1991): 70.
11. Richard Rorty, "Religion in the Public Square: A Reconsideration," *Journal of Religious Ethics* 31, no. 1 (2003): 142.
12. For more on Richard Rorty on these points, see Shannon Sullivan, "Prophetic Vision and Trash Talkin': Pragmatism, Feminism and Racial Privilege," in *Pragmatism, Nation, and Race: Community in the Age of Empire*, ed. Chad Kautzer and Eduardo Mendieta (Bloomington, IN: Indiana University Press, 2009), 186–205.
13. Marilyn Frye, *The Politics of Reality* (Freedom, CA: Crossing Press, 1983), xvi.
14. Frye, *The Politics of Reality*, 175.
15. This paragraph and the one that follows have been adapted from Sullivan, "Prophetic Vision and Trash Talkin'," 196–97.
16. See, for example, Pamela Sue Anderson and Beverley Clack, eds., *Feminist Philosophy of Religion: Critical Readings* (New York: Routledge, 2004).
17. See Catharine MacKinnon, *Feminism Unmodified: Discourses on Life and Law* (Cambridge, MA: Harvard University Press, 1987), and *Are Women Human? And Other International Dialogues* (Cambridge, MA: Harvard University Press, 2006).
18. See, for example, MacKinnon, *Are Women Human?* 128–29.
19. Cornel West, "The Historicist Turn in Philosophy of Religion," in Cornel West, *The Cornel West Reader* (New York: Basic Civitas Books, 1999), 361.
20. West, "The Historicist Turn in Philosophy of Religion," 364.
21. Taylor, *A Secular Age*, 4–5, emphasis in original.
22. For a contemporary example of this, see the blog of "The Black Atheist," who aims to contribute to "'The New Atheist' movement of the 21st century" from the perspective of "the minority atheist community," theblackatheist.blogspot.com/ (accessed July 7, 2009).

23. Cornel West, *The American Evasion of Philosophy: A Genealogy of Pragmatism* (Madison, WI: University of Wisconsin Press, 1989), 233.
24. Robert E. Birt, interviewed in *African American Philosophers: 17 Conversations*, ed. George Yancy (New York: Routledge, 1998), 346.
25. Fredrick Harris, *Something Within: Religion in African American Political Activism* (New York: Oxford University Press, 1999), 8.
26. Harris, *Something Within*. 4.
27. M. Jacqui Alexander, *Pedagogies of Crossing: Meditations on Feminism, Sexual Politics, Memory, and the Sacred* (Durham, NC: Duke University Press, 2005), 326, 323.
28. Layli Phillips, "Womanism: On Its Own," in *The Womanist Reader*, ed. Layli Phillips (New York: Routledge, 2006), xx.
29. Michele M. Moody-Adams, interviewed in *African American Philosophers: 17 Conversations*, ed. George Yancy (New York: Routledge, 1998), 131.
30. Howard Thurman, *Jesus and the Disinherited* (Boston, MA: Beacon Press, 1976), 29.
31. Roberto S. Goizueta, "*Nosotros*: Toward a U.S. Hispanic Anthropology," *Hispanic Anthropology* 27, no. 1 (Winter 1992): 58.
32. Ada María Isasi-Díaz, La Lucha *Continues:* Mujerista *Theology* (Maryknoll, NY: Orbis Books, 2004), 1.
33. Isasi-Díaz, La Lucha *Continues*, 24–36.
34. Cornel West, interviewed in *African American Philosophers: 17 Conversations*, ed. George Yancy (New York: Routledge, 1998), 42.
35. West, *The American Evasion of Philosophy*, 233, 232.
36. West, *The American Evasion of Philosophy*, 212.
37. West, *The American Evasion of Philosophy*, 228.
38. West, *The American Evasion of Philosophy*, 228.
39. West, *The American Evasion of Philosophy*, 233.
40. West, *The American Evasion of Philosophy*, 233.
41. Cornel West, *Race Matters* (New York: Vintage Books, 1993), 144.
42. Cornel West, "Prophetic Christian as Organic Intellectual: Martin Luther King, Jr.," in Cornel West, *The Cornel West Reader* (New York: Basic *Civitas* Books, 1999), 427.
43. Cornel West, "Subversive Joy and Revolutionary Patience in Black Christianity," in Cornel West, *The Cornel West Reader* (New York: Basic *Civitas* Books, 1999), 437.
44. Charles Mills, *Blackness Visible: Essays on Philosophy and Race* (Ithaca, NY: Cornell University Press, 1998), 3.
45. This paragraph and the one that follows have been adapted from Sullivan, "Prophetic Vision and Trash Talkin'," 197, 200.
46. Mills, *Blackness Visible*, 2.
47. Lewis Gordon, interviewed in *African American Philosophers: 17 Conversations*, ed. George Yancy (New York: Routledge, 1998), 110–11.
48. Another one, for women of color in particular, can be radical separatism. bell hooks has argued that a feminist insistence on radical separatism implicitly has excluded women of color, who often want and need to work closely with men of color in political struggle against racism. hooks' analysis of the unspoken racial (and potentially racist) effects of radical separatism on feminism has inspired my argument concerning religion here. See hooks, *Feminist Theory: From Margin to Center* (Boston, MA: South End Press, 1984) 64–81.
49. West, "The Historicist Turn in Philosophy of Religion," 368.
50. Connolly, *Why I Am Not a Secularist*, 6.

9

Philosophy's Whiteness and the Loss of Wisdom

Susan E. Babbitt, Queen's University

Introduction

Soon after I began teaching philosophy in 1990 I was involved in organizing a panel at the Canadian Philosophical Association on racism and (the discipline of) Philosophy.[1] Charles Mills presented statistics about the number of Blacks and First Nations people gaining Ph.Ds in Philosophy across the U.S. and Canada. The numbers were in single digits. Mills pointed out then that these numbers had changed little over the preceding decade. Apparently, they have changed little since.

What struck most of us on that panel was the sheer difficulty of raising questions about racism and Philosophy. We intended the panel to address the question of why Philosophy is so white. Yet we only managed to generate discussion about racism itself—what it is, what it is not. The facts about Philosophy's whiteness are not controversial. Thus, we thought the panel would address questions about the organization of the discipline, including curricula. Some of us even thought the panel might provide occasion to recognize and state that Philosophy, as we practice and teach it, is possibly racist. For the relative absence of non-whites in the discipline reflects the reality that Philosophy departments mostly, even only, teach the work of whites, specifically the work of English-speaking white men of northern European descent. And if we are teaching, or even giving students the impression, that all relevant thinking about the human condition has been done by whites, are we not promoting white supremacy?

At one level it seems obvious that there is a problem. Philosophy is part of the Humanities and as such we understand it to address questions about the human condition. Forty years ago, U.S. philosopher and social critic Thomas Merton said that we can no longer understand the Humanities to include only the thinkers of the West. We must also include the contemplative traditions of Asia. He added then in 1967 that, in his view, our survival, spiritual and physical, may well depend upon such inclusion.[2] Indeed, I know no professional philosopher who would deny that "humanity" includes the peoples of Asia, Africa, Latin America and Aboriginal peoples. And no one would deny that these peoples have complex histories, and ingenious cultures and ideas. Yet still, in the Anglo-American tradition at least, we teach philosophy as if only certain peoples have contributed to and are likely to contribute to our understanding of the human condition.

Yet some will say that it is not reasonable to expect small Philosophy departments to teach courses in Asian, Latin American, Aboriginal, and African philosophies. Philosophy departments cannot teach everything. However, we could be teaching philosophy in such a way that students understand that the philosophies of other traditions and cultures matter to us as human beings. We could be teaching students to raise questions about the philosophical tradition they know, and we could be showing students that and how raising such questions is hard. For we become attached to certain ways of seeing the world and then have difficulty even recognizing that we see the world in such ways. Raising questions about the discipline itself requires that we see that Philosophy could be otherwise by which I mean that the fundamental questions could be otherwise. And this means, at least arguably, seeing that we could be otherwise, that is, that we could think otherwise of ourselves as human beings. For that is what, as I understand it, Philosophy is ultimately about—what it means to live in the world, and get along, as human beings.

I don't believe university Philosophy teachers do this very well, or that we even intend to. Hilary Putnam pointed out that raising questions requires bold imaginative conceptualization together with conviction. For in order to see that there is something that has not been understood and that needs to be understood, that is, in order to raise a question, we need to see that the world could really be other than we expect it to be and that moreover it makes sense to think that it could be otherwise. For instance, Putnam argued that there could never have been questions about Newton's theories if Einstein had not first demonstrated that the world can be conceived of otherwise.[3] Einstein developed an alternative conceptual scheme that made it possible to question deep-seated beliefs about physics, beliefs that could not have been questioned before, precisely because they were so deep-seated. It did not make sense until Einstein, for instance, to question belief in the well-established formula "$f=ma$," so much so that any empirical evidence showing that formula to have failed would be thought to have involved experimental error. It would have been dismissed. The evidence suggesting that "$f=ma$" could be wrong, which existed, gained importance only when there was something for that evidence to explain, which was the possibility of error, a possibility that Einstein's conceptualization made plausible.

It is obvious that Philosophy is one of the whitest disciplines in the Humanities. It is well-known that not only can a student in Canada or the U.S. gain an undergraduate degree studying almost nothing but the work of white English speaking men of northern European descent but that also students are subtly encouraged to do so. Yet there seems to be no question about why this is

Philosophy's Whiteness and the Loss of Wisdom 169

so, that is, no demand for an explanation. By this I mean that there is no real surprise at the fact that this is so and therefore no reason for trying to discover why the discipline is this way, how it got there and what it would take to change it.

In what follows, I suggest that if there is no question about why Philosophy is so white, it is because there is no general expectation that Philosophy ought not to be so.[4] As we know from the Philosophy of Science, it is not evidence that determines interest in new possibilities but rather interest in new possibilities that makes feasible the discovery of and the importance given to the evidence for such possibilities.[5] Thus, in order for there to be some evidence that Philosophy ought not to be so white, and that students really should be learning about the human condition from Africans, Latin Americans, Asians and Aboriginal peoples also, there has first to be a real *interest* in the possibility. By this I mean that there has to be some expectation that a tradition of mostly white English speaking men of northern European descent just might not be getting it all right and that it could be a good thing, therefore, to find out what other traditions might offer.

My other point in what follows is that this question of whiteness, and the difficulty of resolving it academically, has to do, fundamentally, with the nature of Philosophy as the pursuit of wisdom. I suggest that it is not possible to appreciate the rich philosophical contributions of "other" traditions if certain popular philosophical assumptions of the Anglo-American tradition are not questioned. In particular, I have in mind a popular commitment, particularly among political philosophers, to the view that freedom is defined, roughly, by ability to choose, under the right conditions, among a wide array of meaningful options. There is, arguably, plenty of evidence that this sort of view is in fact false and that freedom results instead from the right sorts of understanding and awareness, not primarily from capacity to choose, although choice is important. Yet it is almost impossible to argue against this view of freedom without encountering a certain kind of emotional resistance and the accusation that the alternative to such a view is to endorse a kind of repression. That is, if ever it is suggested that it may not be the case that it is *always* better to choose for oneself rather than be coerced, one is suspected of endorsing repression. However, as it turns out, it is quite often the case that choosing for oneself is not in fact better than arriving at a state or set of conditions by other means.[6]

I suspect that professional philosophers' attachment to this view of freedom is largely unexamined and mostly a matter of existential security. That is, I suspect the view is comfortable but unfounded, and that it could be known to be unfounded if it were not so comfortable. My point here, though, is not primarily about freedom, although I will say more about this view below. I use the question of freedom as an example. My point, instead, is that if professional philosophers, because of personal commitment to certain views, are unable to raise the sorts of questions that critically identify deep-seated assumptions about who we are as human beings, we might wonder whether the dominant academic practice of Philosophy, at least in the English-speaking traditions, is really about wisdom after all. It might be, instead, as a student regretfully commented to me recently, about correctness. I will suggest that the pursuit of wisdom requires a kind of humility that is not a usual characteristic of the academic practice of Philosophy, at least in the English-speaking world. Philosophy as we teach it is instead often characterized by an obsession with clarity and precision, and a fear of precisely the sort of healthy confusion and uncertainty that might get us somewhere, philosophically. And I am not arguing here against clarity and precision.

The Indifference Contract

More than a decade ago, in *The Racial Contract,* Charles Mills commented on the paucity of African Americans in the profession of Philosophy, only about 1% of the North American total.[7] In *Contract and Domination*, written more recently with Carole Pateman, Mills points out that this figure has not changed proportionally.[8] He adds that the number of women within the group of African Americans is lower than that of men. At the time of his writing, he guesses that there are not more than 30 African American women in the profession of Philosophy in all of the United States. The numbers of Asians and Latin Americans are even lower, and the number of Native Americans in Philosophy is not more than 5 or 6 for the entire country.

Non-whites, and especially women of colour are, then, as Mills points out, "space invaders," "trespassers," marked by race and gender as doubly "out of place" in a discipline that pretends to be universal. It is notable, according to Mills, that the most famous woman of colour with a philosophy background, Angela Davis, does not teach in a Philosophy department or publish in Philosophy journals. Well-known Nigerian-American philosopher, Nkiru Nzegwu, no longer teaches in a Philosophy department. Those women of colour who stay in Philosophy report bearing the burden of "integrating the bus," as Uma Narayan describes it. Narayan, an Asian American philosopher, writes about being treated as hotel staff at American Philosophical Association meetings and of her career-long desire to see the discipline of philosophy integrated so that future generations of philosophers of colour do not bear the enormous burden that she has born within the academic world.[9]

Yet Mills' own solution to the problem that he has done much to identify is indicative of the nature of the problem and its difficulty. In *Contract and Domination*, which is a discussion between Charles Mills and Carole Pateman about the long-established and popular tradition of contract theory, Mills argues that contract theory does indeed provide a model for defining justice. Contract theory is a philosophical device that defines justice in terms of what certain people would agree to under the right conditions. It is an idealization on the basis of which arguments are made for some or other conception of social justice. For instance, we ask what certain people would desire for themselves if they were choosing without knowing their own class or social position, and with a knowledge of relevant social facts, and we arrive from such a consideration at an understanding of what would be required for social justice. Pateman disagrees with this project, arguing that the fundamental philosophical conceptions—of freedom, the self, the community—upon which contract theory rests need to be reexamined. I do not intend to examine here Mills' arguments for revising contract theory to answer problems of historic systemic injustice or Pateman's specific argument against his defense. I am interested instead in one of Mills' reasons for wanting to make the argument for social contract in the first place. Social contract theory should be revised, according to Mills, to address the problems of exclusion in society at large, including Philosophy. He writes that "the overwhelming rationale for seeking to engage with contract theory is that it's already there and is hegemonic."[10] Indeed, "liberalism and the discourse of rights are globally triumphant and contract theory is the best established vehicle for expressing these normative commitments [to justice and equality]."[11]

Thus, Mills wants to defend contract theory as an answer to systemic injustice, including the whiteness of Philosophy, because contract theory is philosophically hegemonic. Mills also writes that there are no alternatives to liberalism, or at least none that have been successful. He asks, begging a number of important questions: "What's the alternative? Besides, what's wrong with moral equality, autonomy, self-realization, equality before the law, due process, freedom of expression, freedom of association, voting rights, and so forth?"[12] Mills suggests here, without argument, that there are no alternatives because marxism is "presently moribund," communitarianism is relativistic and feminists are turning toward justice again after insisting initially on an "ethic of care." Contract theory should be defended, according to Mills, because it is well-established, because it has been successful and because there are no alternatives.

Yet Nkiru Nzegwu, in *Family Matters: Feminist Concepts in African Philosophy of Culture*, points precisely to philosophers' uncritical acceptance of the foundations of their own culturally specific discipline to explain why the activities and theories of the Igbo women of West Africa can never be a source of philosophical insight, but are instead only of anthropological interest for U.S. feminists.[13] Nzegwu, mentioned above, was trained in Philosophy but now teaches in the Department of Africana Studies at Binghamton University. She is one of those who no longer teaches in a Philosophy department, and she does not publish her work in Philosophy journals.

Nzegwu's recent book, *Family Matters,* tells the story of the history and organization of Igbo women of east Nigeria. While some North American feminists have pointed to analysis in terms of gender as a defining aspect of feminist scholarship, Nzegwu argues that Igbo society is not organized according to gender, or at least it was not so organized prior to colonization. In Igbo society, there are jobs typically done by women and others typically done by men. But it is common for women to do work usually done by men and vice versa. For instance, women take responsibility for certain sorts of agricultural development, yet if the need arises, they could undertake the responsibility that is usually allotted to men. (The same is true for men.) An interesting aspect of this phenomenon is that a woman will not be considered male in undertaking these activities, as some have assumed, nor would a man who supported her in such a role be considered female.[14]

Nzegwu's book shows how Western scholars, and even Igbo historians themselves, get it wrong about Igbo society when they analyze it in terms of gender. If gender is based on sexual differentiation that accords women as a group a lower status than men, understanding Igbo society requires that we think about equality without gender-based constraints. Nzegwu argues that equality within a non-gendered society is not a matter of *sameness* according to pre-established norms but rather of the results of equal sharing of duties and responsibilities to the community at large. The category "gender" as understood in the West just does not apply in this situation.

This example of social organization—called a dual-sex system—is of philosophical interest: It is typical to think of equality in terms of how two groups are the same where what it means to be "the same" depends upon what we start with. So, for instance, equality for women is defined in terms of what men have within the current society. The conception of social equality demonstrated by the Igbo conception of society does not depend in such a way upon the current arrangement; instead, what it means to have social equality depends upon what happens within the society when those whose equality is at stake are given equal duties and responsibilities. It is not that a certain conception of the society determines what people ought to have and to do; rather, in the Igbo situation, it is assumed that a certain respectful conception of what people ought to have and to do will determine the ideal of social equality in general.

The organization of Igbo society into a dual-sex system puts the questions of equality differently. It is not necessary to start with a conception of society and the groups that make it up in order to ask what those groups should have in order to be *the same* within that society. Instead, the question is about how groups within the society can live and work best for the good of the community, with equal respect and opportunity, and to derive from this consideration a conception of the society and its needs for justice. The focus is not on the *sameness* of groups, or even on the groups at all, but on the conditions according to which people can best work and live productively in harmony. As Nzegwu argues, the Igbo social organization offers up sensible and innovative conceptions of the family, sex, marriage, responsibility for children, children's rights and relationships between individuals and society. But none of these is easily understandable without understanding the general conceptualization of social equality in society at large. And yet, as she demonstrates in a fascinating docudrama in chapter four of *Family Matters*, it is typical for North American scholars to try to understand each particular concept on the basis of assumptions underlying the organization of North American societies but that are not typical of some African societies. It is in regard to this well-known point about Western bias in scholarship of Africa that Nzegwu points out the dangers for Philosophy of the *personal* commitment to philosophical frameworks, a point I return to below.

The question that is raised about Philosophy in *Family Matters* is: Why is a discussion of Igbo women not treated as *philosophically* interesting, that is, as contributing to a discussion about how equality in general is conceptualized but is instead treated as *anthropologically* interesting, that is, as a discussion not about human beings in general, but about the empirically established differences between one group and another, in this case, between Americans and Igbos? When we approach an example as anthropologically interesting, it makes sense to look at the example as *other*, that is, in terms of its differences from what is familiar. Of course, anthropology teaches us about human beings in some general sense but it does so by identifying similarities and differences. Philosophy, at least on some understandings, looks for more universal sorts of understandings. We look for differences but we do so in order to identify false universalizations. So, for instance, when women entered Philosophy, with experiences and perceptions different from those of most men, it became clear that general philosophical accounts of, for instance, autonomy and moral development were inadequate, derived from the experience of men, and not in fact characteristic of human experience in general. Differences are philosophically interesting but not primarily as differences; instead, differences are important for identifying and understanding *sameness*. So Nzegwu asks why the experience of Igbo women is not an example that raises questions about false generalizations about equality, ones based primarily upon the experience of North American and European societies. Why, instead, is the experience of Igbo women, including understandings of family, sex, children's rights and social roles, dismissed as irrelevant to North American and European societies precisely because it does not fit with generalizations based upon such societies?

Nzegwu's answer to this question is, as I understand it, self-satisfaction—specifically satisfaction about national identity, defined in particular by certain conceptions of freedom and individuality. The contract theory that Mills is determined to defend is a view that takes for granted certain fundamental conceptions. It takes for granted the view, for instance, that what people choose in specific conditions defines, or mostly defines a person's real interests.[15] When Mills says, as noted above, "Besides, what's wrong with moral equality, autonomy, self-realization, equality before the law, due process, freedom of expression, freedom of association, voting rights, and so forth?" he takes it to be a rhetorical question.[16] It is not a rhetorical question; it is one with an answer. There *is* something wrong with moral equality, autonomy, self-realization, etc., when such concepts are defined in terms of popular (liberal) assumptions of Anglo-American philosophy. And what is wrong with these concepts has been identified by marxist and feminist philosophers—scholarship he ignores. It is precisely in regard to this sort of question-begging dismissal that Nzegwu identifies an "epistemological crisis" within North American philosophy. She is referring to a self-satisfied unwillingness to question precisely those deep-seated, successful, "hegemonic" conceptions that provide security to the discipline and ultimately to a sense of identity.[17] And among these conceptions are all the ones Mills lists.

Mills is right to think that no one can reasonably be against moral equality. But moral equality is conceptualized differently by the Igbo people of east Nigeria and the Igbo conception makes sense. This is what *Family Matters* demonstrates. Yet, if it is assumed without argument, as Mills does, that there is no question about moral equality, then whatever the Igbos are talking about cannot be moral equality, because it is not the same.

What Nzegwu refers to as an "epistemological crisis" is an unwillingness to question certain well-established and comfortable conceptions, such as freedom and individuality, the presumption of which rules out the philosophical plausibility of some of the world's important traditions. At least it rules out the plausibility of such traditions as ones telling us about moral equality, autonomy, freedom, and so on.

While Mills considers the hegemonic status of contract theory to provide a reason for its defense, Pateman argues, importantly, that what she calls "the contract of *indifference*" is more fundamental than either the sexual or racial contracts.[18] The *indifference contract*, she says, is that contract according to which "we" identify ourselves as human beings in such a way as to make certain others aliens. The *indifference contract*, Pateman suggests, is that sense of *sameness* that makes 80% of the world's populations *other* in the relevant sense, that is, other than human. It is an implicit assumption about who matters, i.e., about who constitutes the generalized "we" in discussions of the human condition. The *indifference contract* is a certain sense of complacence about the question of what it means to be a human being that rules out any need to investigate the views of people outside North America, northern Europe and a few other societies.

The *indifference contract* explains how it is that most of the world disappears from our thinking. Thus, for instance, Italian journalist Gianni Miná, in the "Prologue" of *Un continente desaparecido,* suggests that many of us end up with bizarre expectations about human wellbeing. We seem to believe life and aspirations have been guaranteed, by some sort of Divine Right, to the 29 nations of the world who control the markets (e.g., Canada, United States, Europe, and Japan), and who represent only a fifth of the world's population.[19] And of course, it is not surprising that the richest 20% of the world's population does not see the evils of the system we benefit from. But why is there no shame? According to some plausible definitions of human flourishing, it is not possible to live well with shame (e.g. Sen 1965, x). And the 20% are supposedly living well. So there must be, in general, no shame.

Miná asks what sort of "verdadera incomprehensión cultural"[20] protects us from the horrified gaze of those on the other side of what Fidel Castro calls the new iron curtain along the Rio Grande River, separating the U.S. and Mexico? And what sort of reasoning explains surprise that the other four fifths of the world's population, who have lost their resources to the richest fifth, and who cannot now find a decent life where they are, are trying to jump the wall to reach the North for some chance of survival? It must be that the 80% just don't matter, or at least don't matter in relevant ways. This is what Pateman refers to as the indifference contract.

The Mills/Pateman book provides a useful example of the difficulty of addressing the whiteness issue in Philosophy within the Anglo-American tradition. Mills suggests, without argument, that there are no alternatives to the liberal view. Yet there certainly are alternatives. And some are well worked-out, and have been for millenia. But such views—feminist, marxist humanist, Buddhist, the views of the ancient Chinese philosopher Chuang Tzu—cannot be alternatives to liberal views about moral equality, autonomy, and so on, unless they can *be* views about moral equality, autonomy, and so on. And this cannot be possible unless there is some question about such liberal views, that is, some expectation that such views might be wrong, thus making it plausible to reconsider them. Pateman, for one, suggests such views might be wrong. But her argument is harder to make and Mills easy dismissal of the important questions about liberalism shows why.

The Cuba Example

I now consider an example of what is involved in investigating presuppositions about *sameness*, that is, in questioning the presuppositions of ideology informing national identities.[21] Cuba is a country in our hemisphere that is rich in ideas. It is, for instance, the birthplace of José Martí, a nineteenth century philosopher, poet and military general whose ideas about political unity, freedom and moral development continue to inspire new Latin American and Caribbean generations concerned for global justice. Yet I am often struck by the tendency of professional philosophers, even otherwise progressive ones, to dismiss Cuba entirely because Cuba "is not free," where "free" is left undefined and unargued for.[22]

I take it that this is how Pateman's "indifference contract" works. Scholars try to understand Cuba, or the Igbo women, by gathering empirical information, but then draw conclusions from that collection of data without bothering to consider the conceptual issues upon which the analysis of such information is based. At least, they do not consider the relevant conceptual issues, which are precisely those pertaining to fundamental questions about human reality, such as freedom. So, for instance, people go to Cuba to investigate democracy in Cuba and take the central question to be the existence of a single party system. They note that there is only one political party and they make an effort to find out whether there are plans to introduce a second party. It is important to point out here that I am referring not to enemies of Cuba but to those who are sympathetic. Friends of Cuba, concerned with the issue of democracy, examine the possibility of a multi-party system and they excuse Cuba for its single party system because Cuba exists under the threat of U.S. invasion and cannot afford to "open up" during such a period of national insecurity.[23]

Yet it is obvious to anyone who knows even just a little about Cuba that there exist serious intelligent people who think that democracy can indeed exist with a single party system. They have arguments for this position, arguments rooted in rich philosophical traditions. In Philosophy, we teach students that in order to be fair in argument, it is important to understand an opponent's arguments in a way that attributes to that opponent intelligence and moral responsibility. In other words, it is not considered fair argument to construe the opponent's views as stupid or morally irresponsible; at least, it is not fair to start out with that assumption. First we try to understand the argument in a way that makes sense, assuming our opponent's intellectual and moral equality, and then we ask whether the argument so formulated holds up. Yet it is quite common in the case of Cuba for well-intended scholars to say, "I cannot understand how anyone can think that there can be democracy with a single party" and then to just move on from there as if just because they cannot understand it, it cannot be possible. They do not bother to seriously consider the arguments.

Rhetorical questions can represent a kind of question-begging, the suggestion without argument that the opposing position is wrong. For instance, someone can say, "How can anyone think that there can be democracy when there are only a few thin newspapers in the streets?" And yet, there is an answer to this question that could be pursued. The problem is that there wouldn't be a reason to seek the answer out if one didn't first have some expectation that such an answer might matter, that is, if one didn't first have an interest in understanding an answer. For instance, there would not be a reason to take the question seriously if one did not first expect that—just perhaps—piles of thick newspapers in the streets are irrelevant to genuine democracy. As Putnam pointed out in regard to Newton, in order for there to be a question, there has to be some expectation that the world could in fact be other than previously taken for granted. This would include the expectation that those who think it could be otherwise have views worth trying to understand.

In 2001 I began taking large groups of Canadian students to study at the University of Havana for two weeks and I insisted that the course be a Philosophy course.[24] This was for an important reason. I did not intend to take students to Cuba for a field trip to see some other part of the world, so that they could see how people live elsewhere. In particular, I did not want to be introducing students to the Third World so that they could understand how privileged they are in Canada, although of course this would happen. The objective of the course was primarily philosophical. I introduced the course and undertook the enormous organizational hurdles with the objective that the students learn something about fair and constructive engagement—philosophical engagement—with people whose philosophical traditions, as well as their historical, economic and geographical conditions, are different from their own. I tried to make it clear to students that I was not taking them to Havana so that they could learn about Cubans, although certainly they would learn a lot about the Cuban situation. Instead, I was taking them there so that they would learn something about themselves, as persons. By this I meant, not that the trip should be a voyage of self-discovery, although often it was, but that they should do the work to understand what the philosophical ideas they encountered in Cuba, and Latin America more generally, implied for their thinking about issues affecting them here in their own country. I wanted students to see that ideas, and not just culture and revolution, come from Latin America. And I wanted them to understand, even just to begin to understand, what this means for them as scholars, if they really want to be, as students generally do, "citizens of the world."

My own interest in Cuba has been multifaceted. I went to Cuba for the first time, for a Philosophy conference, in June 1993. This was the year that the economic crisis, following the collapse of the Soviet Union, was kicking in. It was being widely predicted that Cuba could not survive. In Cuba, there were almost famine conditions. Few goods were entering the country and many people were trying to cross the 90 miles between Cuba and the US. But there at the Faculty of Philosophy and History, at the University of Havana, professors and students, without pens or lights, were working on philosophical questions. I found interesting, not the question of why people were leaving the island, which had an obvious answer given the crisis, but rather the question of why people were staying, as they were, steadfastly. I was intrigued, and moved, by the example of and ensuing friendship with people who really believed that they could make their society better, even under such difficult conditions, and who continued to work for that. From 1993–1995 I went twice a year to the University of Havana and from 1996–1999 I spent 3–4 months a year there, becoming fluent in the language and familiar with Cuba's complexity and interest. Impressively, even as they struggled to survive, Cuba gave priority to children and youth. Indeed, it was during the difficult decade of the 90s that Cuba finally brought its infant mortality rate to below 10, a significant feat for a poor, embattled country.

The fact that Cuba has survived and has moved forward economically and socially, in many ways, demands explanation. So, besides being impressed by Cuba's many accomplishments, I was primarily intrigued from the beginning by the question of why there is no question about Cuba's successes. So much is known about Cuba's achievements in health, education, sport, emergency response, culture, agriculture and many other areas. And so much more could be known. I was fascinated by Cuba's development program as well as by its unique system of government that had made such programs possible. But my primary interest, being a philosopher, was in the question of understanding. Why is such a powerful example so easily dismissed by the world at large and by philosophers as well? And what does it take for it to be understood fairly?

I wanted students to see what it meant to engage fairly in argument when doing so means raising questions about fundamental assumptions, ones related in particular to their own sense of who they are in the world, assumptions they were undoubtedly attached to. As it turns out, though, even for students to understand the philosophical foundations of the Cuban revolution, they had to have some experience of this sort of questioning: Students had to be able to question their own ideological foundations, or at least see that there could be a question, in order to consider Cuba's philosophical foundations worth-pursuing. But they also had to do this, or at least see that it could be done, in order to understand Cuba's philosophical roots. For two of the important theorists of the Cuban Revolution, Martí, and Che Guevara in the twentieth century, both argued that we only come to understand and realize ourselves as human beings when we become able to identify and critically examine the implicit presuppositions, inherited from tradition and upbringing, of our very sense of ourselves as individuals. For it is these sorts of inherited values, beliefs and preferences that rob us of our freedom.[25]

Martí, who was not a marxist, and Che Guevara, one of the most important contributors to 20th century marxist humanism, both argued that freedom is not a matter of the availability of choice; instead, freedom is possible *only* as a result of a cultured understanding of the arbitrary influences, rooted in the social, educational, family and religious traditions one happens to be born into, compelling one to favour some options and reject others. This is what Martí meant when he said that "Man's first task is to reconquer himself."[26] He didn't mean the kind of psychological awareness that results from introspection. Quite to the contrary, Martí thought real *self*-awareness arises from understanding the universe and one's place in it. Only in the context of such engagement with nature, and appreciating one's small place in it is there the possibility of more adequate perspective, and freedom from relevant aspects of an arbitrarily derived background.[27]

Martí understood that freedom cannot be defined by deep-seated desires, preferences and so on, for the person who relies only upon herself to know her interests is doomed to be controlled by the mostly arbitrary patterns of her particular and narrow past. And so, as Martí emphasized, one ends up like an oyster, seeing the shell and thinking the world is dark: "He who lives under an autocratic creed is like an oyster in his shell, seeing only the prison that traps him and believing, in the darkness, that it is the world. Liberty gives wings to the oyster. And what seemed a prodigious battle when heard from within the shell turns out to be, in the light and open air, the natural movement of the vital fluids driven by the energetic pulse of the world."[28]

Now it is not my position that we should try to understand the arguments in order to justify the positions such arguments support. Instead, we should try to understand the arguments in order to see whether they are persuasive. Just because Martí, who was one of the theorists of the Cuban revolution, argued persuasively that freedom is only possible through education and culture, with his own special understanding of both education and culture, does not mean that the Cuban government, by emphasizing education and culture, has pursued freedom and democracy. It does mean, however, that it is unfair to dismiss such arguments because they do not prioritize the existence of multiple parties. It is also uninteresting.

Students were expected to understand the arguments for a single party system and to see how such arguments make sense in terms of the arguments' own philosophical conceptions. They didn't have to agree that the arguments make sense, but they had to do the work to see how such arguments *might* make sense.[29] Having understood the arguments and their foundations in Martí and Guevara's conceptions of freedom, they could then argue against such views, defending their own understandings of freedom and democracy. However, if they have in fact understood the philosophical foundations of the Cuban system, they cannot, arguing fairly and respectfully, assume without argument that an individual's or a society's interests are defined by what would be chosen under the right conditions, as on liberal philosophical views. They cannot just assume without argument that freedom is best understood in terms of metaphorical "openness."[30] If it is reasonable to think otherwise they have to now *argue* that their understanding is preferable. In defending their views against a reasonable alternative, they will have deepened their understanding of their own position, even if they haven't changed their position.

It doesn't make sense to make an argument for a position for which there is no sensible alternative. It is when we recognize that we could reasonably think otherwise that it becomes necessary to argue for one view rather than the other. This recognition, though, sometimes comes about as the result of an emotional, not primarily an intellectual experience. For in the case of Cuba, the ideological forces discouraging fair understanding are considerable. And sometimes people only begin to try to understand Cubans' arguments when they find they really *like* Cubans or *like* Cuba, or when they are moved by an experience there. In the much reprinted article, "Cuba Libre," 1960s radical Leroi Jones describes how he came to be able to identify the ideology of his country, the United States, as a result of an emotional experience.[31] Jones went to Cuba determined not to be "taken in" by the communists. He was, as was typical of Americans in the 1960s, suspicious of communists. But he interacted with Cubans in Cuba and describes his experience of their happiness. Jones' personal, emotional experience in Cuba contradicted his expectations that these people should be dismissed. He had expected that these people might be somewhat crazy. But as a result of the contradiction between his expectations and what he felt when he shared the Cubans' happiness, he became aware of such expectations and became able to question them. Then, when he returned to the U.S., Jones describes becoming aware of the "thin crust of lie that we cannot even detect in our own thinking" and from that awareness he went on to become a radical and effective critic of his own society.

Jones could easily have dismissed the contradictions between his deep-seated beliefs and his actual experiences in Cuba, and remained with his more comfortable assumptions. If he had relied upon his intellectual analysis of the situation, this is what he might have done. What he experienced with the Cubans could be explained away, for instance, as craziness or weirdness, just as evidence against $f=ma$ could be explained away as some kind of mistake with the experiment. Rationality often, and correctly, works this way: In many cases, we should not reject deep-seated beliefs because of a momentary emotional or intuitive perception; instead, we depend upon established background beliefs and assumptions to provide reason for rejecting a strong emotional sense of connectedness, or an intuition. But in the story Jones tells, he cared enough about the people with whom he engaged in Cuba, and what their reality might suggest for him, to ask a question and to pursue more adequate explanatory resources. And, as a result, he came to realize that some of his established beliefs were false and that he had good reason to question other such beliefs.

Many people only become able to identify and eventually question their own ideological foundations when they have a personal emotional experience that is in some sense transformative. In taking students to Cuba I wanted them to see how some understanding is not acquired primarily through intellectual analysis, although it will involve intellectual analysis. In particular, I wanted them to see how, in some situations, the very possibility of intellectual analysis depends upon emotional experience, for it requires the existence of a question, that is, some doubt about deep-seated presuppositions, including philosophical ones. I hoped that they would understand this as a result of their own efforts to engage fairly with the Cuban reality. But they would also know this if they studied the Cuban philosophical traditions directly. Like Marx, Martí thought we become estranged from ourselves, and others, when we allow ourselves to be guided only by intellectual reasoning, identifying, usually unself-consciously, with intellectual abstractions, including national ideals, group identities, political ideals and so on. In a beautiful passage about authenticity, Martí describes how he found his own voice, not by writing "in academic ink" but "in my own blood": He writes, "None of [my verses] has emerged from my mind, warmed over, artful and beautified; they have come like tears springing from the eyes or blood spurting out from a wound . . . . I am responsible for the copy. I found some garments that were torn and others that were whole, and I wore these colours. I know they are not worn out. I love difficult sonorities and sincerity, even when it may seem brutal."[32]

This sort of emotional, experiential understanding is not given much place in Anglo-American philosophy but it is the highest form of wisdom in Eastern philosophies. Martí was deeply aware of the brutality of colonialism and the deadening force of imperialist ideology.[33] He knew the confusing effects of an ideology that, as Simón Bolívar declared, has sent us nothing but misery in the name of liberty.[34] For this reason, perhaps, Martí knew from his own experience that when we rely only upon intellectual argument, i.e., upon "academic ink," whatever does not fit with established concepts can be dismissed. However, when we are emotionally moved by an experience or a perception, and we feel that experience or perception to be of a certain sort—beautiful, perhaps—it is much harder to dismiss it. If scholars engage with the situation and peoples of either Cuba or east Nigeria to such an extent that, as Martí says, "I found some garments that were torn and others that were whole, and I wore these colours," they might not so easily prejudge the significance of such stories and may instead find reason to pursue more adequate understanding.

Perhaps because of the priority given to experiential understanding, Merton says, as mentioned above, that our spiritual and maybe even our physical survival could depend upon really teaching the Humanities, including the contemplative traditions of Asia.[35] Experiential, emotional understanding is at the heart of some Eastern philosophies, but it is marginal in Western philosophies. Marxists and existentialists recognised, and insisted upon, the danger of alienation through identification with intellectual abstractions. But Merton, for one, thinks that neither marxists nor existentialists fully understood the power of their own insights into the nature and need for authenticity.[36] Although Eastern philosophies, particularly Buddhism, are sometimes dismissed in the West as being quietistic, as involving withdrawal from the world, the emphasis on meditation and solitude is, as Merton argues, the most radical response to the problem of alienation. For among the ideals that we substitute for real life experience are ideals about ourselves, including such personal ideals as being "progressive," "mindful" or "self-aware."[37] But questioning abstractions related to ourselves—i.e., the sense of presuppposed *sameness* referred to as the *indifference contract*—cannot be an issue about introspection, arrived at through self-regard. It is, instead, an issue about experiencing—really experiencing—the world around us, with respect and humility, and discovering in the process that some cherished beliefs about the world and our place in it might be wrong.

I have to mention here that, although I took students to Cuba for five years, I do not think it is necessary to travel somewhere to be sufficiently moved to ask relevant questions about one's own expectations and stabilizing beliefs. What is necessary, though, is humility. Einstein wrote that in the case of science, real expertise requires humility because science is not just about solving problems, which any good scientists can do, but about identifying new questions, new priorities. Einstein thought that great scientists must be the most "religious" (in his sense) of persons because of the need for respect for the mysteries of the universe and human existence.[38] Such respect, Einstein suggested, is incompatible with arrogance and self-absorption. As Marti commented in his remark about the oyster, someone who is guided by self-importance ends up mistaking the oyster shell for the world, and thinking the world is dark.

Analytic Anglo-American philosophy does not have much theoretical room for Einstein's sense of mystery or Martí's perception of beauty. Or so it seems to me after almost twenty years of teaching in this tradition. Certainly the ideas are there in much of the work of feminists, but they are not dominant in the tradition. Those of us who teach them do so in courses that are electives, or we do so for short periods and then our courses are cancelled (as my Cuba course was suddenly—without consultation, process or explanation). But the core courses in Philosophy do not encourage students toward the sort of humility that would lead them to seek out the arguments for alternative views. Indeed, there is a kind of argument that is all too familiar in Philosophy discussions in which someone who is presenting a different sort of view—feminist, Nigerian, Buddhist—is responded to by saying, "I cannot understand why someone would think. . ." and the fact that this is not understood is presented as an argument against the view being presented. Now I don't want to be misunderstood: There are some views that should be dismissed. There are some views for which there are good reasons to think they are indeed nutty, even without much examination. But when whole continents of people have followed certain views—Buddhist, for instance—there is reason to think that such views might be worth trying to understand, and to understand fairly.

A year ago, in Havana, I asked the well-known and much respected Cuban philosopher, Rigoberto Pupo Pupo why he thought it was that some of the exciting developments in Latin American philosophy, about which he is so passionate in his close collaboration with Mexican philosophers, are never talked about, even mentioned, at the American and Canadian Philosophical Associations. I knew the answer, but I wanted to hear him say it in his quietly passionate, dignified way. He said, "The analytic tradition is the dominant one. They don't need to listen. But human beings are so complex. How can we think that human beings learn only in one way—through reason and logic? We learn in so many ways—through metaphors, stories, feeling, perceptions of beauty. How can we think philosophical understanding is so limited?" I had learned from Pupo about Martí's commitment to the perception of beauty as the foundation of *all* philosophical understanding and I had learned from his example what this might mean. I have since found ways to explain this—to students at least—within the analytic tradition that I mostly teach. Martí's contribution is profound. While his contribution is not the subject of this chapter, its importance is.

"Freedom" is Dead

I want to turn briefly now to the hegemonic views about freedom that make it hard to give importance to philosophers such as Martí whose commitment to freedom is different. A few years ago, I published a paper on the issue of raising philosophical questions about popular conceptions of freedom and individuality, without which, in my view, it is impossible to appreciate the full philosophical richness of a philosopher like José Martí, of the tradition of marxist humanism, and of Eastern philosophies such as Buddhism. I based that paper upon an anecdote told by (Nobel prize winning writer) José Saramago at the World Social Forum in Puerto Alegre, Brazil.[39] The story went like this: In a village in Italy, near Florence, in 800 A.D., it was the custom that the church bells were rung whenever someone died. One day the bells rang and everyone returned from the fields. People looked around to see who had died, but everyone seemed to be present. They asked the bell-ringer, "Who has died?" His answer was: "Justice has died."[40]

I take it that the point here is that just as in ancient times, the village church bell tolled to mark someone's death, the global village bell needs to be rung to signal the death of justice and to claim the importance of that death. Saramago goes on to suggest that the traditions defining political direction, including those of unions and left-wing political parties, need to be named for what they are. In particular, he suggests, we need to see, and state loudly and definitively, that what is being defined as justice is not justice at all: "Each time [justice] dies, it is as if it never existed for those who trusted in it, for those that expected what we all have a right to expect: justice, simply justice. Not the kind that . . . confuses us with flowery, empty legalistic rhetoric" but one that recognizes the "rational, sensitive dignity we once assumed to be the supreme aspiration of mankind."[41]

According to Saramago, we have come to expect of democracy and the Universal Declaration of Rights something much less than justice. Our expectations for democracy do not include any real effect on the single force that governs the world, namely, the "economic power . . . managed by multinational corporations in line with strategies of domination that have nothing to do with the common good to which, by definition, democracy aspires."[42] Saramago refers to "some sort of verbal and mental automatism" that keeps us from seeing the "raw, naked facts." Unless we first see that "justice is dead," or even that it might be, there cannot be any discovery about justice, for there is no question. The bells have to ring to announce that justice is dead if it is to make sense to ask what happened to justice, and what ought now to happen if we are to pursue it anew.

Saramago's point is that it is necessary to see and proclaim that justice is dead, that freedom is not freedom, that democracy in Latin America is, as Eduardo Galeano writes, "encaged," in order for it to make sense to ask how we might more adequately understand freedom and democracy. In Saramago's anecdote at the World Social Forum, the point was that certain deep-seated expectations about justice have to be denounced and abandoned before we can begin to see that they are wrong. Otherwise, the "automatism" continues to inform expectations about any evidence to the contrary, of which, arguably, there is much. Even if we, as philosophy teachers, did teach students to value the wisdom gained from what is *felt*, so that they might see for themselves the explanatory inadequacy of some beliefs taken for granted, the real lessons of traditions such as those of the Buddha and Martí can be dismissed as philosophically implausible before they have been understood, just as Mills so quickly dismisses the supposedly unworked out alternatives to liberalism.

Mills is right that the ideas represented in contract theory are hegemonic. Political philosophers take it to be uncontroversial that it is always better to "live life from the inside," with true beliefs[43] and that "it is always better to choose than to be compelled."[44] But in fact, as it turns out, it is *not* always better to choose than to be compelled. There are at least three reasons for thinking this. One reason for this is that when I choose something, I identify myself with that choice. Choice is a relationship, as Christine Korsgaard points out, between the subject conceived as such and the object, conceived in a certain way.[45] There are some events that we are better off not being identified with, even if we cause them to happen.

For example, in the novel, *Sophie's Choice,* Sophie is forced to *choose* which of her two children will live and which one will die.[46] Sophie must make the decision herself; otherwise, the commander will send both children to die. Sophie thinks that perhaps if she had not argued with the commander, demonstrating that she spoke German, he would not have made her choose. She looks for an explanation for the *choice.* For the memory that kills her is not of what occurred but that she had a choice about what occurred, that she was in some sense the cause of her daughter's death, even though she was not the explanation. If she had been coerced, even though the result would have been the same, she may have been able to free herself.

One might think that it was not really a choice, because Sophie was forced to make the decision. But the position of philosophers like Claudia Mills is that it is irrelevant whether it was a *real* choice or not. What matters is that it be *our* choice. Mills thinks that it is always better to choose than to have been coerced because when we choose we have a sense of authenticity, however minimal, and it is that sense of authenticity that provides greater well-being. She argues that the value of choice consists in being the author of one's life, and that this has to do with "giving a conscious moment of assent to the way the world is, which need not be the way we chose or would have chosen it to be."[47] But in Sophie's case, it is precisely that authenticity, or even the illusion of it, that eventually destroys her.

A second reason for resisting the dominant view is that there are goals and values—like self-respect—that those who are lucky in life never have to choose, but that those who are less lucky consider a choice. This sort of case has to do with the role of institutions in making or eliminating choice: if an individual's way of being, and relationships, are supported by institutions, that is, if they are socially expected, she does not have to *choose* such a life, or set of relations. Thus, the fact of having a choice may not be an indication of well-being, but rather of exclusion and limitations.

Institutions—that is, practices giving rise to rights, roles, and obligations— sometimes actually free us up by removing choice about crucial human possibilities. Someone who is *compelled* toward choices reflecting well-being and self-worth is in fact better off than someone whose circumstances make available an array of feasible options for doing otherwise. In an argument about self-respect, Robin Dillon applies the term "basal self-respect" to that feeling of worth people have when they have always been *regarded* by others as worthy, and when as a result there is then no question of self-respect for them.[48] People who have *basal self-respect* have no need to *choose* to pursue self-respect. One has to choose if there is a question, that is, if it is feasible that one *not* possess worth and self- respect. If there is no question about one's worth, one is, in a sense, compelled toward the realization of well-being, without choice. According to Dillon, questions about self-respect arise more frequently for women than for men. This is not because self-respect is a different issue for men, but rather because the worth of men is recognized by society, and hence men do not have to raise questions about it.[49] Men are lucky to be without that choice.

A third reason for doubting the primacy of choice in discussions of freedom is the one that Martí and Guevara offer, and that seems obvious to anyone who considers the reality of systemically unjust societies: Just because someone chooses something, even under all the right conditions, it does not mean that whatever has been chosen is somehow in her interests. For globally unjust systems supported by morally depraved ideologies can make the wrong sorts of choices seem right. This popular view of choice gets things the wrong way around, and Martí and Guevara, among others, made this point. It is not deep-seated desires, plans and preferences that explain a person's best interests, but rather a person's best interests—that is, the acting upon and bringing about of what is in fact a more humane situation for that person—that explain appropriate personal desires, plans and preferences. The latter view is the most sensible, and the most explanatory when we consider the state of the world, and the deep-seated, mistaken views about justice that Saramago refers to, and that now rule the world. Fidel Castro is one of the few on the world stage who point out that the world's problems will not be solved through reasonable argument.[50] He is not advocating armed revolution. Instead, he is referring to Martí's rather simple point about the danger of trying to work things out through "academic ink" alone and the philosophical ease with which new solutions can be discounted as unreasonable just because they are new.

In practice, the dominant and popular liberal philosophical conceptions of moral equality, autonomy, freedom and so on do not work. I have not argued this here. I have tried to suggest that the arguments could be made but they will not be unless there are real questions about such concepts. As with justice, the bell may have to be rung to declare that freedom is dead, or at least that it might be, before there will be any real questions about freedom.

The award-winning Brazilian film, *To the Left of the Father*,[51] tells the story of someone who tried to think differently about freedom and unity. The film was described by the main actor as a cry against the globalized annihilation of culture, the cry of those who have no place at the table of the rich. It is about a large family in Brazil, the father of which is sternly religious and fiercely committed to family unity, to the value of work, to patience as the most significant of all virtues. The mother, who sits at "the left of the father" at the hierarchically ordered dinner table, provides the protagonist (the second son) with his introduction, through her warmth and affectionate touch, to passion. The second son leaves the family, not because he has illusions about what lies beyond but because the unity, the patience, the harmony of the family is overwhelmingly *not* what it is supposed to be. As a child he saw and felt the erotic beauty of his surroundings and relations, but found no expression for such perceptions and feelings in the language of religious and family unity. When the eldest son goes after him to bring him back to the fold, telling him that he has destroyed the unity, the second son tries to explain that the unity is not real, that it was broken long ago, and that many desires within the family went unspoken.

The film portrays the tortured effort of the run-away son to explain to his older brother that there is something beneath or beyond the "words" of the house, having to do with deeper, more fundamental human connection. Finally, with his elder brother, the "prodigal son" returns. He tries to explain to his father, who wants to understand. But the father does *not* understand and the second son, recognising that the father cannot understand, gives up, and tells his father what the father wants to hear, namely, that unity and family harmony are most important, and that he, the second son, is grateful for his place at the table. The party to celebrate his return begins. But the yearning that finds no expression in conversation between father and son, finds expression at the party. The sister, who best understood the departure of the second son, dances erotically and freely. As she becomes more free, the clapping becomes restrained and the relatives watching become afraid. The parents become nervous, the mother tries to capture her, to stop her dance, and finally the father, in terror, kills her.

Luis Fernando Carvalho, director of the film, says that imagination causes fear, because it is an act of freedom, of transgression, of citizenship. Perhaps his point is that imagination, as Eduardo Galeano suggests, allows us to interpret the world in terms of what it might be, not just in terms of what it is. Only when we imagine what could be does it make sense to ask about what is. According to Galeano, to do otherwise is failure to respect reality. Thus, it is hard for the second son to raise questions about freedom and love because what exists now—in the family—*already is* freedom and love. And if there is no imagination or expectation of anything else, it is not meaningful to ask about what exists now. But the sister's actual expression of freedom in dance demonstrates that what exists now might not in fact be what it is supposed to be and the second son's view becomes plausible.

If, as the father insists, the family provides all the freedom and love necessary, the son's message of dissatisfaction cannot be *about* freedom and love. The second son's cry cannot constitute resistance to a way of interpreting the world and people's needs if it doesn't even refer to such interpretations, if it is not *about* them. Instead, the second son's message, as long as it is *just* difference, is an illness, something to be tolerated, something that requires patience, not something to be understood.

When *To the Left of the Father* was presented at the New Latin American Film Festival in Havana, it was presented as the cry of those who have no place at the table of the rich. It happens that "the table of the rich" is where the discussions about freedom and democracy were taking place, at the time of the film, in discussions of hemispheric free trade. It is true that, in such discussions, many voices are involved and many stories are being discussed. But if it is taken for granted that nothing more needs to be said about freedom and democracy, that the story has already been told, some views will never be heard, even if presented. If such stories are to be learned from, if they are even to be recognized as worth pursuing, we need to expect that previous stories could be wrong, that there might be something left out—something important.

Mills is wrong to defend contract theory because it is hegemonic. We live in a world with a single dominant ideology—taken for granted by the world's richest societies—that lacks explanatory capacity. The ideology of freedom as choice does not explain why those who can choose to possess almost anything they desire are not free to control our own lives, to live as we might really want to—in peace and harmony with others and with nature—rather than as dictated by desires and preferences inherited from arbitrarily positioned traditions. But it may be as difficult to show that the liberal "living life from the inside" view is wrong as it would have been—before Einstein—to show empirically that "f=ma" is wrong.[52] As long as there is just one dominant ideology about freedom and democracy, that philosophers in all sorts of subtle ways endorse, the *indifference contract* will retain its force, and Philosophy its whiteness.

The Lost Love of Wisdom

Eduardo Galeano tells the following story in *El Libro de los Abrazos*: A friend was taking his small boy to see the sea for the first time. At first, as they approached, the sea was just a smell, a very intense smell, but when finally it was in front of them, in its immensity, the boy was quiet. He was speechless before the unexpected beauty. When eventually he was able to speak, he said simply, "Papá, help me to see."

According to Galeano, the function of art is to help us to see: "Estamos entranados para no ver. Estamos entrenados para no vernos. Yo quisiera escribir una literatura que ayude a mirar. En qué consiste el oficio de escribir? En la búsqueda de palabras que ayuden a mirar."[53] If the function of art is to help us to see, perhaps the function of philosophy is to help us to see that we *don't* see, and to see that, and how, it is *hard* to recognize that we don't see. Philosophy must do the work of showing what *might* be, which is the only way that it makes sense to question what *is,* that is, to suggest, strongly enough to make it meaningful to raise questions and pursue them, that what *is* might not be what *ought* to be. I've tried to suggest that unless we do the work of understanding how the world can be relevantly otherwise, including philosophically, some stories will never be heard as stories about *us* as human beings, or about the concepts—like freedom—that concern us. Instead, they will be stories about *difference,* to be tolerated, but ultimately, morally, dismissed.

The problem, even contradiction, that may exist for Anglo-American Philosophy is that whenever we question the sense of *sameness* that disallows such stories, we end up in a situation of existential insecurity, which is what it is because of theoretical insecurity, something analytic philosophers detest. As Thomas Kuhn pointed out in 1962, people often become seriously agitated when concepts fail to describe what is seen and experienced.[54] According to the famous psychology experiment that Kuhn cites, people often prefer to not see what is there in front of them than to *understand* that in fact they cannot identify what is there.

Analytic Anglo-American philosophy does not seem to have much space, in theory or practice, for the uncertainty involved in recognizing that we do not understand what we thought we understood, at least not as regards concepts like moral equality, autonomy, and so on. It is true that feminists have made some progress in this area, but it is U.S. feminists who are the target of Nzegwu's book.

Wisdom would seem to have something to do with perspective. It is not the same as knowledge but is rather the position from which we give importance to knowledge, the perspective from which we judge what matters. Even in the Philosophy of Science there is recognition that perspective has to do also with who we are.[55] Scientists' "subjective" intuitions play a role in the reliability of beliefs when such intuitions are explained by the scientists' engagement with the object of the research.[56] How much more then should it not also be the case that in philosophical research into questions about moral equality, autonomy and other aspects of human well-being, it matters who the researcher is, and whether she possesses real interest in human well-being?

As Martí knew, and some Eastern philosophies insist, there is a role in the practice of Philosophy for questions about who we can be, and for the insecurity that results when we recognize that we are not who we thought we were. The ancient Chinese philosopher, Chuang Tzu, thought that whenever philosophers concern themselves with *the good* as something to be attained, however they identify *the good*, the pursuit of such an object leads to alienation and delusion (Merton 1992 21). It was not the idea of the good that Chuang Tzu resisted. Quite the contrary. Rather, it was the idea that it can be an object to be objectively analyzed, the pursuit of which distracts from the real good with which one is endowed by the very fact of existence, the good realized through the humility of a simple moral life. There is much more to say about this view. The point here is that Chuang Tzu insisted, as Einstein recognized in his remarks about scientific achievement, that the self-righteousness and arrogance of achievement and clever analytical debate can undermine the real possibility of discovery.

Philosophy is about solving problems. This is true. But it is also famously about raising questions. If Philosophy is to become less white, given the state of the discipline of Anglo-American analytic Philosophy [57] right now, philosophers should consider the importance of questions about how we live and who we are, and the kind of work this requires of us. This is difficult within Western traditions for several reasons, one being a kind of arrogance about the discipline itself. I have suggested that there needs to be recognition that Anglo-American philosophy may be wrong in some of its deepest, identifying philosophical commitments, particularly about the nature of human freedom. Without the capacity for such recognition, and the commitment to keep alive and actively pursue the questions raised, or that could be raised by such recognition, this dominant Western philosophical tradition may not be about wisdom after all.

Notes

1. For the purposes of this chapter, I will capitalize "philosophy" to refer to the discipline of Philosophy, that is, philosophy as taught within English-speaking universities of United States, Canada and Britain. What I say in this chapter is not meant to apply to all philosophers. The question of whiteness has arisen in particular about the tradition of Anglo-American analytic philosophy.
2. Thomas Merton, *Mystics and Zen Masters* (New York: Farrar, Strauss and Giroux, 1967), 80.
3. Hilary Putnam, "The Analytic and the Synthetic," in *Mind, Language and Reality. Philosophical Papers Vol. 2*. (New York: Cambridge University Press, 1975).
4. Of course, there are some, such as the authors included in this book, who have thought so.
5. See Richard N. Boyd, "Metaphor and Theory Change," in *Metaphor and Thought*, ed. A. Ortony (New York: Cambridge University Press, 1979), 348–408; "Scientific Realism and Naturalistic Epistemology" in *Proceedings of the Biennial Meeting of the Philosophy of Science Association*, Vol. 1980, Volume Two: Symposia and Invited Papers (1980) 613–62; "Observations, Explanatory Power and Simplicity: Toward a Non-Humean Account," in *Observation, Experiment and Hypothesis in Modern Physical Science*, ed. P. Achinstein and O. Hannaway (Cambridge, Mass.: MIT Press, 1985); Richard W. Miller, *Fact and Method*, (Princeton, NJ: Princeton University Press, 1987).
6. I have argued this in "Reasons, Explanation and Saramago's Bell," in *Hypatia: A Journal of Feminist Philosophy* Special Issue: Analytic Feminism, ed. Anita Superson and Samantha Brennan, 20 No. 4 (Fall 2005), 144–63.
7. Charles Mills, *The Racial Contract* (Ithaca, NY: Cornell University Press, 1997), 2.
8. Charles Mills and Carole Pateman, *Contract and Domination* (Cambridge: Polity Press, 2007), 167. I am grateful to Katherine Drummond for introducing me to this book and its importance
9. Mills and Pateman, *Contract and Domination*, 168.
10. Mills, in Mills and Pateman, *Contract and Domination*, 23.
11. Mills and Pateman, *Contract and Domination*, 115.
12. Mills and Pateman, *Contract and Domination*, 102.
13. Nkiru Nzegwu, *Family Matters: Feminist Concepts in African Philosophy of Culture* (Albany, NY: SUNY Press, 2006).
14. For example, see Ifi Amadiume, *Male Daughters, Female Husbands: Gender and Sex in an African Society* (Atlantic Highlands, NJ: Zed Books, 1987).
15. I'm simplifying the view here but I've discussed it at length in Susan Babbitt "Feminism and Objective Interests: The Role of Transformation Experiences in Rational Deliberation," in *Feminist Epistemologies*, ed. Elizabeth Potter and Linda Alcoff (New York: Routledge, 1992), 245–64; and *Impossible Dreams: Rationality, Integrity, and Moral Imagination* (Boulder, CO: Westview Press, 1996).
16. Mills, in Mills and Pateman, *Contract and Domination*, 102.
17. Toni Morrison, *Playing in the Dark: Whiteness and the Literary Imagination* (New York: Vintage Books, 1992).
18. Pateman, in Mills and Pateman, *Contract and Domination*, 155–64.
19. Gianni Miná, *Un Continente Desaparecido* (Havana, Cuba: Casa Editor, 2000), 28. The translation of the title is *A Disappeared Continent*.
20. Real cultural misunderstanding. In Miná, *Un Continente Desaparecido*, 34.
21. For example, Morrison, *Playing in the Dark*, 1992.

22. Susan Babbitt, "Freedom and Democracy in Cuba: A Question about Understanding," in *Moral Issues in Global Perspective*, ed. Christine Koggel. (Peterborough, On: Broadview Press, 1999a), 235–54; "Stories from the South: A question of logic," in *Hypatia: A Journal of Feminist Philosophy* 20, no. 3 (2005a): 1–21.
23. For example, Interview with John Kirk, CBC Radio 1 "The Current," April 16 2008, http://www.cbc.ca/thecurrent/2008/200804/20080416.html (accessed August 4, 2009).
24. For information on this, see www.queensu.ca/philosophy/cuba (accessed August 4, 2009).
25. Ernesto Che Guevara, "Socialism and Man in Cuba," in *The Che Guevara Reader*, ed. David Deutschmann. (Melbourne: Ocean Press, 1997), 197–214.
26. José Martí, *José Martí: Selected Writings*, ed. Esther Allen (New York: Penguin Books, 2002), 49.
27. Albert Einstein expressed similar views, for example in *Ideas and Opinions*, (New York: Wings Books, 1954), 40.
28. Martí, *José Martí: Selected Writings*, 187–88.
29. For an example of such arguments, see Arnold August, *Democracy in Cuba and the 1997-98 Elections* (Havana, Cuba: Editorial José Martí, 1999).
30. I have discussed elsewhere the plausibility of the idea that freedom is not best described as "openness" but rather in terms of direction. Che Guevara, for instance, said that freedom requires a *narrow* dialectic, because freedom depends upon direction, that is, upon changing circumstances and conditions so that more humane sorts of choices become possible. See my 1999a, cited above, as well as Susan Babbitt "Moral Risk and Dark Waters," in *Racism and Philosophy*, ed. Susan Babbitt and Sue Campbell (Ithaca: Cornell University Press, 1999b), 235–54; and "Cuba, Democracy and the Armed Owl," in *Journal on African Philosophy*, ed. Olufemi Taiwo, Ayotunde Bewaji, and Pamela Abuya 1, no. 1 (2002): http://www.africanphilosophy.com/vol1.1/babbitt.html (accessed August 4, 2009).
31. Leroi Jones, "Cuba Libre," in *Home: Social Essays*. (New York: William Morrow, 1966), 11–62.
32. Martí, *José Martí: Selected Writings*, 57.
33. Just a day before he died he wrote in his diary that everything he had done with his life until then had been for this goal: "To prevent, by the timely independence of Cuba, the United States from extending its hold across the Antilles and falling with all the greater force on the lands of our America," 347.
34. Simón Bolívar, *El Libertador: Writings of Simón Bolívar* (New York: Oxford University Press, 2003).
35. It does not here matter what is meant by "spiritual"; the point is that understanding in general—in a world of injustice—requires a more adequate perspective, and such a perspective includes also understanding who we are.
36. Merton, *Mystics and Zen Masters*, 284–88.
37. Merton, *Mystics and Zen Masters*, 30–32.
38. Einstein, *Ideas and Opinions*, 41–49.
39. Susan Babbitt, "Reasons, Explanation, and Saramago's Bell," in *Hypatia: A Journal of Feminist Philosophy* 20, no. 4 (2005b): 144–163.
40. José Saramago, "From Justice to Democracy by Way of the Bells," *World Social Forum*, March 9, 2002, Puerto Alegre, Brazil. www.znet.org/content/visionstrategy/saramagobell./cfm (accessed July 2002).
41. Saramago, "From Justice to Democracy by Way of the Bells."
42. Saramago, "From Justice to Democracy by Way of the Bells."

43. Will Kymlicka, *Liberalism, Community and Culture* (Oxford: Clarendon Press, 1991), 12.
44. Claudia Mills, "Choice and Circumstance," in *Ethics* 109 (1998), 154–65.
45. Christine Korsgaard, *The Sources of Normativity* (Cambridge, UK: Cambridge University Press, 1996), 30–48.
46. William Styron, *Sophie's Choice* (New York: Vintage books, 1979).
47. Mills, "Choice and Circumstance," 165.
48. Robin Dillon, "Respect: Moral, Political, Emotional," in *Ethics* 107 (1997): 226–249.
49. Dillon, "Respect," 247.
50. Or he was. Now he makes the point in retirement through writing.
51. Directed by Luiz Fernando Carvahlo, 2001.
52. Putnam, "The Analytic and the Synthetic."
53. We are trained to not see. We are trained to not see ourselves. I want to write literature that helps to see. What is involved in the job of writing? The search for words that help to see.
54. Thomas Kuhn, *The Structure of Scientific Revolutions* (Chicago: University of Chicago Press, 1962), 66.
55. For example, see Peter Railton, "Marx and the objectivity of science" In *PSA* 2 (1984): 813–825; Philip Kitcher, "The Naturalists Return" in *Philosophical Review* 101 (1992): 53–114.
56. Boyd, "Scientific Realism and Naturalistic Epistemology."
57. Of course Analytic Anglo-American Philosophy is just a part of Western philosophy. It is, however, the part I am familiar with and so I am restricting my remarks to this tradition.

10

Against the Whiteness of Ethics: Dilemmatizing as a Critical Approach

Lisa Tessman, Binghamton University

> "When you get right down to it, a lot of philosophy is just white guys jerking off."
>
> —Charles Mills[1]

The Whiteness of Ideal Theory

Charles Mills has critiqued the whiteness of the discipline of philosophy by pointing to the distinction between ideal and non-ideal theorizing, arguing that while the former has dominated Anglo-American philosophy and functions there as a kind of ideology that supports the continuation of white supremacy, it is the latter that is necessary for attending to the realities of racialized lives. I accept Mills' point, and in this chapter, investigate how idealization within my own primary subfield of philosophy—ethics—leads mainstream ethical theory to be inattentive to, and therefore fail to reflect, moral life under racial, as well as other, forms of domination and oppression.[2] I propose that recognizing the high level of *dilemmaticity*[3] that moral life may exhibit under certain (non-ideal) conditions can help produce both better descriptive accounts of moral life in racist societies and hopefully more useful—and less alienating—normative claims. I take it that racial domination and oppression are closely related to and intertwined with other forms of domination and oppression. Since the whiteness of the discipline of philosophy is due at least in large part to mainstream philosophers' failure to attend to racial domination and oppression, my thinking about how to undo the whiteness of the discipline focuses on how, particularly within ethics, to become and remain attentive to (moral life under) racial domination and oppression. While there will be some specificities to attending to racial injustice, as distinguished from other forms of injustice, much of what I say pertains not just to racial but also to other injustices. Emphasizing the non-ideal in ethics by foregrounding dilemmaticity—that is, utilizing the critical tool of *di-*

lemmatizing—should reveal something about the texture of moral life in societies that support many interrelated forms of domination and oppression.

In an essay entitled "Non-Cartesian *Sums*: Philosophy and the African-American Experience," Mills sets for himself the task of identifying "the *conceptual* or *theoretical* whiteness of the discipline" of philosophy.[4] After noting that while women are frequently and directly degraded in the philosophical canon, "for the most part blacks are simply not mentioned in classic philosophy texts,"[5] thus suggesting that the masculinism and the whiteness (or to use Marilyn Frye's term, "whiteliness"[6]) of philosophy follow somewhat different patterns, Mills claims that it is because the life experiences of blacks are so thoroughly ignored and left out of mainstream philosophy that such philosophy is consistently alienating to many black people:

> Either philosophy is not about real issues in the first place but about pseudo-problems; or when it is about real problems, the emphases are in the wrong places; or crucial facts are omitted, making the whole discussion pointless; or the abstractness is really a sham for what we all know but are not allowed to say out loud. The impatience or indifference that I have sometimes detected in black students seems to derive in part from their sense that there is something strange in spending a whole course describing the logic of different moral ideals, for example, without ever mentioning that *all of them* were systematically violated for blacks. So it is not merely that the ideal was not always attained but that, more fundamentally, *this was never actually the ideal in the first place.*[7]

For Mills, "the defining feature of the African-American experience under conditions of white supremacy" is that of "subpersonhood,"[8] and this is the feature of experience that is excluded from rather than reflected in mainstream philosophy. The central problems that arise in mainstream philosophy are not the problems that preoccupy blacks whose personhood is constantly denied or challenged. So, for instance, Mills contrasts Descartes' central problem—proving that his own existence can be known to him given his doubts about what can be known—with the problem faced by Ralph Ellison's invisible man—convincing white people of his existence as a person, given the white supremacist context in which his personhood is (at best) in doubt.[9] The life experiences of blacks in white supremacist societies likely include, as they do in the case of the invisible man, the experience of struggling for full personhood. Theorists who develop concepts that apply to full persons, such as the concepts of equality, justice, freedom, flourishing, and so on, may take one of two problematic approaches. 1) They might assume (but not explicitly state) that blacks do not count as full persons and so assume simultaneously that the concepts apply to "everyone," i.e., to all persons, and that the concepts do not apply to blacks;[10] their implicit exclusion of blacks from full personhood (and from their theorizing) can be deduced from a performative contradiction between their theory and their practice, if, say (Mills uses the case of Locke to illustrate this), they embrace the ideal of equality for all while investing in the slave trade. This is the sense in which Mills claims that real, inclusive equality must have never truly been the ideal, since what is revealed by the theorist's practice is an "ideal" of racial/gender/(etc.) hierarchy coupled with equality for full persons. 2) They might assume that their theories do apply to everyone including blacks (whom they themselves count as full persons) but overlook the fact that black experiences do not fit the mold of people whose personhood is not routinely questioned; thus they include blacks but only by assuming that black people are just like white people. What they exclude are the distinctive experiences of blacks in a white supremacist society, experiences of particular struggles.[11] The problematic theories thus either exclude blacks from full personhood and from the domain of the theories, or, at the very least, they exclude from consideration an experience typical of blacks in white supremacist societies, namely the experience of struggling for full personhood. In either case, the theories, because of what they exclude, are alienating to blacks.

The way to avoid the exclusion of blacks or black experiences—or more broadly the experiences of people of color—from theoretical significance is fairly clear: start with descriptive accounts of *actual* experience, including the experiences of people of color in white supremacist societies. This is the position that Mills develops in "'Ideal Theory' As Ideology," where he moves from his critique of the whiteness/whiteliness (and masculinism) of the discipline of philosophy to the identification of ideal theory with this characteristic whiteness/whiteliness (and masculinism) and to the suggestion that it behooves theorists of liberation such as feminist and critical race theorists to develop the non-idealizing approach of looking at actual experiences, practices, beliefs, and so on. Moral life in idealized societies will be imagined, posited, or stipulated as something quite distant from and alien to moral life in unjust societies; non-idealizing approaches should better equip the theorist to capture the relevant aspects of moral life in actual, non-ideal societies (including societies that support domination and oppression) and to offer normative claims that are not inapplicable, irrelevant, ill informed, and alienating.

There are two ways in which it can be argued that theory (focusing now especially on ethical theory)—*when undertaken as ideal theory*—functions to favor white (and otherwise privileged) people. The first argument depends on a claim of epistemic privilege—loosely, that the most reliable knowledge about white supremacy is produced within the communities of those who are subjected to racial domination and oppression—and contends that because ideal theory does not begin with descriptive accounts of the moral practices (and—to borrow a term from Margaret Urban Walker—moral understandings)[12] of *any* community, let alone communities of color, it is epistemically disabled.[13] Mills invokes the claim of epistemic privilege and argues that ideal theory cannot produce adequate knowledge of how to end white supremacy.[14]

Even if one is reluctant to accept the claim of epistemic privilege upon which standpoint theory relies, there is still a second argument to make about the whiteness/whiteliness of ethical theory that is undertaken as ideal theory: by basing the idealized version of moral subjectivity on what really mirrors more closely the subjectivity of the (racially) privileged than the subjectivity of the victims of racism, and by basing the idealized version of the background conditions for morality on what really tend to be closer to the life conditions of the (racially) privileged than to the life conditions of the victims of racism, ideal theorizing produces moral prescriptions that are especially and drastically ill suited for people of color. Ideal theorizing will leave certain questions unanalyzed (such as questions about how to cope with the challenges of oppression) and will instead focus on questions that are irrelevant for the actual lives of many people of color (for instance, questions that arise only for people in positions of significant control). Furthermore, ideal theorizing may make the moral choices of people of color appear aberrant or condemnable, precisely because they are de-contextualized, that is, removed from the contextual features of the relevant moral subjectivity and background conditions. As Mills argues, in doing this, ideal theory serves an ideological purpose.[15]

Mainstream ethics is white, or whitely, then, in the sense that it is not race-conscious, that is, conscious of and attentive to the actual phenomena of racial domination and oppression and its effects; most mainstream (white) ethicists ignore racial domination and oppression because they ignore domination and oppression more generally,[16] which is something that they are ideologically motivated to do and which they accomplish through an approach of idealizing moral life rather than examining actual moral lives, that is, moral lives that take place in non-ideal(ized) societies. Because domination and oppression are social phenomena of enormous moral relevance and, I would suggest, serve as a major factor in making societies non-ideal[17] (one might make the contingent claim that the injustices of domination and oppression are major imperfections of all actual, contemporary non-ideal[ized] societies), any non-idealized approach to ethics should find ways to remain conscious of and attentive to domination and oppression, including its racialized versions. While no one lives under ideal conditions, victims of injustice live under conditions that are especially far from ideal.

Mills endorses a naturalized approach to ethics as a methodology that guards against idealization.[18] I too take non-ideal theorizing in ethics to be best carried out through a naturalized approach, and I find Margaret Urban Walker's naturalized approach to ethics to offer a useful starting point, though I do depart from her in a way which I will note below. Walker takes morality to be (nothing but) a product of actual social groups, inseparable from the group's other social practices, and argues that the normative authority of moral practices derives (only) from their ability to withstand a sort of critical inquiry—which she calls "transparency testing"—where practices are tested in light of the (revisable) shared moral understandings of the group.[19] I think of Walker's "transparency testing" as a form of ideology critique since it ferrets out those practices that must appear to be something other than what they are in order for practitioners to maintain their confidence in them. If ideology is functioning to make practices appear to be something other than what they really are, then transparency testing will reveal this; that is, the practices will be revealed as ideological through their failure to pass the transparency test.[20] Because morality itself is found in the special authority that moral practitioners accord to practices that pass a transparency test, a naturalizing approach can only arrive at normative claims by examining the moral understandings of actual social groups and specifically by seeking understandings that have (actually, and not just hypothetically) been developed through a critical practice like transparency testing. Thus naturalizing ethics entails critical engagement with accounts of *actual* lives, accounts that might come from direct experience, empirical studies, narrative, history, and so on.

A naturalized approach to ethics may help guard against the ways in which an idealized approach could favor white (and otherwise privileged) people. If one accepts the claim of epistemic privilege and is concerned with the epistemic limitations of using ideal theory to theorize how to end white supremacy, then by using a naturalized approach one can argue that it will be in the moral understandings of actual communities of color that one is likeliest to find the resources with which to authorize racially liberatory moral practices and to de-authorize white supremacist practices. Walker does not explicitly make use of (and I suspect that she would reject) a claim of epistemic privilege that might have led her to an examination of the moral understandings of particular oppressed communities, understandings that would not be visible from other standpoints. Instead—and in this I would disagree with her—she seems to assume that the egalitarian norms of liberal democracies can be the basis upon which non-egalitarian moral practices can be effectively exposed as masquerading as something other than what they are (for instance, masquerading as "fair" or even as "natural"), and thereby denied moral authority.[21] While the moral understandings expressed by these norms are not dependent upon an epistemically privileged standpoint, Walker recognizes that they do come from a particular historical context, a context within which, in Walker's view, enough people are sufficiently committed to egalitarianism to support an opposition to power abuses. Thus she argues that there are resources from within liberal democratic understandings with which one can de-authorize oppressive practices. However, if one were willing to invoke a claim of epistemic privilege one could argue that some liberal democratic practices themselves might be de-authorized from the standpoint of certain oppressed communities whose moral understandings include more radical claims. The *actual* history of liberal democratic societies that are meanwhile white supremacist societies suggests either that transparency testing (or some other form of ideology critique) has not taken place or not been effective or widespread enough in these societies, or that a naturalizing approach that does not insist on focusing on the actual lives of people of color, including the moral understandings that may be possible only from an epistemically privileged standpoint, may be inadequate for revealing the workings of white supremacy.

The ill-suitedness of the conclusions of ideal theory for many people of color can also be addressed by a naturalized approach in which one is not only committed to focusing on actual moral subjects and moral conditions (as opposed to idealized abstractions of both) but is also committed to choosing purposefully to focus on the lives of people of color; such focusing enables one to increase the relevance and the usefulness of moral philosophy to people of color. Thus a crucial step toward unwhitening the field of ethics is the task of gaining multi-disciplinary familiarity with the lived realities of people of color and incorporating this familiarity into one's ethical theorizing. Whether or not one accepts the claim of epistemic privilege and argues that better knowledge of the workings of white supremacy can be gleaned from the moral understandings of people of color, one could still, simply in order to increase the relevance of ethical theory to people of color, be motivated to start theorizing with descriptive accounts of what moral life is like under domination and oppression, or more widely but somewhat differently, what moral life is like for those who are conscious of domination and oppression in an unjust society (even if they themselves do not belong to any subordinated or oppressed group).

I propose that an ethicist's consciousness of domination and oppression will be evident in her/his recognition of the fundamental *dilemmaticity* of moral life, and that either the experience of being subjected to domination and oppression or the awareness of the injustice of domination and oppression will typically give rise to a certain pattern of dilemmaticity in one's moral life; the critical tool of *dilemmatizing* can serve as an aid for the ethicist in remaining conscious of injustice, and in crafting ethical theory that is both attentive and responsive to moral agents who are subordinated or oppressed.

The Dilemmaticity of Non-Ideal(ized) Moral Life

I take a moral dilemma to be a situation in which there is a compelling moral reason to enact each of two possibilities, where it is not possible to enact both, either because one possibility is to do x and the other is to not do x, thus making it logically impossible, or because some contingent factor makes it impossible to do both.[22] Dilemmas may be irresolvable, such as when the conflicting moral reasons can both be expressed in terms of the same principle or value but are equally strong or weighty when compared with each other, or when the conflicting moral reasons are incommensurable or incomparable because they cannot both be expressed in terms of the same principle or value.[23] Or, they may be resolvable because, for instance, one of the conflicting moral reasons is stronger than and overrides the other; in this case the conflict will count as a genuine moral dilemma if and only if the resolution does not cancel or otherwise fully eliminate the overridden moral reason. In either the case of an irresolvable dilemma or the case of a resolvable dilemma whose resolution does not cancel the overridden moral reason, when the agent acts, she/he necessarily acts against (or fails to act according to) what remains a compelling moral reason or a moral requirement. A moral dilemma can thus be thought of as a situation in which moral failure or wrongdoing is "inescapable."[24]

There are several strands of argument developed by ethicists who endorse the genuineness of moral dilemmas. I am most interested in what has come to be known as the experientialist or phenomenological approach, including work that begins with Bernard Williams' argument that conflicting moral requirements are more like conflicting desires than like conflicting beliefs, for when desires conflict and one decides in favor of one desire, the other does not disappear, but may "remain" and generate a feeling of regret. After navigating a resolvable dilemma and acting in accordance with one of the conflicting moral requirements, a "moral remainder" may be manifested in emotions such as regret, guilt, or anguish about the "*ought* that is not acted upon," even when one is convinced that one made the best possible decision about how to act in the face of the dilemma.[25]

Williams' move of drawing on moral experience for insight about the genuineness of moral dilemmas is consistent with naturalized approaches to ethics. I take Williams' account to refuse the idealizing move of conceiving of the moral agent as having a perfect decision procedure for resolving moral dilemmas without remainder and thereby as free from the threat of facing such dilemmas and having to live with their fallout. Williams' introduction of the idea of a moral remainder, in conjunction with his insistence that moral conflicts cannot be avoided—at least not without losing out on all that is of value that may give rise to such conflicts[26]—suggests that it is wrong to think of the task of ethical theory as (limited to) supplying correct answers to questions about how to resolve moral conflicts. If Williams is right that "moral conflicts are neither systematically avoidable, nor all soluble without remainder,"[27] part of the task of ethics must be to account for the moral experience of navigating moral dilemmas that are either irresolvable or resolvable only with a remainder.[28]

If, as I assume, one would ideally not act contrary to a compelling moral reason or violate a moral requirement, then in facing a dilemma, one faces a situation where no matter what one does one must act in a less-than-ideal way. It is by definition, then, that dilemmatic conditions are, in at least a weak sense, non-ideal conditions, and the recognition of the genuineness of moral dilemmas undermines idealization in ethics. Under fully ideal(ized) conditions it must be assumed that moral agents do not face any genuine moral dilemmas; the moral conflicts that they do face count only as apparent dilemmas, conflicts that can be resolved by applying the correct decision procedure. Likewise, fully ideal(ized) moral agents would not experience emotions such as regret or guilt in the wake of a moral conflict, since ideal(ized) moral agents would be perfectly rational and these emotions are irrational given that moral dilemmas are only apparent. Fully ideal(ized) moral agents can thus be said to live free from the moral threat of finding themselves in a genuine dilemma. One powerful way to idealize in ethics, then, is to deny that there can be such a thing as a genuine moral dilemma, and to argue to the contrary that there is a perfect or infallible decision procedure available to any (rational) moral agent facing an apparent dilemma.[29] The anti-dilemma theorists (I cannot help but think of these as the quintessential "white guys jerking off" alluded to by Mills) use a variety of arguments to deny that there are any genuine moral dilemmas. For instance, they may argue that in any case of apparently conflicting moral reasons, at least one of the reasons must be only a prima facie reason that in fact is eliminated by one's finding that it is overridden by the other reason, which holds in an "all things considered" way. Monist theories of value express all moral requirements in terms of a single value and thus may claim that two requirements can always be compared to determine which weighs more heavily, with the less weighty being eliminated (and moral permission to act on either requirement if they weigh equally). The anti-dilemma theorists are all able to posit a world in which one never must act against a (non-cancelled) compelling moral reason, that is, a world in which one never must act morally in a less than ideal way.

My intention here is not to enter into the debate about whether or not there are any genuine moral dilemmas. Rather, I join those who recognize genuine moral dilemmas but I take their analyses one step further because I am interested in the question of how attention to dilemmaticity as a variable characteristic of moral conditions can help one to describe the texture of moral life (especially moral life under different forms of domination and oppression) and to make normative claims that are informed by this attention. I expect that attention of this sort will help the ethicist to notice what Mills is most concerned to bring into view—the experiences tied to being denied full personhood under white supremacy—but will be in some ways more encompassing, as it will also entail consideration of other experiences associated with various forms of domination and oppression. It is not the mere *existence* of moral dilemmas that I am highlighting here as the relevant feature of moral experience; the dilemmaticity of moral conditions vary, and the relevance of this variation must be recognized. Patterns of dilemmatic conditions are typically tied to other socially patterned features of life conditions. Certain systemically patterned dilemmatic conditions—especially if the degree of dilemmaticity is also high—will complicate and degrade moral life, reducing the possibilities of acting in a morally "clean" way, even for the agent who always does the very best that is possible in the face of any given dilemma. It is this sort of dilemmaticity—dilemmaticity that is systemically patterned and therefore tied to other patterned features of life including patterns of domination and oppression—that needs to be attended to by the ethicist who wishes to remain race-conscious (and conscious of gender, etc.), and to offer both good descriptive accounts of the texture of moral life, and appropriate normative claims about how one might live under actual, given conditions.

The systemic patterns that dilemmas may follow are numerous and varied in part because the conditions of different forms of domination and oppression—as well as other structural phenomena (such as exploitation)—are so varied. For instance, under some conditions one will typically encounter dilemmas that arise out of conflicts of particular incommensurable values, such as the "care" vs.

"justice" conflicts that are more prevalent for people engaged in care labor (including those who are unjustly saddled with more than their share of care labor, or with unfair expectations about what a care worker is responsible for). Other conditions, such as conditions of poverty, may be typified by choices between different life-necessities that cannot all be afforded. People living in poverty constantly make choices of which essential aspects of life to sacrifice (with a morally compelling reason not to sacrifice any): work a second job and have no time to spend with one's children, pay the rent but go without heat or without health insurance for one's family, enlist in the military or else have no way to get an education or job training, save on subway fare but walk through neighborhoods that have a high crime rate. Whichever choice is made in each of these common dilemmas leaves the other "oughts"—such as "one ought not neglect one's own health" or "one ought to spend (a certain amount of) time with one's children"—still in place, ineliminable but unfullfillable. What would be best—having a reasonably short work day, time with one's children, good housing, health care, education, safe living environments, and so on, all without having to "dirty one's hands" in exchange—is not available. This version of a highly dilemmatic moral life thus entails the ongoing sacrifice of some moral requirement, for instance, the requirement to provide or care adequately for one's dependents, the requirement to refrain from using morally forbidden means—such as killing or exploiting others—to an otherwise acceptable or commendable end, or the requirement not to engage in a morally problematic self-sacrifice.[30] For another example, and one that speaks directly to Mills' concern with the denial of personhood: blacks whose full personhood is relentlessly denied will experience a related sort of everyday dilemmaticity; they may face persistent dilemmas in which they must choose between asserting their full personhood at the expense of sacrificing some benefit, or bowing down (not insisting on recognition as a full person) in order to be rewarded with some benefit that is accorded to black people only if they acquiesce in their subordinate status. Coping with any of the patterned forms of abuse or violation that unjust societies support also requires navigating dilemmas. Women (and occasionally men) with abusive partners have sometimes faced the question of whether to kill their abuser, seeing it as their only way out; they violate a moral requirement if they kill, and likewise if they sacrifice their own lives by staying with the abuser or by leaving but remaining in constant fear that the abuser will pursue them. Members of a black community face a dilemma of whether or not to call the police to intervene if they (or their children, and so on) are abused, raped, or otherwise violated by another member of the community, given that the violator will himself (or herself) likely be treated unjustly by the legal system; there is a moral requirement to stop, say, child abuse, but so too is there a requirement that even if overridden is not thereby cancelled, to refrain from using a racist judiciary and from perpetuating racist stereotypes of blacks as criminals. Anti-racist whites also face this dilemma if they are ever violated by a black person, since whites are clearly in a position to use a racist judiciary to their advantage and/or to perpetuate the image of black (male) predator/white (female) victim; for them, the moral requirements stemming from their anti-racist commitments can conflict with the moral requirement to protect themselves from violation. The good or ideal option in this sort of case is hard to imagine because it is so counterfactual—a non-racist judicial system? Or perhaps a world in which anarchist collectivities have replaced practices of punishment with practices of prevention? And finally, for a more general characterization of a patterned kind of dilemmaticity that arises in non-ideal/unjust societies: any person targeted by domination and oppression may encounter a recurring pattern of dilemma in which surviving or getting ahead by means of complicity contends with engaging in resistance, or in which individualistic strategies vie with collective ones; even those who are not themselves victims of a particular form of injustice may encounter a recurring pattern of dilemma if they are committed to opposing that form of injustice, because they too will face the dilemmas that force a choice between different sacrifices that must be made, or perhaps violence that one might engage in,[31] in fighting injustice. If the morally good option is in each case ruled out by the unjust conditions of the society, then anyone who aims at moral goodness where such goodness is understood to require standing against injustice (and this includes not just the victims of injustice) will find themselves living a moral life that is, perhaps relentlessly, troubled by its shortcomings and filled with disturbing moral remainders.

Naturalized approaches to ethics can avoid a particular kind of idealizing that occurs either through (in the extreme) the denial of the possibility of genuine moral dilemmas or through the recognition of genuine moral dilemmas but the failure to consider how dilemmaticity may vary under the varying life conditions that are tied to social positioning in unjust societies. Non-idealizing, naturalized approaches depend upon familiarity with empirical studies, narrative accounts (and so on) for information about moral experience; my claim is that one relevant dimension of moral experience that ethicists who take these approaches should attend to is the (patterns of) dilemmaticity of the moral conditions that people live in and how this may vary with race, gender, class, and other aspects of social position.[32] While the theorists who defend the genuineness of dilemmas avoid idealizing moral conditions in the extreme way that the anti-dilemma theorists do, as far as I can tell even they do not have the *very* non-ideal conditions of domination and oppression in mind, nor do they think about moral conditions as typically evidencing a particular pattern of dilemmaticity that is tied to (other) socially patterned features of life. The dilemmas that they have in mind may either be not very strong (for instance, the moral dilemma may be easily resolvable because the moral considerations in favor of at least one of the possibilities in the dilemma will be weak, as in the case when I break my promise to meet a friend for coffee because I stop to assist an accident victim on the way, thus incurring an extremely weak moral remainder that is then discharged with an explanation—"sorry, but . . ."—to my friend), or they may be strong and terrible but few and far between, wildly hypothetical, and typically instigated by a bout of rare and unexpected bad luck (it is, after all, not every day that one finds oneself on a sinking boat deliberating about whom to cast overboard[33] or a random encounter with a coercive and evil agent (beginning with Aristotle's case of the tyrant holding one's family hostage and asking one to do something base)[34] rather than a systemic pattern. The quite real disasters that abound in the actual lives of subordinated and oppressed people are sidelined while unlikely, hypothetical encounters with moral conflicts are exaggerated.[35]

Claudia Card, in introducing the notion of the "unnatural lottery"[36] into the discourse on moral luck, called attention to the fact that while all human lives are vulnerable to bad moral luck (at least according to those who do not deny that there is such a thing as moral luck), victims of oppression are specially vulnerable to a systemic sort of bad moral luck. My claim about dilemmaticity parallels Card's claim about moral luck: while the experience of encountering moral dilemmas can occur in any human life (at least according to those who do not deny that there is such a thing as a genuine moral dilemma), domination and oppression create a patterned, and in fact ongoing encounter with dilemmatic conditions of a certain sort. Just as the recognition of moral luck alters one's understanding of what moral life is like, and the more so the more prevalent moral luck is, so too does the recognition of the genuineness of moral dilemmas alter one's understanding of what moral life is like, and the more so the greater the degree of dilemmaticity is and the more systemically patterned the dilemmas encountered are. As Card has suggested that certain sorts of bad moral luck are especially pervasive in the lives of oppressed people, I am suggesting here that domination and oppression give rise to dilemmatic conditions that have a special character and a special sort of constancy due to their systemic sources.[37]

Domination and oppression, in constraining possibilities of either self-determination or flourishing,[38] place subordinated or oppressed moral agents in an ongoing way in situations where all options that they face are morally problematic. These moral agents are in a position where they must choose from amongst a set of options that can range from the merely non-ideal to the truly terrible. Sometimes all of the available options may be truly terrible. As Marilyn Frye's memorable birdcage metaphor suggests, the oppressed face double binds; any direction they may turn, there is another wire of the cage, i.e., some bad or at least less-than-ideal option.[39] But to say this is just to say that these moral agents will tend to find themselves continually facing dilemmas; they live under highly dilemmatic conditions. It is not that dilemmas occur *only* when options are constrained because of domination and oppression; any constraint on options that makes it impossible to act on two conflicting but compelling moral reasons will create a dilemma. However, in systemically or institutionally constraining what would otherwise be good, morally endorsable possibilities, the phenomena of domination and oppression spawn what I take to be a special, systemic sort of dilemmaticity. This contrasts with the portrait drawn by those who accept that there are genuine moral dilemmas but do not recognize the role of oppression and domination in generating dilemmas, and it contrasts even more strongly with an idealized portrait of a society in which the theorist can always represent (at least) one option for the members of that society as a *good* option (where "good" here could be understood in terms of some desideratum for the society, such as justice). The parties to John Rawls' original position, for instance, can through stipulation be cast as choosing from a variety of contending principles of justice, where at least one (set) of them is a good choice, a choice that if implemented (with strict compliance) would result in a just society.[40]

To summarize and conclude: Non-ideal theorizing and in particular naturalized approaches seem most promising for producing work in ethics that remains race-conscious and that therefore has a chance at giving accurate characterizations of the moral lives of people of color in white supremacist societies (and that likewise remains conscious of gender, class, and so on, and can characterize the moral lives of people subject to various kinds of domination and oppression) and making normative claims that are appropriate for such moral lives. There are many aspects of moral life that domination and oppression alter or affect and more needs to be done to identify them. I am making the limited claim that *one* of these aspects of moral life can be revealed through attending to features of the dilemmaticity of the moral conditions that people of color typically encounter.

Critical social theorists make regular use of the approach of *problematizing*: taking an apparently normal or innocuous situation, practice, or claim and casting it differently, as evidencing problems—often systemic problems or problems that stem from injustice—that then call for change or opposition. To *dilemmatize* is to reexamine moral life, which pre-dilemmatizing may appear as cleanly governed through the application of principles or rational procedures that yield (ideal) solutions, in such a way that problems of a certain sort—genuine dilemmas that cannot be solved or whose solution leaves a troublesome remainder—are revealed. Sometimes what will be revealed are not only dilemmas, but a certain pattern of dilemmas that track other unjust, socially structured features of life. Dilemmatizing obviously requires that one not start with a framework that denies the possibility of genuine moral dilemmas. But beyond this, for dilemmatizing to function as a critical tool, dilemmatizing, like problematizing, requires that one keep an eye out for patterns that suggest a systemic source of the dilemmas/problems. Dilemmatizing can thus reveal patterns of dilemmaticity that are characteristic of the moral lives of people living under the constraints of domination and oppression.

The shift in ethical thinking that would result from ethicists' attention to patterns of dilemmaticity is one part of what seems like a promising, larger shift from ideal(ized) (and alienating) theory to non-idealizing ethical thinking, thinking that begins with accounts of actual moral life, taking these accounts to lay out the conditions under which any moral evaluations or prescriptions must hold up. The descriptive accounts of moral life that manifest attention to patterns of dilemmaticity cannot be expected to "solve" any moral problems. Rather, their role is to convey the awesome responsibility—in some cases an absurd responsibility—that falls on people who face highly dilemmatic moral conditions. As Jean-Paul Sartre says that he remarked to the young man who was torn between staying with his otherwise desolate mother and joining the Free French Forces: "You are free, therefore choose—that is to say, invent. No rule of general morality can show you what you ought to do: no signs are vouchsafed in this world."[41] Sartre's remark does not offer the young man a solution; for Sartre, a resolution can only be invented, in the form of the value that comes to be by virtue of being chosen. Facing a dilemma means being in ("condemned to") this situation of having to invent, and of having responsibility for the value that is chosen; and, one might add, this responsibility is, often painfully or sorrowfully, a responsibility for the rejected path—for not caring for one's mother, for not contributing to the struggle. Accounts that characterize the moral subject as being regularly in the position of choosing between terrible options—a position often created by the constraining structures of domination and oppression—might reveal moral life as both tragic and comic,[42] but certainly not as clean or easy.

Notes

1. Charles W. Mills, "Non-Cartesian *Sums*: Philosophy and the African-American Experience" in *Blackness Visible: Essays on Philosophy and Race* (Ithaca, NY: Cornell University Press, 1998), 4.
2. I am borrowing from Iris Marion Young (*Justice and the Politics of Difference* [Princeton, NY: Princeton University Press, 1990]) the idea that domination and oppression are two phenomena that jointly comprise injustice (and so I use "unjust societies" interchangeably with "societies that support domination and oppression"). She conceives of domination as "the institutional constraint on self-determination" and oppression as "the institutional constraint on self-development" (37). I do diverge some from Young because I prefer to tie oppression to flourishing, thus I follow Selin Gürsözlü (unpublished work) in adapting Young's account of oppression to a eudaimonistic framework and thinking of oppression as the "institutional constraint on" flourishing.
3. Some help with the usage: *dilemma* is to *dilemmatic* as *problem* is to *problematic*; *dilemmatic* is to *dilemmatize* as *problematic* is to *problematize*; *dilemmatic* is to *dilemmaticity* as *elastic* is to *elasticity*.
4. Mills, "Non-Cartesian *Sums*," 2; italics in the original.
5. Mills, "Non-Cartesian *Sums*," 2.
6. Marilyn Frye, "White Woman Feminist" in *Willful Virgin: Essays in Feminism* (Freedom, CA: The Crossing Press, 1992).
7. Mills, "Non-Cartesian *Sums*," 4; italics in the original.
8. Mills, "Non-Cartesian *Sums*," 6.
9. Mills, "Non-Cartesian *Sums*," 8–9; Ralph Ellison, *The Invisible Man* (New York: Signet Books, 1947).
10. Mills, "Non-Cartesian *Sums*," 4.
11. Mills, "Non-Cartesian *Sums*," 9.
12. Margaret Urban Walker, *Moral Understandings: A Feminist Study in Ethics* (New York: Routledge, 1998).
13. Charles W. Mills, "'Ideal Theory' as Ideology," in *Moral Psychology*, ed. Peggy DesAutels and Margaret Urban Walker (Lanham, MD: Rowman & Littlefield, 2004), 167.
14. Mills, "'Ideal Theory' as Ideology," 172–74.
15. Mills, "'Ideal Theory' as Ideology," 170.
16. I say "most" because one could also point out that some white feminist ethicists ignore racial injustice even while attending (though badly, if they ignore the intersections) to another form of injustice, such as gender injustice.
17. Other kinds of moral luck—that is, those kinds of moral luck that, unlike injustice, do not stem from what Claudia Card has dubbed "the unnatural lottery"—are other such major factors. See Claudia Card, *The Unnatural Lottery: Character and Moral Luck* (Philadelphia: Temple University Press, 1996).
18. Mills, "'Ideal Theory' as Ideology," 168.
19. Walker, *Moral Understandings*; and Walker, *Moral Contexts* (Lanham, MD: Rowman & Littlefield, 2003).
20. See for instance Walker, *Moral Contexts*, 109.
21. Walker, *Moral Understandings*, 73.
22. For those who claim that there are genuine moral dilemmas, this is a fairly standard way of defining a moral dilemma; it closely follows Christopher Gowan's definition (Christopher Gowans, ed., *Moral Dilemmas* [Oxford: Oxford University Press, 1987],

Introduction). For another summary discussion of the definition of a moral dilemma, see Walter Sinnott-Armstrong, *Moral Dilemmas* (New York: Blackwell, 1988), chapter 1. Those who deny that there are genuine moral dilemmas tend to define dilemmas such that any resolvable conflict does not count as a dilemma. I favor a definition that counts both resolvable and irresolvable moral conflicts as dilemmas, as long as the resolution does not eradicate the obligation that is not fulfilled. A wide range of work on moral dilemmas is collected both in Gowans, ed., *Moral Dilemmas*, and in H.E. Mason, ed., *Moral Dilemmas and Moral Theory* (Oxford: Oxford University Press, 1996). There are also excellent discussions of dilemmas in Michael Stocker, *Plural and Conflicting Values* (Oxford: Oxford University Press, 1990); Christopher Gowans, *Innocence Lost: An Examination of Inescapable Moral Wrongdoing* (Oxford: Oxford University Press, 1994); and Rosalind Hursthouse, *On Virtue Ethics* (Oxford: Oxford University Press, 1999).

23. Initial discussions of this latter sort—where dilemmas are irresolvable because the values are incommensurable—can be found in E.J. Lemmon, "Moral Dilemmas," *The Philosophical Review* 70 (1962): 139–43 and 148–58; Bas C. van Fraassen, "Values and the Heart's Command," *The Journal of Philosophy* 70 (1973): 5–19; and Thomas Nagel, "The Fragmentation of Value," in *Mortal Questions* (Cambridge: Cambridge University Press, 1979). All three are reprinted in Gowans, ed., *Moral Dilemmas*.

24. See Gowans, *Innocence Lost*.

25. Bernard Williams, "Ethical Consistency," in *Problems of the Self* (New York: Cambridge University Press, 1973), 175; italics in the original.

26. Williams, "Ethical Consistency," 179.

27. Williams, "Ethical Consistency," 179.

28. I emphasize here Williams' phenomenological account of navigating moral dilemmas and being left with regret or other moral remainders, because I want to contrast the non-idealizing approach of looking at moral experience with the idealizing approach of rationally deducing moral prescriptions from *a priori* moral principles or from an assumed monistic value such as utility. However, as an aside I will note that Williams actually takes two approaches to demonstrating the possibility of genuine moral dilemmas: 1) he points to moral experience, and 2) he also supplies a direct objection to those who argue against the possibility of genuine moral dilemmas on the basis of their producing a contradiction when combined with the rules of deontic logic (which they do not question). Williams chooses to sacrifice a rule of deontic logic rather than sacrifice the possibility of genuine moral dilemmas. Supposing that there is a genuine moral dilemma in the form of *I ought to do a; I ought to do b; I cannot do a and b*, and also accepting the assumption that ought implies can, he ends up rejecting what he calls the agglomeration principle (a standard rule in deontic logic): that *I ought to do a* and *I ought to do b* implies that *I ought to do a and b*; he thus denies that asserting the existence of the moral dilemma entails accepting that *I ought to do a and b* and thereby avoids the following contradiction: *I ought to do a and b; I cannot do a and b; ought implies can* (and so *I cannot* implies *it is not the case that I ought); thus it is not the case that I ought to do a and b* (Williams, "Ethical Consistency," 179–84). There are several other ways one might oppose the claim that genuine dilemmas are ruled out because of deontic logic: one could reject a different rule of deontic logic, namely that *ought implies can* (this is my strong inclination), or, as Ruth Barcan Marcus does, one could argue that while inconsistency between the rules the deontic logic and the possibility of genuine moral dilemmas would indeed call deontic logic into question, there is in fact no such inconsistency even though genuine moral dilemmas are possible. In "Moral Dilemmas and Consistency" (in Gowans, ed.,

Moral Dilemmas, 188–204) Marcus argues that principles that are consistent according to her way of defining consistency ("rules are consistent if there are possible circumstances in which no conflict will emerge" [195]) can still conflict, producing genuine moral dilemmas. She agrees with Williams that genuine moral dilemmas can leave troublesome remainders, and pointing to this fact and to the desirability of avoiding such remainders, concludes that there is another *ought*, a "second-order" ought: one ought to act in such a way that one will not find oneself in a genuine moral dilemma; however, she adds, provocatively, that "this second-order 'ought' does *not* imply 'can,'" since given the "contingencies of this world" it may be impossible to avoid all moral dilemmas (200; italics in the original).

29. A few theorists have noted that those who invoke deontic logic to argue against the possibility of genuine moral dilemmas demonstrate that in *ideal* worlds there can be no genuine moral dilemmas, but this fails to disprove the possibility of genuine moral dilemmas in the actual, nonideal world. See John Holbo, "Moral Dilemmas and the Logic of Obligation," *American Philosophical Quarterly* 39, no. 3 (2002): 259–74; and Sven Ove Hansson, "Ideal Worlds—Wishful Thinking in Deontic Logic," *Studia Logica* 82 (2006): 329–36.

30. I do not take moral and prudential concerns to be at odds with each other. Employing a loosely eudaimonistic framework, I take adequate attention to one's own well-being to be a moral (as well as prudential) concern. Because subordinated people (and this is so especially for women) may be expected and socialized to exhibit a damaging sort of self-sacrifice, I think it is especially important to insist that engaging in self-sacrifice is a moral harm.

31. See Jean-Paul Sartre's play "Dirty Hands," in *No Exit and Three Other Plays*, translated by L. Abel (New York: Alfred Knopf, 1949 [French, 1948]).

32. Some of Carol Gilligan's work could be said to focus on the experience of dilemmaticity; for instance, in speaking of her study of women's experience of their abortion decisions, she comments that "the findings pertain to the different ways in which women think about dilemmas in their lives" (*In a Different Voice* [Cambridge, MA: Harvard University Press, 1982], 72); she compares women's responses to actual dilemmas and to hypothetical dilemmas such as the Heinz dilemma. Gilligan's (early) work has been well critiqued for failures to attend to race and class differences. Some essays taking or engaging with an empirical approach to moral dilemmas, and attentive to at least some dimension of social positioning, are collected in Carol Gibb Harding, ed., *Moral Dilemmas: Philosophical and Psychological Issues in the Development of Moral Reasoning* (Chicago: Precedent Publishing, Inc., 1985). What is now being called "experimental ethics" (for an overview, see Anthony Appiah, *Experiments in Ethics* [Cambridge, MA: Harvard University Press, 2008]) does not, in my view, count as the sort of empirical engagement with moral experience that reveals much about the relation of moral experience to social positioning, in part because the "experiments" cited tend to be ones that produce data on how subjects in idealized, hypothetical or staged situations respond to moral conflicts (e.g. hypothetical variations on the trolley problem, the staged situation of walking by a person in need when one is/is not in a hurry, and so on) rather than on how people experience moral conflict in their actual lives. For instance, the experiments do not reveal anything about who is more likely to experience which sorts of moral conflicts given their life conditions. The findings of moral psychology that fall under "experimental ethics"—including those that rely on measurements of brain activity through the use of fMRI, or a purposeful manipulation (e.g. through hypnotic suggestion) of moral "intuitions," and so on—could potentially yield information useful for connecting moral experience to social position, but I do not think this is the current direction of the field.

33. As Marilyn Friedman has noted in another context: "The moral world of mainstream ethics is a nightmare of plane crashes, train wrecks, and sinking ships. Wives and children drown in this literature at an alarming rate." (*What Are Friends For?* [Ithaca, NY: Cornell Uniersity Press, 1993], 71).
34. Aristotle, *Nicomachean Ethics* in *The Complete Works of Aristotle: The Revised Oxford Translation*, ed. Jonathan Barnes (Princeton: Princeton University Press, 1984), 1110a5–11.
35. Christopher Gowans, in "Moral Theory, Moral Dilemmas, and Moral Responsibility" (in Mason, ed., *Moral Dilemmas and Moral Theory*, 199–215), characterizes the split between the pro-dilemma and anti-dilemma theorists as a split between those with, respectively, experientialist and rationalist leanings (where experientialism "seeks to understand moral practice primarily from the standpoint of the moral experience of persons" [201] and rationalism "regards moral practice primarily as a form of human rationality" [200]), and discusses (approvingly) the methodology of appeal to moral experience, noting that "experientialism looks to history, biography, literature, and the like, not as (at best) a storehouse of possibly useful illustrations of points already established by philosophical analysis, but as a significant resource for expanding the horizons of our own personal experience, and hence as having an important role to play within philosophical analysis" (201). I agree with his characterization; however, my point is that it is necessary to pay attention to *whose* experience one consults. The pro-dilemma theorists who take the experientialist or phenomenological approach do not consider how social positioning affects one's experience of dilemmaticity.
36. Card, *The Unnatural Lottery*.
37. There is also, of course, good moral luck; similarly, as Rosalind Hursthouse (following a suggestion by Philippa Foot in "Moral Realism and Moral Dilemma," *Journal of Philosophy* 80 [7] [1983]: 370–98) has pointed out, there are "pleasant" dilemmas, such as choosing between equally wonderful birthday gifts that one could buy for one's child (Hursthouse, *On Virtue Ethics*, 66–67). Obviously, these are not the dilemmatic patterns that would typify life under domination or oppression.
38. See endnote 2
39. Marilyn Frye, "Oppression," in *The Politics of Reality* (Trumansburg, NY: The Crossing Press, 1983).
40. John Rawls, *A Theory of Justice* (Cambridge, MA: Harvard University Press, 1971).
41. Jean-Paul Sartre, "Existentialism is a Humanism," in *Existentialism from Dostoevsky to Sartre*, ed. Walter Kaufmann (New York: Penguin, 1956), 356.
42. I borrow this characterization from Cornel West, "Black Strivings in a Twilight Civilization" in *The Cornel West Reader* (New York: Basic Civitas Books, 1999).

11

The Whiteness of Anti-Racist White Philosophical Address

Cris Mayo, University of Illinois at Urbana-Champaign

> In all jazz, and especially in the blues, there is something tart and ironic, authoritative and double-edged. White Americans seem to feel that happy songs are *happy* and sad songs are *sad*, and that, God help us, is exactly the way most white Americans sing them—sounding, in both cases, so helplessly, defenselessly fatuous that one dare not speculate on the temperature of the deep freeze from which issue their brave and sexless little voices.
> (Baldwin, *The Fire Next Time*, 41-42)

> I am sure that many women here are telling themselves they aren't racists because they are capable of being civil to Black women, having been raised by their parents to be anything but. It's not about merely being polite: "I'm not racist because I do not snarl and snap at Black people." It's much more subtle than that. It's not white women's fault that they have been raised, for the most part not to know how to talk to Black women, not knowing how to look us in the eye and laugh *with* us.
> (Barbara Smith, "Racism and Women's Studies,"
> *But Some of Us are Brave*, 49)

This chapter examines white antiracist philosophical forms of address and contrasts them with black traditions of deceptive etiquette, convoluted insult, and subversive humor. Philosophy has a long tradition, too, of oblique argument, staged personas, and riddles. But white philosophical work against racism generally avoids attempting to teach or create arguments indirectly via hyperbole, irony, or provocative statement, presumably because such tactics are complicated by their implicatedness in the structural formation of whiteness. White antiracist philosophers, by and large (there are exceptions), work through direct argument and direct evocation of emotion and commitment. White philosophers speaking with certainty or even earnest uncertainty are still speaking through a philosophical tradition and a structural identity that converts even strongly felt, thoughtful intervention into gestures of mastery. Philosophy that pretends its indecision isn't anything more than the false modesty of whiteness covering its own power simply shows how whiteness operates. In other words, the mechanisms of philosophical address, even when they attempt to decenter the white philosopher through critique of whiteness and racism, concretize the power and certainty, and thus the whiteness of philosophy.

By suggesting that antiracist white philosophizing is complicit in structural racism in general and in racism in philosophy in particular I am not saying anything that antiracist white philosophers do not already centralize in their work. We all understand that philosophy's task and thus even our own interventions are part of what Lucius T. Outlaw Jr., refers to as "the legitimation of 'the order of things,'" a process that can explain racism and ethnocentrism as well as opposition to racism and ethnocentrism.[1] That the tools of philosophy are ambivalent and complicit is not surprising and that white antiracist philosophers would carefully select particular tools, I think, shows their understanding of not only their social position as whites, but also their critical understanding of the history of philosophy, too aspects of whiteness that they understand themselves to be complicit in even as they attempt to undo each.

I will put this white antiracist complicity into two interrelated conversations. The first is an examination of the rhetorical tactics that white antiracist philosophers use. As a contrast to the seductive crypto-dominance of white philosophical address—a form of false modesty that so many of us engaged in philosophy embrace even when we attempt to undo our power—I turn to oppositional forms of address in black philosophies and practices that use indirection to challenge white hegemony. These black traditions of indirect communication derive not only from strategies of communicating with black people in the midst of white people, but also from complex forms of dealing with oppression in ways that attempt to deflect the damages of that oppression. Black counter-narratives of pointed, hyperbolic, provocative, or subtle engagement with bias simultaneously show the perpetual problem of white supremacy and its equally perpetual gaps and fissures.

I begin by attempting to undo what I have already said cannot be undone through philosophy. While I am also wary of the pose of humility because it too easily looks like the guilty seeking absolution or is simply a performative contradiction because humility craves recognition, I will start here by saying that as a white philosopher of education who is concerned about the perpetual problem of recentering whiteness, I have indulged in the kinds of address I am critiquing. By positioning other white philosophers as less thoughtful or dangerously self-fascinated by their whiteness, even while I have attempted to stay out of the game of white exceptionalism that Audrey Thompson warns against,[2] I set myself out as exceptional. One potential effect of my critique of other anti-racist white philosophers has been to make a white philosopher appear to think she is one rung higher on the conceptual ladder of antiracist philosophy. Even in the midst of arguing that we need to see whiteness as a form of structural inequality that we ought to be dismantling not rearticulating, by engaging in philosophical conversation on the subject—describing the world, not changing it—I am engaged in rearticulating the category, not substantively undoing the forms of power that maintain it. One might argue that this is not the whiteness of philosophy per se but an indication that philosophy and strategies of whiteness fit together particularly well. Most of my comments are directed at white women working against whiteness. White men, especially Race Traitors,[3] mobilize hyperbolic, nearly comic forms of masculinity in their proposed interventions in white practices but I'm honestly never convinced they are self-conscious about their exaggerated attachment to white masculinity so it is possible that I am reading their masculinity more critically than they would. Even in making these comments I continue to point out better and worse forms of inhabiting and articulating critiques of whiteness.

Any act of white philosophizing against racism repeats these problems. But herein lies the conundrum of white antiracist philosophy: its intervention is always complicit in the system it critiques, indeed our legitimacy as seemingly thoughtful philosophers grows as we intervene in weighty topics like racism. Our white antiracist legitimacy, however vexed that might be, is derived from a history of philosophy predicated on the inferiority of people of color and women of any race or ethnicity. The tools that we use have had multiple uses, some for justice and to justify the racist, sexist status quo. By appearing to be more thoughtful, more reasonable, more attuned to the affective or structural dimensions of the institutions, histories and power relations we inhabit, even antiracist philosophers mark out for themselves a space apart, largely because philosophy and thought are often conceived as situated in time differently, for the workings of inequality. But by thinking of our thinking as an indication of the creation of a critical space apart, I believe we are shortsighted in how much that space apart is not apart at all.

Less Whiter than Thou and Other Follies

Rather than citing sources on contemporary white antiracist philosophy and once again starting a cycle of recrimination and distinction, I want to gloss the tactics that many of us have used as in our attempts to get out of our white complicity, even as we delve deeply into it to dismantle it. These tactics are characterized by clarity of address and strength of purpose, but, for all of that, they generate a troubling series of pitfalls to that seeming clarity. In contrast to the antiracist black forms of address to which I turn in the second half of this chapter, the clarity and dangers of white antiracist address create all the more difficulty because they emanate from people who have structural privilege. If their dangers, in other words, can more readily have an effect, their complications nonetheless do damage and maintain white complicity. Examining these tactics gives a counterpoint to the forms of black address in the second half of this chapter. But in making this contrast I am not suggesting that white address should be changed into the more complex forms that black address takes. White address cannot easily be different than it is because it is shaped not only by the intentions of white philosophers but by the structure of whiteness. Because whiteness itself too often hides itself in strategic forms of erasure of its own workings and specificity, white antiracist address has had to mobilize obvious, earnest, seemingly transparent forms of communication strategically to work against the erasure of whiteness. That these forms have their own problems is as obvious to those using them to work against other attendant problems of whiteness as they are to any critic of whiteness.

White antiracist philosophy also suffers from its own lack of competence in working through the complexity of race. As whites come from traditions that have expended much more energy on perpetuating racism than challenging and covering up white privilege than critiquing it, we do not have the same strategies of thinking and rhetorical devices for communicating about the complexity of the system we inhabit. Even our own earnestness motivated by commitment to antiracism has echoes of white demands for truth and agreement that structured etiquette under slavery. In his study of etiquette and race relations, Bertram Wilbur Doyle noted that whites required agreement from black people to the point that "Negroes . . . usually agreed with any statement made by a white person, so that, in many instances they were accused of evasion, if not deceit."[4] While this is an historical example, it remains relevant because whiteness functions as a demand for the truth and certainty about the social order. Our relative naivete about our own structural position as whites and how it has shaped us means that our thinking remains as yet simplistic, more focused on working against the too easy fall back position of not thinking than trying to find multiple ways into the problem of whiteness. We are still mired in whiteness's demand for the truth of itself and still also bound in its subtle and pervasive techniques of domination. Whiteness structures our rhetorical approaches to critique of whiteness as much as it structures the actions, habits, and identities we inhabit.

White Identity

The first rhetorical tactic in white antiracist philosophy is to self-identify as white and to indicate by so doing an understanding of the importance of standpoint epistemology, thus the limits of one's intervention into racism. This tactic works against the unmarkedness of philosophy's position and makes explicit the whiteness of philosophers, particularly those whose work on race, multiculturalism, and difference occupies the space of reasoned intervention in heated political discourse. On the one hand, this self-identification inevitably mobilizes a whiff of the confessional, but on the other hand, it is also a tactic of deauthorization. In more than a few discussions of antiracist philosophy, students of color have remarked that the white authors do not know enough about the experience of racism even if some of their arguments about how it is perpetuated are compelling. The indication of whiteness, then, is not confession in search of redemption. Rather, it is the indication of a deficit of perspective and complicity in a system that maintains that deficit. White students, too, have remarked that white people cannot know enough about racism to write about and this raises another conundrum in white philosophizing about racism. White people do, of course, know plenty about racism, being the source of it. The difficulty, though, in crafting arguments for undoing racism is that while white people have been the source of a white-perpetuated system of inequality, they have not been the central source of work against racism. White standpoint epistemology can provide nuanced accounts of how racism is taught in white families, schools, communities, and institutions. But people of color have access to that insight through their own experience of those institutions and relations. In other words, the expertise of the white perspective provides expertise on the problem, not the solution generally, so it does remain a deficient perspective from which to address changing white superiority.

A related tactic to identifying as white is to identify as white but to complicate it. It is easy to critique this attempt at complication as an attempt to sidestep responsibility for the white "part" of oneself by providing another aspect of one's class, gender, sexuality, or some other form of identity that shows the intersection of multiple vectors of subjectivity, alliance, and experience. Disability theorists and activists have long argued against the kind of simplistic approach to bias that closes down discussions of differences that might be put in conversation rather than opposition, arguing that one can no more rank forms of pain and exclusion than one can rank forms of oppression. People's identities are a complex constellation of race, class, gender, sexuality, religion, region, disability, and so on, and it is crucial to understand how the intersections of those forms of identity work together. But because racism is a topic so frequently avoided, the attempt to complicate whiteness can be a tactic of trying to claim common cause without examining noncommon experience of particular bias. The gesture of analogy or complication seems an ill-timed attempt at connection with people of color in a discussion that is about racial division.

White Power

Indicating an understanding of the social, economic, and political power that one wields as a white person can be similar to indicating white identity. But focusing on the structural elements of whiteness and white superiority evinces a fuller understanding of the meaning of whiteness, moving past the confession of a particular kind of standpoint epistemology and into an interrogation of the effects of that position. Unlike the tactic of examining white self-identity, interrogating one's structural whiteness illuminates the possibility of using white power to undo white power. Even as I have argued against this tactic, by using my institutional legitimacy to do so I have also contributed to it: the philosopher is a legitimate commentator on the follies of others who think they can use the master's tools, etc. White antiracist philosophers have put their ideas into action and written about how they have used their institutional position to leverage things that students of color were unable to access for themselves. Even a self-critical understanding of the problematic of racist patronage created by this intervention cannot undo the problematic, but it is not unreasonable to also point out that at least students benefited from something they would not otherwise have accessed. Using white power for racial justice, white philosophers understand, is a stopgap approach that gives concrete examples to the problem of complicity. One is complicit in whiteness even when engaged in the purported nonexercise of one's white power as much as one is complicit in the exercise of one's white power. As long as there is white power, the dilemmas entailed by putting it into antiracist action remains a vital ethical problem for white people and simply ignoring or not owning up to it does no good. Clearly reveling in one's white charitable, missionary burden is beyond the pale. Indulging in sarcastic derogation of other white people for their whiteness is also wrong.

White Frustration

Discussions of white frustration over the conundrum of whiteness—too often unmarked, too dangerous when marked and indulged in, and often simply replicating the problem of racism as they attempt to undo it—bring together the address that uses identity with the tactic of trying to use white power.[5] Almost all writings on the frustrations of whiteness, including the problematic of continuing to proliferate whiteness even as one attempts to address it are directed firmly at whiteness as the problem. But there are moments when white frustration includes frustration toward people of color who are not sympathetic to the particular vexing pangs of responsible whiteness. White frustration verges into frustrations that people of color want white people to work against racism but then they do not appreciate the mistakes we make when we do so—most often these are stories told about other white people, not stories of the author her/himself, but sometimes they are that too. This white frustrated address makes the political problem of racism keenly manifest in white individual emotional experience, threatening to convert structural critique into how one person feels (enough about dismantling racism, let's talk about me). As much as structural definitions are in binary relations, frustration is generally a characteristic of a person, thus, at the risk of making the only point I have repeatedly, whiteness as a structural identity is converted through narratives of white frustration into a personal and emotional identity that is then conceived of as on the same level of the personal, community and political identity as people of color. People whose complicity in structures of bias derives from their unintended social and political position cannot undo their complicity through intentioned action individually. These are social and political issues and as much as individual attitudes and actions are part of the process of changing social and political arrangements, one cannot "feel" better until there is a better context in which to feel.

But even the character of all the sentences this critique is outlining have the same sense of certainly and clarity that they rail against. In the context of writing about sexuality, I would be inclined to circle around points, use (hopefully) subtle humor to jab at heterosexism. In the context of writing about whiteness, I am much more inclined to the manifesto-like assertion that is the source of the critique in the first place. Dodging through the maze of bias and understanding how to hide from it are not strategies I embody or use in the discussion of whiteness because the experience of the dominant position, a racial position in no way tempered by any other experience of nondominance, cannot easily translate into deft or jarring manipulations of language. This does not bring me to the kind of tears of frustration that some antiracist white philosophers have described but rather to nausea.

Fear of Falling, Fear of Resentment

I have suggested elsewhere that rather than arguing for positive forms of white identity, antiracist philosophy should examine what it would mean to shift to a vertiginous relationship to whiteness,[6] an image that comes from Minnie Bruce Pratt's classic essay, "Skin Blood Heart," in which she describes her inability to follow her father up the stairs of a tower to look over the town from a superior perspective allowed him by race and gender privilege.[7] Vertigo is as much a fear of the difference between the space one occupies and another space as it is an odd sort of potentially self-destroying pleasure in the possibility of the dangers created by the gap between one space and another. Vertigo does, however, entail an understanding that one is in a space, on the one hand firmly different from the space one is looking at, but on the other hand, a space one might potentially leave.

In turning to vertigo, and invoking the associated concept of "falling"—certainly a fear common in representations of the crisis of whiteness and its attendant middle class panic based on the fear that white privilege and middle class status are only tenuous forms of privilege that might be challenged by whoever is at the gates at any moment—I think we move to a sense of panic that may explain why whites thinking about whiteness can largely only be serious. "Falling" marks the dangers of changing thought and action, and as much as falling itself can be a rush, hitting the ground is usually unpleasant. Fear of falling, though, is both a fear of heights and a fear that one will not control one's impulse to see what a fall would be like. This dangerous temptation brings us to the useful part of vertigo—the contemplation of a new space that could entail the end of one's starting space. If whiteness can be conceived as structural, white frustration might be converted out of an affective response to the conundrums of white antiracist action and into a vertigo of seeing the position whiteness occupies now and considering what will happen should the space of whiteness be, as the race traitors put, abolished. The feeling of vertigo, I think, does get to the difficult balance that antiracist white philosophers try to strike in both bringing in our own experiences and failures and also understanding that those are not unique, they are part of what it means to occupy white space.

Vertigo is a state in which straight and easy thinking is not possible, the potential for change creates dissonances and instabilities that work against clear argument. White philosophers turn to earnest communication and finely honed distinctions among kinds of white talk and action because we do understand that as much as whiteness disappears in self-effacing strategies or solidifies in its effects against people of color, it is nonetheless not itself a certain and complete system. Understanding whiteness and its relation to oppression require a kind of movement—as we will see in a moment, this may be the kind of movement similar to the uses of humor in black antiracist projects. It is possible that even whiteness conscious whites cannot yet approach the disruptions of humor for our project. Given the history of white laughter about racial injustice,[8] not against racial injustice, white-led white laughter may still pose too many risks. As much as I think a vertiginous relationship to whiteness is necessary, I also recognize that fear of "falling" can easily convert to white resentment, whiteness as a structural position almost has its own agency (albeit with all white people's complicity) to reconfigure any traitorous act into white supremacy. Yet white antiracist philosophers, even as they describe whiteness as an omnipotent, omnipresent system, understand its internal contradictions. Whiteness itself has gaps and inconsistencies and ridiculous[9] expressions of power but to ridicule it from the perspective of the source of its ridiculousness is a very difficult and perhaps impossible task.[10]

Joking or Mad

It is this ridiculousness and dangerousness of white superiority that Black philosophers, critics, and writers, work with, through, and against. In his exaggerated exchange about racial superiority with a fictionalized white interlocutor, Van Dieman, W.E.B. Du Bois says, "I sit here and maintain that black folk are much superior to white. 'You are either joking or mad,' he says. Both and neither. This race talk is, of course, a joke, and frequently it has driven me insane and probably will permanently in the future."[11] When I have talked with colleagues who largely teach people with whom they do not share an identity, we find in common our use of humor to diffuse what the divide means. And we share in common a large store of anger at contexts that drive us into using humor to slide around uncomfortable engagements, to ease student fears about us, and to even just try to insert a little levity into contexts that seem to become so important and formal if we talk about our difference. There are still differences between my experience as a white person doing this and another colleague's experience as a black professor in a white majority school, so I do not raise this to say I know how all of it feels. But I do raise the issue of using humor as defense, offense, and just simply self-amusement in a difficult situation because that much I do share.

The constant possibility that humor will be taken as deferential performance, with all its historical resonances of minstrelsy, makes race-based humor dangerous even as it is a staple in the history of black resistance to white power. As one interviewed former enslaved black put it:

> Us slaves watched white folks' parties where the guests danced a minuet and then paraded in a grand march, with the ladies and gentlemen going different ways and meeting again, arm in arm, and marching down the center together. Then we'd do it, too, but we used to mock 'em, every step. Sometimes the white folks noticed, but they seemed to like it; I guess they thought we couldn't dance any better.[12]

That humor might be taken as harmless, in addition, also allows the expression of dangerous ideas in contexts where their danger is diminished by the expectation that socially inferior people will be amusing and even sort of offensive. Dexter Gordon argues that African American humor "confounds" canonical understandings of how humor functions and who can be humorous, disrupting the traditional rhetorical positioning of humor as a device of the socially superior.[13] Indeed much philosophizing about humor rehearses Aristotle's or Hobbes's contention that humor is an expression of social superiority, erasing the intentionally subversive forms of humor that are evident in traditions as disparate as foolery, minstrelsy, and trickster lore. These are forms of humor based on risk, even if some forms may seem to recuperate hierarchy in their studied and scripted forms.

But the veneer of humor, even the occasion of white misunderstandings of what is not humorous, provide a strategic context for risky communication. White people did convert subversive black humor into buffoonery and did recount the "antics" of black people to justify white power. Hobbes's observation that humor is an act of superiority is then partially accurate. African American humor though reconfigures superiority, shifting the basis of superiority away from simple social power and into intellectual, political, and aesthetic superiority. As Du Bois humorously constructs his dialogue, the provocative point that black people are superior to whites generates the comment that it is either a joke or mad, noting that either way, the discussion is meant to upset conventional understandings, even if it must do so through a form of humor verging on insanity. Yet it is quite clear from the rest of Du Bois's characterization of the quality of white society, his critique is quite serious:

> If their factories gave us gracious community of thought and feeling; beauty enshrined, free and joyous; if their work veiled them with tender sympathy at human distress and wide tolerance and understanding—then, all hail, White

Imperial Industry! But it does not. It is a Beast! Its creators even do not understand it, cannot curb or guide it. They themselves are but hideous, groping hired Hands, doing their bit to oil the raging devastating machinery which kills men to make cloth, prostitutes women to rear buildings and eats little children. Is this superiority? It is madness. We are the supermen who sit idly by and laugh and look at civilization.[14]

The hypocrisy of white claims to superiority, then, provides ample sources for laughter, even if the exercise of white power is not particularly amusing. Humor or the expression of knowing laughter can comment more pointedly, in some ways, than specific social critique, born as it is of common experiences and common frustrations. In groups with shared experience, laughter indicates both the strength of critique in its near reflex response to shared understandings; and, at the same time, laughter is a break from words, a reaction that indicates language and reasoning has come to an end.

Indeed the fictionalized dialogue in *Dusk of Dawn* has a strikingly different form and address than the rest of this volume of Du Bois's autobiography. It comes at a point where Du Bois has just recounted his own racial history and his intellectual history of engaging with definitions of race. Du Bois explains his experience with "scientific racism" by noting:

The first thing that brought me to my senses in all this racial discussion was the continuous change in the proofs and arguments advanced. I could accept evolution and the survival of the fittest, provided the interval between advanced and backward races was not made too impossible. I balked at the usual "thousand years." But no sooner had I settled into scientific security here, than the basis of race distinction was changed without explanation, without apology.[15]

He moves into a fictionalized dialogue with a white friend, then, because his own family history and the academic tools available do not provide a sufficient way into a real, felt discussion of race, those tools obscure their object. Earnestness and seriousness, in other words, are screens to what race means and thus his turn to humor is a turn to better forms of truth-telling about the shifting terrain of racial superiority. As Gordon puts it, "At its base, then, African American humor is very serious." Hypocrisy, even if laughable, is highly damaging and Du Bois indicates this damage is done to both races.[16] Indeed racism is so damaging that direct and simple speech about it cannot get to the point, cannot communicate in a way that two antagonistic audiences might find a way to better understanding. The break caused by racism, then, breaks into rationality, science, and history and, according to Du Bois, has to be addressed via other forms of communication that can account for complexity.[17]

Because African American humor is often a critique of race relations and situated in dangerous relations with whites, then, it often has "to address at least two audiences across the color line."[18] Frederick Douglass understood the time and place of earnest address, and used it especially with white abolitionist audiences who expected to hear an authentic, heartrending experience of slavery. He also understood how to use humor to allow more latitude in saying risky things in risky ways to risky audiences. Granville Ganter argues that Douglass's use of stereotypes of slave behavior combined with his ridicule of white slaveowners took the source of white audience laughter from "their prejudiced habits of laughing at plantation stereotypes and moves them toward communal laughter at the slaveholders' hypocrisy."[19] Ganter contends that "Douglass's skill at rearranging and reorienting the boundaries of self-and-society is the engine that drives some of his most humorous and violent rhetoric."[20] Ganter recounts a risky situation Douglass defused with convoluted humor. Responding to a speaker who had discoursed for an hour on how black people were descended from monkeys, Douglass takes the stage and is warned, "'Don't speak disrespectfully, or I'll knock you down.' Somewhat threatened by Rynders' presence, Douglass replies, 'No, I won't' (speak disrespectfully), which some people in the crowd heard as 'No, you won't' (knock me down). In this moment of tension, Douglass assured the crowd there would be no riot. Using himself as a foil, he responded to Grant's speech by saying, 'There is no danger of our being thrown into confusion by a monkey.'" His antagonist, Rynders, points out that Douglass is half white, at which point Douglass then claims himself as half brother to Rynders, much to the amusement of the crowd and even the grudging admiration of Rynders.[21] But clearly Douglass's humor has risen to the challenge made to him; it is no backing down but rather an aggressively defensive and offensive series of moves, both initially disarming Douglass's own position and then manipulating bias into advantage, stymieing his opponent who would have to object to his own position in order to best Douglass.

Douglass has manipulated hypocrisy into a new series of incongruous statements that change the undergirdings of the initial forms of bias he encountered. He understands the volatility of the situation and knows he cannot strategically make his arguments directly through reason. Instead he must make use of the rhetorical turn to insult what his interlocutor has initiated. At that point, the audience's laughter is as much a mark of shared frustration at his audacious response to canonical discourses of bias as a new, clear understanding. As John Morreall explains it, using a Freudian approach to laughter, the source of laughter may not itself be pleasant but "if the 'shift' of psychic energy is somehow pleasing, laughter results."[22] Mary Douglas, among others, suggests that some laughter is relief at the passing of a threat and that jokes rely on "the congruence of the joke structure with the social structure " that creates the threat.[23] Laughter can thus be a mechanism that indicates to a social group that what had appeared to be threatening—in this case, the specter of a black man besting a white man—is something that a group can appreciate, can, to put it in its most idealistic terms, help a social group rethink its initial position. While Mary Douglas's account explains how dangerous jokes can be recuperated to support a social structure, Frederick Douglass's use of humor highlights the multiple audiences that can experience humor both differently and similarly and that can change the social context as they learn from humor. Douglass's humor moves people from one place in thought and action to another with a doubled gesture that plays on their expectations and allows his innovation to make sense to them.

Yet, at the same time, Douglass may move his various audiences to new places. The threat entailed by challenging racist structures may have only passed temporarily. Douglass's challenges to traditional forms of bias continue past the moment of interaction. In effect, his words continue to threaten that structure and while he may have allowed some in his audience relief that no riot took place at that moment, his challenge to racist structures means they are permanently challenged. The logic of white bias is undone by the way he folds it back on itself and at that point there is no relief at the passing of a threat. Indeed, the threat is all the clearer given that the ridiculousness of the grounding of oppressive power has been exposed by Douglass' critique that generates laughter rather than violence from the crowd. Other forms of subversive humor communicate to other black people but apparently leave white people in a more conflicted state of obliviousness than their recounting of humor may indicate. It is the power of whiteness to recuperate challenges to itself that I think are behind white antiracist use of earnestness rather than these complex forms of humorous critique. Humor can be complex, unstable, and divergent in its effects: it "works" differently for different groups of people causing each to laugh but at different parts of the same utterance. Humor sometimes directly communicates to insiders and leaves outsiders baffled yet able to construct something funny out of the situation even if it is not the same understanding that makes the insiders laugh. The differently raced understandings of humor structure the next section, showing that black subversive humor can be used by whites to construct a nostalgia for the past, largely based on misunderstanding black humor.

White Racist Humor and Why Antiracist Whites Need Earnestness

In his collection of racist humor, William F. Roberts, whose fond recollections of plantation days structure the book, notes, "Even the solemn interest in freedom was used as a theme for humor." He cites:

> My ol' Mistus promised me
> When she die, she set me free.
> Lived so long till her head go bal'
> Give out the notion of dyin' a'tal.[24]

Clearly the song describes racist white behavior not a black humorous take on freedom, thus the humor has, at least in the way Roberts has framed his recollection, worked in its effort to present something comfortingly humorous to a white man steeped in nostalgia, even while it communicated to black people a warning against whites who seemed like they would finally be generous in death. In his introduction to the book, Roberts shows his conflicted understanding of race relations and white supremacy as he shifts between white-centered memories of slavery and claims to want to improve race relations in his 1942 present: "The recollections of my childhood and youth are filled with memories of Negro stories and mule tales . . . . [Including] the fun and humor we find among the Negroes and mules on the plantation." But also he wants "to make this a handbook of dependable information and correct understanding as to the outstanding phases and characteristics of Negro life in the South where whites and blacks live together."[25] The frontispiece is a photo of a statue of Booker T. Washington and the book ends with a (purported) black man's testimony that "the future of the black man lies in the South."[26] I raise this particular example because it represents a genre of white writing on slavery that indicates simultaneously that race relations were better than historical memory would indicate—though he does himself note that white children chanted their dislike of black people as part of their play[27]—and attempts to use humor as an indication that there was appreciation of black people, even during times when racism structured that humor. His book, then, attempts to both refigure racist humor and intervene in inequality though it reads as no more than a thinly veiled attempt to make legitimate a collection of stories that re-assert white superiority by lampooning black people.

Black subversive humor enables social critique to be spoken publicly, either to be heard only by sympathizers or to jolt even opponents into a new space, but white subversive humor—and Roberts' collection seems to be just that—reconfirms the racial hierarchy while gesturing at appreciation of race relations (as they were before abolition). When white humor is used to reconfirm racism it is not surprising that white antiracist philosophical address would prefer earnest approaches. The subtlety and complications of black humor are directed largely at black audiences skilled at reading doubled texts and finding ways to work against white power while keeping their white audience mistakenly amused (and amusing their black audience at the limited ability of whites to discern complex messages).

When I was in elementary school, one of my white liberal teachers told the class of white students that we were always thinking of the N-word. No matter how liberal our families were or how well we had been brought up, for white people, that invective was always immediately accessible and we would use it or think it even if we thought we were well-meaning and better than that. White privilege guarantees that the word will be there and that white people can slide into using it, as easily as we slide into occupying positions of privilege or use discourses that relegitimize white power. Perhaps antiracist whites risk too much misunderstanding by trying to make a critique of racism too subtle or too complex because it is too easy for white audiences to assume that what that subtlety or complexity really means to be doing is reasserting white superiority—any word we say does that. In other words, it may be that even antiracist whites understand that racism structures all white utterances, actions, and strategies and that the break entailed by humor is potentially a break that can too easily convert intentioned white antiracist action back into the all-too-easy-to-assume gestures of white superiority.[28] While earnest white antiracist philosophizing has its shortcomings, it may remain the only path to white intervention in white racism until the structures of racism have been dismantled. White philosophers, until then, will have to be content with only partially describing the world of race, and also engaging in action to change racist structures.

Notes

1. Lucius T. Outlaw, Jr., "On Race and Philosophy," in *Racism and Philosophy*, ed. Susan E. Babbitt and Sue Campbell (Ithaca, NY: Cornell University Press, 1999), 73.
2. See Audrey Thompson, "Tiffany: Friend of People of Color: White Investments in Antiracism," *Qualitative Studies in Education* 16, no. 1 (2003): 7–29.
3. See Noel Ignatiev and John Garvey, eds., *Race Traitors* (New York: Routledge, 1996).
4. Bertram Wilbur Doyle, *The Etiquette of Race Relations in the South: A Study in Social Control* (Chicago: University of Chicago Press, 1937), 12.
5. Liz Ellsworth refers to these as the "double binds of whiteness," in "Double Binds of Whiteness" in *Off White: Readings on Race, Power, and Society*, ed. Michelle Fine, Lois Weiss, Linda C. Powell, and L. Mun Wong (New York: Routledge, 1997), 259–69.
6. "Vertigo at the Heart of Whiteness." Response to Barbara Applebaum and Erin Stoik, "On the Meaning and Necessity of a White, Anti-racist Identity," in *Philosophy of Education 2000*, ed. Lynda Stone (Urbana, Ill.: Philosophy of Education Society, 2001), 217–20.
7. Minnie Bruce Pratt, "Skin Blood Heart," in *Yours in Struggle: Three Feminist Perspectives on Anti-Semitism and Racism* (Ithaca, New York: Firebrand Books, 1988).
8. Ellsworth cites Carr's "An American Tale: A Lynching and the Legacies Left Behind" as an example of a white person trying to come to grips with the history of the lynching of a black man, a story told and retold in her family to laughter, and who "returns to that laughter over and over" as a source of her shame about the lynching (259).
9. Michel Foucault in *Abnormal* (New York: Picador, 1999) describes this as a new form of judicial power as "Discourses that can kill, discourses of truth, and the third property, discourses . . . that make one laugh" (6) and although his focus in not on whiteness per se, the use of expert testimony to make ridiculous yet supposedly scientific claims has a strong example in judicial decisions on race-related issues in the U.S. Further, his understanding that "one" will laugh indicates that the audience of these discourses are positioned as if they were not implicated in them, but beyond as passive spectators—they will not be laughed at, for instance.
10. There is disagreement among white antiracist philosophers, for instance, on Sandra Bernhardt's performance of white ridiculousness in *Without You I'm Nothing*, a performance I take to be a rare moment of a white performer self-consciously mimicking and inhabiting the fetishization of black culture. Others disagree, arguing that the performance, no matter the intention of the performer, is simply a hyperbolic statement of cultural appropriation. blackpeopleloveus.com is a goofier rendition of this kind of white satire of white racial appropriation.
11. W.E.B Du Bois excerpt from *Dusk to [sic] Dawn* in David R. Roediger, ed. *Black on White: Black Writers on What It Means to Be White* (New York: Schocken, 1998), 30.
12. Quote from Marshall and Jean Stearn's *Jazz Dance*, cited in Roediger, *Black on White*, 152.
13. Dexter B. Gordon, "Humor in African American Discourse: Speaking of Oppression," *Journal of Black Studies* 29 no. 2, (Nov. 1998): 254–76.
14. W.E. B. Du Bois in Roediger, *Black on White*, 36.
15. W. E. B. Du Bois, *Dusk of Dawn*, (New York: Harcourt, Brace, 1940), 99.
16. Gordon, "Humor in African American Discourse," 256. Du Bois describes some of the damage that whites experience from racism: "My friend Van Dieman is not my only white companion. I have others—many others; one and one especially I want to bring to

your attention not because of his attitude toward me but rather because of his attitude toward himself. He represents the way in which my environing white group distorts and frustrates itself even as it strives toward Justice and all because of me. In other words, because of the Negro problem. The average reasonable, conscientious, and fairly intelligent white American faces continuing paradox" (*Dusk of Dawn*, 153).

17. In recalling his early understanding of race, Du Bois says, "All human action to me in those days was conscious and rational. There was no twilight zone." (*Dusk of Dawn*, 282). In the end, he argues, without changing the economic and political structure of white supremacy, white racist thoughts and habits will not change.

18. Gordon, "Humor in African American Discourse," 272.

19. Granville Ganter, "'He Made Us Laugh Some': Frederick Douglass's Humor," *African American Review* 37 no. 4, (2003): 535–54.

20. Ganter, "'He Made Us Laugh Some,'" 538.

21. Ganter, "'He Made Us Laugh Some,'" 543.

22. John Morreall cited in Ganter, "'He Made Us Laugh Some,'" 545.

23. Mary Douglas, "Jokes," in *Rethinking Popular Culture: Contemporary Perspectives in Cultural Studies*, ed. Chandra Mukerji and Michael Schudson (Berkeley: University of California Press, 1991), 300.

24. William F. Roberts, *Dixie Darkies: Negro Stories, Mule Tales, Race Relationships* (Boston: Bruce Humphries, 1942), 140.

25. Roberts, *Dixie Darkies*, 9.

26. Roberts, *Dixie Darkies*, 150.

27. Roberts, *Dixie Darkies*, 144.

28. See, for instance, Eric Lott, *Love and Theft: Blackface Minstrelsy and the American Working Class* (New York: Oxford University Press, 1993) for an examination of the ambivalent and complex racial identifications structuring white participation in blackface.

12

Colonial Practices/Colonial Identities: All the Women are Still White[1]

Sarah Lucia Hoagland, Northeastern Illinois University

The analytical concept of "racialization" suggests that the color line does not merely divide and separate; it involves a dynamic process through which social groups can be bound, defined, and shaped. The process not only creates stereotypes of the colonized as "other" and as inferior; . . . the colonizer too develops a cultural identity that survives well past the formal context of colonial rule.

—Satya Mohanty[2]

My concern in this chapter has to do with ways Western gender discourse embeds us in and is embedded in colonial formations, ways hegemonic and white academic feminism animate colonial identities. A question I find useful is asked by Michael Horswell: What happens when two hybrids meet? For purposes of this chapter, I take the question to be, what happens when two not framed at the center meet, in particular, what happens when white academic feminists approach other women? My concern is with ways Western training encourages academic feminists to hold, to maintain, the center by the relationships we animate and the practices we enact. Susan Brison describes the massive denial of her rape and attempted murder, which "takes the shape of attempts to explain the assault in ways that leave the observer's worldview unscathed."[3] Women of color have described and analyzed the massive denial of U.S. racial formations which takes the shape either of ignoring or of taking up racism in ways that leave Western academic discourse unscathed. Uma Narayan, for example, critiques Western feminist epistemologists for targeting positivism rather than colonialism: "Western feminists, despite their critical understanding of their own culture, often tend to be more a part of it than they realize. If they fail to see the contexts of their theories and assume that their perspective has universal validity for all feminists, they tend to participate in the dominance that western culture has exercised over nonwestern cultures."[4]

227

The center holds when we embrace objectivity, commensurability and (Western) rationality as universal articles of faith. The center holds when our work is grounded in presumptions of transparency and translation. The center holds when we practice an epistemology of ignorance by using the Modern Western cognitive framework of gender to access, read, interpret, and assess another culture. My concern has to do with ways in which we, as white academic women approach or ignore women of color, enact colonial practices and animate colonial identities.

Listening to and working *donner avec,* to "give on and with,"[5] the scholarship of writers from the colonial margins involves being willing to be vulnerable, to be open, to epistemic shifts, open to ways of understanding that will challenge normalcy and our place in its reproduction. One shift involves recognizing that those practices of colonization, enslavement and genocide, begun with the Spanish conquest of what is now called the Americas and continued through heterogeneous practices during the next centuries of Anglo-European formation and development, are not accidental to or even oppositional to but formative of European Modernity and Enlightenment ideals. Another involves understanding that Modern Anglo-European racial and gender formations, developed through processes of Spanish colonization and subsequently through various colonial, genocidal, and enslavement practices, are what have been naturalized by Anglo-European science in the late 18th and early 19th centuries. A third is that there is no "post" to colonialism: The complete restructuring of cultures—economically, historically, institutionally, socially, linguistically, spiritually, and epistemically, stands Modern Ibero-Anglo-European colonialisms apart from earlier practices. And although many, certainly not all, areas colonized have achieved *political* independence, economic, social, political and epistemic colonial structures remain; moreover the restructuring of cultures continues unchecked (today in the name of development or democracy), including gendered and racialized codification of differences. This is the coloniality of power. I have come to understand the "after" of "post-colonialism" is an aftermath that includes virtually seamless continuations of colonial re-orderings: identity formation, economic exploitation, epistemic ordering, and patterns of violence. This aftermath informs U.S. academic institutions, including its intellectual canons, and even thrives in progressive intellectual productions.

Colonial Productions

Understanding the coloniality of power involves understanding the strategies of colonial reconstruction and orderings of societies in the deployment of power. One strategy involves the colonization of language.[6] Walter Mignolo details processes whereby aspects of *Mexica* culture were translated into Spanish by colonizers and thereby reframed as being like Spanish productions but inferior because "primitive." An example he offers is the Mexica *amoxtli,* grasped and translated by the Spanish as *libro* (book). There are significant differences between *amoxtli* and *libro*. In the case of *libros,* we understand the author as central to its production, postmodern deconstruction notwithstanding, while the reader is a more passive participant. In the case of *amoxtli,* however, the *tlacuilo,* producer of *amoxtli,* is a technician and the one reading the *amoxtli* is an interpreter, a reader of signs of the world as well as of the *amoxtli,* and thereby central to cultural reproduction. Thus, as Walter Mignolo writes, "the Spaniards and the Mexicas had not only different material ways of encoding and transmitting knowledge but also—as is natural—different concepts of the activities of reading and writing. Mexicas put the accent on the act of observing and telling out loud the stories of what they were looking at (movements of the sky or the black and red ink). Spaniards stressed reading the word rather than reading the world, and made the letter the anchor of knowledge and understanding."[7]

In this way, Walter Mignolo explains, Spanish colonizers ultimately erased the differences between the two cultures using their own descriptions and cultural productions as a universal frame of understanding such that *amoxtli* came to be understood as a primitive form of book. What the Spanish encountered in the Mexica was a distinct civilization. However, Walter Mignolo notes, "the Spanish never understood that, if the Amerindians lacked letters, they themselves by the same token lacked *quipus* and *amoxtli.* And while the Spanish had men of letters, the Incas had *quipucamayoc* and the Mexicas *tlamatinime.*" In the 100 or so year process of colonizing the Mexica, the Spanish produced the discourse of the denial of coevalness that ultimately constructed the Mexica civilization not as distinct but rather as primitive: the same-but-backward-in-time.[8]

That is, before there was the construction of the Other (e.g., British Orientalism), there was the construction of the Same-but-backward-in-time. It is this construction which makes possible a second strategy, namely the Myth of Modernity. This myth imagines Europe as predating industrialization, as beginning in a state of nature that enjoys a linear, evolutionary, historical process culminating in "mankind's" arrival at modern Anglo-European civilization. Concepts such as "linear history," "progress," and "development," began to take shape and construct a colonizer imagination. Social contract theory emerged, and the indigenous of the Americas figured in the background of the fiction of the state of nature.[9] These concepts are foundational to subsequent Enlightenment thinking such that modernity and rationality have come to be understood as exclusively European products and experiences.[10]

Citing Immanuel Kant's "What is Enlightenment" and Georg Hegel's *Lectures on the Philosophy of History,* Enrique Dussel articulates premises of the Myth of Modernity: that Europe is the superior civilization; that it is obliged to develop others; that the development should follow Europe's; that where these efforts are opposed violence is necessary; that victims are a redemptive sacrifice; that barbarians are in a state of guilt; and that the suffering of others is inevitable. For Georg Hegel, Modern Christian Europe, thus, has nothing to learn from other cultures, and this embodiment of world history endows Europe with a kind of universal right. This is Eurocentrism, a universalizing univocal project that constituted the Modern Anglo-European ego as at the center and end of history. As Enrique Dussel argues, this means that the experience of conquest is central to the development of the cogito and hence the Modern Anglo-European individual ego. "I conquer" is not only prior to but also formative of "I think." Moreover, Modernity as myth always authorizes its violence as civilizing whether propagating Christianity, or democracy and the free market,[11] or socialism.

Anibal Quijano argues that another strategy of colonial ordering involves racial codification. Racialization in its modern meaning began to be developed during the Spanish colonization of the Americas in codifying differences between conquerors and conquered. Racialized beings replace the idea of beings who are superior or inferior as a result of domination; that is, domination was reconceived as biological, and hence natural. Thus, he argues, the idea of race was a way of granting legitimacy to the colonial reordering of conquered peoples, ultimately naturalizing colonial relations.[12] Colonizers took Aztecs, Mayas, Incas, Toltecs, Zapotecs, Chimus, Aymaras, Chibchas, Cuñas and many others, and translated them as Indians, while reframing Ashantis, Yorubas, Zulus, Bantus, Fons, Igbos Congos, Bacongos, Hausas, among others, as Africans or blacks. Dispossessing peoples of their identities and their place facilitates constructing them as inferior and promotes a cognitive model in which non-Europe becomes the past, if not always in fact, then at least in description, "primitive," and thereby inferior.[13] Noting that blacks were not only exploited but colonized, Anibal Quijano argues that as time went on, colonizers codified the phenotypic trait of the colonized as color, "this category probably being initially established in the area of Anglo-America."[14]

He argues that Anglo-American globalization has its roots in colonialism, and articulates two axes of a new model of power. One is racial codification while the other, yet another strategy of colonial ordering, involves the creation and development a new structure to organize and control labor, its resources, and products: Slavery, serfdom, indentured servitude, petty commodity production, reciprocity, and wage labor were reconstituted or developed to produce commodities for the world market and thus articulated to capital. That is, Anibal Quijano argues, all previous forms of labor were reorganized toward commodity production and thus became aspects of capitalism. In the process, forms of labor were racialized, wage labor being reserved for whites, non-productive labor for indigenous and others, slavery for blacks. The new historical identities (black or African, Indio or indigenous) enabled race and the division of labor to remain systematically and structurally linked. "In the course of the worldwide expansion of colonial domination on the part of the same dominant race (or, from the eighteenth century onward, Europeans), the same criteria of social classification were imposed on all of the world population."[15] Anibal Quijano goes on to argue that control of a type of labor was also the control of a people, and the two elements appear today as naturally associated through identity formation.[16] For example, white property owners still accept that those designated as non-whites should work for them (but not that whites should work for non-whites).[17] Certainly I have observed very hardworking, cash-strapped white laborers in Michigan refusing to do specific kinds of labor they understand to be labor appropriate to migrant workers from Mexico.

Beginning with these analyses from Walter Mignolo, Enrique Dussel and Anibal Quijano, María Lugones articulates yet another strategy of colonial ordering and a third axis of the modern colonial system—the development and introduction of new concepts of gender. She argues that colonialism was not a process of imposing preexisting European gender arrangements on colonized people. Instead it "imposed a new gender system that created very different arrangements for colonized males and females than for white bourgeois colonizers. Thus, it introduced many genders and gender itself as a colonial concept and mode of organization of relations of production, property relations, of cosmologies and ways of knowing."[18] That is, the new gender system is also critical to colonial re-orderings of cultures. She explains that "Those changes were introduced through slow, discontinuous, and heterogeneous processes that violently inferiorized colonized women," and involved subordination of females in every aspect of life and their forced dismissal from the public sphere. Certainly two indicators I have come across used to declare a culture to be primitive, not civilized, are collectivity (in contrast to Western individualism), and women's sexual autonomy & authority. María Lugones argues that understanding the imposition of this system involves understanding its role in undermining indigenous and other cultures by means of disintegrating "communal relations, egalitarian relations, ritual thinking, collective decision making and authority;" it involves re-cognizing the nature and scope of changes in social structure that the processes constituting colonial/modern racialized, gendered Eurocentered capitalism imposed.[19] That is, the modern colonial gender system was developed and imposed to facilitate the destruction of frameworks, epistemes, economies and cosmologies of conquered cultures.

These strategies of colonial ordering: the denial of coevalness, the myth of modernity, racialized commodity production, and racialized gender codification, all have become central to Modern Western cognition understood not as a particular worldview, but as universal. My interest here is to attend to (some) ways white and hegemonic academic feminism come out of and remain rooted in this colonial heritage, and, in deploying gender analysis, enact colonial material and conceptual relationalities and identities which reproduce this framework and leave these re-orderings intact, unscathed.

Animating Colonial Identities

Chandra Mohanty introduced the notion of discursive colonization as a practice of Western feminist researchers who position themselves to analyze the lives of marginalized women. She describes ways Western feminist scholars presuppose Western culture and "codify others as Other" (which she notes can also happen among Third World scholars embedded in Western scholarship). Concerned with Western feminist use of an ahistorical, acontextual, universal, analytic category of woman, she challenges the category's embedded assumption that "men and women are already constituted as sexual-political subjects prior to their entry into the arena of social relations," when in fact "women are produced through these very relations as well as being implicated in forming these relations." As a consequence, "Western feminists alone become the true 'subjects' of this counterhistory. Third World women, on the other hand, never rise above the debilitating generality of their 'object' status." Moreover, the only discourse for articulating Third World women's lives is an Anglo-European one.[20] Indeed, disciplinary research methodologies dictate that the only agents in the relation are presumed to be the knowing (authorized) subjects, and within authorizing institutions, theirs is the prerogative of interpretation and packaging of information. Western disciplinary practice thus positions the academic as a judge of credibility and a gatekeeper for its authority, thereby maintaining the coloniality of knowledge.[21]

Discursive colonization flourishes and the center holds because it is white bourgeois women who have consistently counted as the model for analyses of gender in hegemonic and white feminism. Thus for example when developing their work on liberty and the enfranchisement of women, John Stuart and Harriet Taylor Mill were clearly not thinking of Indian women. Although John Stuart Mill argued for the enfranchisement of women, he also held a high post in the British East India Company. And while in *On Liberty* he says he is not aware that any community has a right to force another to be "civilized," elsewhere he argues that despotism is the best means of civilizing a people.[22] The circularity/auto-validation of the "higher" and "lower" pleasures of his utilitarian argument is obvious. The center holds in academic feminism when a feminist philosopher takes up John Stuart and Harriet Taylor Mill's work without taking up its relationship to colonial society and culture. Such ignoring, possibly regarded as irrelevant because the work can be allegedly universalized, i.e., decontextualized, manages to preserve, unmarked and unremarked, the racialized and gendered implications of the Mills' theorizing and, more importantly, the racialized and gendered nature of the rights and liberties and responsibilities to be obtained and defended.

Jin Haritaworn notes that nineteenth century European women performed superiority over "Oriental women" and enacted their own agency by working to liberate "Oriental women" from "backward, patriarchal cultures."[23] Taking up

Lady Mary Montagu's "defense" of Turkish women in *Turkish Embassy Letters*, Meyda Yeğenoğlu analyzes how Lady Montagu positions herself as a supplement to Western masculinist Orientalism, providing the one thing European men couldn't obtain: access to Turkish harems, to "the scene of 'stark naked' truth/essence of the other/woman."[24] In other words, gaining the trust of upper-class Turkish women and access to their spaces, Lady Montagu gained her own voice and authority by informing on them and writing about the one thing European men could not in Orientalist discourse, thereby completing the men's work.[25]

Moreover Meyda Yeğenoğlu highlights the symbolic representation of the "Oriental woman": her condition is morally condemned as a sign of the oppressive nature of the culture, and she is used to indicate that the "Orient" must modernize by means of a radical break from tradition. "The metonymic association between the Orient and its women, or more specifically the representation of woman as tradition and as the essence of the Orient, made it all the more important to lift the veil, for *unveiling and thereby modernizing the woman of the Orient signified the transformation of the Orient itself.*"[26]

Jennifer Morgan points out that if we don't understand how race and gender animate each other, we are left with a "one-dimensional sense of how the categories were mobilized and why they resonated with such clarity and violence in the lives of early Modern Europe."[27] Arguing that the colonial Atlantic Slave trade was an integral part of the process of the material reorganization of gender, she details how "confronted with an Africa they needed to exploit, European writers turned to black women as evidence of a cultural inferiority that ultimately became encoded as racial difference. Monstrous bodies became enmeshed with savage behavior as the icon of women's breasts became evidence of tangible barbarism. African women's 'unwomanly' behavior evolved an immutable distance between European and African on which the development of racial slavery depended." As a result, Europeans "conjure[d] a gendered and racialized figure that marked the boundaries of English civility even as she naturalized the subjugation of Africans and their descendants in the Americas."[28]

María Lugones has noted that white academic feminists, in responding to women of colors' anger at glaring and subtle omissions and distortions in white and hegemonic feminist theorizing, have put effort into figuring out ways to fix the theory rather than into figuring out ways to take up the invitation to dialogue. For example, Jasbin Puar complains about the reception and use of black feminist theorizing of intersectionality in ways that reify standpoint epistemology.[29] bell hooks exposed an increase in white supremacy in the academy since the political challenges of the 1970s as a result of where white academic women have sought support, engagement, and authority. First, there was the move to sever theory from practice, insisting proper theorizing required academic discipline, a distancing from activists to gain academic credibility. Then, in response to challenges by women of color, there was the move to work with white academic men to determine standards for theorizing, a distancing from the women of color seeking to engage white women.[30]

Initially the anger from women of color was an invitation/challenge to dialogue. But this challenge was not a request to be included in what already existed, it was an invitation to respond to a different set of interlocutors who offer different sets of challenges. Indeed, Meyda Yeğenoğlu argues, "Western feminism, as it attempts to represent cultural difference by reiterating the economy of sameness, is inextricably complicitous with masculinist Orientalism and imperialism."[31]

"In other words, all the women are still white."[32]

Jennifer Morgan argues that centering the lives of enslaved women during the colonial period is not about inclusion but is rather a method for rewriting early American history.[33] For example she offers a significant reframing of motherhood, remarking that intricate and complex studies of the body, of reproduction, and of childbirth "are notable for the persistence with which they mobilize the category of 'woman' unmodified by race."[34] Motherhood will be understood quite differently when taken up in the context of "both the overwhelming commodification of the bodies of infants and their mothers, and the potential impulse women may have felt to interrupt such obscene calculations.... In any such account, a rejection of emotional connections, a refusal to protect, would be just as rational and likely a configuration of the mother-child relationship as was the bonds of motherhood that created Harriet Jacobs' stunning seven-year ordeal—a story that has become an archetype of enslaved motherhood."[35]

For the modern colonial gender system, María Lugones argues, has a dark and a light side. The hegemonic characterization of white Anglo-European women as fragile and sexually passive, a characterization many have been working to destabilize for decades, opposes them to nonwhite women, including female slaves who were "characterized along a gamut of sexual aggression and perversion and as strong enough to do any sort of labor." Moreover, she argues, "there was no extension of the status of white women to colonized women even when they were turned into similes of bourgeois white women."[36] Spanish and later British colonizers and others developed and imposed a Christian sexuality as they worked to destroy women's sexual autonomy and community authority in indigenous cultures. And as indigenous women were brought under colonial systems, they were not understood to deserve the rights and liberties and status of white women. Moreover their status and labor, along with the status and labor of indigenous men, enabled the construction of (privileged white) women as fragile and in need of defense.[37]

Andrea Smith argues that the demonization of Native women is a strategy by white men to maintain control over white women. Native women were portrayed as immoral, non-human, hyper-sexed animals. In this context, white women, to prove their humanity, sought purity, virginity, subservience. And Native men were labeled ruthless savages, rapists from which white women needed the protection of white men, while quite the opposite was true. It is Native women who needed, and continue to need, given the development and imposition of U.S. law in relation to tribal law, protection from white men.[38]

As María Lugones notes, in colonial impositions, females excluded from white womanhood were not just subordinates, they were understood to be like animals in a deep sense of "without gender," sexually marked as female but without characteristics of femininity.

Again, there is a light and dark side to the Modern colonial gender system and many genders. Understanding this means also understanding that efforts to enact white feminist goals in "formerly" colonized cultures become, *ipso facto*, enactments of colonial agendas and identities. Such efforts presuppose the continued imposition of Western ontology, episteme, economics, politics, and cosmology. This is one reason feminists focusing on positivism instead of colonialism is a problem, as Uma Nayaran argues. Disciplinary structures created during the four centuries of Ibero-Anglo-European colonization structure Western academic relationality and imagination today, including white and hegemonic feminism.

Working to spread Western feminist values means working to spread, for example, Western individualism, autonomy, and individual rights, rights marinated in racialized and gendered framings and enacted as accruing to certain members of society who are maintained by Others. This is a discourse presupposing a disappeared subordinate. Meyda Yeğenoğlu argues that the point is not simply to criticize, but also to understand what is at stake in Western universal ideals of feminism. The colonial move interpellates others into a Western discourse.[39] In the process, white and hegemonic feminists reinforce twofold a subordinate status for women of color within the order of things—subordinate in relation to Western culture and subordinate in relation to the construction of white women within Western culture.[40]

Gender is not about finding and identifying females, it is about reading, interpreting, framing a culture, *ipso facto* imposing Western cultural orderings which inferiorize women of color. Again, María Lugones is arguing that new concepts of gender were developed and imposed on colonized women during the process of colonization, including white women's gender authority in relation to women of color.

All the women are still white because when two not framed at the center meet and one is a white Western woman, we translate and impose colonial culture through our notions of gender, using it to imagine universal inclusion or to analyze other cultures. We don't work to enter other cosmologies but instead remain focused on white male academic practices; when moved to consider others we focus on commonality and inclusion, act to maintain authority over women of color; we work from a white Western model of gender and maintain our status as gatekeepers, we remain supplements to the canon; we impose Western cultural values as if they were or should be universal, and remain loyal to our disciplines even when critically engaging them, keeping our worldviews intact, unscathed. We don't think to address ways we are called to replicate the coloniality of power by animating colonial identities/relationalities.

Donner-avec

Thus while developing critical discourse within Western ideology, we nevertheless resist ways of thinking and engaging that might leave our worldviews and our place in them scathed. Again, gender is a conceptual, interpretive tool.

Oyèrónké Oyewùmí argues that "men" and "women" are naturalized Western categories understood to be universal, fundamental elements around which communities and cultures organize and where one category dominates the other. Due to imperialism, Western debates about roles and identities have been universalized, exported and injected. Analyzing Yorùbá language and culture, she argues that gender did not exist as a social category in precolonial Yorùbá society: "The body was not the basis of social or political roles, inclusions or exclusions, not the foundation of thought and identity."[41] Indeed, "Yorùbá language is gender-free, which means that many categories taken for granted in English are absent. There are no gender specific words denoting son, daughter, brother, or sister. Yorùbá names are not gender-specific; neither are *Qko* and *aya*—two categories translated as the English husband and wife, respectively."[42] She argues that we will misunderstand Yorùbá society if we follow feminist scholars' deployment of gender, presupposing "woman" as a social category understood to be "powerless, disadvantaged, and controlled by men."[43]

Some may be tempted to argue that they can nevertheless *find* gender in precolonial Yorùbá culture, taking issue with Oyèrónké Oyewùmí's analysis of Yorùbá language, insisting on commensurability at some level and hence pushing for transparency and translation into gender categories. But this is a violent rewriting of culture. For example, Richard Brandt wrote a book, *Hopi Ethics*. He acknowledged that while within the Hopi language, there is no phrase which corresponds to the English phrase, "Your duty is. . . ." Nevertheless, presupposing a deontological system as universal, as the essence of ethics, he argues that "we" can ask: "(since we do not want to call a term 'ethical' unless it is equivalent to one of the English terms like 'duty,' 'blameworthy,' and so on), what concepts are expressed by those Hopi terms which interpreters regard as the nearest equivalents of 'right,' 'duty,' 'blameworthy,' etc., when applied to conduct? This is an empirically decidable question."[44] In other words, Richard Brandt considers *duty* a factual, observable, phenomena which can be detected (even if practiced unselfconsciously) and studied, providing an analysis to show that the Hopi really do have ethics even if they don't understand this, or can't verbalize this, about themselves. Thus the Hopi become ethically the same, but backward in time.

Just as the Spanish deployed *libro,* "book," to name a Mexica phenomenon, *amoxtli,* and Richard Brandt deployed *duty,* U.S. white feminists deploy *gender* as a means, not of engaging, but of grasping other cultures, of rendering them the same . . . and therefore backward in time. And that universalizing is a colonial move for the naming is not a simple denotation, not an empirically decidable question, it is an interpellating into Western semiotics and practices, and thereby delineating the possibilities and limitations available (equal rights, e.g., that is, Western possibilities and limitations).

Cognitive frameworks permeate our thinking.[45] And gender enters us into a cognitive framework. Oyèrónké Oyewùmí writes, "Researchers always find gender where they look for it."[46]

Moreover, we've inherited a practice from Descartes[47]: if it doesn't make sense to me, if I can't see the logic, I can doubt it. So the burden is on the other to enter my logic and translate it for me. As Rodolfo Kusch notes, "we wield ignorance like a metric stick."[48]

My interest in this chapter concerns the conceptual maneuverings by which academics are epistemically positioned to practice knowledge inherited from colonial formations; ways other forms of knowledge racialized and gendered by the coloniality of knowledge are erased, dismissed; ways those of us educated in Western traditions are taught, when we wish to explore something new, to translate it into something we know and understand, rather than working to enter a distinct conceptual framework, a different cosmology, rather than working to inhabit and move among disparate logics, multicenters of meaning.

Rodolfo Kusch worked to open up the understanding of an América populated by (at least) two disparate ideologies and so worked to move among distinct logics, arguing that we can't really understand indigenous thought using concepts that are central to academic production, concepts such as causality. He contrasts what he calls seminal (indigenous) and causal (Modern Western) thinking. For example, he contrasts Martin Heidegger's *Dasein* with the Aymara *utcatha. Dasein* involves *being* that is located but thrown there, suggesting alienation, or possibly something to be transcended. *Utcatha,* on the other hand, is connected with domicile, dwelling, plaza, womb, vital center; it is a *being there* linked to shelter, a place of germination, of possibilities.[49] These are incommensurable worldviews. But that does not mean that someone from one can't interact with someone from the other. What we must be willing to engage in is an epistemic shift, shifts in practices of knowing—not grasping, but extending with generosity: *donner-avec,* "gives on and with."[50] It is interesting to think of the communiqués of the Zapatistas as exemplifying "seminal" thinking while the government's approach to the Zapatistas exemplifies causal thinking. Thus rather than understand the Zapatistas as going for something like liberation, as Westerners understand liberation, or rights, we can engage the Zapatistas as defending their dwelling, where they are from, as part of their being. It is not individual rights but a way of *being* that is under attack and being defended.[51] This does not percolate in a concept such as *Dasein.*

What if we enacted different relationalities, different epistemic practices? What if we engaged in epistemic shifts, shifts in practices of knowing—again, not grasping, but extending with generosity, something other than totalitarian certainty?[52]

Jennifer Morgan, Oyèrónké Oyewùmí, and Sylvia Marcos argue that gender has to be freed from Modern European identity and cosmology.

> Among the Igbo, the creator was Chineke—representing both male (Chi) and female (Eke)—whose unity and complementarity formed the crux of Igbo cosmology.[53]

> It is significant that in Yoruba cosmology, when a body part is singled out it is the *orí* (head), which is elaborated as the seat of individual fate *(orí)*. The word *orí* thus has two closely intertwined meanings—fate and head. *Orí* has no gender.[54]

> The idea of a divine pair is deeply rooted in Mesoamerican thought . . . . Man and woman, death and life, evil and good, above and below, far and close, light and dark, cold and hot were some of the dual aspects of one same reality. Not mutually exclusive, not static, not hierarchically organized (at least not in the modern pyramidal way), all elements and natural phenomena were construed as a balance of dual valences.[55]

Drawing on primary sources, colonial documents and ethnographies, Sylvia Marcos works to describe a precolonial cosmology. The Nahua world view involves duality, fluidity and balance: "The urge for balance gave duality plasticity: since the critical point of balance had to be found in continuous movement, it redefined itself from moment to moment. Change and flux in the entire cosmos had an impact on the way things here on earth were conceptualized. This bipolar fluid, shifting, and yet balanced universe framed the perception of beneficial as well as harmful events and actions, of good as well as evil forces, giving their relations a nostalgic, non-rigid quality. The duality implicit in all Mesoamerican cosmologies gave its impulse to everything: divinities, people, objects, time, and space with its five directions."[56] Moreover, this cosmology is still alive, and Sylvia Marcos interviewed curanderas, graniceras, shamans and midwives whose practices are rooted in Nahua cosmology. She notes that "gender" in this cosmology involves a fluid continuum of identities "kept in balance through a homeorrheic equilibrium."[57]

This is not translatable into Western cosmology, into a factual, observable, phenomena which can be detected, perhaps assumed to be practiced unselfconsciously; this is not commensurable with Western gender. Indeed, María Lugones suggests that it is not even clear that we who have been disciplined solely in Western gender thinking can use gender to understand social relations in since gender is so marinated in Western constructions.

What if white women engaged, took up understandings of, accepted invitations from, broke bread with, women (and men) of color rather than seeking acknowledgment and validation from white academic men who remain grounded in the canon? What if white academic women did not make women of color gain intellectual authority by navigating their work through some member of the canon, and instead encouraged them to develop their own trajectories? What if white feminists worked to destabilize not only the hegemonic characterization of white Anglo-European women in relation to white Anglo-European men, but also the hegemonic characterization of white Anglo-European women in relation to women and men of color? What if we ceased animating colonial practices and identities? Would the center, our racialized gender center, still hold?

Notes

1. This phrasing comes from Jennifer Morgan (6) and refers to the anthology: *All the Women Are White, All the Blacks Are Men, But Some of Us Are Brave*, ed., Gloria T. Hull, Patricia Bell Scott, and Barbara Smith. This chapter is deeply informed by ongoing conversations with María Lugones, Jackie Anderson, Anne Leighton, Alison Bailey, Crista Lebens. I presented an earlier version of this chapter at the 5th Annual California Roundtable on Philosophy and Race, University of California, Berkeley, and The Association for Feminist Epistemologies, Methodologies, Metaphysics, and Science Studies (FEMMSS) in conjunction with the University of South Carolina Women's and Gender Studies Conference, The politics of Knowledge.
2. Satya P. Mohanty, "Drawing the color line: Kipling and the culture of colonial rule," in *The Bounds of Race: Perspectives on Hegemony and Resistance*, ed. Dominick La Capra (Ithaca, NY: Cornell University Press, 1991), 314.
3. Susan J. Brison, *Aftermath: Violence and the Remaking of a Self* (Princeton, NJ: Princeton U. Press, 2002), 9.
4. Uma Narayan, "The Project of Feminist Epistemology: Perspectives From a Nonwestern Feminist," in *Gender/Body/Knowledge: Feminist Reconstructions of Being*, ed. Alison Jaggar and Susan Bordo (New Brunswick, NJ: Rutgers University Press, 1990), 263.
5. Édouard Glissant offers the concept of *donner avec*, translated by Betsy Wing as "gives on and with" as a concept of understanding, indeed an epistemic positioning, in contrast to the Modern Western idea of *grasping*.
6. Walter Mignolo also offers intricate analyses of the colonization of space and the colonization of memory.
7. Walter D. Mignolo, *The Darker Side of the Renaissance* (Ann Arbor: The University of Michigan Press, 1995), 105. Moreover, Walter Mignolo notes the critical role *book* played in colonization—to be Asante, one has to be born Asante; to be Maori, one must be born Maori and continue to return to practice critical rituals during the year; to be Christian, one can simply profess beliefs. On the other hand, he notes, religions grounded in the idea of the book can be spread. "Christianity in the book can force the same, giving it the status of truth," (Mignolo, *The Darker Side of the Renaissance*, 82–3).
8. Mignolo, *The Darker Side of the Renaissance*, 93. Johannes Fabian articulated the denial of coevalness in analyzing the rise of anthropology during the rise of capitalism and colonial expansion as a means of establishing Western primacy and justifying Western dominance. See Johannes Fabian, *Time and The Other: How Anthropology Makes Its Object* (New York: Columbia University Press, 1983).
9. Thus, for example, Walter Mignolo notes that the idea of evolution frames current histories of the book as historians begin the history of books with the production of scrolls rather than recognizing the advent of the book as a rupture (Mignolo, *The Darker Side of the Renaissance*, 77) as is the current shift to the use of the internet.
10. Anibal Quijano, "Coloniality of Power, Eurocentrism, and Latin America," *Neplanta: Views from South* 1, no. 3 (2000), 542. Significantly, subsequent forms of colonialism, such as British and French forms as well as many resistances to colonization, take the notion of progress and some element of linear history for granted. It becomes established as a pattern of thought, cognitive framework.
11. Enrique Dussel, 1995. *The Invention of the Americas: Eclipse of "the Other" and the Myth of Modernity*. Trans. Michael D. Barber (New York: The Continuum Publishing Co., 1995). See 19–23, 66, and 136–38.

12. Quijano, "Coloniality of Power, Eurocentrism, and Latin America," 534.
13. Quijano, "Coloniality of Power, Eurocentrism, and Latin America," 551.
14. Quijano, "Coloniality of Power, Eurocentrism, and Latin America," 534.
15. Quijano, "Coloniality of Power, Eurocentrism, and Latin America," 536.
16. "The fact is that from the very beginning of the colonization of America, Europeans associated nonpaid or nonwaged labor with the dominated races because they were 'inferior' races." At first Amerindians were simply worked to death, disposable labor. This ended in the 1700s with the end of the encomendero system. But with the new organization, Indios were not advanced to wage labor. Quijano, "Coloniality of Power, Eurocentrism, and Latin America," 538.
17. Quijano, "Coloniality of Power, Eurocentrism, and Latin America," 535–39.
18. María Lugones, "Heterosexualism and the colonial/modern, gender system," *Hypatia*. 22, no. 1 (2007): 186–209, quotation on 186.
19. Lugones, "Heterosexualism and the colonial/modern, gender system," 201–2.
20. Chandra Talpade Mohanty, "Under Western Eyes: Feminist Scholarship and Colonial Discourses," in *Third World Women and the Politics of Feminism*, ed. Chandra Mohanty, Ann Russo, and Lourdes Torres (Bloomington: Indiana University Press, 1991), 59, 71.
21. Sarah Lucia Hoagland, "Epistemic Shifts: Feminist Advocacy Research and Resistant Negotiation," in *Feminist Epistemology and Philosophy of Science: Power in Knowledge* (Kluwer, forthcoming). In discussing women who were captured in the Atlantic Slave trade, Jennifer Morgan continuously reminds the reader of the agency of the women she is discussing while simultaneously refusing to foreclose meaning through interpretation. "I am in search of an expansive methodology employed in the service of, and open to the possibility of, contingency and the unknowability of the past" (Jennifer Morgan, *Laboring Women: Reproduction and Gender in New World Slavery* (Philadelphia: University of Penn. Press, 2004), 201). She is not a gatekeeper, or as Khoo Lee remarked to me, a zookeeper.
22. John Stuart Mill, *Considerations on Representative Government*, ed. with an introduction by R. B McCallum (London: Oxford University Press, 1861/1946), 39, from Bruce Mazlish, *James and John Stuart Mill* (New York: Basic Books, 1975), 394.
23. Jin Haritaworn, "Loyal Repetitions of the Nation: Gay Assimilation and the 'War on Terror,'" *darkmatter*. http//:www.darkmatter101.org/site (Posted May 2, 2008).
24. Meyda Yeğenoğlu, *Colonial Fantasies: Towards a Feminist Reading of Orientalism* (Cambridge, MA: Cambridge University Press, 1998), 90–91.
25. Yeğenoğlu, *Colonial Fantasies*, 90–91.
26. Yeğenoğlu, *Colonial Fantasies*, 99. In taking up nationalist struggles, she also notes: "However, although the veiling and unveiling of women appear to be reverse strategies of responding to Western hegemony they are both in fact conditioned by and therefore the products of Orientalist hegemony" (Yeğenoğlu, *Colonial Fantasies*, 136).
27. Morgan, *Laboring Women*, 197.
28. Morgan, *Laboring Women*, 49.
29. Puar, Jasbir, Ben Pitcher and Henriette Gunklel, "Q&A with Jasbir Puar," *darkmatter*. http//:www.darkmatter101.org/site (Posted May 2, 2008)
30. bell hooks, *Teaching to Transgress: Education as the Practice of Freedom* (New York: Routledge, 1994), 63. Recently two academic feminists discussing separate announcements of conferences have appealed to the mainstream to justify centering white male fears, defenses and ignorances:

I am working with a quite diverse reading & organizing committee some of whom were very much concerned that the conference appeal to mainstream interests.
And
I wanted this conference to get notice in the "mainstream" and we know how many women make a major impact to that audience.

31. Yeğenoğlu, *Colonial Fantasies*, 86. Arguing that a positive depiction of subjects to counter negative masculinist images does not undermine Orientalism but misses the colonial move, she explains that the power of Orientalism comes not from negative images deployed nor from distortions of "reality." Orientalism is the power to animate a regime of truth about the Other which thereby authorizes, indeed establishes the identity of, the One, the authorized knowing subject (Yeğenoğlu, *Colonial Fantasies*, 89–90).
32. Morgan, *Laboring Women*, 6.
33. Morgan, *Laboring Women*, 11.
34. Morgan, *Laboring Women*, 6.
35. Morgan, *Laboring Women*, 200–01.
36. Lugones, "Heterosexualism and the colonial/modern, gender system," 202–3.
37. Lugones, "Heterosexualism and the colonial/modern, gender system."
38. Andrea Smith, *Conquest: Sexual Violence and American Indian Genocide* (Cambridge, MA, South End Press, 2005); Sarah Deer, "Federal Indian Law and Violent Crime: Native Women and Children at the Mercy of the State," in *The Color of Violence: The Incite! Anthology* (Cambridge, MA: South End Press, 2006). As U.S. and tribal law interact and function today, white men can, and do, rape Native women on reservations with impunity.
39. Yeğenoğlu, *Colonial Fantasies*, 90, 102.
40. Lugones, "Heterosexualism and the colonial/modern, gender system."
41. Oyèrónké Oyewùmí, *The Invention of Women: Making an African Sense of Western Gender Discourses* (Minneapolis: U of Minnesota Press, 1997), x–xiii). "The assertion that 'woman' as a social category did not exist in Yorùbá communities (Oyewùmí's assertion) should not be read as antimaterialist hermeneutics, a kind of poststructuralist deconstruction of the body into dissolution. Far from it—the body was (and still is) very corporeal in Yoruba communities. But, prior to the infusion of Western notions into Yorùbá culture, the body was not the basis of social roles, inclusions, or exclusions; it was not the foundation of social thought and identity" (Oyewùmí, *The Invention of Women*, x).
42. Oyewùmí, *The Invention of Women*, 29.
43. Oyewùmí, *The Invention of Women*, x–xiii.
44. Richard Brandt, *Hopi Ethics: A Theoretical Analysis* (Chicago: University of Chicago Press, Midway Reprints, 1974), 91, 82–3.
45. Sylvia Marcos, *Taken from the Lips: Gender and Eros in Mesoamerican Religions* (Boston: Brill, 2006), 1.
46. Oyewùmí, *The Invention of Women*, 31.
47. Rene Descartes, *Meditations on First Philosophy* (Indianapolis, IN: Hackett Publishing Company, Inc., 1979).
48. Rodolfo Kusch, *Indigenous and Popular Thought in América*. Trans. María Lugones and Joshua Price (Durham, NC: Duke University Press, forthcoming). Originally published as *El Pensamiento Indigena y Popular en América*.
49. Kusch, *Indigenous and Popular Thought in América*.

50. Édouard Glissant, *Poetics of Relation*. Trans., Betsy Wing (Ann Arbor: University of Michigan Press, [1981] 1989).
51. Subcomandante Marcos and the Zapatista Army of National Liberation, *Shadows of Tender Fury*. Trans. by Frank Bardacke, Leslie López, and the Watsonville, California, Human Rights Committee (New York: Monthly Review Press, 1995).
52. Glissant, *Poetics of Relation*.
53. Morgan, *Laboring Women*, 64.
54. Oyewùmí, *The Invention of Women*, 38.
55. Marcos, *Taken from the Lips*, 14.
56. Marcos, *Taken from the Lips*, 33–34.
57. Marcos, *Taken from the Lips*, 13.

13

Is Philosophy Anything if it Isn't White?

Cynthia Kaufman, De Anza College in Cupertino

That philosophy is a very white field seems obvious. In the U.S., most of the texts philosophers use have been written by white authors and the vast majority of professional philosophers are white. But is philosophy's whiteness an essential quality? What kind of existence would philosophy have if it weren't white? And how is its whiteness related to racism?

There isn't a word in Vietnamese for philosophy. And yet in Vietnam, people think rigorously, they have discursive means of resolving disputes, they contemplate the nature of the universe, of knowledge, of human action, and of politics.[1]

During one quarter, in my critical thinking class, a Vietnamese student spoke up and said that if he were to argue the way I was suggesting within a Vietnamese context, he would be rejected for being rude. Several other Vietnamese students chimed in in agreement. Is there anything universal about the value of engaging in conversation about ideas through trying to refute the other person's ideas? Does it matter that a person from a non-Western background must let go of some dearly held cultural practices to succeed in a philosophy classroom? To what extent do our students code switch, and use philosophy instrumentally to help them survive in Western dominant contexts? To what extent is philosophy a virus for spreading Eurocentrism?

The derivation of the term philosophy from the Greek "love of wisdom" points to a wide-open field of possibilities for the reflection on all sorts of things, using all sorts of approaches. And yet, the term "philosophy" is usually understood to have a far narrower reference. A trip to almost any dictionary will find something like the following from the Oxford English Dictionary: philosophy is "love, study, or pursuit (through argument or reason) of wisdom, truth or knowledge." One can imagine a deeply multiracial and multicultural philosophy that was based on studying, investigating, comparing and analyzing, using a variety of methods, the forms of wisdom that arise in a rich variety of cultural contexts. Such a philosophy would not have to be "white," nor would it have to be racist.

But stuck in the middle of the OED's wide definition is one of the fulcrums for maintaining and reproducing the whiteness of Philosophy. The parenthesis that limits philosophy to pursuit "through argument or reason" expresses a limit on philosophy that many see as crucial to its definition. How notions of reason and argumentation are conceptualized is a core node from which much of the whiteness of philosophy emanates.[2]

The boundaries of those concepts are policed vigilantly and with severity. In my experience, those trying to question dominant forms of rationality are regularly met with reactions which violate the expressed norms of rational discourse: rather than being open to being swayed by the force of the better argument, our interlocutors often become stiff, defensive, and dismissive. Positions that question dominant notions of the rational are mocked and rejected through name-calling. Papers that make arguments for alternative approaches to reason are rarely accepted in major journals, and people who hold those positions are regularly denied tenure.

The battle to maintain the whiteness of philosophy is raging in often quiet ways, in philosophy departments, in journals, at conferences, in classrooms. Those working to maintain the whiteness of philosophy often have no idea that this is what they are doing. And yet the cultural work of creating and maintaining forms of cultural hegemony is being done every day in decisions about what texts to teach, how to interpret them, who to listen to, who to dismiss, and how we argue with one another.

There are many situations in which people, when presented with new information, will change their views, or at least consider new ideas in a relaxed and open way. But other ideas can send these same, generally open, people into what looks like a state of panic. Under these circumstances, suddenly the affect changes from relaxed engagement to a defensive combative pose, suddenly attempted refutations are thrown out at a rapid pace without much consideration, the intellectual level of the conversation drops to a surprisingly low level. Personal insults are likely to fly, and all of the norms of good argumentation are thrown out the window.

What I believe is happening in these cases is that the person defending mainstream approaches to philosophy has been thrown into a state of panic by their perception that a core pillar of their sense of self is about to be challenged. If what they are being told is true, then their sense of self will be rocked. Their sense of themselves as smart, because they are "smarter" than someone else, and their sense of security that they have a method that is reliable, and their sense of themselves as special, because they are part of a culture that is "superior," will be vulnerable to being challenged. We spend years in school accumulating cultural capital, and if what we learned was wrong or in need of being decentered, then we are not as well-educated as we were before. Our value on the cultural market will have declined.

Martin Bernal argues that much of the really serious work of creating philosophy as a white discipline happened in the 19th century when self-consciously racist people reinterpreted historical texts in ways that wrote anything black, Egyptian, or Mesopotamian out of our understanding of the history.[3] At that time, the superiority of the European tradition was asserted, argued for, and defended. Those of us working in the present time have been handed a tradition with serious racism embedded in it, and unless we undo that work of the 19th century, we will be carrying on their racist work.

Any questioning of the superiority of the Western cannon puts in question the superiority of those of us constructed as part of the West. And while it is often white males of upper class backgrounds who can easily adopt this mantle, many people of color, working class people and women, have been allowed membership in the club of the West, and have not wanted to give up the sense of self that comes from being constituted by the so-called greatest lineage in the history of the world.[4]

Rationality has played an important role in helping to maintain the notion of European superiority. It is a placeholder term. As a short hand for "good thinking" it can be used to distinguish ways of thinking that are approved from ways of thinking that are to be rejected. As a core term of judgment within the Western tradition, it has powerful rhetorical force for doing the cultural work of creating hegemonic tools that can be used to create the distinctions that help to provide the intellectual underpinnings to perpetuate racism within Western culture.

Among other possibilities, rationality can refer to thought that is logical, thought that is non-emotional, and thought that leads to progress. In each of these uses, rationality functions as a measuring stick to judge the validity of ways of thinking. And yet, in each case, there is an insufficiency to the grounding of the measuring stick. In each case the insufficiency leaves open a space into which whiteness often gets braided deeply into the concept of rationality. This chapter will explore three different uses of ideas of "rationality" to see how the whiteness of philosophy is both constituted and hidden. The following sections look at rationality as logic, rationality as non-emotional, and rationality as Habermas' universal reason.

Philosophy's whiteness is not just a problem for philosophy, or for people of color who would like to be "philosophers." Philosophy plays an important cultural role as the discourse on discourse,[5] as the master key to the master narrative. And if we are able to disrupt the circuits through which rationality positions white thinkers as superior, we help transform widely circulating cultural logics that rely on these philosophical conceptions. And so increasing our ability to interrupt hegemonizing uses of rationality within philosophy, we can also weaken the racism inherent in dominant ways that the world is understood in the West and increasingly around the world.

Rationality as Logic

When we talk about thought that is rational, for many people that means thought that is logical. Claims of an idea or a system of thinking being "logical" are often used in imprecise ways. People will charge others with being illogical when they merely disagree with their conclusions, the assumptions they are using to begin their argument, or when they don't like the ways that they are reasoning. Rarely do people making this charge actually mean that a person has violated a rule of deductive reasoning in their thinking. The charge that thinking is illogical carries heavy rhetorical force, but often with little philosophical grounding.

When philosophers are pushed to be more precise in making distinctions between the logical and the illogical they usually rely heavily on the law of non-contradiction. Since Aristotle, the law of non-contradiction has been taken in Western philosophy to be the cornerstone of rational inquiry, and the core principle for distinguishing logical from illogical thought. The law of non-contradiction is taken to be the most basic principle of deductive logic, and its use is often taken to distinguish logical thought from illogical, and good thought from bad. The claim that a discursive practice is logical or illogical has also been used in problematic ways to denigrate the thinking of non-white people and indeed of whole cultures.

This denigration is enabled by equivocation, enacted frequently by philosophers and the public more broadly, on the question of whether the rules of logic apply when one is practicing formal deductive logic, or whether they can be applied outside of that domain. If you were constructing a proof using deductive logic, then it would be wrong to accept as valid a conclusion that included a contradiction (both A and not-A). That would be a violation of the rules of the game of deductive logic.

But is it correct to reject, as Aristotle seems to do, Heraclitus' "We step and do not step into the same rivers?" Is Heraclitus being illogical and irrational, or is he making a statement outside the domain of deductive reasoning? In rejecting Heraclitus, Aristotle means to reject as incorrect thinking that does not accord with the law of non-contradiction.

And, yet Aristotle himself accepts the fact that he can offer no solid grounding for the law of non-contradiction. Aristotle writes:

> There are some who, as we said, both themselves assert that it is possible for the same thing to be and not to be, and say that people can judge this to be the case. And among others many writers about nature use this language. But we have posited that it is impossible for anything at the same time to be and not be, and by this means have shown that this is the most indisputable of all principles. Some indeed demand that even this shall be demonstrated, but this they do through want of education. For it is impossible that there should be demonstration of absolutely everything.[6]

The law of non-contradiction has been used to powerful effect in the development of Western logic, and Western philosophy more broadly. The language game that is deductive logic has been used to powerful effect through the history of Western philosophy and Western science.[7] Even if logic is not a self-grounding practice, we can still appreciate its power as a way of organizing thought: we can accept it as a useful language game, in the sense that Ludwig Wittgenstein uses that term. Logic, like chess, offers a set of rules which, once accepted, can be used to distinguish objectively better from objectively worse moves, but whose rules, like those of chess cannot themselves be objectively validated. The "objectivity" obtains within the game, but cannot be used to judge other games.

If we understand logic this way, we can still play its game, to much good effect. But if we understand logic as a valued language game then we should be careful in how we understand the relationship between this language game and others.

At my college, when our curriculum committee instituted a new policy that classes should contain perspectives from multiple cultures where possible, the most powerful members of the philosophy department reacted with outrage when asked if we could make our logic classes reflect multicultural perspectives. Surely logic is simply logic. It isn't a cultural practice, and so there are not multiple cultural approaches to it. I found that claim so fascinating that I began to investigate.

In the *Encyclopedia of Philosophy* there are entries for Indian logic, Arabic logic, and Chinese logic.[8] Arabic logic is an important part of Western logic, and does not constitute an independent tradition. A multicultural approach to logic would need to mention the history of logic and in that history give due attention to the contributions from Arabic thinkers. Chinese and Indian logic appear to be largely independent traditions. In both of those traditions, people have attempted to reduce thought to its most basic rules, and to use those rules to judge the validity of statements.

Around 200 C.E. the Buddhist thinker Nagarjuna developed a deeply complex system of philosophy based on Buddhism and logical argumentation. Nagarjuna used *reductio ad absurdum* to challenge the views of his opponents, but he also employed paradox in complex ways, seeming to both accept and not accept the law of non-contradiction. For Nagarjuna what we would take to be standard rules for deductive reasoning hold for the everyday material world. But when asking deeper questions about the nature of ontology, contradiction is required. Nagarjuna uses the tetralemma, widely accepted in Indian rhetoric and logic, according to which any statement has 4 possible truth-values:

S is P
S is not-P
S is both P and not-P
S is neither P nor not-P.

According to Graham Priest and Jay L. Garfield:

> Indian epistemology and metaphysics, including Buddhist epistemology and metaphysics, typically partitions each problem space defined by a property into four possibilities, not two. So Nagarjuna in *Molamadhyamakak* considers the possibility that motion, for instance is in the moving object, not in the moving

object, both in and not in the moving object, and neither in nor not in the moving object. Each prima facie logical possibility needs analysis before rejection.[9]

Similarly the Jains developed a tool for analyzing discourse using the doctrine of sevenfold predication (sapta-bhangi-naya):

1. Positive Attribution
2. Negative Attribution
3. Positive and negative attribution
4. Inexpressibility
5. Positive attributions and inexpressibility
6. Negative attributions and inexpressibility
7. Positive attributions, negative attributions, and inexpressibility.

Using this and a few other techniques, they developed elaborate ways of analyzing discourse, and were very interested in including notions of the multiplicity of perspective in their reasoning.

These Indian thinkers are doing something that looks quite a bit like Western deductive logic, and yet both systems allow for the analysis of statements that do not accord with the law of non-contradiction.

Much Chinese thinking, especially in the Taoist and Buddhist traditions, is fascinated with the complex nature of contradiction. When the Taoist Lao Tzu writes that we must "do by not doing"[10] he is not being irrational. He is making a profound statement, which, like Heraclitus' statement above, attempts to get at a truth, which is difficult to render straightforwardly. Paradox is used here to point to a truth beyond the literal meaning.[11]

It is possible when encountering a statement like Lao Tzu's to reject his philosophy as irrational. One can also simply put it aside as poetry rather than philosophy. But Taoism begins from the assumption that there is something philosophically important about exploring seemingly contradictory statements.

Some who have looked into this debate have taken the Chinese and Indian approaches to contradiction to prove that, however interesting what they were doing was, it was not logic, since by definition logic is founded on the law of noncontradiction. The claim then becomes tautological: logic is based on the law of noncontradiction, and anyone not using the law of noncontradiction is not doing logic. And the fact that all logic uses the law of noncontradiction proves that logic has a universal nature.

There is much to be learned from studying the logical systems that arose in these very different traditions. As Western thinkers are increasingly interested in understanding the nature of ambiguity, change, and the relations of parts to wholes, it is likely that there are some valuable insights to be learned from an investigation of Chinese and Indian approaches to contradiction.

Claims of being logical can mask attempts to put forward as superior one's own cultural ways over the cultural ways of others. In academic philosophy, logic is often used as a gate for separating the real philosophers from those who should be weeded out. Feminists have made a strong case that logic is often deployed in ways that keep women from being interested in philosophy.[12] Philosophers and supporters of the dominant culture routinely reject the ideas of others as illogical. This charge carries a powerful rhetorical force, and part of that force derives from the vague belief that certain ways of being in the world are superior because they are based on more logical ways of thinking.

Logic is often taken as a cornerstone to the ways of thinking that have led to the ascendance of the West, politically, technologically, scientifically, and culturally. When rationality is equated with the logical, and when logic is a cultural particular masquerading as a universal, we have a vortex scrambling our thinking about the reasoning process.

In this confusion, a variety of prejudices are often enabled and given legitimacy. Thinking that works with paradox is disparaged. Thinking that is highly attuned to context and ambiguity are often rejected. Ways of understanding the world that begin from a unity of the emotional, spiritual, and material domains are rejected out of hand. The cultural assumptions that underlie dominant Western ways of understanding the world are dogmatically understood as linked with logical, and therefore "good," reasoning. And all of this without any sound philosophical grounding.

Rationality as Dispassionate

A second common place where the concept of rationality is used in ways that constitute and hide whiteness is around the notion that reason is a form of clear thinking that we can tap into when we shut out the confusions that arise from our bodies.

Plato is an important source for the idea that the body is a source of error in our thinking. In *The Republic,* Plato writes:

> Now children, women, and slaves, and (among so-called men) the rabble who constitute the majority of the population are the ones who evidently experience the greatest quantity and variety of forms of desire, pleasure, and pain . . . . Whereas simple and moderate forms, which are guided by the rational mind with its intelligence and true beliefs, are encountered only in those few people who have been endowed with excellence by their nature and their education.[13]

Later in this section Plato distinguishes passions, which can drive us to good things from emotion, which he conceptualizes as something like impulses, and which always lead us astray. In *The Symposium,* Plato elaborates a rich and complex notion of the relationship between reason and emotion. Our desire for a lover who is a good truth loving person will inspire our search for truth. The physical side of Eros starts us on a process of exploration that leads to a love of wisdom: or philosophy. In *The Republic,* passion is spoken of as potentially positive[14] and indeed as crucial to the pursuit of philosophy: a passion for wisdom. But that passion is limited, and it is clearly distinguished from emotions as a whole.

Feminists have argued that many emotions are crucial to good thinking. Good ethical reasoning requires care. The search for wisdom requires a passion for wisdom. The intuition that there is a problem drives inquiry and critique. But much of the Western tradition has followed Plato in a fairly crude way by leaving out the complexity of his notion of passion, and in seeing emotions as nothing more than impulse, and hence as nothing but impediments to good thinking. Reason is taken as the Other of emotion, and one is good where the other is bad.

The negative value judgments put on emotion and the body, as the source of emotion, are then imposed on people whose social roles put them more in touch with their physical being. Women and members of the laboring classes are seen in Plato and Aristotle as inferior and unable to pursue philosophy well because of their immersion in the concerns of the body.[15] The ancient idea that the poor cannot do philosophy has been transposed through the history of slavery and colonialism into a widespread cultural rejection of the humanity of people of color.[16]

Many authors have explored the psychodynamics of what happens for dominant forms of Western consciousness as privileged people suppress their own bodily passions, such as eroticism, and project that repressed material onto others.[17] Suddenly the world is populated by rational, dispassionate, philosophically oriented white people, savage and lustful people of color, and women of all races who are temptresses.

This idea can be seen alive and kicking in many schemas of developmental psychology and ethics, such as those of Lawrence Kohlberg and Jean Piaget. In my classes, students will fairly often make statements with profound racist implications about the ability of others to do philosophy, and justify them using Abraham Maslow's hierarchy of needs which they are learning about in their psychology classes. According to Maslow, people's needs exist in a hierarchy, starting at level one, with basic physiological needs, and ascending through a series of stages, to level five, the needs of self-actualization (which includes needs for "morality, creativity, spontaneity, problem solving, lack of prejudice, and acceptance of facts") followed by level six- the need to know and understand and level seven- aesthetic needs. Only when we have satisfied our lower order survival needs are we able to move into a concern with higher needs, such as needs for self-development. Only those people who have satisfied their basic needs are able to engage in things like philosophical reflection and moral development.

This idea is often used by people sympathetic to the poor to claim that people's basic needs must be attended to. But along with that concern for the physical well-being of others goes an unstated paternalism: surely the poor aren't very good thinkers or artists. It would be too much to expect that of them: they are still taking care of their lower order needs.

Of course there is no empirical evidence to support the claim that people who are taking care of their survival needs do not engage in art, music, spirituality or philosophy. Indeed, much of the great art of the world (as long as we don't tautologically confine art to the classical forms created by the privileged) is done by people whose lives are very unstable (level two) and insecure economically (level one). Serious philosophy does take time, but there are many poor people in this world today who spend more time thinking about the nature of things than your average busy professor of philosophy. A person's class position does not correlate with how much time they have for serious reflection, nor with how important that reflection is to them, or how philosophically rich it is.

There are also some reasons to believe that the poor and those doing physical work have quite a bit to offer philosophically. People with more privilege may have their thinking distorted by desires to protect their privilege. They may be thinking about the kinds of things that are relevant to their own experience and not to the experiences of the poor. The poor are likely to be quite good at thinking about how to survive under harsh circumstances, how to make a meaningful and satisfying life under harsh circumstances, and about the nature of the social systems that cause them harm.

The idea that we can use the metric of non-emotionality of thought to judge its rationality is fraught with peril. A distinction between well-considered versus impulsively obtained conclusions is helpful in many contexts for distinguishing better from worse ways of deciding validity. But beyond that, thinking which is non-emotional is likely to be thinking which is devoid of ethical content, which is deaf to the contextual complexities of the situation in which it arises, and which is unable to resonate very deeply with those it addresses.

We should be very judicious in making claims for the superiority of a judgment based on its being non-emotional when we know the history of the ways that the thought processes of whole groups of people have been disparaged. If women's context sensitive forms of intuition have been rejected because a man who uses a more constrained thought process cannot understand her, whom should we take to be the better thinker? If a person of color, whose survival requires him to read body language and see what a person looks like when they are lying, decides someone is lying when he does not have the information to ground that judgment argumentatively, should we call his decision to treat something as a lie irrational? When an "uneducated" person refuses to change a belief in the face of a mountain of scholarly evidence, because it just doesn't feel right, can we be sure that the scholarly evidence is correct, and the judgment to not accept irrational?

People make many judgments on the basis of intelligent uses of emotion. Sorting out which are better and which are worse judgments is complex and requires forms of discourse analysis that are sensitive to the contexts and emotions present in a situation. The dogmatic rejection of emotion simplifies this process, but it is not "rational" and is unlikely to help us in making better judgments.

Plato had a deep passion for philosophy. That passion drove him on his spiritual quest for Truth. Philosophers are human beings full of emotions in everything we do. Philosophers of emotion have only begun to scratch the surface

254 Cynthia Kaufman

of how to distinguish better from worse uses of emotion in philosophy.[18] Until we are more sophisticated in our ability to talk about the intelligent use of emotion, we would be well-advised to not reject thinking because we can see a trace of emotion in it.

Jacques Derrida's theory of deconstruction helps us to understand how positively asserted terms, like reason, often rely for their creation on their opposition to a denigrated opposite term, like emotion. The form of rationality which is constructed through this opposition relies for its rhetorical force on unconsciously held beliefs about emotion, and much of the power behind the negation of emotion is grounded in negative views of those constituted as emotional: women, people of color, and the poor. The construction of philosophy on the basis of a form of reason which is buttressed by the negation of emotion is one of the key places where whiteness is woven deeply into the core of our practice.

Rationality as Habermas' Universal Reason

Jürgen Habermas has devoted quite a large body of work to pushing back against the relativism he believes is implied by postmodernism, and has given a very influential contemporary articulation of the defense of universalistic approaches to rationality. In the process of making that argument, Habermas relies on beliefs about Western superiority to ground his notion of the universality of reason.[19]

For Habermas, there is no a priori content to what views are to count as rational. Rather, for him, a rational viewpoint is one that was reached through a process of good argumentation. Thus, someone is said to be rational to the extent that they are willing to defend their views through arguments and respond to the force of the arguments of the partner in argumentation. From this it would follow that we could engage in arguments to settle disputes, and could use this method to undermine the abuses we have uncovered in current discourses of rationality, while still engaging in legitimizing practices.

In place of a correspondence theory of truth Habermas argues for a consensus theory of truth. Against the charge that what he is speaking about here is not truth, but a method for ascertaining truth, Habermas claims that the method for redeeming truth claims is not external to the meaning of truth. Following John Dewey, he defines truth as "warranted assertability." The truth of a statement lies in the warrantedness of what is asserted.[20]

Since the truth of a proposition is judged through the settlement of differences through argumentation, the best basis for saying that a certain proposition is true is that it was arrived at through good argumentation and that all those participating in the discussion agree to its truth.

Yet clearly, if consensus is to count as the mark of a true proposition, there must be some way to distinguish valid from invalid forms of consensus. If one participant in the discussion wields a sanction of death over other participants if they disagree, it would be hard to imagine why we should accept the agreed upon proposition as true. A rationally motivated consensus (and therefore a consensus which yields truth- or "warranted assertability") is one in which what determines the outcome of the argument is nothing but the unforced force of the better argument (*der zwanglosen Zwang des besseren Arguments*). In order to be sure that this is the case, the participants must allow for a stepwise radicalization in which increasingly deep questions as to the context of the discussion can be raised.

There is a tendency in the literature to understand Habermas' argument to be that rationality is grounded in the concept of the force of the better argument, and yet a careful reading of the first section of the *Theory of Communicative Action* shows that Habermas is aware of the fundamental openness of what can be taken to be a satisfactory argument. Surely people can use open methods of argumentation to come to all sorts of conclusions. For this reason, the idea of an ideal speech situation is not enough to ground the claim that there is some sort of universality to reason. This is why Habermas develops another, more empirical side to his argument. And this is where we will see the implicit racism of his position.

Acknowledging that something more than the force of the better argument is needed to ground his theory of rationality, Habermas writes:

> Even when we are judging the rationality of individual persons, it is not sufficient to resort to this or that expression. The question is rather, whether A or B or a group of individuals behaves rationally *in general*; whether one may systematically expect that they have good reasons for their expressions .... When there appears a systematic effect in these respects, across various domains of interaction and over long periods (perhaps even over the space of a lifetime), we also speak of the rationality of a lifeworld shared not only by individuals but by collectives as well.[21]

Habermas then goes on to ask what lifeworld structures go into making rational action orientations of individuals possible. He pursues the answer to this question through an engagement with the various essays collected in the book *Rationality*.[22] These essays, written mainly by anthropologists and sociologists, deal with the question of whether or not it is possible to talk about rationality cross-culturally.

In this section, Habermas attempts to make clear what it is that distinguishes the modern from mythical worldviews. For him, mythical worldviews are characterized by their totalizing power. "The deeper one penetrates into the network of a mythical interpretation of the world, the more strongly the totalizing power of the savage mind stands out."[23] All information is processed through a single interpretive framework. One consequence of this is that people with mythical worldviews are not able to make the distinctions we moderns take to be fundamental. In particular, they do not permit a clear differentiation between nature and culture. "We can understand this phenomenon to begin with as a mixing of two object domains, physical nature and sociocultural environment."[24]

One of the problems with a mythical worldview according to Habermas is that from within its parameters, judgments can only be dogmatically asserted. This he argues is because:

> mythical worldviews prevent us from categorically uncoupling nature and culture, not only through conceptually mixing the objective and social worlds but also through reifying the linguistic worldview. As a result the concept of the world is dogmatically invested with a specific content that is withdrawn from rational discussion and thus from criticism.[25]

What Habermas sees as a dogmatic conflation of the subjective and objective worlds prevents the raising of validity claims that require the ability to step back from the culture and view it externally. Thus, Habermas argues that what distinguishes mythical from modern worldviews is their differing degrees of openness. A closed worldview is characterized by an "insufficient differentiation among fundamental attitudes to the objective, social, and subjective worlds; and the lack of reflexivity in worldviews that cannot be identified as worldviews, as cultural traditions."[26]

At the end of this section, Habermas makes clear that with this distinction between closed and open worldviews he still has not grounded the rationality of open worldviews. "Of course this does not yet prove that the supposed rationality expressed in our understanding of the world is more than a reflection of the particular features of a culture stamped by science, that it may rightfully raise a claim to universality."[27] This necessitates the next step to the argument, an answer to the question as to why we should take the "openness" of a worldview as indication of its rationality.

Central for this part of Habermas' argument is his engagement with the work of Peter Winch who argues that there is no perspective from which we could ground the universality or superiority of our own worldview. Because each language has its own notions of reality and truth, there is no neutral perspective from which we could say that science registers them correctly.[28] Winch is critical of anthropological approaches that claim the peoples they study are irrational because of the logical contradictions that could be found in the statements they make. This claim is based on a category mistake, the beliefs of members of the studied culture are not scientific theories at all, and thus should not be seen as bad scientific theories. Where we might see logical contradictions, we may be missing something like shifts in level of meaning.

Habermas answers these objections he raises from Winch by using Robin Horton's idea that open worldviews promote learning and hence promote species development. According to Habermas and Horton, Winch may be right that we cannot judge the rationality of a worldview on the basis of its sharing with us views we take to be scientifically grounded, nor on the basis of our being able to find what look to us like logical contradictions in their utterances about the world. But he believes that we can make that claim on the basis of a judgment about the openness of a worldview.

Habermas quotes from Horton's essay:

> In other words, absence of any awareness of alternatives makes for an absolute acceptance of the established theoretical tenets, and removes any possibility of questioning them. In these circumstances, the established tenets invest the believer with a compelling force.[29]

Habermas claims that the distinction "closed versus open" provides a context independent standard for judging the rationality of worldviews.[30]

Habermas raises the point that in a scientific culture there are many beliefs held as sacred, that is, as not open to criticism. He argues, however, that this means that our culture is not as completely open as it could be. One such position is our hypostatization of cognitive-instrumental rationality as the only legitimate form of rationality. Here, Habermas attempts to slip his own conclusions into the discussion without support. Why this does not count as an example of the closedness of our worldview rather that the claim that there is such a thing as a universal rationality, or that the West is more progressive than the rest of the world, for example, is never explained.

The problem with Habermas' view here is that the elements of the Western world view which we must hold as sacred are precisely those required for Habermas' own conclusions. An open worldview *must* distinguish between nature and culture because otherwise how could we ground our theory of communicative action? And we need some way to ground the rationality of at least some aspects of our modern worldview because without this we fall into relativism, which cannot account for the progress he claims we know to be exhibited by modern Western culture.

Habermas fails in his attempt to ground reason as a universal measure for the validity of statements. His attempt to provide a grounding more firm than that provided by an open notion of the value of argumentation gets braided together with assumptions of the cultural superiority of the West. Habermas seems to hope that his readers will share some of his cultural prejudices, and that those holding those common assumptions will together feel satisfied that their views are grounded. For those not sharing those values, Habermas' argument ends up reading like a shaggy dog story that trails off into an infinite void.

What Habermas is doing here is the cultural work of creating hegemony. His complex craftsmanship helps to create a view of the world that simultaneously puts forward the superiority of Western ways, while claiming its universality. This leads to the belief that in the West we somehow found the truth and a more rational way of being in the world. Of course we will be generous enough to share these discoveries with others, but in the process, they will be articulated into a particular cultural practice and the traces of that parochialism will be buried.

Conclusion

The Hegelian notion of the false universal is helpful for understanding what's going on with these three examples of reason and whiteness. For Hegel, concepts which arise in a particular situation or context, and which can help us understand a part of reality, under some circumstances, can sometimes come to be understood as having universal validity and applicability and the traces of their historical and parochial lineage come to be obscured.

In all three of the cases explored above, a cultural particular is presented through academic philosophy as a universal. Logic is understood to be a universal measure, and it is used to measure statements that are based on other language games. Non-emotionality is taken to be a standard for judging the validity of statements, and whole populations are rejected as being too emotional in their thought processes. Western ways of understanding the world are taken in a circular fashion to ground the superiority of judgments typical of Western thinkers.

By presenting a cultural particular as a universal, philosophy itself as an academic practice helps to buttress culturally white ways of understanding the world and colludes in making whiteness invisible but socially potent. White forms of reason become like magnetic fields, invisibly drawing and holding together forms of meaning while remaining largely unnoticed. As long as philosophers continue to produce and enable these equivocations, philosophy will be a site for the reproduction of racist social outcomes.

One of the most pernicious uses of the forms of equivocation and fantasy explored in this chapter is that the whole history of colonialism and slavery ends up being submerged. It is replaced with a story of European influence over the world because of superior thought processes. This belief is widely held and is used all over the world to explain and justify the spread of Western political, economic, and cultural forms.

It is crucial as we enter into the next period in world history, where capitalist forms of development are leading to global warming, where over a billion people in the world regularly do not have enough to eat and where languages and cultures are going extinct at an alarming rate, that we have a realistic view of the nature of the history of the West.

Philosophy has so far played an ignominious role in helping to create an image of a West that has come to prominence as a result of its "superior philosophy." As long as philosophers remain silent about the ways that Eurocentrism is wrapped into some of philosophy's most prized conceptualizations of the world, they will be complicit in upholding ways of understanding the world that lead to devastating outcomes.

They will also be doing bad philosophy. So long as we are reactive when we get questioned about the non-Western history of Western philosophy, when we bristle at the idea that there may be "rational" ways of understanding the world that don't rely on the law of non-contradiction, when we repeat distorted versions of our history which leave out the contributions of people from outside of Europe, when we hold on to the idea that there is something superior about Western thinking that is the cause of Western economic domination, we will be playing into racism, whether we know it or not.

Reason and rationality are enabled in playing the destructive roles outlined in this chapter in part by the tenacity with which many thinkers, who are not necessarily motivated by Eurocentrism, hold onto something that will give them security in their ability to make good judgments. Surely we want to be able to make judgments, and it has seemed to many that universal forms of rationality are indispensable for doing so.

And yet many philosophers, pragmatists, and postmodernists among them, have done important work, articulating the vast epistemological world that exists between a relativism that permits anything and a universalism that operates as an iron law found in the universe.

Postmodern philosopher Jane Flax argues that our moral judgments are likely to be more well-considered when we take responsibility for them and see them as judgments we are making from our own situated positions, rather than as truths that justify themselves:

> To take responsibility is to firmly situate ourselves within contingent and imperfect context, to acknowledge differential privileges of race, gender, geographic location, and sexual identities, and to resist the delusory and dangerous hope of redemption to a world not of our own making. We need to learn to make claims on our own and others' behalf and to listen to those which differ from ours, knowing that ultimately there is nothing that justifies them beyond each person's own desire and need and the discursive practices in which these are developed, embedded, and legitimated.[31]

Developing sophistication around those discursive practices is an important place philosophy can be useful. Flax argues for a philosophy which is modest in its claims and open to a multiplicity of perspectives, and which lives with uncertainty and ambiguity.

Following Dewey, I believe that it is helpful to see philosophy as a practice that living human beings engage in to help us to figure out ways of living well together and ways of engaging with the world.[32] Since there is no universal language-game-transcending human culture and ready to authorize our statements, we must do our best to get along in the world with the faculties that we have: the ability think, to engage in dialogue, to question, to wonder, and to disagree. We develop argumentative tools and discursive strategies, and we use them because they work. When others question how well they work or what blind spots they may carry, we reflect on their nature and remain open to revising them. Philosophers are well-trained at using these tools of analysis and reflection. Philosophy trains us in intellectual flexibility, in the arts of ascending ladders of inquiry and analysis. It trains us to wonder, to question received truths, to revise our most basic conceptual schemas.

Like so much racism in the contemporary West, the forms of racism that philosophy helps to reinforce are largely perpetuated by well-meaning people who do not intend to be racist. The kinds of racism that persist today are much more insidious and more subtle than older forms, and for this reason, professional philosophers have an important role to play in rooting them out with our well-honed skills at analyzing cultural logics.

When we look at what is left of philosophy when we get rid of the notion that it is a universal method for getting to the truth that has led the West to achieve "greatness," we still have quite a bit left. We have a marvelous process, deeply reflective, open in its methods and available to people from all cultures, of all genders, and at all class levels in any society to practice: sustained and careful reflection, wonder and inquiry. We have philosophy as love of wisdom.

*Thanks to: George Yancy for asking me to write the chapter and for all of his encouragement. Thanks also to Ron Sundstrom, Tram Nguyen, Wendy White, Rebecca Gordon, and David Borsos for reading drafts and giving very helpful comments.

Notes

1. Thanks to my colleague Tram Nguyen for this insight.
2. In addition to referring to a particular approach to knowing the world, the term "philosophy" also refers to a particular historical tradition or lineage. The boundaries of that lineage are obsessively policed, in ways that assure that philosophy remains constituted as a white European tradition. The ancient Greeks were not engaged in a white practice when they did philosophy. They were neither white nor European. At that time, "race" didn't exist and neither did "Europe" as a unifying concept. According to Herodotus, the Greeks saw themselves as members of a relatively insignificant society living in the shadows of intellectual giants such as the Egyptians. See Martin Bernal's *Black Athena: The Afroasiatic Roots of Classical Civilization* (New Brunswick, NJ: Rutgers University Press, 1987).

Plato's argumentative methodology is probably Greek in origins, being rooted in the rhetorical strategies of the sophists. But it seems likely that his basic belief that there is a unitary truth that transcends the shifting vagaries of experience, that is to be pursued for it's own sake, was deeply influenced by Egyptian metaphysics. So the rationalism that is so central to philosophy's self-conception may not have been white in its origins. If a color can be posthumously attributed to rationalism, that color is probably somewhere between black and brown. In standard histories, Plato is seen as originating rationalism and he is usually understood to have been white.

There are a few other central nodes where the Western tradition is constructed as white. Rather than acknowledge the centrality of Muslim North African Philosophers in carrying the lineage forward in the middle ages, the tradition is taught as if a light went out somewhere around 400 C.E. only to be magically flipped on again in the Renaissance. (See María Rosa Menoçal, *The Ornament of the World: How Muslims, Jews, and Christians Created a Culture of Tolerance in Medieval Spain* [Boston: Little Brown, 2002].) Core ideas to Western philosophy, such as democracy, which have important sources of origin in the Americas are truncated, and their histories mangled to fit the story of the Western origin of everything good.

While there was a flurry of interest in these issues of non-Western roots of Western philosophy in the 1990s, discussion of them has largely gone dormant. My reading of that literature led me to believe that the multi-culturalists won the rational argument, but lost the battle for hegemony. Those who have attempted to trace Western philosophy's lineage beyond the mythical origin of the Greeks have been shunned, ostracized, and mostly ignored, but many of their core claims stand.

Those issues are complex and contentious and will hopefully receive the attention they deserve in a new generation of scholarship.

3. Bernal, *Black Athena*.
4. Pierre Bourdieu and Richard Nice, *Distinction: A Critique of the Judgment of Taste* (Cambridge, MA.: Harvard University Press, 1987).
5. This expression comes from Luce Irigaray. See *This Sex Which is Not One*. Trans. Catherine Porter and Carolyn Burke (Ithaca N.Y: Cornell University Press, 1985), 74.
6. Aristotle, *Metaphysics* Bk. 4 Ch. 3 1006a, 2–9, in *The Basic Works of Aristotle*, ed. Richard McKeon (New York; Random House, 1941), 737. For an excellent discussion of the status of the law of non-contradiction see the entry Dialethism (2004) Graham Priest. In the Stanford Encyclopedia of Philosophy: http://plato.stanford.edu/ search/searcher.py?query=Dialethism (accessed July 1, 2009).
7. It should also be noted that the role of logic in science has often overstated: while logi-

cal thinking helps to clarify thought, scientists use many other techniques: such as careful observation, the creation of compelling narratives, studying the work of others, and intuition, in the development of and deliberation over scientific discoveries. Logic is one tool among many.

8. Paul Edwards, ed., *Encyclopedia of Philosophy* (New York: MacMillan, 1972/1967), vol. 4, 512.

9. Jay L. Garfield and Graham Priest, "Nagarjuna and the Limits of Thought," in *Beyond the Limits of Thought*, ed. Graham Priest (New York: Oxford University Press, 2002). Found at: www.metareligion.com/Philosophy/Articles/Epistemology (accessed July 1, 2009).

10. Lao Tzu, *Tao Te Ching*. Trans. Charles Muller (New York: Barnes and Noble Classics, 2005).

11. For an excellent discussion of how contemporary White American and Chinese thinkers vary in their use of principles of reasoning in their everyday judgments see: Richard E. Nisbett, Kaiping Peng, Incheol Choi, and Ara Norenzayan, "Culture and Systems of Thought: Holistic Versus Analytic Cognition," *Psychological Review*, 108 no. 2, (Apr 2001): 291–310.

12. Andrea Nye, *Words of Power: A Feminist Reading of the History of Logic* (New York: Routledge, 1990).

13. Plato, *Republic*. Trans. Robin Waterfield (Oxford, UK: Oxford University Press, 1993), 138. Section 431 c.

14. Plato, *Republic*, 150–1. Sections 439–441.

15. Nancy Tuana, *Women and the History of Philosophy* (St. Paul, MN: Paragon House, 1992).

16. See David Theo Goldberg, *Racist Culture: Philosophy and the Politics of Meaning* (New York: Wiley-Blackwell, 2009).

17. Frantz Fanon, *Black Skin White Masks* (New York: Grove Press, 1967); Joel Kovel, *White Racism: A Psychohistory* (New York: Columbia University Press, 1984).

18. See David Haekwon Kim, ed., *Passions of the Color Line: Emotion and Power in Racial Construction* (Albany, NY: SUNY Press, forthcoming).

19. This is a compressed version of my paper: "The Unforced Force of the More Familiar Argument: A Critique of Habermas' Theory of Communicative Rationality," *Philosophy Today* 43, no. 4 (1999): 348–60.

20. For an interesting criticism of this view as confusing the meaning of "truth" with a criterion for truth see: Alessandro Ferrara, "A critique of Habermas' Consensus Theory of Truth," in *Philosophy and Social Criticism* 13, no. 1 (1987): 39–68 and "Critical Theory and its Discontents: On Wellmer's Critique of Habermas," in *Praxis International* 8, no. 3 (Oct. 1989): 305–20.

21. Jürgen Habermas, *Theory of Communicative Action. Volume 1*. Trans. Thomas McCarthy (Boston: Beacon Press, 1981), 43.

22. Bryan R. Wilson, ed., *Rationality* (Oxford: Basil Blackwell, 1970).

23. Habermas, *Theory of Communicative Action*, 45. It is interesting to note that translator Thomas McCarthy adds scare quotes around savage mind that are not in the original [wilden denkens].

24. Habermas, *Theory of Communicative Action*, 48.

25. Habermas, *Theory of Communicative Action*, 51.

26. Habermas, *Theory of Communicative Action*, 52.

27. Habermas, *Theory of Communicative Action*, 53.

28. Habermas, *Theory of Communicative Action*, 57.

29. Habermas, *Theory of Communicative Action*, 61.

30. Habermas, *Theory of Communicative Action*, 62.
31. Jane Flax, "The End of Innocence," in *Feminists Theorize the Political*, ed. Judith Butler and Joan W. Scott (New York: Routledge, 1992), 461.
32. John Dewey, *The Quest For Certainty* (New York: Putnam Group, 1960).

Index

a theory of justice, 2
aboriginal peoples, 168, 169
African American experience, 27, 35, 159, 195
African American philosophy, 4, 30, 33, 42
African American women, 170
Alcoff, Linda Martín, 4, 6, 8, 9, 20
Alemán, Ana Martínez, 44
Alexander, Jacqui, 159
alliance, xx, 20
alligare, xx
Althusser, Louis, xv
ambiguity, 58, 106, 121, 126, 127, 251, 259
American Indian Movement (AIM), 56
American pragmatism, 36, 157
Amerindians, 229
Anderson, Jackie, 108
Anglo-American globalization, 230
Anglo-American philosophy, xi, 4, 173, 175, 180, 181, 188, 193
anti-dilemma theorists, 200, 202
Anzaldúa, Gloria, 51, 52, 53, 70, 106
Archimedean point, xv
Aristotle, 51, 80, 248, 252
arrogance, xx, 13, 100, 106, 107, 109, 181, 188
arrogant perception, 58, 105
Auschwitz, 15
autonomy and moral development, 173
Aymara, 230, 237

Aztecs, 230

Baier, Annette, 13
Bakhtin, Mikhail, 38
Bantu, 230
Bartky, Sandra, 1, 3, 10, 11
Benhabib, Seyla, 17
Bernal, Martin, 246
betrayal, 100
Biden, Joseph, 7
birdcage metaphor, 203
Birt, Robert E., 1
black authenticity, 33, 43
black gaze, 31
black male rapist, xviii
black penis, xvii
black space, 35
black women, 52, 233
Bolívar, Simón, 180
Bordo, Susan, 68
Brandt, Richard, 236, 237
Brison, Susan, 227
British East India Company, 232
British Orientalism, 229
Britzman, Deborah, 13
Brown, Angela, 139, 140
Buddhism, 181, 182, 249
Butler, Judith, 17

Cannon, Katie, x, 28
Card, Claudia, 203
Carvalho, Luis Fernando, 186

Castro, Fidel, 174, 185
center, xix–xx, 11, 34–36, 38, 40, 62, 70, 112, 154, 163, 219, 227, 228, 230, 232, 235, 237, 239
center of whiteness, xix, xx
civil death, 122
Civil Rights Movement, 159
Clinton, Catherine, 27, 28, 32, 35
Collins, Patricia Hill, 36, 55, 67
colonial formations, 227, 237
colonial history, 59
colonial violence, 120
colonialism, 52, 53, 56–59, 62, 65, 66, 68, 112, 180, 228, 230, 231, 235, 239, 258
color non-realism, 143–44
color universalism, 139, 143
color variability, 134, 137, 140
colorblindness, 41
color-emotion relativity, 143
community of inquiry, 33
conceptual or theoretical whiteness, xix, 122, 125, 194
conceptual whiteness, xix, xx, 65, 163
Connolly, William, 154, 164
Crandall, Prudence, 100
Crenshaw, Kimberlé, 55, 56, 67, 69
critical race feminist philosophy, 61, 62
Cuban philosophical traditions, 180
Cuban Revolution, 178
Curry, Blanche Radford, 103
Cuñas, 230

Daly, Mary, 108
dark languages, 136
Davis, Angela, x, xviii, 36, 53, 100, 101, 117, 119, 120, 121, 122, 170
de-authorization, 214
degree of dilemmaticity, 200, 203
Delpit, Lisa, 14, 16, 37, 38
denials of complicity, 3, 4, 8–13
Derrida, Jacques, 38, 254
Descartes, Rene, 13, 79–81, 237
Dewey, John, 38, 254, 259
different relationalities, 238
dilemmaticity, 193, 198, 200–205
Diller, Ann, 16
Dillon, Robin, 184

disability, 124, 125, 215
disciplinary comfort zones, 58
disciplinary formation, 118
disciplining of philosophy, 125
dismantling racism, 216
Doane, Woody, 11
Douglass, Frederick, 35, 69, 101, 221, 222
Doyle, Bertram Wilber, 214
Du Bois, W.E.B., 36, 39, 218–20
Dussel, Enrique, 230, 231

Eastern philosophies, 180–82, 188
Einstein, Albert, 168, 181, 187, 188
elements of whiteliness, 104
Ellison, Ralph, 70, 194
embodiment, xvi, xviii, xix, 230
emotional resistance, 169
emotional trauma, 13
engaged listening, 15
enslavement, xviii, 228
epistemic privilege, 195, 197
epistemically disabled, 195
epistemological crisis, 173, 174
epistemologies of ignorance, 8, 106
Eros, 251
ethnocentric racist, 104
Eurocentric, 38, 69
European superiority, 247

false universalizations, 173
Farnham, Christie, 27, 28, 32, 35
Fellows, Mary Louise, 2
feminist philosophy, x, xii, 51, 52, 53, 58, 60, 62, 99, 102, 103, 124, 126, 127, 157
feminists of color, 12, 58, 69, 100, 105, 106
Flax, Jane, 259
Fon, 230
Foreman, Tyron, 5
Foucault, Michel, 51, 118
Frankenberg, Ruth, 12
freedom, xi, 36, 39, 55, 63, 169, 171, 173–75, 178, 179, 182, 183, 185–87, 194, 222
Freire, Paulo, 38
Friends of Cuba, 175

frustrations of whiteness, 216
Frye, Marilyn, x, 83–84, 104, 156–57, 194
fuckor/fuckee, xvii
Furbee, N. Louanna, 135, 138

Galeano, Edwardo, 183, 186, 187
gatekeepers, 235
genocide, 69, 157, 228
God-talk, 161
Goizueta, Roberto, 160
Gordon, Dexter, 219, 220
Gordon, Lewis, 1, 20
Grimke sisters, 101
Guevara, Che, 178, 179, 185

Habermas, Jürgen, x, 254–57
habits of whiteness, 61
Hall, Kim, 64
Hall, Stuart, 38
Haraway, Donna, 123
Harding, Sandra, xix, 6, 51, 123
Harper, Frances E.W., 101
Hausa, 230
Headley, Clevis, 1
Hegel, G.W.F., 258
Heidegger, Martin, 155
Heldke, Lisa, 18, 77
Heraclitus, 248
heroic individualism, 20
Higgenbothan, Elizabeth, 10
Hispanic identity and culture, 160
Hoagland, Sarah, xix, xx, 227
Hobbes, Thomas, 219
Honorary Octoroon, 27, 32, 33
honorary white, 32
hooks, bell, x, 36, 38, 43, 52, 105, 233
Hopi language, 236
Horswell, Michael, 227
Horton, Robin, 256–57
Houston, Barbara, 18
Hoy, David, 117
Huggins, Nathan, 28
Hull, Gloria, 53
human freedom, 28, 37, 188
Hume, David, 77, 79, 80–93
Hurricane Katrina, 5
hyper-sexed animals, 234

Hytten, Kathy, 11

Igbo, 171–75, 230, 238
Igbo women, 171, 173, 175
imperialism, 59, 234, 236
imperialist ideology, 180
Incas, 229, 230
Indian curry, 145
indifference contract, 174, 175, 181, 187
indirect communication, 212
interdisciplinary pollination, 118
interpellation, xv, xvi
intersectional analysis, 119
intersectionality, 51, 53–57, 60, 62, 67–69, 118, 119, 120, 233
Invisible Man, 13, 123, 194
Isasi-Díaz, Ada María, 160

Jackson, Jesse, 156
Jacobs, Harriet, 234
Jesus Christ, 160
Jim Crow, 153
Jones, Jacqueline, 27–29, 32, 35
Jones, Leroi, 179–80

Kay, Paul, 134, 138
King, Martin Luther, 156
Kleinman, Sherryl, 12
the Knower, 111
Kohlberg, Lawrence, 252
Korsgaard, Christine, 183
Korsmeyer, Carolyn, 85
Kuku-Yalanji, 136

Laub, Dori, 15
Lewis, Amanda, 5
liability model, 18, 19
liberalism, 171, 175, 183
Lindsey, 139, 140
linguistic relativity, 138, 141, 142, 143
lived experience, 52, 54, 56, 105, 154, 158, 163
Lloyd, Genevieve, 79–82, 125
Locke, John, 68, 194
logic of purity, 121
logical positivism, 158
Lorde, Audre, 53, 101

love of wisdom, 245, 251, 260
loving perception, 104–6
Lugones, María, x, 15, 16, 32, 51, 58, 60, 65, 104, 105, 106, 121, 231, 233–35, 239
lynching, 153

MacKinnon, Catherine, 157
Malcolm X, 36
Malkoc, 134
Man of Culture, 77–79, 81–83, 85, 90, 91, 93
Man of Reason, 77–81
Martí, José, 175, 178–83, 185, 188
Maslow, Abraham, 252
matrices of domination, 56
May, Vivian, 5, 8
Mayas, 230
McIntosh, Peggy, 5, 11
McIntyre, Alice, 11
Merton, Thomas, 167, 181, 188, 191
Mestizaje, 121, 160
Mignolo, Walter, x, 229, 231
Mill, John Stuart, 232
Mills, Charles, x, xix, 1, 2, 7, 9, 10, 52, 65, 122, 123, 125, 162, 167, 170, 171, 173–75, 183, 184, 187, 193–96, 200, 201
Miná, Gianni, 174
Miner, Myrtilla, 101
miscegenation, 121
Mis-Education of the Negro, 39
model of responsibility, 18–20
Modern Western cognition, 231
Mohanty, Chandra, x, 232
Moody-Adams, Michele, 159
moral philosophy, 13, 122, 198
moral responsibility, 3, 8, 18–20, 176
Morgan, Jennifer, 233, 234, 238
Morrison, Toni, 42
motherhood, 63, 234
Moya, Paula, 105
mujerista theology, 160
mysteries of the universe, 181
myth of modernity, 231

Nagarjuna, 249
naïve realists, 145

Napper, George, 43
Narayan, Uma, x, 52, 170, 227, 235
Native women, 56, 62, 66, 234, 235
naturalized approaches to ethics, 196, 197
negative liberties, 63
Nietzsche, Frederick, 155, 156
non-Cartesian Sums, 123
non-ideal theorizing, 193, 196
Nopper, Tamara K., 108–11
normalizing of whiteness, 31
Norplant, 62
Nzegwu, Nkiru, x, 170–74

Obama, Barack, 7
objectivism, 131, 133, 140, 141, 143, 146, 147
Olenquist, Andrew, 16
Oliver, Kelly, 15
openness, 15–17, 179, 255, 256
oral contraception, 62
Oriental woman, 232
Ortega, Mariana, 52, 60, 100, 104–7
Outlaw, Lucius T., 212
Owen, David, 131
Oyewùmí, Oyèrónké, x, 236–38

Pateman, Carole, x, 170, 174, 175
patriarchy, 52, 55, 65, 67–69, 110
people of color, ix, xi, 10, 30, 32, 34, 43, 52, 60–62, 69, 82, 103, 107, 108, 110, 131, 132, 141, 143, 147, 153, 158, 160, 162–64, 196, 198, 204, 213, 215, 216, 218, 247, 253, 254
philosopher as troublemaker, 127
philosophical Neanderthal, 155
philosophical subjectivity, 126
philosophy of religion, xi, xix, 155, 157, 158
philosophy of science, xix, 51
philosophy's hostility to religion, 153–55, 157
philosophy's white center, 20
Piaget, Jean, 252
Plato, 82, 251, 253
plurality, 51, 53, 57–62, 64, 67, 69, 70, 143

political philosophers, 154, 169
political philosophy, xix, 123, 126, 154
positive liberties, 63
post-supremacist philosophy, 57, 59
pragmatism, 38, 161, 162
Pratt, Minnie Bruce, 217, 225
prophetic pragmatism, 158, 161, 162
prophetic vision, 161
proxy agency, 19
psycho-ontological, 162
Pupo Pupo, Rigoberto, 182
Putnam, Hilary, 168, 176

race traitors, 213, 218
racial entitlement, 30
racialization, 66, 79, 124, 227
racialized commodity production, 230
racism, ix, x, xvii, 1, 3, 5, 7, 9, 10–13, 17, 20, 30, 39, 42, 43, 54–59, 67, 68, 94, 99–103, 105–8, 110, 113, 119, 127, 158, 159, 162, 164, 167, 196, 212–17, 220, 224, 225, 227, 245–47, 255, 259, 260
racist anti-racist, 109
rape, 69, 157, 227
rationality, xi, 38, 62, 80, 99, 101, 105, 106, 112, 125, 220, 228, 229, 245, 247, 251, 252, 254–59
rationality as white, 105, 106
Rawls, John, x, 2, 3, 17, 123
Razack, Sherene, 2
real philosophers, 126, 250
religare, xx
reproductive justice, 64, 65, 68
resistance to whiteliness, 100, 111
Revel, Jean-François, 91–93,
Riley, Dianne, 108
Roberts, Dorothy, 63
Roberts, William F., 222–23
Robertson, Emily, 16
Roelofs, Monique, 79, 94
Rorty, Richard, 156, 159, 165
Rosenblatt, Louise, 38

Santa Claus, 156
Sapir, Edward, 138
Saramago, José, 182, 183, 185
Scheman, Naomi, 17

secular, 154, 159, 161, 164
secularism, xi, 156, 164
self-other dialectic, xv
self-regard, 181
sexism, xvii, 55, 56, 99, 100, 110, 113, 119
sexual autonomy, 231, 234
sexual violence, 68, 69, 120
sexualization of knowledge, 120
silencing, x, 108, 109
Smith, Andrea, 69, 120, 234
Smith, Barbara, 53, 211
Smith, William, 37
social connection, 19, 20
social locations, 18, 55
sociality, xv
solidarity, 44, 45, 100, 101, 110158, 159, 162
Sophie's Choice, 184
soul food, 77, 78
Spelman, Elizabeth, 15, 16, 65
Spinoza, B., 80, 83
Spinoza's ideal, 80
Spivak, Gayatri, 127
Srivastava, Sarita, 12
standpoint epistemology, 214, 215, 233
standpoint theory, 195
Stanton, Elizabeth Cady, 101, 113
stereotypes, 201, 221
sterilization, 56, 63
structural injustice, 19
structural racism, 212
structure of whiteness, 214
Stubblefield, Anna, xv, 13, 57
students of color, 29, 30, 34, 41, 42, 44, 45, 163, 214, 215
subpersonhood, 194
subversive black humor, 219
super-sex addict, xvii
suspension of prejudice, 91
systemically privileged, 7, 15
systems of subordination, 56

Taliaferro, Charles, 155, 165
Taylor, Charles, 154, 158, 163, 165
theoretical whiteness, 13, 52
Third World, 57, 65, 176, 232

Thompson, Audrey, 15, 16, 27, 212, 225
To the Left of the Father, 185, 186
Toltecs, 230
Torres, Edén, 44
transcendental norm, xvi
transparency testing, 196, 197
troublemaker, xvi
trust, xvi–xviii, xx, 29–32, 44, 45, 233
Truth, Sojourner, 101
Tswana, 136
turf, 120
Tye, Michael, 137, 148
Tzu, Chuang, 175, 188
Tzu, Lao, 250

unbreakapartability, 119, 120
unearned privilege, 12
Universal Declaration of Rights, 183
universal validity, 227, 258
University of Havana, 176, 177
unnatural lottery, 203, 207
untrustworthiness, 30

Van Dieman, 218, 225
vertigo, xvi, 218
vigilant, xviii
vulnerability, 14, 16

Walker, Margaret Urban, 195–97
Warren, John, 11
Washington, Booker T., 33, 223
Webster, 134
well-intentioned white people, 10
West, Cornel, x, 36, 38, 156–58, 161–63
Western feminist values, 235
Western gender thinking, 238
Western logic, 248, 249
white abolitionist audiences, 220, 221
white academic feminism, 53, 227, 233
white academic women, 228, 233, 239
white antiracist philosophers, 212, 218, 225
white authority, 53
white authors, 214, 245
white bourgeois women, 66, 231
white complicity, 18, 20, 213

white demographic, 61
white dominance, 32, 45
white domination, 65, 153, 158, 159
white entitlement, 30, 32, 45
white feminist(s), xix, 2, 12, 52–54, 56, 57, 59–61, 64, 99–102, 105–8, 111, 112, 235, 237, 239
white feminist philosopher(s), 2, 53, 58, 59, 61, 69, 105, 112
white guilt, 61
white ignorance, 1, 3–6, 8, 9, 11, 13, 32, 52, 60, 69
white male, xix, 131, 132, 141, 143, 235, 247
white male academic practices, 235
white people, 1, 3–10, 15, 16, 18, 20, 31, 59, 104, 105, 107, 110–12, 142, 153, 163, 164, 195, 215, 216, 218, 222, 223, 248, 252
white philosophizing, 212–14
white power, 215, 216, 219, 220, 223
white privilege, xvii, 12, 31, 42, 43, 54, 67, 104, 108, 153, 214, 217
white self, xvi, xx, 215
white superiority, 65, 215, 218, 224
white supremacy, ix, xv, xix, 4, 9, 10, 20, 28, 31, 33, 35, 39, 42, 43, 52, 55, 59, 64–67, 69, 102, 106, 108, 111, 112, 159, 167, 193–96, 198, 200, 212, 218, 223, 233
white talk, 11, 218
white teacher's supportiveness, 30
white theories, 131, 148
white Western male, 145
white women philosophers, x, xix, 127
white-centered institution, 44
whiteliness, 83, 84, 100, 104–9, 194, 195
whitely, 58, 83, 84, 89, 90, 104–6, 109, 112, 196
whiteness as method, 119, 127
whiteness of philosophy, xv, xviii–xx, 2, 13, 14, 20, 52, 82, 83, 124, 154, 163, 164, 212, 213, 246, 247
Whorf, Benjamin, 138
willful ignorance, 5, 8
Williams, Bernard 199
Winch, Peter, 256

wisdom, xi, 37, 170, 180, 183, 189, 245, 251
without gender, 66, 172, 235
Wittgenstein, Ludwig, 51, 249
Woodson, Carter G., 36, 39
women in philosophy, 124
Women of All Red Nations (WARN), 56
women of color, x, xviii, 2, 16, 44, 52–54, 56–66, 68, 69, 71, 100, 102–9, 111, 112, 119, 159, 228, 233–36, 239

Wretched of the Earth, 158, 162

Yancy, George, 4, 71, 94, 121, 127, 132, 142, 148, 260
Yeğenoğlu, Meyda, 233–36
Yorubas, 230, 238
Young, Iris Marion, 3, 18, 19, 206

Zack, Naomi, x, 51, 57
Zapotecs, 230
Zulu/Zulus, 136, 230

About The Contributors

Barbara Applebaum is Associate Professor in Cultural Foundations of Education at Syracuse University. She has published in *Educational Theory, Teachers College Record,* the *Journal of Moral Education and Educational Foundations.* Her current research projects focus on the relationship between agency and complicity, rearticulating white moral responsibility, and what she refers to as "white complicity pedagogy."

Susan E. Babbitt teaches Philosophy at Queen's University in Kingston, Ontario, Canada. She is the author of two books on rationality and moral imagination, and coeditor (with Sue Campbell) of an anthology on racism and Philosophy. Her recent research has been on women and development in Cuba. She is currently editing an anthology on the work of Cuban philosopher José Martí.

Alison Bailey directs the Women's and Gender Studies Program at Illinois State University where she is also a professor in the philosophy department. Her philosophical interests are largely motivated by questions of social justice. She recently co-edited a special issue of *Hypatia* on "The Reproduction of Whiteness: Race and the Regulation of the Gendered Body," with Jacquelyn N. Zita. Her recent work on philosophical issues related to racism and resistance has appeared in *Hypatia, Whiteness: Feminist Philosophical Perspectives, Feminist Ethics Revisited,* and *Race and Epistemologies of Ignorance.* She and Chris Cuomo have just coedited *The Feminist Philosophy Reader.*

Berit Brogaard's current research is located at the intersection of philosophy of language, philosophy of mind, and epistemology; she has authored or coauthored papers which have appeared in various journals and edited volumes, including: *Noûs, Philosophy and Phenomenological Research, Australasian Journal of Philosophy, Philosophical Studies, Philosophical Quarterly, Philoso-

phical Perspectives, *Philosophy Compass*, *American Philosophical Quarterly*, *Analysis*, *Mind and Language*, *The Monist*, *Pacific Philosophical Quarterly*, *Synthese*, and *Canadian Journal of Philosophy*. She currently holds a visiting fellowship from the RSSS Philosophy Program and Centre for Consciousness at the Australian National University, and is an Associate Professor of Philosophy at University of Missouri, St. Louis.

Lisa Heldke is Professor of Philosophy at Gustavus Adolphus College, where she also holds the Sponberg Chair in Ethics. She writes and teaches as a pragmatist feminist philosopher who is particularly influenced by John Dewey, Jane Addams and W.E.B. Du Bois. She is most interested in questions of epistemology, and questions about teaching and learning, and has pursued those questions by exploring the seemingly-unlikely topic of food. She is the author of *Exotic Appetites: Ruminations of a Food Adventurer* (Routledge), and co-editor of three anthologies: *Cooking, Eating, Thinking: Transformative Philosophies of Food* (Indiana); *Oppression, Privilege and Resistance* (Macmillan); and *The Atkins Diet and Philosophy* (a volume in the Open Court Popular Culture and Philosophy series). She is co-founder of Convivium: The Philosophy and Food Roundtable, and a member of the Radical Philosophy Association and the Society for the Advancement of American Philosophy. She is also the co-editor of *Philosophers on Holiday*, an intermittent 'zine in the philosophical travel and leisure genre (on the web at http://www.gustavus.edu/~poconnor).

Sarah Lucia Hoagland is Professor of Philosophy and Women's Studies at Northeastern Illinois University in Chicago. She specializes in Lesbian philosophy. She is author of *Lesbian Ethics: Toward New Values*. This book's thesis is that the values from Anglo-European ethical philosophy undermine rather than promote lesbian connection. The book develops an ethics relevant to Lesbians under oppression, one that avoids both blaming the victim and "victimism," embraces the spirit of lesbian resistance, and encourages plurality. She is also co-editor of *For Lesbians Only* with Julia Penelope, and *Re-reading the Canon: Feminist Interpretations of Mary Daly* with Marilyn Frye. Sarah is a collective member of the Institute of Lesbian Studies in Chicago, a staff member of the Escuela Popular Norteña, and a Research Associate of the Philosophy Interpretation and Culture Center, Binghamton University in Binghamton, New York.

Cynthia Kaufman is the author of *Ideas for Action: Relevant Theory for Radical Change* (South End Press, 2003). She is the chair of the department of Philosophy at De Anza College in Cupertino, California. She has worked as a racial justice activist for many years, working against police abuse, writing and teaching about white privilege, and most recently in institutional transformation work at De Anza College.

Crista Lebens teaches philosophy and women's studies at the University of Wisconsin-Whitewater. She works primarily in social ontology, specifically working on praxical theories of resistance to multiple oppressions and the coalescence of gender, race, class, and sexuality in identity. Her articles have been published in *International Studies in Philosophy, Discourse: an Interdisciplinary Philosophy Journal;* and in *Battleground: Women and Gender.*

Cris Mayo is Associate Professor in the Department of Educational Policy Studies and the Gender and Women's Studies Program at the University of Illinois at Urbana-Champaign. Her work examines the intersections of sexuality, gender, race, and educational philosophy and includes *Disputing the Subject of Sex,* (Rowman and Littlefield, 2004, 2007), as well as a variety of articles in *Educational Theory, Philosophy of Education,* and *Philosophical Studies in Education.*

Alexis Shotwell is an Assistant Professor of Philosophy at Laurentian University in Sudbury, Ontario. Her academic work addresses racial formation, unspeakable and unspoken knowledge, gender, and political transformation. Her writing has appeared in *Hypatia, Sociological Theory, Upping the Anti,* and several book collections. She has recently completed a book entitled *Knowing Otherwise: Implicit Understanding and Political Change,* forthcoming from Penn State Uiversity Press.

Shannon Sullivan is Head of Philosophy and Associate Professor of Philosophy, Women's Studies, and African and African American Studies at Penn State University. She is the author of *Revealing Whiteness: The Unconscious Habits of Racial Privilege* (Indiana UP, 2006) and *Living Across and Through Skins: Transactional Bodies, Pragmatism and Feminism* (Indiana UP, 2001). She has co-edited (with Nancy Tuana) a special issue of *Hypatia* on Feminist Epistemologies of Ignorance (Summer 2006) and an anthology on *Race and Epistemologies of Ignorance* (SUNY Press, 2007).

Lisa Tessman is the author of *Burdened Virtues: Virtue Ethics for Liberatory Struggles* (Oxford University Press, 2005) and co-editor with Bat-Ami Bar On of *Jewish Locations: Traversing Racialized Landscapes* (Rowman and Littlefield, 2001). She is an Associate Professor of Philosophy and Women's Studies at Binghamton University.

Audrey Thompson is a professor in the department of Education, Culture and Society, University of Utah. Her research interests include whiteness theory, African American epistemologies and pedagogies, pragmatisms, writing and research epistemologies, feminist ethics and epistemology, and feminist and anti-racist pedagogy.

George Yancy is Associate Professor of philosophy at Duquesne University. He has published in numerous scholarly journals, including *Philosophy & Social Criticism*, *The Journal of Social Philosophy*, *The Journal of Speculative Philosophy*, and *African American Review*. He is the editor of over 10 books, three of which have received *Choice* Outstanding Academic Book Awards. He is the author of *Black Bodies, White Gazes: The Continuing Significance of Race* (2008), which received an Honorable Mention from the Gustavus Myers Center for the Study of Bigotry and Human Rights. In 2008, Yancy was nominated for Duquesne University's Presidential Award for Faculty Excellence in Scholarship.